D0076833

Derrida and Religion

Derrida and Religion

OTHER TESTAMENTS

EDITED BY

YVONNE SHERWOOD & KEVIN HART

Routledge
New York • London

Published in 2005 by
Routledge
Taylor & Francis Group
270 Madison Avenue
New York, NY 10016
www.routledge-ny.com

Published in Great Britain by
Routledge
Taylor & Francis Group
2 Park Square
Milton Park, Abingdon
Oxon OX14 4RN U.K.
www.routledge.co.uk

conf. Nov 2002 (p.4)

Copyright © 2005 by Taylor & Francis Books, Inc.

Routledge is an imprint of the Taylor & Francis Group.
Printed in the United States of America on acid free paper.

All rights reserved. No part of this book may be reprinted or reproduced or utilized in any
form or by any electronic, mechanical or other means, now known or hereafter invented,
including photocopying and recording or in any information storage or retrieval system,
without permission in writing from the publishers.

Library of Congress Cataloging-in-Publication Data.

Derrida and religion: other testaments / edited by Yvonne Sherwood & Kevin Hart.
    p. cm.
  Includes bibliographical references and index.
    ISBN 0-415-96888-7 (hardcover : alk. paper)—ISBN 0-415-96889-5 (pbk. : alk. paper)
  1. Derrida, Jacques—Religion. I. Sherwood, Yvonne. II. Hart, Kevin, 1954-
    B2430.D484D485 2004
    194—dc22

                                                                        2004002089

for Jacques Derrida

Contents

VI   Revelation(s)

VII   La/Le Toucher (Touching Her/Him)

Acknowledgments

Yvonne Sherwood would like to thank all those who helped, in any way, with the organization of the conference *Other Testaments: Derrida and Religion*. In addition to the protagonists and friends who appear on these pages, she would like to thank all those local friends and colleagues who supported her during the years and months of organization (chiefly, but by no means exclusively, Mark Brummitt, Julie Clague, Alastair Hunter, and Heather Walton). Acknowledgment is also due to the Robertson Bequest at Glasgow University for assistance with the final proofreading of the manuscript, and to Richard Davie for his generous assistance with sub-editing. Helen, John, and Thomas Sponton contributed to the final stages of this manuscript in ways that they probably know nothing about.

Kevin Hart would like to thank Brook Cameron for assistance with transcribing the interview.

The editors would jointly like to thank all those connected with Routledge—particularly Bill Germano, Damian Treffs, Gilad Foss, Linda Manis, and Amy Rodriguez—for seeing the book into print with such efficiency and enthusiasm. Special thanks are due to Scott Moringiello for help in checking proofs and in preparing the indexes.

Yvonne Sherwood and Kevin Hart

About the Contributors

George Aichele is a professor in the Department of Philosophy and Religion at Adrian College. He is author of *Jesus Framed* (1996) and *The Control of Biblical Meaning: Canon as Semiotic Mechanism* (2001), and was a member of the Biblical and Culture Collective, the collaborative author of *The Postmodern Bible* (1995).

Marcella Maria Althaus-Reid is a senior lecturer in christian ethics and systematic theology at the School of Divinity, The University of Edinburgh, Scotland. She is a Latin American theologian known for her pioneer research on liberation theology and queer theory and is the author of *Indecent Theology: Theological Perversions on Sex, Gender and Politics* (2001) and *The Queer God* (2003).

Gil Anidjar is an assistant professor of comparative literature in the Department of Middle East and Asian Languages and Cultures at Columbia University. He is the editor of Jacques Derrida's *Acts of Religion* (Routledge, 2002) and the author of *Our Place in al-Andalus: Kabbalah, Philosophy, Literature in Arab Jewish Letters* (2002) and *The Jew, the Arab: A History of the Enemy* (2003).

Ellen T. Armour is an associate professor and chair of the Religious Studies Department at Rhodes College in Memphis, Tennessee, where she currently holds the R.A. Webb Professorship in Religious Studies. She is the author of *Deconstruction, Feminist Theology, and the Problem of Difference: Subverting the Race/Gender Divide* (1999) and coeditor of the forthcoming *Bodily Citations: Religionists Engage Judith Butler.*

Timothy K. Beal is the Harkness Professor of Biblical Literature and Director of the Baker-Nord Center for the Humanities at Case Western Reserve University in Cleveland, Ohio. His most recent books are *Religion and Its Monsters* (2002) and *Theory for Religious Studies* (2004), both published by Routledge.

Daniel Boyarin is the Taubman Professor of Talmudic Culture in the Departments of Rhetoric and Near Eastern Studies at the University of California at Berkeley. His most recent publications are *Sparks of the Logos: Essays in Rabbinic Hermeneutics* (2003) and *Border Lines: The Partition of Judaeo-Christianity* (2004).

Virginia Burrus is a professor of early church history at Drew University. She is the author, most recently, of *The Sex Lives of Saints: An Erotics of Ancient Hagiography* (2003).

John D. Caputo is the David R. Cook Professor of Philosophy at Villanova University where he has taught since 1968. His more recent publications include *On Religion* (2001), *The Prayers and Tears of Jacques Derrida* (1997), and *Deconstruction in a Nutshell* (1997). His work is the subject of *Religion Without Religion: The Prayers and Tears of John D. Caputo* (Routledge, 2001) and *A Passion for the Impossible: John D. Caputo in Focus* (2003).

David Dault is a graduate of Columbia Theological Seminary. He currently divides his time between Berlin and Nashville, where he is a teaching fellow in the Graduate Department of Religion at Vanderbilt University.

Robert Gibbs is a professor of philosophy at the University of Toronto. He is the author of *Correlations in Rosenzweig and Lévinas* (1992); co-author, with Peter Ochs and Steven Kepnes of *Reasoning After Revelation* (2002); and coeditor, with Elliot R. Wolfson, of *Suffering Religion*. His most recent book is *Why Ethics? Signs of Responsibilities* (2000).

Kevin Hart is a professor of English at the University of Notre Dame. His recent books include the expanded edition of *The Trespass of the Sign* (2000); *The Dark Gaze: Maurice Blanchot and the Sacred* (2004); *Postmodernism* (2004); and, with Geoffrey Hartman, *Maurice Blanchot: The Power of Contestation* (2004). His selected poems, *Flame Tree*, appeared with Bloodaxe in 2003.

Robyn Horner is a lecturer in theology at Australian Catholic University in Victoria, and a research associate at Monash University. Her research focuses on the intersections of theology with contemporary French thought, particularly as it is expressed in the works of Jacques Derrida, Emmanuel Lévinas, and Jean-Luc Marion. She is the author of *Rethinking God as Gift: Marion, Derrida, and the Limits of Phenomenology* (2001), and *Jean-Luc Marion: An Introduction for Theologians* (forthcoming), as well as the co-translator for Marion's *In Excess: Studies in Saturated Phenomena* (2002).

Grace M. Jantzen is a research professor of religion, culture, and gender at the University of Manchester. She is the author of many books and articles, most recently *Becoming Divine: Towards a Feminist Philosophy of Religion* (1998) and *Power and Gender in Christian Mysticism* (1995). She is currently at work on a multivolume project titled *Death and the Displacement of Beauty*. She is a Quaker.

Richard Kearney holds the Charles Seelig Chair in Philosophy at Boston College. He is also a visiting Professor at University College Dublin. His most recent publications include the trilogy, *On Stories; Strangers, Gods and Monsters;* and *The God Who May Be.*

Cleo McNelly Kearns writes and lectures on comparative literature and the philosophy of religion. She is the author of *T. S. Eliot and Indic Traditions: A Study in Poetry and Belief* (1987) and of essays on, among others, Lacan, Derrida, Kristeva, and Irigaray. She is currently a fellow at the Center for the Study of Religion at Princeton University and is completing a book on the figure of the Virgin Mary in cultural memory.

Catherine Keller is a professor of constructive theology at Drew University and executive director of the Drew Transdisciplinary Theological Colloquium. She is the author of numerous works in philosophical theology, including *From a Broken Web* (1988); *Apocalypse Now and Then* (1997); and, most recently, *The Face of the Deep* (2003).

Gregg Lambert is an associate professor and director of graduate studies, Department of English, Syracuse University. He is author of *Report to the Academy: The New Conflict of the Faculties* (2001), *The Non-Philosophy of Gilles Deleuze* (2002), and *Return of the Baroque in Modern Culture: The Art, Theory and the Baroque in the Modern Age* (2004).

Tod Linafelt is an associate professor of biblical literature at Georgetown University in Washington, D.C. He is the author and editor of several books and numerous scholarly articles, including *Surviving Lamentations* (2000).

Walter Lowe is a professor of systematic theology at the Candler School of Theology and Graduate Division of Religion, Emory University. He is the author of *Evil and the Unconscious* (1983) and *Theology and Difference: The Wound of Reason* (1993), the latter treating Barth, Derrida, and Kant. Having contributed essays to a number of recent volumes on God and postmodernism, he is currently writing an introduction to Christian theology.

John P. Manoussakis teaches philosophy and directs the European School in Humanities at Boston College. He is the author of numerous articles on the philosophy of religion published in *Modern Theology, The American Catholic Philosophical Quarterly,* and *Journal for the Psychoanalysis of Culture & Society.* He is the coeditor of *Traversing the Imaginary: An Encounter with the Thought of Richard Kearny* (2004), and *After God* (2005).

Stephen D. Moore is a professor of New Testament at Drew University Theological School. His recent books include *God's Gym: Divine Male Bodies of the Bible* (Routledge, 1996) and *God's Beauty Parlor: And Other Queer Spaces in and Around the Bible* (2001). He is currently working on a further book on postcolonial studies and early Christianity.

Hugh S. Pyper is a senior lecturer in biblical studies and head of the School of Humanities at the University of Leeds, England. He has published widely on the literary study of the Bible, postmodernism, Kierkegaard, and the pedagogy of biblical studies. He is also coeditor for the *Oxford Companion to Christian Thought* (2000).

Tyler Roberts is an associate professor of religious studies at Grinnell College in Grinnell, Iowa. He is the author of *Contesting Spirit: Nietzsche, Affirmation, Religion* (1998). His current work explores the relevance of contemporary continental philosophy for rethinking the study of religion.

Regina M. Schwartz is a professor of English and religion at Northwestern University. She is the author or editor of numerous books including *Remembering and Repeating: On Milton's Theology and Poetics* (1993), *The Curse of Cain: The Violent Legacy of Monotheism* (1997), and

Transcendence: Philosophy, Theology and Literature Approach the Beyond (Routledge, 2004).

Yvonne Sherwood is a senior lecturer in OT/Tanakh and Judaism at the University of Glasgow, where she is also co-director of the Center for Literature, Theology, and the Arts. Previous publications include *The Prostitute and the Prophet* (1996); *A Biblical Text and Its Afterlives: The Survival of Jonah in Western Culture* (2000); and *Derrida's Bible* (2004). She is currently writing a monograph on the "sacrifice" of Isaac/Ishmael in ancient commentary and contemporary cultures under the working title *Isaac/Ishmael's Scar.*

Inge-Birgitte Siegumfeldt is an associate professor at the Department of English at Copenhagen University. She is currently working on a study of "circumcision" as a figure in Derrida's writing.

Edith Wyschogrod, J. Newton Rayzor Professor of Philosophy and Religious Thought Emerita at Rice University, is currently working on theories of altruism. Her most recent book is *An Ethics of Remembering: History, Heterology and the Nameless Others* (1998).

SECTION I
Introduction

CHAPTER 1

Other Testaments

YVONNE SHERWOOD AND KEVIN HART

An inheritance is never gathered, it is never one with itself. Its presumed unity, if there is one, can only consist in the *injunction to reaffirm by choosing*. *You must* [il faut] means you must filter, select, criticise, you must sort out among several of the possibilities which inhabit the same injunction.... If the legibility of a legacy were given, natural, transparent, univocal, if it did not simultaneously call for and defy interpretation, one would never have to inherit from it. One would be affected by it as a cause—natural or genetic....

Inheritance is never a given, it is always a task. It remains before us, as incontestably as the fact that, before even wanting it, or refusing it, we are inheritors, and inheritors in mourning, like all inheritors ... *To be...* means...to inherit. All questions about being what one is to be (or not be) are questions of inheritance.... We *are* inheritors, which does not mean that we *have* or that we *receive* this or that, that a given inheritance enriches us one day with this or that, but that the *being* we are *is* first of all inheritance, like it or not, know it or not.[1]

When one writes, one is always trying to outsmart the worst. Perhaps so as to prevent it from taking everything away...[2]

In early 2000, a small group of people got together to prepare a place for Elijah (Elie) Derrida at the joint annual meeting of the American Academy of Religion and the Society of Biblical Literature (AAR/SBL).[3] For noninitiates, the AAR/SBL is the largest worldwide conference on religion and is also, hardly coincidentally, Anglophone and North American, echoing back to Derrida all that he has said about "religion" as a word that "circulates in the world…like an *English word* [*Comme un mot anglais*] that has been to Rome and taken a detour to the United States."[4] The result was the conference "Derrida and Religion: Other Testaments" (Toronto, November 23–26, 2002) which this volume represents. We want to begin by saying, simply, thank you. Thank you particularly to George Aichele, John Caputo, Cleo McNelly Kearns, David Odell-Scott, and, above all, to Jacques Derrida, whose good faith ensured that this project did not languish forever in the *à venir* or flounder on the inherent fragility of a promise made in Paris. We hope that this anthology captures at least something of the excitement of the event—not least the plenary interview, which, with a turnout of well over a thousand people, made those of us on stage feel bizarrely like evangelists at a mass revival meeting. However, our aim was only "evangelism" in a very qualified sense.

"Fall" and "Evangelism"

Why *Derrida and Religion*? What did we want from the encounter that we called "Derrida and Religion: Other Testaments?" Not to celebrate the return of the once-erring, seemingly Nietzschean but now softer, whiter-haired, more Lévinasian prodigal, as if he had suddenly changed roles like a character in a soap. Not to say that *Derrida and Religion* is a more self-evident or natural connection than those other "Derrida ands" or "Deconstruction ands" that he lists in those half-smiling conjunction tables in "Et cetera."[5] Not, certainly not, to preach a new Derridean religion or elaborate a *devotio postmoderna*. Not to calibrate Derrida's religiosity and assess how far he has kept, or spilled, the precious vial of an inherited Jewishness. And not to showcase a "Jacques in a box,"[6] as if everything could be gambled in one interview or one throw—so repeating a situation that Derrida has parodied in the past:

> Now we are in an academic casino. Standing behind the gaming table, holding the card of deconstruction (there is only one card, obviously "Paul de Man's war"), I alone represent "Deconstruction", all gathered into one for this last throw, this last chance. Oh yes, I almost forgot: it must be the last chance, at the last moment,

at dawn. And if I lose, the croupiers will declare "Deconstruction" in ruins, bankrupt. Exit "Deconstruction."[7]

Rather, given all that Derrida has given to religion, we wanted to acknowledge the gift without "fantasizing proportionality", without allowing a domesticating "thank you" to imply that a self-evident legacy had been successfully received, as if products labelled "Grammatology" (1970s), "A-theology" (1980s) or "Religion without Religion" (1990s) were now passing out of sight along the swift conveyor belt of theoretical production.[8] Above all, we wanted to "evangelize" in the modest sense of spreading the words and responding to a perceived debt of telling.

By Derrida's account, all acts of writing and thinking are driven by a fall that has always and already happened: an awareness that we have not yet told enough, been sufficiently faithful to the other person, and that we can never perfectly coincide with ourselves (with oneself as "subject"). Because it is inseparable from the desire to save oneself and to present oneself as completely naked or true, all autobiography is confession. (Occasionally even God, in the becoming-literature-of-God that is the Hebrew Bible, seems to realize that he has not "done something that cannot be improved upon" in those curious moments where he repents or regrets).[9] If all our endeavors with proper names and corpora are motivated by a sense that justice is still to come, this must be the case, and acutely so, with the name of "Derrida." No other name has been so thoroughly substituted by media rumors or by slogans attached to prestige labels of their own: "Habermas," "Jameson," "Abrams," the "Blooms" (Allan and Harold), and "Eagleton." Consider, for example, how Fredric Jameson's slogan the "prison-house of language" (1972) has echoed around M.H. Abrams' "sealed echo-chamber" (1977), René Wellek's "prison-house of language that has no relation to reality" (1983), and Terry Eagleton's condemnation of deconstruction as that which makes us "prisoners of our own discourse" (1983).[10]

As if in parody of Derrida's careful work on the way in which the name comes apart from the corpus and mourns in advance the one who signs, "Derrida" and "deconstruction" have been pressed into double service: as the names of absolute impotence and absolute danger.[11] They have been divided by way of quasi-religious mystification and secular demystification; encroaching totalitarianism and encroaching relativism; the troglodyte's club and the newly patented academic gadget that, in the siege-and-defense culture of academic business as usual, offers sophisticated schools and machines that always beat modernity's spinning jennies and combustion engines.[12] Viewed from the left, Derrida signifies the threat of totalizing power that has been achieved, paradoxically, through impotent bookishness. He represents a regression into ivory tower scholasticism and, at the same time, scary acceleration into a *laissez-faire* University that churns out "pomo" neologisms like so many violin tunes to accompany the burning of Rome.[13] He serves as cipher for perilous regression (into childhood "play," or the occult world of Jewish mysticism), and also for dangerous acceleration beyond the borders of the humanities and the human and humane.[14] Primarily, he is cast as the one who folds the human—touch, skin, love, blood—into the whiteness of specters, absences, vapors, holograms, and the one who rotates words that are only ever words, not *locked on* to politics, context, actuality, matter and all that matters, and therefore, as people say, "unengaged."[15] Strangely, he has been characterized by those writing from the political right wing in similar ways. Here he signifies both the impotence and irrelevance of a "philosophical cloud cuckoo land" and the force that, with its ranks of disciples, is on the verge of ruining not only the universities but the very heavens and the earth by bringing off the most technocratic death of God (and man) to date.[16]

Ironically, these mass-produced Derridas, like the cloned faces of an Andy Warhol print, demonstrate precisely what their manufacturers and sponsors allegedly most resist: the infidelity of the signifier that floats above all responsibility, content, or debt. Herman Rapaport documents their genealogy, charting their genesis in a conservative politics that requires a myth of *Kulturkampf* to call it into being (what more justifying of "defensive" war than reports of rapidly accumulating weapons of mass deconstruction?) but also, more oddly, in left-wing critiques that erect a "white" Parisian Derrida while forgetting his work on margins, white mythology, the creolization of philosophy, and his unceasing campaign against the deracinating paleness of abstraction.[17] What interests us here is the way in which these accusing fingers point to contemporary anxieties and pressures precisely in the wildness of their gesticulations. There is something very old, even biblical, in the horror story of the world being rolled up into a scroll—something apocalyptic in the collision of *Endzeit* and *Urzeit* in ruined landscapes of negation where the deconstructive bogeymen howl or quietly pare their nails. There is something mythical about the way in which "Derrida" as a sign of excess is extrapolated in mutually exclusive directions, as overly rational and prerational, too far left and too far right. There is something that resonates, albeit at a distance, with the diffuse effects of Derrida's presumed Jewishness.[18]

There are elements of this confusion that point to persistent traces of the religious in the secular world. Spectres both Pauline and Romantic seem to haunt the common assumption that the very worst thing that Derrida could say would be "All the world's a text (and we are merely players)," as though Jacques were Jaques in a postmodern performance of

As You Like It. The antithesis between dead letter and living spirit survives and mutates. Conversely, there are symptoms of a belated coming to terms with modernity from the side of religion. To read some sensational accounts of The Brutal Death of the Transcendental Signified—spread by certain opponents *and* advocates of "deconstruction"—one would think that Derrida had simply written another version of the critique of transcendence, as developed by Kant, Feuerbach, Marx, and Freud. The morality play scenarios performed on the stage of Derrida and Deconstruction crudely mirror genuine fears. The equal and opposite performances of Totalitarianism Against Individualism or Collectivities Against Solipsisms (with Derrida playing the villain in both) exorcise, by simplifying, the perceived moral ambiguity of (unifying or violent) wholes and (fragmenting or freeing) parts. The specter of Derrida as word spinner and dealer in theoretical market forces reflects a growing public awareness of the role of financial, political and verbal currency in constructing, "sexing-up" and generally mediating the world we live in.[19] It signals a creeping sense that internal insufficiencies and economies of trade are compromising even our most self-evidently good stories such as The Rise of Democracy and The Extension of Individual Human Rights.

In short, the cultural holograms of Derrida and deconstruction are important because they reveal a massive overdetermination: too much has been revealed, too much of it is contradictory, so much of it unstitches our world—and so perhaps the end is coming. The sense of contemporary apocalypse (not unlike the apocalypse analyzed by Catherine Keller and Stephen Moore in this volume) is interesting because, by *blurring* the roles of Christ and Anti-Christ, it intimates real confusion over the direction in which redemption and disaster are to be found. Far from suggesting that we inhabit a different world to Derrida (he in "cloud cuckoo land" and we on *terra firma*) all the accusing fingers show that the questions he raises are not so new to us, and suggest that we are already using the specter of deconstructive anarchy or images of impotent "undecideability" to name other fears. Does the fragility of our concepts lead to chaos? Does a saturation of legacies and contexts render us unable to make important decisions? Irony of ironies: Derrida engages precisely the questions that assemble, as a confused rabble, to cry out against the prospect of their forgetting that they choose to call by the name of "Derrida." Slowly and carefully, he works through relations between techno-science and the natural, the individual and the totality, the historical and the transcendental, the religious and the secular, and also the crisis of the University and the nature of academic work.[20]

Beyond the "Deconstructionism" Room

The conference halls of religion—perhaps particularly the sections devoted to studying so-called "Judeo-Christianity"—have, as predicted, "many rooms" (John 14:2) now furnished with conference tables and overhead projectors, and "deconstructionism" is thought to belong in a very high, very chilly loft space. Here, rumor has it, scholars work on hyper-advanced textual studies; engage in wild hermeneutical games; and experiment to see whether, if sufficiently strong doses of anti-bodies are applied, theology will eventually decay into a-theology. This presumed confinement is unfortunate, as Derrida has timely things to say to many different rooms in Religion's house without fully endorsing business as usual in any of them. Not only does he think through the legacies of those who laid the foundations for the labors that take place in different rooms (the "founding fathers" of, say, anthropology, psychology, linguistics), but he engages with the different desires by which we distinguish between different spheres of study: the desire to do justice to the archive, to generate universal statements about religion, or to hold religion accountable to its social conditions and political effects. The promise (and threat) of Derrida is not that we will be amalgamated under a new brand name. In fact, one of the most important things that Derrida can give us is a means of questioning the process whereby new celebrity theories or methods, with seemingly ever shorter half-lives (and shelf-lives), rapidly decay and are equally rapidly replaced.

For ironically, while the "postmodern" is still seen as a special suite of rooms apart, its rather lazy tropes increasingly preside, as if by default, over us, confining us in cul-de-sacs of thinking from which Derrida gives us the resources to escape. One of these is the idea of perspectival multiplicity that in fact perpetuates cultures of mutual indifference, thereby legitimating an atomized academy bound only by what Rapaport amusingly calls "the approach approach."[21] Another related paradigm is the quest for the new (quasi-messianic?) theory that, when it comes, will be far more productive than anything we have applied to date.[22] Derrida seems deliberately to defy these fantasies by placing his own name within the texts of others, by working with "old" names, and by maintaining that all "isms," all wearying discourses of limits and edges, rely on the very old structure of *apokalypsis,* which makes newness by repatching old wineskins and cloth. By arguing that the solid secure "subject" of the textbooks never really existed for anyone—certainly not for Descartes, Kant, and Hegel—he spoils the postmodern retrojection of the modern as the place of blind men who once upon a time believed in "the subject" and practiced philosophy as if it were a branch of Newtonian physics, and he studiously avoids reductive

"Postmodern" reinventions of certain features of Romanticism and German Idealism (with neologisms sprinkled on top).[23] He deliberately puts as much distance as possible between his own acts of writing and paradigms such as the "*turn*" to the subject, in which the world is contracted into the pupil of the all-creating "I." And he stands at an equally suspicious distance from what John Caputo calls "heteromorphic" postmodernity and its idioms of the "inexhaustiblerichness of meaning" and the "transcendence of semantic excess."[24] Orientating his work more in the direction of "heteronomic" difference, in which the "I" is turned toward the other and constituted or gathered in response to the other,[25] he carefully guards against degeneration into a Sunday School Ethics about embracing the "other"—an expression already almost "used up rhetorically" or in danger of becoming a "ghost," as he often half-smilingly comments.[26] His circumfessions disabuse us of the assumption that one can give one's identity as easily as one can give a postcode, in an act of giving that presumably (in return) gives one immunity in wielding "it" thereafter. And he resists identity politics, or discourses of the "Other" that rely on too stable a dichotomy between enemy and friend. His concentration on what comes before the subject—phenomenologies of social relation such as giving, forgiving, and promising—enables us to question the methodological neatness of social scientific models, so prevalent in Religious Studies, that tend to work forward from subjects who are already fixed. As Rapaport observes, Derrida offers us ways of thinking about the subject beyond the impasse of postmodern theories that sometimes seem to lurch, often in the same work, between the passive (subjected) subject, inscribed in a world of language, and the voluntarist subject who seems to kick off the web of constructs, and really *do* things with words.[27] Derrida believes that words *do* things, and strives, in "chang[ing] language [to] change more than language." But this can hardly be a predictable, preprogrammable act in a context where language does not submit to being the "governable instrument of a speaking being or subject" and where there is no hyper-performative cog-mechanism through which "words" unproblematically turn the wheels of "world."[28]

Acts of Writing as Acts of Faith

Derrida's very qualified, but very considerable, *faith* in words leads to acts of writing that—a long way from the dream of deconstruction as something like the supreme weapon in the arsenal of criticism—foregrounds the deciphering, wagering, hoping, (typing and deleting), thinking-without-knowing that attends anything that we try to *do* with words.[29] When Derrida risks some least bad definitions of deconstruction, he ventures "the movements of…ex-appropriation," a questioning of *pouvoir* as power/being able, and the experience of *suffering* as "not being able," as if there were something mortal and fragile about deconstruction.[30] For Derrida, writing must *act*, in acts of writing that can never be purely constatitive, but that are always (in Derrida's case overtly) performative, and therefore subject to the risk of the perverformative,[31] and (so) writing *labors*, to elicit the best and outsmart the danger of the worst. Writing fears because it is not underwritten with any insurance and because by never saying enough it runs the risk of always saying too much. In the absence of knowledge of who or what is coming, writing can only calculate, risk, adopt certain strategies and sacrifice others (even our modest introduction composes and decomposes itself around the impossibility of imagining all you "yous" who are not one). Above all, writing must *believe*, which is why one cannot be an unbeliever and a writer: faith is required by acts of writing that open out into a giving to be read that is always, also, "a leaving to be desired."[32]

It may be symptomatic of what is loosely called the times that this writing is seen, by some, to waste time: it is not efficient and productive enough, its yield is too slow. Not only does it not add to our pile of academic goods (apart from some neologisms that can easily be snatched from it) but it seems to subject some of the goods we already had to dispossession. Moreover it seems actively to dispossess us of the security of our disciplinary languages; it is symptomatic, Derrida says, of how much we believe in the ownership of "our" words that we deeply resent difficulties at home here in language, whereas we would expect them in physics or maths.[33] For some, there is something deeply frustrating about the way in which Derrida strives to perform, in slow motion, the inherent complexity and vulnerability that attends the labor of our thinking, especially here in religion and humanities (and yet what could be *less* straightforward than the structures of response that shape religion and human relations?). There is also something rather offputtingly *weak* about writing that foregrounds the fear, labor and risk that haunts any act of writing striving to get itself read and to matter (not just to get itself published)—a fear for which the conventions of untroubled doctoral discourse seem to serve as both antidote and mask. And yet, for others, the importance of Derrida seems to lie precisely in the meticulous boldness and delicate hubris of these acts of writing, and in their performative assault on the edifice of philosophy as, *by definition*, a form of knowledge that places its holder in a position of strength.[34] And it is this overt performance of the *faith* required by writing that, among other things, makes Derrida's writing resonate with the "religious": a word that gets attached to the Derrida corpus not only to testify to the many religious works, terms, and motifs that can be found there, but also for want of another word to define the pervasive sense of the "for want of," the giving to be read in the sense of "leaving to be desired."

Derrida/Theology and Derrida/Religion

That we can even venture the conjunction "Derrida and Religion" testifies to a certain move beyond the reception of Derrida in the 1970s and 1980s, partly characterized by a deconstruction of Christian theology. Although quite different in their responses to deconstruction, Christopher Norris and Gayatri Spivak disseminated deconstruction's assumed power to demystify religion and to convict theology of the metaphysics of presence.[35] More generally, the deconstruction of Christian theology was conducted without reference to the diverse currents of modern theology. If the *Church Dogmatics* of Karl Barth was opened up to new readings, little was said about Hans Urs von Balthasar's "theology of the middle" or Eberhard Jüngel's rejection of the metaphysical God and rethinking of faith in the Crucified One.[36] Trinitarian theology underwent a revival in the 1980s and 1990s, with fresh understandings of the differences and relations between the three *personæ* being developed; yet all this went unnoticed by almost all Christian advocates of deconstruction whenever they spoke of God. At times the period was marked by bold appropriations of Jewish spirituality and hasty attempts to slot Derrida into one or another Jewish tradition, as alleged defender of the liberating "Hebraic" as opposed to the repressive "Hellenic."[37] Christianity was frequently treated as the negative pole in this equation and subtleties of doctrine, diversity, and historical development were not given the care and attention that deconstructive readings should solicit. The prevailing assumption was that the God of Christianity can be framed exclusively in metaphysical terms. By the 1990s we find theological critiques of deconstruction, the loudest of which gains its considerable energy by mistakenly aligning it with nihilism.[38] Yet, not even the most detailed of these has proven convincing either to theologians or to deconstructionists.[39]

The once timid, now increasingly confident "and" in our title intimates a reciprocal influence between "Derrida" and "religion": as Derrida draws on religious texts and phenomena to write of, say, the performative risk of the word, the bereavement of experience, or the opening to a justice to come, so his acts of writing suggest new ways of thinking about religion, a long way from limited secular tropes of possession and identity, such as having a religion, being religious, or having a God. Fascinatingly, Derrida goes out on a very fragile limb to talk about naïve things that fall under the Kantian notion of *parerga*—things like sacrifices, angels, gifts, talliths, ghosts, alms, prayers, confessions—in acts of writing that stand out like Gaudi's Sagrada

Familia against the skyline of more sober, "scientific" Religious Studies.[40] Importantly, he does not only concentrate on religious border-effects such as mysticism or marranism, but also explores how aporiae inhabit central, orthodox things. An unsettling logic structures such central figures as biblical apocalyptic, the breaking of the tablets on Sinai, the sacrifice on Mount Moriah, the touch of Jesus. And Derrida's Abraham is bound as tightly as the marrano in the strange logic of the secret.

Derrida and Religion by no means represents the dream of what Timothy Beal and Tod Linafelt call the restoration of "Times New Roman": the return of pristine belief to the individual, the academy or the state. Derrida has clearly marked his difference from that other North African, Augustine, on the grounds that the Catholic saint seems to be in a position to make a symmetrical confession in which the self, like the prodigal son, wanders from its true homeland only to return with prayers and tears. He constantly questions the idea of the "return of the religious" understood either as the resurgence of some dangerous fundamental or fundamentalist essence *or* as the uncovering of the true light that had been buried beneath the bushel of the secular. He does not credit the traditional stories of battles between Faith and Reason, or Religion and Science, as if one were ultimately to put an end to the other, and maintains that in their theoretical composition, and their social and political outworkings, the relations between religion and modernity are "uneven, unfulfilled, relative and complex."[41] Against those who, perhaps with too much faith in epochs, would configure "the religious" and "the secular" as pure heteronomy and pure autonomy respectively, he maintains that secularization is only a "manner of speaking": indeed, he responded to one of the interview questions put to him in Toronto with the observation that something like a struggle between autonomy and heteronomy seems to be taking place in midrash and the Bible, which at this point clearly fail to conform to their preordained roles as sites of submission, "tutelage," and the prostrate other of secularism. Intriguingly, he risks a new understanding of religion:

> However little may be known of religion in the singular, we do know that it is always a response and a responsibility that is prescribed, not chosen freely in an act of pure and abstractly autonomous will. There is no doubt that it implies freedom, will and responsibility, but let us try to think this: will and freedom without autonomy. Whether it is a question of sacredness, sacrificiality or of faith, the other makes the law, the law is other: to give oneself back, and up, to the other. To every and to the utterly other (*tout autre…*).[42]

He also counters the popular image of fundamentalism as the nemesis of the modern by writing, unexpectedly, of the "*rationality* of the said 'fundamentalisms' [which] can also be *hypercritical* and not even recoil before what can sometimes resemble a deconstructive radicalization of the critical gesture."[43] Resisting the classical antitheses, he ventures the view that religious revelations and Enlightenments *cross* around metaphors of light, elucidation, and revelation and around a desire for the most promising, fervent concepts (such as "rights," "democracy," and "truth") that have an inbuilt messianic quality, a striving for perfection that is always yet to come.[44]

Although Derrida sees similarity between the structures of the lights of Revelation and Enlightenment, he does not argue that these lights are even roughly the same. Rather, his task is to analyze the conceptual tools and the chances and perils that religion offers in negotiation with the most positive inheritances of the Enlightenments. (See for example his analysis of the onto-theological legacy of sovereignty in the "light" of the ongoing unfolding of "democracy" in *Philosophy in a Time of Terror*.[45]) His work on religion is hospitable but by no means apologetic. Indeed, the aspect of "Derrida and religion" that makes it so promising and threatening is the development of a dark trajectory that runs through Søren Kierkegaard and Rudolf Otto and that leads us in the shadows of the holy; the fear and trembling; the divine-demonic; and what is going on, often so badly, in the name of religion today.[46] Here "evil" and "violence" are not cast as unexpected intruders into religion, but are seen as emerging from religion's own structural traits. For if religion can be defined, empathetically, as the affirmation of the dignity of life whereby "life has absolute value by being worth more than life," this logic *also* leads Abraham up Mount Moriah to sacrifice his son in the name of that which is greater, more beloved than life.[47] Similarly, the indemnifying reflex that characterizes the desire for the holy, the saved, the safe, the one, and tugs it toward the realm of hyperbole, beyond all compromise, is also the force that renders the monotheisms fundamentally inhospitable to one another. According to the logic of the perverformative, "any religious utterance, act, or gesture, stands in the shadow of—more or less, but never totally avoidable—perversion, parody, kitsch ... blasphemy."[48] (This is a fact that traditional religious interpreters have acknowledged, albeit more gingerly than Derrida, in acts of writing that attempt to outsmart the worst and place the precious legacies securely in the realm of the best.)[49]

For Derrida, we cannot choose whether to respond to religion or focus our response on surface "signs and wonders" such as the rise of religious terrorism or the phenomenon of the American and British premiers being asked (in a rather different tone to that in which Derrida was asked in Toronto) whether they pray.[50] The specters of religion structure our thinking in general and haunt unevenly detheologized terms such as "sovereignty" and "nation state." If to be is to inherit, and inheritance is not something given or passed on quasi-genetically (like a meme), but a task, then we must think religion in the tangled contexts in which we live, move, and have our being. This means drawing out the most challenging concepts of religion; filtering them; and, if need be, more than euphemistically criticizing them.

Editorial

Such is the task assumed by the "quasi-community" of people gathered here who signal their reception of "religion" and "Derrida" by "going off elsewhere" in the most generous, faithful-ungrateful, rebellious-affirmative response that attends the scene of the gift.[51] This is not a cohesive community and certainly not a worshipping one. Assembled here are postcards that were penned in response to a call for papers from different disciplinary addresses that necessarily lack the intrinsic connectedness of the "occasional" writings that make up the Derrida corpus.[52] The contributors do not believe in the entwined hands of the master and disciple-scribe, as in the double hand of the Farfa Bible reprinted on the front cover of this book. And they parse *Derrida and Religion* in different ways. Some work intimately with the Derrida corpus while others brush against it at a tangent, and there is a rapport with Derrida's many styles and spirits. Some come closest to the spirit of care, rigor, and exactitude that carefully delineates and delimits: where exactly Derrida is located in relation to Lévinas or Marion; where precisely Derrida's work on "revelation", "gift," or "sacrifice" falls within the inheritances of phenomenology; what exactly Derrida says about "Christian sacrifice," in relation to the New Testament, Nietzsche, Baudelaire. Others draw closer to spirits of radical invention or intervention, solicitation, impropriety (see especially the work of "indecent theologian" Marcella Althaus-Reid.)[53] None of this separation was preprogrammed by us, with the exception of the hinged readings by theologians and biblical scholars whom we invited to work together across the gulf that often separates theology and biblical criticism.[54]

The result is a body of work for which we, as editors, are quite unable to perform the usual service of gathering the essays into a collective purpose, or conducting an introductory tour in which (subscribing to what Daniel Boyarin terms the dream of the "magic language"), the editors presume to distill out the soul of each of the papers in a couple of apposite sentences apiece. At the same time, we want to do more than puff at our pipes, stretch out our legs, and relax into comfortable armchair-metaphors of rich ecumenism, multiple perspectives, yawningly belabored "impossibility" and licensed indifference masquerading as *différance*. Always more edited than editing, Derrida has never subjected the motif of the "collection" to the same close scrutiny that he has devoted to the "preface."[55] Yet we can speculate on what he might say about the retrospective marshalling of papers into a coherent narrative, the assumption that these papers represent us, as we represent them, and that we all speak authoritatively for *Derrida and Religion*. We can imagine what he might write about the problems of appropriation and countersigning that attend the dream of the omniresponsible, omnihospitable, editorial pen. Hugh Pyper's more faithful reading notwithstanding, as we worked on this anthology we began to see the scene from the Farfa Bible as the performance of the wish fulfillment dream of an editor: the main figure (appropriately enough with two faces) is the composite "editor," and the docile contributors have conveniently stacked themselves *en masse* to pass him a single pen through a single representative, whereupon this two-faced figure converts them into a single sheet, the "Introduction," which he raises, triumphantly, over their heads…

Gathering Points

Without recourse to such fictions, we have had to settle for the more modest editorial activities of nudging the papers under slightly revised headings and drawing some tentative lines between them. One might expect more consolidation: after all, our membership is only slightly broader than the colloquium on Capri.[56] Although women are represented here there is still no Hindu, Buddhist, or representative of any other religious group. We can only witness to the existence of important work on Derrida and Hinduism, Buddhism, and the so-called ethno-philosophies (such as Tao, Zen, Sunyavada, Nagarjuna, varieties of Sufi) and confess that here we write only of and in the Abrahamic, indeed within a potentially all-consuming corner of the Abrahamic that excludes (and projects images of) the very religion that gives us the term Abrahamic.[57] For here, too, there is no Muslim. Following Fethi Benslama and Gil Anidjar, we want to highlight the importance of Derrida's "little *Arab-Jew*" for dislocating the mutually obsessed gaze of Christian and Jew. But it would be saying far too much to say that—at least for here, for now (as for Derrida)—Islam figures as anything more than a strategic pressure exerted from the wings.[58]

What unites us in these pages is perhaps a sense of not being at home. This is not because few of us in this temporary community have ever professed or confessed together in the same synagogue, church, conference room, or even edited collection, before. Nor is it simply because some come from a Christianity that is centered on Rome, another from Greek Orthodoxy (centred on Constantinople), another from a particular history of the Latin in so-called "Latin America," and others from a detour between Rome and the U.S./Northern Europe that runs through Wittenberg or Geneva.[59] We are not all at home in the sense that what unites us is the feeling that the legacies of the "Jewish" and the "Christian" are not a gathered context for us, and that we must work our way through their different possibilities soliciting, delimiting, risking. Our shared sense of the unsettledness of these inheritances collides with the almost universal assumption that the "Judeo-Christian" and the "biblical" are self-evident things that (with a little help from Plato) form the bedrock of our culture, giving us the Book; the Logos; and God-the-Father, who, like a contemporary equivalent of the Gnostic Demiurge, spawns the bad world that we call Western Metaphysics. In these pages the "Jew" and the "Christian" appear in rather less familiar roles, and it is those very old Old and New Testaments that accommodate the "Other Testaments" so boldly announced in our title. And it is that most homely of figures—the "Abrahamic"—that unsettles the familiar and the familial.

Without in any way wanting to deny or qualify the important and solid fact of our Abrahamic, Judeo-Christian particularity, it is clear that there is more than enough difference, and far more than we can begin to take account of, in the complex space that is the "Judeo-Christian": not least of all in that tiny hyphen that joins and separates them. One of the places where our anxieties and labors converge is on that hyphen, that link that simplifies and naturalizes a history of entanglement far closer to a DNA spiral than a straight line.[60] Working from the side of the Christian, Hugh Pyper, Timothy Beal, and Tod Linafelt demonstrate how those mega-metaphors traditionally used to manage relations between Old-New and Jew-Christian—the "supersessionist theo-logic" of the cataract or the veil, the "Old" as retrospective shadow cast by the Christian son/sun—are deconstructed by the Bible's micro-metaphorics of light. They show how the Bible's own optical metaphors and mini-hyphens (Saul-Paul, Paul-Moses) reveal the space between the testaments not as an abyss but as a slip of the tongue or a folding of the veil. The strange thought of "two testaments perpendicular to the light, neither the source of light," or the reconfiguration of the hyphen as a folded cloth, blinking eye (or mere moment, instant, *Augenblick*) intersects with Walter Lowe's question about what it might mean to reverse the hyphen's direction of vitriolic flow and to inject concepts such as the "living letter" and "living law" into the

triumphalism, subjectivism, and freedom of Christianity. This is a movement that goes well beyond an autoimmune gesture by a Christianity keen
to purge itself of *its* anti-Judaism, and one that suggests a Christianity so
unlike itself that it almost touches Daniel Boyarin's and Regina Schwartz's
reworkings of a Jewish "letter" and Jewish "law". Schwartz's claim for a
radical biblical vision where the law *is* justice; Boyarin's assertion that
Tanakh and Midrash have "no Logos, no Phallus, no father"; and Robert
Gibbs's discussion of the weak messianism of disjunctive, interrogative
historiography are all ventured from the side of Jewishnesses that cannot
be uncoupled from Christianities and that must strategically counteract
Christianity's symbolic pull.

All this pressure on and in the hyphen recalls what Derrida has circumfessed about the experience of undergoing circumcision (euphemistic
"baptism") and bar mitzvah (euphemistic "communion") and rebelling
against a Judaism of exteriority, legalism, and Pharisaism seen through
already-Christian eyes. This story, precisely because it is neither "his" nor
a "story," serves as a microcosm of a larger philosophical problematic:
namely that there is no Jewish philosophy that can be written without
passing through the Christian and the Greco-German-Latin of the
philosophical languages. This means that the names of Rosenzweig,
Blanchot, Lévinas, and Derrida do not represent, as some naively say, the
coming-to-light of a new, self-evidently "Jewish" philosophy, so much as a
"wait[ing] [and labouring] for a singularity which can be called Jewish
and which *waits*, to keep on being thought."[61] This has everything to do
with Derrida's elaboration of the aleatory givens of "his" own story around
the problematic of cutting from/cleaving to "Judaism"—a figure probed in
Inge-Birgitte Siegumfeldt's attempt to flesh out Derrida's "foot"-note
about circumcision being all he's ever talked about, and in the chance
meeting set up by David Dault between Derrida and Rosenzweig on the
day of reconciliation and parting that is Yom Kippur.[62]

Just as several papers gather around what might be called a deconstruction of Christianity from the direction of "the Jew," so others exert
pressure on the homo-fraternal and filial structures of religion from the
direction of "woman" (the quotes not signalling, as some fear, confinement in the spectral realm of nonbeing, but rather the function of woman
as a lever of intervention, working through the traditions that put her in
her place).[63] Cleo McNelly Kearns' Mary is one such lever, promising to
reach out across the hyphens of the Jewish-Christian-Islamic and also,
crucially, to extend that hospitality beyond sexual indifference and the
economy of the father, son, and brother. In practice, however the
desedimenting effects of what could be called the "Maryamic" show that

her movements are no more straightforwardly hospitable than those of the Abrahamic (no Lévinasian figure of *natural* hospitality, womb-house, or trope of wide-eyed ecumenism, "she"). Grace Jantzen and Gregg Lambert consider how two other Marys, Mary of Egypt and Mary Magdalene, expose, in different ways, the ends (desires and limits) of man. Jantzen's Mary of Egypt flickers, spectrally, between seducer and confessor, and Lambert exposes how the "sense of the body of woman" as the site of openness to touch and prohibition against touch, brushes close to the untouchable yet touchable body of Christ, thereby inscribing "her body" as the origin and limit of the Christian tradition. As Ellen Armour says in an earlier work, it seems that "God's place, and questions of woman's place are intimately connected."[64] Or, as she supplements that argument here, that woman and the divine cross at the point where the gendered, raced, sexed, and divine others touch and repel one another in complex mirroring effects that go beyond the simple structure of antonyms and synonyms. The figure of the sexual other, like that of "the animal" and like that of "the divine", is intrinsic to the construction of concepts such as sovereignty, subjectivity, immanence, transcendence, death, embodiment, and desire, which is why the reconfiguring or shifting of these concepts necessarily involves "re-sexualiz[ing] a … [theological] discourse that has been too neutralizing."[65]

These pressures exerted from the specific sites of the "Jew" and "woman" cannot be trivialised as a simple accident of our identities: "Jews" and "Christians," men and women, have written together many times before without so many interventions that seem to demand descriptive phrases such as "X forces" and "Y solicits" rather than usual editorial reflexes such as "X analyses," "Y shows," and "Z suggests." These points of gathering suggest that deconstructions are already happening and that something particular is happening around sexual difference and the hyphen as the most obvious points where theological or anthropocentric sovereignties meet the rigorous challenge, and internal insufficiencies, of "democracy" and "rights."[66] They also point to a perceived need to keep the questions open and to prevent slippage back into moderate "reformations" that would essentially revalidate "Times New Roman." They point to a perceived need to go on deciding, precisely because these interventions are still a long way from being decisive. To read Ellen Armour and Catherine Keller is to hear, clearly, the exhortation that those who work with Derrida and religion should do so in negotiation with the "still small voice" or "few fragile decades" of feminist theology, lest a division between a Derrida subcanon on sexual difference (*Spurs*, for example) and a Derrida subcanon on theology ("How to Avoid Speaking," for example), effectively separates the question of woman and religion from work on the question of woman (in general), and lest a "spectral afterimage, theological ghost, of Derrida" unwittingly revalidates the sexual indifference of the "homogenizing He."[67] Since, as Armour has argued elsewhere, "many of the sites where the economy of *différance* breaks through [the economy of the self-same] carry female markings,"[68] it is hard to imagine how one could go about the expropriation of the proper, the self-same, without encountering the figure of the female (of property)—an observation that *perhaps* also applies, differently, to the figure of the "Jew," slave librarian, keeper of the books, and traditional custodian of Christian theological property.

Welcome

So, welcome to a space that none of us fully owns or disavows. Enter by way of a "hostipitality" committee formed by Edith Wyschogrod, Gil Anidjar, Cleo McNelly Kearns and their treatments of moments at the thresholds of the "Old" and "New" Testaments. Welcome to an Abrahamic family that is, from the beginning, already overextended and divided, and to a Christian God who seems just as overstretched and divided as the family over whom he presides. Welcome to Virginia Burrus's nonlogocentric Logos that seems so unlike itself, so unlike an image of itself that circulates in these regions, and that resonates, in curious poly-temporality, with Marcella Althaus-Reid's and Gregg Lambert's interruptions of the settled doctrine of incarnation as a break with laws of reproduction and sexuality, a bid for relief from monotheistic monotony, and an expropriation of the father: an exposure of the father to death. Welcome to analyses that, far from reposing in the "given," relate the thought of God to the aporia of the gift or the thought of the God who may be; and to attempts to recall the austere theological tradition to metaphorical truths pursued in the sap, blood, ink of their own idioms.[69] Welcome to scriptures marked by historiographical discontinuities, broken tablets, gifts of lack, and unexpected figures such as a Logos that writes without writing, Abraham the brother, strangeangels, and even spooky seven-eyed messiahs. Welcome to analyses that press the promise and risk of God becoming incarnate in different institutional or textual bodies ("old" and "new") and that press the excessiveness and deficiency of a dream of perfect one-ness into the aporiae of an at-one-ment that is no more but one and no longer but one...

At some level these papers simply express, and push, that which is already known, in the background, "here" in religion—namely that only by subterfuge do, say, "Judaism," "Paul," "Origen," shift from the name of a question into terms into which only observations of like type can be corralled.[70] Scholarly business as usual thrives on difference and its management: it needs hyper-Enlightened microscopics; it implicitly agrees with Derrida that even the smallest conceptual atom is subject to fission, and indeed it divides itself into smaller and smaller sections of study to do each atom perfect justice. But, equally, it needs to manage disjunction, which it does through evolutionary narratives or through the related synchronic-rhetorical device whereby cherished truths rise to the surface while their rivals sink back into a general background of "richness." The Babel tower of disciplinary idiolects that is the AAR/SBL knows, as surely as Derrida, that there is no single transhistorical, transcultural edifice called religion, perhaps even senses that this very contested and riven site is the perfect "place" to which to welcome deconstruction, which is always "just visiting." But the smooth running of the conference machine also requires the denial that this is the case.[71] The distinctiveness of this volume lies in the way in which the papers assembled here foreground the movements of *différance* in ways that might be risky for our disciplinary health. Beyond dreams of cohesion and oneness perpetrated by the strangely similar structures of a unifying monotheism and scientific empiricism (the demand to get at what "is," down low beneath all mystification), they perform the risk of choosing, leaping, deciding in places where the "one" is subject to "the rest(lessness)" and where we are not yet saved or even safe.

Stranger yet, these readings resonate with certain notes of very ancient commentary that, as Robert Gibbs provocatively puts it, "recharg[e] the biblical text" in "negotiation and even disappointment in and with [it]."[72] They intimate a sense of mourning and affirming and of imperfect relation that comes from always arriving too late.

References

1. Jacques Derrida, *Specters de Marx* (Paris: Galilée, 1993), pp. 40, 94; *Spectres of Marx*, trans. Peggy Kamuf (New York and London: Routledge, 1994), pp. 16, 54. Here we are following Geoffrey Bennington's translation in "Deconstruction and Ethics," in *Deconstructions: A User's Guide*, ed. Nicholas Royle (Basingstoke and New York: Palgrave, 2000), pp. 64–82 (66–67).
2. Derrida, "Unsealing ('the old new language')" in *Points: Interviews 1974–1984*, ed. Elisabeth Weber, trans. Peggy Kamuf et al. (Stanford: Stanford University Press, 1995), pp. 115–31 (118).
3. For Derrida's secret name Elie/Elijah, see Derrida, *Memoirs of the Blind: The Self-Portrait and Other Ruins*, trans. Pascale-Anne Brault and Michael Naas (Chicago: University of Chicago Press, 1993), pp. 21–23 and "Circumfession" in *Jacques Derrida*, Geoffrey Bennington and Jacques Derrida (Chicago and London: University of Chicago Press, 1993), pp. 83, 88–90.
4. See Jacques Derrida, "Faith and Knowledge: the Two Sources of 'Religion' at the Limits of Reason Alone," in *Religion*, Derrida and Gianni Vattimo (Cambridge: Polity Press, 1998), pp. 1–78 (29). This year, unusually, the conference was held in Canada—North America but not the United States.

5. See Jacques Derrida, "Et cetera… (and so on, und so weiter, and so forth, et ainsi de suite, und so überall, etc.)," trans. Geoffrey Bennington, in *Deconstructions: A User's Guide*, ed. Nicholas Royle (Basingstoke and New York: Palgrave, 2000), p. 283.

6. The phrase is Royle's. See his *Jacques Derrida* (New York: Routledge, 2003), p. 14.

7. Derrida, "Biodegradables," trans. Peggy Kamuf, *Critical Inquiry* 15:4 (1989): 850.

8. The phrase "fantasising proportionality" is taken from Catherine Keller and Stephen Moore, "Derridapocalypse," in this volume.

9. For one of many meditations on the relation between Western cultures of subjectivity and structures of confession, sin, and default, see Derrida, "The Animal That Therefore I Am (More to Follow)," trans. David Wills, *Critical Inquiry* 28:2 (2001): 390. For the repentance or confession of God see "Epoché and Faith," "The Animal That Therefore I Am," pp. 385–386, and *Donner la mort* (Paris: Galilée, 1999), pp. 161–209 (esp. pp. 185–202).

10. The ironic reverberations of the "echo-chamber" can be tracked through Fredric Jameson, *The Prison-House of Language* (Princeton: Princeton University Press, 1972); Meyer Abrams, "The Deconstructive Angel," *Critical Inquiry* 3 (1977): 431; René Wellek, "Destroying Literary Studies," *The New Criterion* 2:4 (December 1983): 3–7; Terry Eagleton, *Literary Theory: An Introduction* (Oxford: Oxford University Press, 1983), pp. 144-145. For an excellent analysis of these and other circulating slogans see Herman Rapaport, *The Theory Mess: Deconstruction in Eclipse* (New York: Columbia University Press, 2001).

11. See the popular dictionary definitions of deconstruction as either (banally) "De+construction: the action of undoing the construction of a thing," or (apocalyptically, madly) the assertion that "readers must eradicate all philosophical or other assumptions when approaching a text." From *The Oxford English Dictionary* (1989) and *Chambers Dictionary* (1998) as gathered by Nicholas Royle, in "What is Deconstruction?" in *Deconstructions*, pp. 1–4.

12. Ironically, the blurb in the program book for the 2002 AAR/SBL meeting, not authored by us, described Derrida as "the one whose work originated the *school of deconstruction*," and the one who "introduced *the deconstructive approach to reading texts*" (italics added). For Derrida's attacks on popular understandings of deconstruction as an interpretive "crowbar," an intricate method smacking of "technical rigor", or a blueprint of a "technical operation used to dismantle systems," see for example, Derek Attridge, ed., *Acts of Literature* (New York and London: Routledge, 1992), p. 2; "Letter to a Japanese Friend" in *A Derrida Reader: Between the Blinds*, ed. Peggy Kamuf (New York: Columbia University Press, 1991), pp. 270–276; Christine McDonald, ed., *The Ear of the Other: Otobiography, Transference, Translation: Texts and Discussions with Jacques Derrida* (Lincoln and London: University of Nebraska Press, 1988), p. 85.

13. For Derrida as "Nero of Philosophy" see R. Harris's letter to the editor, "Fiddle, Fiddle, Fiddle," *Times Literary Supplement* (March 21, 1997).

14. See, for example, Jürgen Habermas's description of deconstruction as regressive mysticism in *The Philosophical Discourse of Modernity: Twelve Lectures* (Cambridge: MIT Press, 1987), p. 182; and Deborah Lipstadt's understanding of "deconstructionism" as an ally of Holocaust in *Denying the Holocaust: The Growing Assault on Truth and Memory* (London: Penguin, 1994), pp. 18–19, 29.

15. See, for example, Habermas's accusations that Derrida "degrades politics and contemporary history to the status of the ontic and the foreground, so as to romp all the more freely, with a greater wealth of associations, in the sphere of the ontological and the archwriting," *The Philosophical Discourse of Modernity*, pp. 181–182; or Gerald Graff's dismissal of the "vanguard professor-intellectual" who markets a fashionable impotence and so diverts radicalism from "legitimate targets—injustice, poverty, triviality, vulgarity, and social loneliness—to a spurious quest after psychic liberation," *Literature Against Itself: Literary Ideas in Modern Society* (Chicago: University of Chicago Press, 1979), p. 116. See also Martha Nussbaum's comment that *Spurs* left her with a "hunger for blood; for … writing about literature that talks of human lives and choices as if they matter" (*Love's Knowledge: Essays on Philosophy and Literature* [New York and Oxford: Oxford University Press, 1990], p. 171). This accusation may lie behind Derrida's meditations on the desirability, and impossibility, of the "pen-syringe" in "Circumfession," pp. 10–12.

16. For examples of denunciations of Derrida in Religion, which have been, if anything, more vehement than in the Humanities at large, see, for example, Kath Filmer, "Of Lunacy and

Laundry Trucks: Deconstruction and Mythopoesis," in *Literature and Belief,* ed. Bruce L. Edwards Jr. (Provo: Brigham Young Press, 1989), pp. 55–64. The phrase "philosophical cloud cuckoo land" can be found on p. 55. See also Alastair McGrath's bizarre description of deconstruction as "the critical method which virtually declares that the identity and intentions of the author of a text are irrelevant to the interpretation of the text, prior to insisting that no meaning can be found in it," Alastair E. McGrath, *Christian Theology: An Introduction* (Oxford: Basil Blackwell, 2nd ed. 1995), p. 114; and the grand claim by the current Bishop of Durham, Tom Wright, that "deconstruction and its pseudo-discourse merely reinscribe empire, allowing the bullies and the bosses to create facts on the ground to their own advantage" ("That Special Relationship," *The Guardian,* [October 18, 2003]: 27).

17. See, for example, "White Mythology: Metaphor in the Text of Philosophy" in *Margins of Philosophy,* trans. Alan Bass (Chicago: University of Chicago Press, 1982), 207–272; *Monolingualism of the Other, or, The Prosthesis of Origin,* trans. Patrick Mensah (Stanford: Stanford University Press, 1998), esp. p. 9; "Faith and Knowledge: The Two Sources of 'Religion' at the Limits of Reason Alone," esp. p. 2. See also Derrida's ongoing struggle with the question of how one might avoid "dissolv[ing] the idioms of difference, the singularities, within a universal, empty, formal language, which as we know is always pretending to be universal" and "reaffirm singularity, specific minority idioms, without giving rise to what we call nationalism in its violent and imperialistic forms," *Talking Liberties: Interviews* (London: Channel 4, 1992), p. 9. Although he frequently writes of his experience as *pied noir,* a noncitizen, or one who grew up on the fringes of the Holocaust universe, Derrida is wary of citing these as subaltern credentials, as if he were strategically "playing the card of the exile and immigrant worker." See *Monolingualism of the Other,* p. 5.

18. While emphatically not saying that the strange functions of Derrida-as-signifier are in any way *attributable* to his perceived Jewishness, we do want to point out a certain similarity between the mythological services of Derrida-as-excess and the more traditional symbolic services of the "Jew." Why does Jürgen Habermas place Derrida close to "Jewish mysticism," cast as anarchic, retrogressive, and curiously proto-fascist? And why does Cornel West seem to link Derrida's Jewishness with bookishness and impotence when he says that "given Derrida's own status as an Algerian-born Jewish leftist marginalized by a hostile French academic establishment (quite different from his reception by the youth in the American academic establishment), the sense of political impotence and hesitation regarding the efficacy of moral action is understandable—but not justifiable"? See Habermas, *The Philosophical Discourse of Modernity,* p. 182, and Cornel West, "The New Cultural Politics of Difference," in *Out There: Marginalisation and Contemporary Cultures,* eds. Russell Fergusson, Cornel West, and Trinh T. Minh-ha (Cambridge: MIT Press, 1990), p. 30. For discussion, see Rapaport, *The Theory Mess,* pp. 48–53, and *Later Derrida: Reading the Recent Work* (London: Routledge, 2003), pp. 15–16.

19. The term "sexing up" is common media parlance, currently, in the U.K., bound up with the Hutton Enquiry, the death of Dr. Kelly, and the battle between the British government and the BBC over the Weapons of Mass Destruction dossier (September 14, 2002). Like its cognate "spin," it points to an increasing public awareness of the mediatization of reality by journalists and governments—hardly an irrelevant concern, and one that seems to find its academic correlate in denunciations of "Derrida."

20. For Derrida's response to the crisis of the natural and to the technological condition (so confusingly expressed in the reification of the deconstructive super-machine and also the demonization of deconstruction as the enemy of the actual) see, for example, "The Rhetoric of Drugs" in *Points,* pp. 244–245; and Derrida and Bernard Stiegler, *Echographies of Television: Filmed Interviews,* trans. Jennifer Bajorek (Oxford: Polity Press, 2002). For his numerous reflections on the role of the University see, for example, "Mochlos: or, The Conflict of the Faculties," trans. Richard Rand and A. Wygant, in *Logomachia: The Conflict of the Faculties,* ed. R. Rand (Lincoln: University of Nebraska Press, 1992), pp. 1–34; "Ja, or the Faux-Bond," in *Points,* pp. 30–77 (esp. p. 63); *Du Droit à la philosophie* (Paris: Editions Galilée, 1990), esp. III and IV; "The University Without Condition" in Derrida, *Without Alibi,* ed., trans. and intro. Peggy Kamuf (Stanford: Stanford University Press, 2002), pp. 202–237.

21. See Herman Rapaport's *The Theory Mess,* p. 155.

22. Scanning the program book for the 2002 AAR/SBL one finds a swarm of new methodologies ("character ethics," "cognitive linguistics," "consumption analysis," "social memory theory"), testifying to the increasing atomisation and proliferation of methodologies.

23. See Christina Howell's careful analysis of what Derrida does and does not do with the subject in *Derrida: Deconstruction from Phenomenology to Ethics* (Oxford: Polity Press, 1998), pp. 142–143. For Derrida's highly amusing parody of eschatological eloquence see "Of an Apocalyptic Tone Recently Adopted in Philosophy," trans. J.P. Leavey, *Oxford Literary Review* 6:2 (1984): 3–37 (20–21). Cf. Walter Lowe's discussion of skewed retrojections of "Modernity" in "Christianity and Anti-Judaism" in this volume.

24. For Derrida's resistance to the death of the Author, "of which too much of a case has been made," see *Signeponge/Signsponge*, trans. Richard Rand (New York: Columbia University Press, 1984), p. 22. For early critiques of the idea of the "transcendence of semantic excess," see "Positions" in Derrida, *Positions*, trans. Alan Bass (Chicago: University of Chicago Press, 1981), p. 46.

25. Derrida *follows* the later Lévinas for whom hospitality is a radical break up of ontology and ego, where "to be" is "to follow" ("Je *suis*"). See, for example, "'Eating Well' or the Calculation of the Subject" in *Points*, pp. 255–87, and "Hostipitality," trans. Gil Anidjar in *Acts of Religion*, Derrida, ed. and intro. Gil Anidjar (New York and London: Routledge, 2002), pp. 358–420 (esp. p. 391). For John D. Caputo's discussion of heteromorphic versus heteronomic difference, see *Against Ethics: Contributions to a Poetics of Obligation with Constant Reference to Deconstruction* (Bloomington and Indianapolis: Indiana University Press, 1992), pp. 53–62.

26. For Derrida's wry comments on the reduction of "the other" to weak homily see "Above All No Journalists!" in *Religion and Media*, ed. Hent de Vries and Samuel Weber (Stanford: Stanford University Press, 2001), pp. 56–93 (81) and *Monolingualism of the Other*, p. 41.

27. See Rapaport, *The Theory Mess*, p. 124.

28. See Derrida, "This Strange Institution called Literature," trans. Geoffrey Bennington and Rachel Bowlby in *Acts of Literature*, pp. 33–75 (55); and *Memoires: For Paul de Man*, trans. Cecile Lindsay, Jonathan Culler, and Eduardo Cadava (New York: Columbia University Press, 1986), p. 96.

29. Cf. Giovanni Borradori, *Philosophy in a Time of Terror: Dialogues with Jürgen Habermas and Jacques Derrida* (Chicago and London: University of Chicago Press, 2003), p. 118: "I decipher, I wager, I hope…"

30. See, for example, Derrida, "Afterword: Toward an Ethic of Discussion," trans. Samuel Weber in *Limited Inc.* (Evanston: Northwestern University Press, 1998), p. 141; "Passages—From Traumatism to Promise" in *Points*, pp. 372–395 (385); "The Animal That Therefore I Am," p. 396.

31. For Derrida, who takes a great deal from his reading of Austin, all constatives have a performative element and vice versa, and the "perverformative" indicates the risk that structurally conditions any performative. For example, for someone to promise it is necessary that he or she might be lying, or joking, or might die before they have a chance to keep the promise—otherwise the promise would not be a promise and would not require credit or credence. For a more fulsome explanation of the performative and perverformative see Royle, *Jacques Derrida*, pp. 28–29. See also Geoffrey Bennington's discussion of the aporia whereby "the necessary possibility of the worst is a positive condition of the (unconditionally demanded) better" in "Deconstruction and Ethics," p. 72.

32. For Derrida's discussion of the risk and faith of writing, see "Force and Signification," *Writing and Difference*, pp. 3–30 (9, 12); "I have a taste for the secret," p. 30; "A 'Madness' Must Watch over Thinking" in *Points*, pp. 339–364 (350).

33. Derrida, "Unsealing ('The Old New Language')," pp. 115–116. On Derrida's response to the frequent accusation that he is wasting his and our time, as well as "the times" see, for example, "The Deconstruction of Actuality" in *Negotiations: Interventions and Interviews 1971–2001*, ed. and trans. Elizabeth Rottenberg (Stanford: Stanford University Press, 2002), p. 89.

34. Compare Michèle Le Doueff's description of the compelling submissive hubris of Pascal—a description that could almost be applied, verbatim, to Derrida. "Long Hair, Short Ideas" in *The Philosophical Imaginary* (London and New York: Continuum, 2002) pp. 100–128 (esp. pp. 123, 127).

35. See Christopher Norris, "Transcendental Vanities," *Times Literary Supplement* (April 27, 1984): 470; Gayatri Spivak, "Translator's Preface," Derrida, *Of Grammatology* (Baltimore: The Johns Hopkins University Press, 1976), p. lxxviii.

36. See Walter Lowe, *Theology and Difference: The Wound of Reason* (Bloomington: Indiana University Press, 1993); Hans Urs von Balthasar, *Mysterium Paschale: The Mystery of Easter*, trans. and intro. Aidan Nichols (Edinburgh: T. & T. Clark, 1990); and Eberhard Jüngel, *God as the Mystery of the World: On the Foundation of the Theology of the Crucified One in the Dispute between Theism and Atheism*, trans. Darrell L. Guder (Grand Rapids: Eerdmans, 1983).

37. See Susan Handelman, *The Slayers of Moses: The Emergence of Rabbinic Interpretation in Modern Literary Theory* (Albany: State University of New York Press, 1982).

38. See John Milbank, *Theology and Social Theory: Beyond Secular Reason* (Oxford: Basil Blackwell, 1990), Part IV.

39. See Catherine Pickstock, *After Writing: On the Liturgical Consummation of Philosophy* (Oxford: Basil Blackwell, 1998).

40. Anyone who has visited the Sagrada Familia and seen the intricate models that Gaudi used to produce his audacious, nongeometrical effects, will understand why we find this an appropriate analogy for Derrida's acts of writing.

41. See "Faith and Knowledge," pp. 5, 28; Borradori, *Philosophy in a Time of Terror*, pp. 116–117; Hent de Vries, *Philosophy and the Turn to Religion* (Baltimore: The Johns Hopkins University Press, 1999), pp. 1–39.

42. Derrida, "Faith and Knowledge," p. 34.

43. Derrida, "Faith and Knowledge," p. 45.

44. On the way in which Enlightenments and Revelations cross around the figure of the eye wide open, see, for example, "The University Without Condition," *passim* but esp. pp. 214–215, and "Faith and Knowledge," pp. 44–45.

45. Borradori, *Philosophy in a Times of Terror, passim*, but esp. pp. 121, 131–32.

46. Though he does not slip so easily into realms or pure irrationality, or supra-rational "feeling," Derrida's ventured "definitions" of religion resonate with Rudolf Otto's *Das Heilege*. For Otto, as in a sense for Derrida, the holy signifies, by definition, a clear "overplus" over ethics, so that, even though the holy intimates intense moral significance, that moral significance never empties out the whole meaning of the word. See Otto, *The Idea of the Holy: An Inquiry into the Non-Rational Factor in the Idea of the Divine and its Relation to the Rational*, trans. John W. Harvey (New York: Oxford University Press, 1965), p. 5.

47. Derrida, "Faith and Knowledge," pp. 50–51.

48. See de Vries, *Philosophy and the Turn to Religion*, p. 11.

49. For example, ancient responses to the sacrifice of Isaac or Ishmael in Judaism, Christianity, and Islam are clearly trying to foreclose the text's dangerous intimation of religion beyond ethics. For discussion, see Yvonne Sherwood, "Binding-Unbinding: Divided Responses of Judaism, Christianity and Islam to the 'Sacrifice' of Abraham's Beloved Son," forthcoming in *JAAR* 72:4 (2004).

50. Returning from Camp David during the inexorable build-up to the war with Iraq, Tony Blair was asked by hostile British journalists whether he and Bush had "prayed together." For Derrida, the so-called rise of religious conservatism in America and the rise of "Islamic fundamentalism" are hardly insignificant features on the present geo-political landscape, but neither are they self-evident symptoms of the "rise of the (purely) religious."

51. See "A 'Madness' Must Watch Over Thinking," pp. 351, cf. 355: "If by community one implies, as is often the case, a harmonious group, consensus, and a fundamental agreement beneath the phenomena of discord or war, then I don't believe in it very much and I sense in it as much threat as promise." On the necessary ingratitude of response, see Derrida, "At This Very Moment in This Work Here I Am," trans. R. Berezdevin, in *Re-Reading Lévinas*, eds. Robert Bernasconi and Simon Critchley (Bloomington: Indiana University Press, 1991), p. 13.

52. For the record, the call for papers went out under the headings "Hospitality: Monolingualism (Monotheism) and the Other," "Sacrifice and Secrets," "Towards the Outside," "La Toucher/Touching Her" and "Reading a Page of Scripture (with a Little Help from Derrida)." Some of the many papers submitted for the "Reading a Page of Scripture..." panels have been ushered into another home: Yvonne Sherwood, ed., *Derrida's Bible*, Religion/Culture/

Critique (New York: Palgrave Macmillan, 2004). The papers presented in Toronto have been supplemented with contributions from Virginia Burrus, John Manoussakis, and Tyler Roberts.

53. For Marcella Althaus-Reid's self-definition as "indecent theologian" see her *Indecent Theology: Theological Perversions in Sex, Gender and Politics* (Routledge: New York, 2000).

54. Three pairs, in which we ourselves participated, were invited to experimentally "Read a Page of Scripture With a Little Help from Derrida": Keller/Moore, Hart/Aichele, and Sherwood/Caputo. The three teams took different approaches: Keller and Moore divided their piece into a game of two halves; Sherwood/Caputo wove the two voices together into a single, though not seamless, piece; and Hart/Aichele acted out a dialogue (it is in their piece that the cracks among our partnerships show most clearly).

55. For Derrida's (out)work on the preface, particularly in relation to Hegel's proliferating prefaces, see especially *Dissemination*, trans. Barbara Johnson (Chicago: University of Chicago Press, 1981).

56. We refer to the Capri colloquium (February–March 1994). Cf. Derrida's comments in "Faith and Knowledge," p. 5.

57. For Derrida and Buddhism (specifically Ch'an mediation and Nagarjuna), see Robert Magliola, *Derrida on the Mend* (West Lafayette: Purdue University Press, 1984); and *Deconstructing Life-Worlds: Buddhism, Christianity, Culture* (AAR Cultural Criticism Series; Oxford University Press, 1997); and David Loy, "The Deconstruction of Buddhism" in *Derrida and Negative Theology,* eds. Harold Coward and Toby Foshay (Albany: State University of New York Press, 1992), pp. 227–253. For Derrida and Bhartrhari, Sankara, Aurobindo, and Nagarjuna see Harold G. Coward, *Derrida and Indian Philosophy* (Albany: State University of New York Press, 1990); and Coward, "Derrida and Bharthari's Vakyapadiya on the Origin of Language" in *Philosophy East and West* 40:1 (1990): 3–16. See also Gayatri Spivak's comments on affinities between deconstruction and the so-called ethno-philosophies in *A Critique of Postcolonial Reason* (Cambridge: Harvard University Press, 1999), p. 429.

58. For analyses that press the figure of the "Arab-Jew" and the conjunction and disjunction of Derrida and Islam, see Gil Anidjar, *The Jew, The Arab: A History of the Enemy* (Stanford: Stanford University Press, 2003); and "'Once More, Once More': Derrida, the Arab, the Jew" in Derrida, *Acts of Religion*, pp. 1-39 (esp. p. 10 n. 32). Also see Fethi Benslama, *La psychoanalyse à l'épreuve de l'Islam* (Paris: Aubier, 2002) and Benslama, ed., *Idiomes, Nationalites, Déconstructions: Rencontre de Rabat avec Jacques Derrida* (Cahiers Intersignes 13; Paris: l'Aube-Toukbal, 1998). See especially Benslama's "Editorial" and "La répudiation originaire," pp. 5–12 and 111–149.

59. Compare Derrida's comments on the Latin and Roman histories of "religion" in "Faith and Knowledge."

60. Cf. Lawrence Hoffman: "Attracted and yet repelled by each other, Jews and Christians established an historical trajectory much like the fabled DNA spiral: swirling round each other in mutual orbit, never coming quite close enough to coalesce, but at the same time, neither one managing to extricate itself from the pull exercised by the other," *Covenant of Blood: Circumcision and Gender in Rabbinic Judaism* (Chicago: University of Chicago Press, 1996), p. 111.

61. See *Monolingualism of the Other*, esp. pp. 52–56; and "How To Avoid Speaking: Denials," trans. Ken Frieden, *Languages of the Unsayable: The Play of Negativity in Literature and Literary Theory* (New York: Columbia University Press, 1989), pp. 3–70, esp. pp. 53 and 31 n. 3. The phrase about Jewish singularity as that which waits is from Blanchot, *The Writing of The Disaster*, trans. Ann Smock (Lincoln: University of Nebraska Press, 1986), p. 25. n. 8. On Blanchot and the Jews, see Kevin Hart, *The Dark Gaze: Maurice Blanchot and the Sacred* (Chicago: University of Chicago Press, 2004), chaps. 6 and 7.

62. "Foot" in biblical Hebrew is, as Derrida knows, a euphemism for penis (which may be one reason for placing his circumfession, as expanded footnote, at the bottom of the page).

63. The feminist or womanist castigation of "Derrida" for depriving woman of voice and essence (just at the moment when she was beginning to find it) seems to be—at least partly—another example of the use of "Derrida" to work out internal problems and pressures. Certainly, as Nancy Holland argues, feminist dismissals of Derrida, like the generally circulating caricatures discussed above, seem to reach in symptomatically opposite directions, condemning him for "doing too much and too little," being "too subjective" and "not subjective enough," and "destroy[ing] old foundations and old authorities but leav[ing] none for our own use," Nancy Holland, *Is Women's Philosophy Possible?* (Savage: Rowman

and Littlefield, 1990), p. 14. Having moved from the unified woman of 70s feminism, to pluralised (but still essentialized) "women," in a move still haunted by the question of the adequacy of all those commas (is it enough to say that one is an "Asian-comma-Buddhist-comma-woman" or a "white-comma-Christian-comma-American-comma-woman?)" commonsense (and thoroughly comma-ed) feminism is itself profoundly in doubt about "woman." It knows, though it says it differently, that the "ism" in feminism marks a problematic passage between the empirical and the transcendental, and now often works not so very far from Derrida's own starting point: the belief that if "she" is not simply to underwrite existing logics and structures, "woman" must function not as a self-evident concept, but as a lever of experimentation and risk.

64. Ellen T. Armour, *Deconstruction, Feminist Theology and the Problem of Difference: Subverting the Race/Gender Divide* (Chicago: University of Chicago Press, 1999), pp. 63–64.

65. Cf. Derrida's emphasis on the need to "resexualis[e] a philosophical and theoretical discourse which has been too 'neutralizing'" in "Choreographies," *The Ear of the Other*, p. 181.

66. For one of many of Derrida's discussions of rights—our need of them and also their need of extension and clarification—see Borradori, *Philosophy in a Time of Terror*, p. 132.

67. For a discussion of the separation of "theology and deconstruction" and "theology and feminism" see Armour, *Deconstruction, Feminist Theology and the Problem of Difference*, esp. pp. 204–205.

68. Armour, *Deconstruction, Feminist Theology and the Problem of Difference*, p. 79.

69. See "Circumfession," p. 121. Also see "The *Retrait* of Metaphor," trans. F. Gasdner, *Enclitic* 2:2 (1987): 3–33 and "White Mythology", *passim*.

70. For how deconstruction replaces the homogenising effect of the proper name (Paul in general, Heidegger in general) with the name of a question, or the micrology of text, see for example Derrida, *A Taste for the Secret*, p. 9; *Of Grammatology*, p. 99.

71. For Derrida's frequent observations that religion is not one, see "Faith and Knowledge," p. 36; for deconstruction as visitor see Derrida, "The Time Is Out of Joint," trans. Peggy Kamuf in *Deconstruction is/in America: A New Sense of the Political*, ed. Anselm Haverkamp (New York: New York University Press, 1995), pp. 14–38 (29).

72. Gibbs, "Messianic Epistemology," Chapter 8 in this volume.

CHAPTER 2

Epoché and Faith: An Interview with Jacques Derrida

JOHN D. CAPUTO, KEVIN HART, AND YVONNE SHERWOOD

Transcribed by Brooke Cameron and Kevin Hart

Yvonne Sherwood: ...It is my very great pleasure to introduce—in French one would say *vous présenter*—Jacques Derrida, who we are so very pleased to say is here, present with us right before our very eyes and ears [*laughter*]. There are numerous ways that I could introduce this man who as an academic signature needs no introduction, but who, because of the persistence of certain caricatures that still stand in for reading, still perhaps, in some sense, does. I could present him, as it is customary to do on these occasions, in terms of his curriculum vitae, but then his work, as he once said of Emmanuel Lévinas, is so large that one can no longer glimpse its edges. I could introduce him in terms of his institutional affiliations, past and present (for example Yale, the Sorbonne, the Ecole Normale Supérieure in Paris and the New School in New York) but I wouldn't want to give you an impression of someone too much in love with institutions, who hasn't asked searching questions about what the University means and does. I could introduce him, as he sometimes has introduced himself, in a slightly tongue-in-cheek "*Ecce Homo*," as a little Arab Jew, a marrano of French Catholic culture, who grew up in a Christianised Judaism that spoke of circumcision as "baptism" and bar mitzvah as "communion," or as someone who regularly watches the Sunday morning TV programs on religion …These things would certainly not be irrelevant to our context here at the American Academy of Religion and the Society of Biblical Literature. Perhaps I should simply reel off a litany of topics that echo around Derrida's work as regularly as they reverberate around discussions at our annual meetings: for example, Augustine, circumcision, confession, Paul, prayer, the spirit and the letter, the Talmud, the tallit, the touch of Jesus, the flood, the tower of Babel, the sacrifice of Isaac (and/or Ishmael), Kierkegaard, messianism, wars of interpretation, Jerusalem, mysticism, Gershom Scholem, kabbalah, religious violence, the limits of ecumenism and tolerance, sacrifice, the sacrifice of woman at the heart of sacrifice, ethics, responsibility and forgiveness, the eschaton, the apocalypse of John, the name of God. Perhaps I should say, just once more, for the record, that Derrida is not an enemy of the good old *Aufklärung*, not an inventor of a machine or school called "deconstruction," not someone who believes that all the world's a text and we are merely players. Indeed, as Derrida has said, one of the requirements of deconstruction is that it touch on "firm structures" and "physical institutions," and that it makes texts answer, precisely to what *matters* to us.

A while ago some of us set an empty chair for Jacques Derrida at the annual meeting because we wanted to acknowledge the debt that many of us here owe to his work and because we wanted to create an opening for something yet to come. We are so glad that Jacques Derrida is here, that he has agreed to speak in English, a language which is not "his," and we would like to say, first of all, welcome.

[*Applause*]

John D. Caputo: In "Circonfession" you said that you are a man of prayers and tears, that you pray all the time and you wonder, as you say to Geoffrey Bennington, "If I ought to tell them that I pray, and describe how that could happen, according to what idiom and what rite, on one's knees or standing up, in front of whom or what books, for if you knew, G., my experience of prayers, you would know everything…?"[1] What do you mean by that? If you rightly pass for an atheist, to whom are you praying? How would your prayers be answered? Who do you expect to answer these prayers?

Jacques Derrida: In the sentence you quote, the signatory of the text says, "G., if you knew my experience of prayers, you would know everything." So I assume you want to know everything [*laughter*]. First, before I start trying to answer Jack's question, I would like to begin with what will in fact be a prayer. I want to thank all of you for this extraordinary hospitality, and to thank Yvonne Sherwood first of all. Your hospitality here is absolutely formidable. Which means that it is terrible for me because, first of all, I'm improvising in a foreign language, and, second, facing questions and problems in which, as everyone knows, I am not competent. And so, I feel very anxious. This is not a fiction: I *am* very anxious. But I will try to do my best.

The invitation to come to Toronto was extended to me in Paris where I met Yvonne at a conference on Judaism or Jewishness, on different Jewish-nesses, and my relations to them. I was already anxious. The conference was in a building in Paris that belongs to a Jewish community. I was terrified, because on the one hand I knew that some of these people would try and denounce me for not being Jewish enough, for not being authentically Jewish. Others would try and convert me to Judaism. And so it was a very strange moment to be invited to come to a conference on religion. I said yes to Yvonne, but I was not expecting such a huge event. In Paris, at that conference, I was not presenting myself as an authentic Jew, nor as a non-Jew; I was not expressing Judaism. Here I am not a Christian either, neither a Muslim nor a Buddhist. I am not a biblical scholar; I am not a theologian. And I have to face the terrible questions that come from the very generous friends who surround me, people who are experts in these fields. So please forgive me. That is my first prayer. I beg pardon for what I will try, in a very shy way, to say before you and before my friends.

Now I will try answer Jack's question. To begin with, my answer would take the form of a question: To whom does one ask *publicly* to say something about prayer? If I were a priest or a theologian or a well-known believer, you wouldn't ask me such a question. If I were simply a nonbeliever, well known as an atheist or as someone totally foreign to prayer, you wouldn't ask me this question. So why am I asked this question in public? Some years ago I would have declined. I would have said, "No, I will not answer this question." And I am wondering why I am now ready to say something. Before saying something in a very naïve and disarmed fashion, I would like to raise another question. In the text you quote, which you know better than others, even better than me, you assume that I am the man who signed it, a man who asks if I ought to tell people that I pray. But you know that the status of this text remains suspended. I have not simply signed this text. The text has the structure of a confession. It is a text that turns around a possible-impossible confession, around circumcision, and around confession. I am not making a confession. I am not signing a confession. I am not speaking in my own name. The text is intertwined with quotations from Saint Augustine. It has a very complex structure, in which it is difficult even for me to decide who is speaking, who is saying something about his prayer, his way of praying, and so on. If I now answer your question, it would have nothing to do with the quotation, because it is not theological, not a confession, not a letter, not … (Had we the time, we could devote a long seminar to the status of the text.) As you know, a prayer is something secret. At least it is for me, to the extent that I pray, if I pray. It is absolutely secret. Of course, there are public prayers. There are people in communities who pray together. And the first thing I will tell you is this: when I was young, my first rebellion against my religious environment was to do with public prayer. So my way of praying, if I pray, is absolutely private. Even if I am in public, even if I am in a synagogue and praying with others, I know that my own prayer would be silent and secret, interrupting something in the community. That is more than one reason for not answering your question! [*Laughter*]

Nevertheless, I will say something. On the one hand, a prayer has to be a mixture of something that is absolutely singular and secret—idiomatic, untranslatable—and, on the other hand, a ritual that involves the body in coded gestures and that uses a common, intelligible language. That is the way I pray, if I pray. And I pray all the time, even now. But there is a problem. My way of praying, if I pray, has more than one edge at the same time. There is something very childish here, and when one prays one is always a child. If I gather images from my childhood, I find images of God as a Father—a severe, just Father with a beard—and also, at the same time, images of a Mother who thinks I am innocent, who is ready to forgive me. This is the childish layer of my prayers, those I perform once a day, for instance, before I go to bed, or a prayer that I might pray right now. There is another layer, of course, which involves my culture, my philosophical experience, my experience of a critique of religion that goes from Feuerbach to Nietzsche. This is the experience of a nonbeliever, someone who is constantly suspicious of the child, someone who asks, "To whom am I praying? Whom am I addressing? Who is God?" In this layer—this layer of a more sophisticated experience, if I can put it that way—I find a way of meditating about the who that is praying and the who that is receiving the prayer. I know that this appears negative, but it isn't; it is a way of thinking when praying that does not simply negate prayer. It is a way of asking all the questions that we are posing at this conference, all of them. These questions are a part of my experience of prayer.

When I pray, I am thinking about negative theology, about the unnamable, the possibility that I might be totally deceived by my belief, and so on. It is a very skeptical—I don't like this word, "skeptical," but it will have to do—prayer. And yet this "skepticism" is part of the prayer. Instead of "skepticism," I could talk of *epoché*, meaning by that the suspension of certainty, not of belief. This suspension of certainty is part of prayer. I consider that this suspension of certainty, this suspension of knowledge, is part of an answer to the question, "Who do you expect to answer these prayers?" That suspension must take place in order for prayer to be authentic. If I knew or were simply expecting an answer, that would be the end of prayer. That would be an order—just as though I were ordering a pizza! [*Laughter*] No, I expect nothing like that. I assume that I must give up any expectation, any certainty, as the one, or the more than one, to whom I address my prayer, if this is still a prayer. Of course, the child who is praying is expecting an answer, expecting some protection for himself, for his beloved ones, for his relations, his wife, children, friends, and so on. But I can't tell if I am praying to someone invisible, to the transcendent one, or if I am praying to those others in myself that I want to address out of love and for the protection of their lives.

At the same time, there is a suspension of any expectation, any economy, any calculation. I am not expecting, I am not hoping: my prayer is hopeless, totally, totally hopeless. I think this hopelessness is a part of what prayer should be. Yet I know there is hope, there is calculation. There is economy, but what sort of economy? Is it the economy of the child or my economy now, as an old man? (If I agree to answer Jack's question—something I wouldn't have done years ago —it's probably because, growing old, I am more of a child than when I was younger. So I say, "Well, now, perhaps I might run the risk of saying something confidential in front of such an audience.") I know that in praying something happens, even if there is no one God in the form of a Father or a Mother receiving my prayer. I know that by the act of praying in the desert, out of love (because I wouldn't pray otherwise), something might already be good in myself: a therapy might be taking place. I know that by doing this, I try—I will not necessarily succeed—to affirm and accept something in myself that won't do any harm to anyone, especially to me. The impression that I do something good for myself or for my loved ones, that's the calculation. If, through this prayer, I am a little better at reconciliation, and if I give up any calculation because I cannot calculate the incalculable, I can become better. But to become better narcissistically is a way of loving in a better way, of being more lovable. That's a calculation; it strives to integrate the incalculable into a calculation. When I pray I experience something strange. The Judaism of my childhood, my experience as a philosopher, as a quasi-theologian, are there; all the texts I've read, from Plato to Saint Augustine to Heidegger, are there. They are my world, the world in which my prayers are prayed. That is the way I pray—at a given time, let's say a fixed moment of the day—and sometimes anywhere, at any moment, for instance, now.

Kevin Hart: I'd like to begin with two general questions about the relations between deconstruction and Christianity. You have pointed out that deconstruction is not to be regarded as a set of theses that can simply be removed from the contexts in which you write and applied to other contexts. It has neither a thetic character nor a proper home. Rather, deconstruction exists in its applications: it is forever mobile, reformulating itself in quite different places and times. In your early work, you came to deconstruction by way of particular philosophical and literary contexts; but, as you know, deconstruction also has a rich Judaic-Christian heritage. One could see Heidegger's *Destruktion* of metaphysics as a folding of Martin Luther's *Heidelberg Disputation* (1518) which folds Saint Paul's warning to the Corinthians, which has itself already folded Isaiah's vision of Yahweh's sentence, "I will destroy the wisdom of the wise." I am not suggesting that "deconstruction" can be translated without remainder by Heidegger's word *Destruktion* or that *Destruktion* can be translated without remainder by Luther's word *destruuntur*. Rather, I am drawing attention to a Judaic–Christian heritage of deconstruction. If this heritage exists and has effects, wouldn't a deconstruction of Christianity be bound to meet an internal limit? I am thinking of Jean-Luc Nancy's current project, *La déconstruction du Christianisme*, needless to say, but more generally of movements of deconstruction already in Christianity, beginning with the formation of the canon and the writings of the Church Fathers. What sort of negotiations do you see as significant in that encounter?

Jacques Derrida: Thank you, Kevin. Well, the word "negotiations" is a very difficult one here, because this negotiation, if there is such a thing, shouldn't be a compromise. It would be a very risky movement. I would totally agree with you: there *is* a Christian heritage, a Judeo-Christian heritage, to deconstruction. Since you mention Jean-Luc Nancy's project let me say something about that. Not everyone here will know the context in which I've been working in France these past few years. Jean-Luc Nancy is one of my best friends. He is currently trying to write what he calls a deconstruction of Christianity. Already in the preface to that book he agrees that Christianity is already self-deconstructed. So the deconstruction of Christianity might be, in a certain way, a Christian achievement. This could be so in many ways, not only because of the tradition that you have recalled, the one that passes through Heidegger's *Destruktion*, but also because I try to do something else with what I call deconstruction. I have the secret hope that it affects this tradition: not betraying it or simply deforming it but affecting it in a new and unexpected way. Now what I am doing is not Heideggerian, as you know, nor is it Lutheran. But this doesn't mean, and I agree with you on this point, that it is totally foreign to Jewish,

Christian, or even Islamic possibilities. Now if the type of deconstruction that I try to do remains let's say Abrahamic—Jewish, Christian, Islamic —this would imply that it's a part of this tradition, it's the memory of this tradition, and also that it affects this tradition in an unpredictable way.

What is Christianity? What is Judaism? What is Islam?

Who knows? Who knows what they will be in the future? Assume that the new Christians or the new Jews or the new Muslims have practiced this unpredictable form of deconstruction, what criteria could we use to establish the new form as Christian or Jewish or Islamic? Now the word "deconstruction" is more closely related to Christianity than to Judaism or Islam. It refers to Heidegger's *Destruktion* and to Luther's *destruuntur*. But the fact that it is literally linked to Christianity doesn't mean that Christianity is more deconstructive than other religions. I can imagine Buddhist, Jewish, or Muslim theologians saying to me, "Deconstruction—we've known that for centuries!" People have come to me from far Eastern cultures telling me just that. And I'm sure that there are Jewish theologians and probably Muslim theologians who would say the same thing. So the fact that deconstruction's link with Christianity is more apparent, more literal, than with other religions doesn't mean that Christianity has a greater affinity with deconstruction.

What Christianity will become in the coming centuries is totally unpredictable. Perhaps it's the religion that is more prepared, more apt, to transform itself than any other. When I spoke of *mondialatinisation* or, in English, globalatinization, I was thinking of globalization as a Christianization, as a Roman Christianization. I was implying that Christianity is the most plastic, the most open, religion, the most prepared, the best prepared, to face unpredictable transformations. So perhaps if the deconstruction of Christianity develops we won't be able to recognize the roots of the Christian religion any more and yet, nevertheless, we will still be able to say that this is Christianity. I think that's what is happening today, especially in a place like this. I have the obscure feeling that something is happening to Christianity, an unpredictable earthquake. And that's not necessarily negative.

Yvonne Sherwood: This might be a question for "Reb Rida." Although you have never invoked the Jewish tradition in any rooted or direct way, there are many resonances between your work and the midrashim. For example when you ask, in *The Gift of Death*, whether the story of the sacrifice of Isaac is predicated on the sacrifice of the woman (in both active and passive senses: woman as object and subject of sacrifice) I think of the ancient midrashim that see the death of Sarah, in Genesis 23, as a *consequence* of Genesis 22. I'm interested to know how you might read a

Isaac [handwritten margin note]

couple of midrashic fragments from Genesis Rabbah, which treat, as you do, subjects of woman, love, blood, sacrifice and circumcision and that seem to read the sacrifice of Isaac as a hypercircumcision. The first is a commentary on God's rather overqualified command in Genesis 22:2 ("*Take your son, your only son, whom you love, even Isaac*"):

> God said "Take your son." Abraham said to Him "I have two sons." He said to him, "Your only one." He said, "This one is the only son to his mother, and this one is the only one to his mother." He said to him, "Whom you love." He said to him, "I love them both." He said to him, "Isaac."

The second stages a drama that precedes the sacrifice:

> Isaac and Ishmael were engaged in controversy: the latter argued, "I am more beloved than you because I was circumcised at the age of thirteen" while the other retorted, "I am more beloved than you because I was circumcised at eight days." Ishmael said to him, "I am more beloved than you, since I was circumcised at thirteen and could have protested, but you were circumcised as a baby and could not refuse." At that moment Isaac exclaimed, "O that God would appear to me and bid me cut off my limbs! Then I would not refuse." (Another version says that Isaac retorted: "All that you did was to lend the Holy One, blessed be He, three drops of blood. But I am now thirty-seven years old yet if God desired of me that I be slaughtered, I would not refuse.")

Jacques Derrida: Thank you. Perhaps at the end of my two answers, I will try and relate the two commentaries. The first one tells us about the terrible experience of facing God, of obeying a God who gives unjustifiable orders in the name of love, in the name of the one you love, and asks someone—in this case, Abraham—to choose between two equally beloved sons. Abraham says, "I love them equally. Both are the sons of their mother, of his mother, and I love them equally." God insists, "You've only one, only one. So you have to elect one." Then Abraham insists, "I love both." And he said, "I love them both." And God said, "Isaac, just one." It's a terrible, terrible situation. Long before the experience of what is called the sacrifice, even before going up to Mount Moriah, there is terror: Abraham has to choose between two equally beloved sons. That's a terrible experience. And we experience it every day.

Abraham experiences at that moment that he must blindly obey an order, a heteronomic order, for which no justification can be provided. Immediately this situation goes beyond any ethical, any human, level.

That's what Kierkegaard says. In fact, Abraham *remains* a criminal: on the level of ethics it's a crime to obey God's order. Abraham accepts that the relation with God is wholly asymmetrical, that God can say to him, "I elect you in order that you elect one of your sons, you must elect him as the one you love. You must love him more than the other in order to kill him." Here we have the experience of a terrible duty. To act in obedience to God you must give up any justification, any humanly intelligible justification. You have to give up having any knowledge of the decision. Abraham's leap is a leap beyond knowledge, beyond ethics, beyond social bonds; it's beyond love and out of love because, as God says, "the one you love." That is the absolute religious experience, if there is such a thing: the pure act of faith, the asymmetrical obedience to an absurd order, an unintelligible order, an order that is beyond ethics and knowledge.

Now the second commentary has to do with two ways of understanding circumcision. On the one hand, we have Isaac who has been circumcised before having to accept circumcision, that is, before having to understand it. That's what happens in the Jewish religion; it's a covenant to which one subscribes. On the other hand, we have Ishmael and Muslim culture. He can say, "Well, at least I was old enough to understand what circumcision is, old enough to transform the heteronomy into an autonomy. I was freely accepting circumcision. So my faith is more intelligible, more authentic, than yours because I was more autonomous that you were." With Ishmael's answer, at least in this logical commentary, we already have the beginning of what I will have to call, in order to save time, a "secularization." It is a way of transforming heteronomy, an asymmetrical situation in which the baby, the young boy, is circumcised before he can understand what's happening, before he can speak. Ishmael is trying to transform an asymmetrical covenant into a somewhat symmetrical, autonomous contract. That is the beginning of secularization: the transition from heteronomy to autonomy. At the same time Ishmael claims that since he is prepared to make this sacrifice at an age when one understands what is involved, he is more ready to enter the covenant that remains asymmetrical. So there is a competition.

The other version you mentioned says, "Ishmael, all that you need is to lend the Holy One, Blessed be He, three drops of blood," and that is circumcision: three drops of blood, even if you are thirteen. "But now I am thirty-seven years old, yet I would not refuse to be slaughtered." There is an option between the two. Now, of course, I was circumcised at seven days without understanding anything. But if God demands or asks me to do even more, to be slaughtered now as an adult, I will accept. So there is an option. There is one who wants to be more obedient, more subject to God, in an asymmetrical way, than the other. And of course it is difficult to read this commentary without having one's eyes in the direction of what is happening today in many parts of the world, in Jerusalem, in this war. Who has been more true to God, more subject to heteronomy? Who has been more of a believer? If I had time, I would go in that direction, in the direction of politics. Needless to say, there is a lot to be said about politics with respect to Judaism, Islam, and Christianity today. When I use the word "political," I point to a human level that has been exceeded by the very first moment in this history, the moment when Abraham received an order by God. At that moment you can have nothing to do with ethics, politics, and the law. How are we to translate this metapolitical, transpolitical situation into the politics of our time? That's what politics are about today.

How can we translate this reference, this Abrahamic reference to this situation, into the geopolitical situation today? It's a matter of translation: not only a commentary on these commentaries but also a question of translation of the nonpolitical, nonethical (or transpolitical, transethical) situation into the political responsibilities that are ours today. It's a matter of negotiations—I come back to that word again—the most risky negotiations. The fact is, if one wants to be rigorous in this negotiation, we have to keep in mind the specificity of ethics and politics and the irreducible specificity of this transpolitical and transethical situation. On the one hand, you have Kierkegaard insisting upon the transethical stage, the religious level, and on the other hand, you have Lévinas who says that the most interesting moment of the story is the angel who suspends the sacrifice. Kierkegaard says that Abraham's sacrifice is a murder, but Lévinas opposes him and says that what matters is not that Abraham was ready to kill his son but that God interrupted the slaughter.

John D. Caputo: How does the "name" of God "work" for you as a "name?" What kind of an "affirmation" does this name contain for you, since in the end, deconstruction is a work of affirmation? In your earlier writings, in *Of Grammatology* and in the 1970s, the name of God seems tied very closely to a kind of "theological closure," to the desire to arrest the play, the desire for a centered discourse or a transcendental signified. But clearly that does not exhaust what the name of God means for you today, where this name has become a more open-ended name, more affirmative, perhaps more a "religious" name than a theological one, and one that you even speak of "saving." Whether you are mentioning this name or using it (and I'm often not sure when you are doing the one or the other), what is going on in and with this name for you now?

Jacques Derrida: A difficult question because on the one hand it is true that there has been a change, not, let's say, in my way of addressing these questions but in the strategy of the text. It is true that at the time I wrote *Of Grammatology* I was speaking in a context in which the name of God was for me what Heidegger would call onto-theological. That is, God as the absolute being, being present, and so on. When I used the word "theological" I meant just what you said. Even today when I speak of sovereignty as an onto-theological phantasm or heritage, I have the name of God in mind. Yet even while writing *Of Grammatology* I had the feeling that the name of God doesn't usually function the way one usually thinks it functions. (There must be signs of the same thing in my other earlier writings.) That is, and Hegel had already said this, God cannot be an example. The name of God is not a name among others. It must function differently. To come to the distinction between meaning and use, to ask whether I am mentioning the name or using it, and to wonder, as you do, whether I am mentioning the name or using it, I have to say that I am not sure, either. If there is something unique in the name of God, in what it names and in the way we name through it, then the distinction between mentioning and using is not pertinent any more. If you want this distinction to work, you have at least to imply that when you use a word there is a referent. "Give me a glass," I say. When I mention the word "glass" I am mentioning the word. I am referring to a word. I am not referring to a thing.

Given this deconstructive move, God could not be the omnipotent first cause, the prime mover, absolute being, or absolute presence. God is not some thing or some being to which I could refer by using the word "God." The word "God" has an essential link to the possibility of being denied. On the one hand, God is far beyond any given existence; he has transcended any given form of being. So I cannot use the word "God" for any finite being. On the other hand, God has an essential link to being named, being called, being addressed. When I use the word "God," I mention it. It is a word that I receive as a word with no visible experience or referent.

This comes back to what I said about prayer. When I pray, if I say "God," if I address God, I don't know if I am using or mentioning the word "God." It is this limit of the pertinence of the distinction between mention and use which makes religion possible and which makes the reference to God possible. That's why in my more recent texts I have been more attentive to the name of God. What are we doing when we name God? What are the limits of this naming? Now we know that in many Abrahamic traditions God is nameless, beyond the name. In Jewish traditions, God is the empty place, beyond any name. But we name the nameless. We name what is nameless. And when we name "what is not," what is or is not nameless, what do we do? That's why being a believer, even a mystic believer, and being an atheist is not necessarily a different state of affairs. I know that the most authentic believers know that they are very close to pure atheism because they know that in using the word "God" they may be merely mentioning it. To mention the word "God" is, in a certain way, already an act of faith. I'm not sure that there is pure faith, but if there is it would consist in asking the question, "When I use the word 'God,' am I referring to someone or mentioning a name?"

A word is not nothing; there is naming, calling. Heidegger draws an interesting distinction between *namen*, to name, and *heissen*, to call. When I mention the name of God, do I give a name, do I name, or do I call? It is difficult to think the experience of naming without referring to the experience of calling. To name is to call. If I am calling God "God," what am I doing? What is it to call? Some nonbelievers say, "Well, you are just calling. That's just mentioning a name." Others would say, "The fact that I call is already not a proof but a sign that God is the one who makes me call to God." The two say different things that are also the same thing. The one says, "When you name God you call God, that's your call; it's an empty call." And the other says, "If I feel the motivation, the impulse, to call God, it means that God is called through me; there is something in me that calls God, and that something is my faith." The skeptical one says that this is a nominalistic experience of calling, but this is a part of faith. Were I sure that when I call there is someone, someone real, at the other end, I wouldn't call. The skeptical person is a part of the faithful person. If God were really present to me, as a certain, as a sure, presence, I wouldn't call. I wouldn't even call Kevin, who is close to me, if I was sure that Kevin is really absolutely present to me. When I call him, it is because I am not sure that he is paying attention to me or that he is simply present. [*Laughter:* Kevin Hart is pouring a glass of water for Jacques Derrida.] That's why between the skeptical person and the believer there is no real contradiction.

Let me add a postscript. What I just said about the uniqueness of the name of God can be transplanted or transposed or translated into anyone's name, even the name of a finite being. It is the same situation. That is why I pick the example of naming or calling Kevin. Calling him has the same structure as calling to God. And that's why faith is at once an exceptional, unique experience and something very common, universal in a certain way.

Kevin Hart: My second general question turns on the relations between theology and deconstruction. Now theology is not one humanities discipline among others: the theologian speaks and writes from within the sphere of faith or, perhaps more exactly, from within an intersection of the spheres of faith and reason. Although you have discussed various topics in mysticism and apophatic theology, and have brooded on sacrifice and the "two sources" of religion, you have never written as a theologian. You have written about faith—about "religious faith" rather than "theological faith," if I might borrow Saint Thomas' distinction—and I would like to ask you a question about faith. Does deconstruction in theology meet an internal limit? If someone has theological faith, confesses to belief in Jesus as the Christ, does that limit what deconstruction can do in that person's thought? Or does it offer another context in which deconstruction works, albeit differently than in other contexts?

Jacques Derrida: I understand that what you call theological faith as opposed to religious faith implies the reference to the historical event that is Jesus. If someone has theological faith, one confesses to believe in Jesus as the Christ, does that limit what deconstruction can do in that person's thought? That is, what is called theology here is a way of relying on revelation, whereas religious faith is something more universal …

Kevin Hart: Theological faith is that faith which arises from grace given by God …

Jacques Derrida: On or about "grace given by God," deconstruction, as such, has nothing to say or to do. If it's given, let's say, to someone in a way that is absolutely improbable, that is, exceeding any proof, in a unique experience, then deconstruction has no lever on this. And it should not have any lever. But once this grace, this given grace, is embodied in a discourse, in a community, in a church, in a religion, in a theology—that is why the word "theological" is a real problem to me—then deconstruction, a deconstruction, may have something to say, something to do, but without questioning or suspecting the moment of grace. Of the discourses, the authorities, the law, the politics, all of which might be consequences of this grace, yes, deconstruction might have something to say or do, while respecting the possibility of this grace. The possibility of this grace is not publicly accessible. And from that point of view, I am really Kierkegaardian: the experience of faith is something that exceeds language in a certain way, it exceeds ethics, politics, and society. In relation to this experience of faith, deconstruction is totally, totally useless and disarmed. And perhaps it is not simply a weakness of deconstruction. Perhaps it is because deconstruction starts from the possibility of, if not grace, then certainly a secret, an absolutely secret experience which I would compare with what you call grace. That's perhaps the starting point of any deconstruction. That is why deconstruction is totally disarmed, totally useless when it reaches this point.

Yvonne Sherwood: Back in 1995, Jack Caputo, as faithful secretary or *Extra-Skriver*, wrote a commentary on *The Gift of Death*. This is how he translated your passage about what if Abraham were to sacrifice on top of Montmartre, instead of Moriah, in Jerusalem, in the incendiary "Middle

9/11

East": "Were a man later this week to take his son and head up to the top of the World Trade Center with the intention of offering his son in sacrifice, we would send a SWAT team to seize the man and put him under arrest for attempted murder, for denying the most elemental command of ethics, which is not to deal in death." Seven years ago, Jack's translation was comically "illustrative" and explicative. Now it makes us tremble in ways we could never have anticipated. My question is: how should we read yours and Jack's glosses on de Silentio and a certain Abraham or Ibrahim at home in Europe and America after 9/11; after the World Trade Center collapsed under the impact of knife and fire (murdering numerous sons and daughters) and after Mohammed Atta, hijacker of American Airlines Flight 11 said, in his will,[2] that his parents should be like Abraham or Ibrahim who willingly offered up their son to death?

Jacques Derrida: That's a very, very dangerous question. I admire the fact that Jack in '95 replaced my reference to Montmartre—very peaceful Montmartre—with the World Trade Center. Although, already in '95—and I don't say this to ignore your point—in '95, already there had been a bombing in the World Trade Center. And the World Trade Center is, of course, the mountain, the highest point in this country, in a certain way. It's a Tower of Babel: not Mount Moriah but a Tower of Babel, which, as you remember, was destroyed by God because of the arrogance of the people who built it. Of course, we could take a number of other examples, today, of terrible sacrifices or murders, collective murders, planes and bombings, and so on. I won't give other examples but would simply like to signal that there are other examples of this situation today. Now Yvonne's question is how should we read her and Jack's glosses on these events. How should we respond to a certain Abraham or Ibrahim at home in Europe and America after 9/11, after Mohammed Atta, the highjacker of American Airlines Flight 11, left a note saying that his parents should be like Abraham or Ibrahim who willingly offered up their son to death?

First, the comparison stops very quickly because even if the parents of Mohammed Atta were ready to offer their sons, in the case of Abraham and Isaac, there was no collective murder. There was just a victim or someone sacrificed. Whereas Mohammed Atta did not commit suicide, he killed thousands of people. Does that mean that the comparison doesn't work at all? If we seriously address the question of the political, military, or historical circumstances of the sacrifice of Isaac in the world since that time, in the name of these traditions, millions of people have been killed and are still being killed. So I don't know what the interpretation might be. My first reaction would be whether one considers the suicidal aspect or the murders, the collective murders, the consequences of this reference to the

divine order to be on the side of death. I cannot see any justification whatsoever for killing. I use the example—the *exemplary* example—of
Abraham and Isaac to say that each time we have to make a choice we are
in this situation. (That's what Jack was writing on.) But even if I use this
situation as paradigmatic, I would not draw the consequence that the
choice of killing, a choice against life, might be justifiable in any way.
Abraham remains a criminal on earth, and so does Mohammed Atta. A
suicide bomber is a criminal, both to himself and to those killed.

As you know, crimes of war and crimes at war are always, especially
now, allegedly justified by religious reasons. Even in President Bush's
discourse, when he speaks of going to war against the "axis of evil," saying
"God bless America," we have fundamentalist religious justification, an
alleged justification. I can find no justification whatsoever in this reference
to a sacrifice. My own discourse would be simply against any allegedly
justified killing and suicide. If I had to address this question politically
today, I would multiply the examples, despite the terrible example that you
chose, despite all the compassion that we have for the victims of 9/11. We
would have to take other examples as well and politically evaluate them
along with the events of 9/11.

John D. Caputo: In October 2001, speaking at the Villanova conference,
you said that while "God is supposed to be absolutely powerful in our
tradition" you are "trying to think of some divinity dissociated from
power, if it is possible." You added that some people would say that "There
is in Jesus Christ some weakness, some vulnerability, some powerlessness,"
but for you "this powerlessness of course is also a sign of the Almighty."
And you concluded, "This would have heavy ethical and political consequences, but it would deserve a long, much longer answer." I am eager to
learn more about this powerlessness of God, what a God dissociated from
power would be like, since it brushes against the grain of the most classical
and ingrained idea of divine omnipotence. What does such an expression
mean for you? In what sense could God lack power and still be God? What
would motivate us to talk about God in terms of powerlessness?

Jacques Derrida: There is nothing original, nothing absolutely original, in
saying that there might be some powerlessness in God: not absolute
powerlessness, of course, but some powerlessness. Even if one considers
God as infinite, we know from the Bible, for instance, that there are
moments in Genesis, in which God—I won't say repents because there is a
problem with translation here—but in which God realizes that he has not
done something that couldn't be improved upon. So there is finitude in
God's infinity. Then in Hegel you could understand that despite God's
infinity, God goes out of himself, enters nature, and becomes finite and, to

that extent, limited in his power. There are a number of examples of this tradition of God being without power.)

But this is not the way that I approach the possibility of a powerless God. My starting point has to do with the problem of sovereignty. I have tried again and again to dissociate two concepts that are usually indissociable: unconditionality and sovereignty. I would like to think of something unconditional in forgiving, in grace, in forgiveness, in the gift, in hospitality—an unconditionality that wouldn't be a sign of power, a sign of sovereignty. So I have tried to dissociate sovereignty and unconditionality. If I think of God on the side of grace, forgiveness, hospitality, unconditional law, then in order not to have to agree with what I call the onto-theological tradition of sovereignty, one has to dissociate God's sovereignty from God, from the very idea of God. We would have God without sovereignty, God without omnipotence. If one thinks of this possibility of the name of God being dissociated from absolute power, then this would be a strategic and political lever to think of unconditionality without sovereignty, and to deconstruct the political concept of sovereignty today, which I would argue is a heritage of onto-theology.

The history of the concept of sovereignty is undergoing a terrible crisis today. There is an earthquake all over the world, with nation states trying to keep sovereignty and others trying to challenge this sovereignty. Today, in terms of international law, the big political problems are problems of sovereignty. We have to think differently about sovereignty, and to deconstruct the onto-theological tradition of sovereignty. And from that point of view, if one wants to keep what I call the unconditional—the gift, hospitality, forgiveness, and so on—we have to dissociate sovereignty and unconditionality. Then we would have to dissociate God and absolute power. Perhaps this comes close to a Christian motif, one you just mentioned. We would have to rethink the vulnerability and powerlessness of Jesus without the absolute power that nonetheless remains in the tradition, the foundation, or the last recourse of Christianity. If it is as weak and vulnerable that Jesus Christ represents or incarnates God, then the consequence would be that God is not absolutely powerful. Or, putting things the other way round, we would say that the weakness, the powerlessness of Jesus, is the human part of the passion, and that God remains absolutely powerful. That's a decision to be made within Christianity. I think we can agree that there are two movements in Christianity.

John D. Caputo: You are suggesting a more radical possibility. The more traditional one would be to say that there is a vulnerability in Jesus, but God retains absolute power.)But to say that there is a vulnerability in God,

(Caputo)

I mean a genuine powerlessness in God, and there Jesus incarnates it, is more interesting.

Jacques Derrida: More interesting, but less common, no?

John D. Caputo: I think so.

Kevin Hart: From time to time you have made use of Heidegger's distinction between *Offenbarung* and *Offenbarkeit*, revelation and revealability. As usually received, the distinction asks us to think about the relative priority of revelation and revealability. Does revelation precede revealability, making conditions of manifestation apparent only after the fact? Or are conditions of revealability in place before a revelation occurs? I would like to invite you to reflect on this distinction. Is it a clear alternative? Or should it be understood, as you hint now and then, as an aporia? You suggested in *Politics of Friendship* that rethinking the alternative by way of iterability might "at least give access to a structure of experience in which the two poles of the alternative cease to oppose one another to form another node, another 'logic,' another 'chronology,' another history, another relation to the order of orders." Could you say a little more about this other structure of experience?

Jacques Derrida: In fact, what I could say would simply go along with what you just suggested: the distinction is an aporia. And as you know, the aporia for me doesn't mean simply paralysis. No way. On the contrary, it's the condition of proceeding, of making a decision, of going forward. The aporia is not simply a negative stop.

Now for those here who are not familiar with this distinction between *Offenbarung* and *Offenbarkeit* that Kevin just mentioned, I would simply summarize the meaning of this distinction, which comes to us from Heidegger. Heidegger says the *Offenbarung*, that is revelation, implies —*implies*, it's not logical, it's not chronological—implies that some revealability, some *Offenbarkeit*, was already there: the "already" has no chronological meaning. For some revelation to take place *Dasein*, the human existence, must be able to open itself to revelation, and this revealability is, let's say, ontologically—not chronologically, not logically—prior to *Offenbarung*, to revelation. If you want to think religious revelation, you have to first go backwards, so to speak, to the possibility of religion, to the possibility of revelation. The question is: Is this the proper order, first in the non-chronological, nonlogical sense, first revealability and the revelation? Or is it more complicated than that?

My difficulty with Heidegger's very strong, very rigorous argument has to do with the possibility that revelation is not simply something that comes to confirm and to fulfill a revealability. Revelation is something that reveals revealability. It is something, an event. Revelation is always an

counter

NB use of "Event" ↔ Meaning of "Event"

event: an event that, in fact, breaks something, so that revealability, *Offenbarkeit*, is open. Revealability is opened by revelation: that's putting it the other way round. But I was not satisfied by this other order, either. I would try to think the relation between the two in a different way. And I don't know which way. I must confess that the logical order, the chronological order, even the ontological order, is not appropriate. So I'm trying to think something that removes the event that one calls revelation from the scheme of veil, revelation, revealability. I'm trying to think the event as something other than an unveiling of a truth or the revelation of a truth, as something that has effects but makes no reference to light, no reference to vision, no reference to unveiling.

Not only human existence but God's existence: what I didn't say to Jack a moment ago is that the weakness, the powerlessness, of God is first of all the possibility of God to be affected by an event. If something *happens* to God, it implies some vulnerability in God. Absolute power is also total insensitivity, total impassibility with regards to an event. Nothing can happen to absolute power, to the sovereign. For something to happen to God, God must be exposed, must be limited in a certain way, must be made finite in his infinity. The event must affect not only human existence but also divine existence. This can be translated into Christian terms: the passion, the crucifixion, happened to God. Yes, it happened to God. This event remains unpredictable, as every event should be. One cannot see it coming. If God could simply predict and, as in providence, could see the passion coming, there would be no event. The event must be totally unpredictable, even to God.

Usually one thinks that there is phenomenologically or ontologically a background, a horizon, against which one sees the event coming. If so, there is no event: if you see it coming, it is not an event. The revelation or revealability is the neutralization of the event. One has to think of an event that affects every living being—human, animal, and God—without any essential revelation or essential revealability. And to that extent the pair of concepts, *Offenbarung* and *Offenbarkeit*, is not useless but it remains secondary by way of thinking what an event is. Of course, with the *Offenbarung* we imply that something happened, whereas with the *Offenbarkeit* nothing has happened. To think the eventness of the event, then, we don't need this couple of concepts.

Yvonne Sherwood: At this conference, there has been an opportunity to see (though not touch) the ossuary[3] that, we are told, is statistically likely to have contained the bones of James, brother of Jesus—to see the container that once allegedly contained, but now no longer contains, the body of the brother of the Christian messiah. How do you interpret this event and the excitement it has generated? What does it say, for example, about the relation between religion and the quest for origins, authenticity, and validation by the proven, empirical truth of a happening; about the alliance between religion and the secret; and about the desire to put one's hands on or into the body or the casket of the body (albeit at several removes)?

Jacques Derrida: If I try improvising an answer to this very, very difficult question, I would be tempted to say that if you want to be true to the alliance between religion and the secret, as you say, between pure faith and the secret—that is, invisible, nonpublic experience—then you have totally to dissociate this experience from science, proof, empirical indications, empirical proofs, and so on. This doesn't mean that science should be given up or disqualified. It means that between science and this pure faith there should be no transition, no passage. There should be an absolute heterogeneity. And on both sides, which means that we shouldn't give up the scientific attempt to explain, in history and in archeology, even in theology; for theology is a science, in a certain way. That's how Heidegger describes theology: "It's a science." On the one hand, we should do whatever we can to let science develop as far as possible. And we know today that it can go very far in terms of archeology and political history. But this should not compete with the order of faith. Which means that we should, on both sides, purify the specificity and heterogeneity of the two movements.

In order to do that, and to find the resources to continue to do that today, to be true to science, knowledge, and to be true to faith, we have to find in our experience, each as a living being, the experience of faith far beyond any received religious tradition, any teaching. That is why I constantly refer to the experience of faith as simply a speech act, as simply the social experience; and this is true even for animals. Animals have faith, in a certain way. As soon as there is a social bond there is faith, and there are social bonds in animals: they trust one another; they have to. (Sometimes they fight, sometimes they don't.) This trust, this bond, this covenant within life, is the resource to understand the heterogeneity between faith and knowledge. Both are absolutely indispensable, but they are indissociable and heterological. That's the ground of our experience of faith as living beings.

Now when I say living beings, I mean first not human beings because we have to ask the question, "What is man?" We have to question the relations between man and animal. And when I say "living being," I include in life death, the possibility of dying and the possibility also of mourning, of introjecting the spectral other, which some animals do as well as human beings. So it is in this experience of faith that is part of life that one can understand and at least think of the heterology between faith and knowledge, between faith and reason.

Your question has to do also with the excitement that this event has generated. I think that it is at once understandable and inauthentic—unhealthy, I would say. Here's something exciting! There is this exhibit in Toronto! Well, I understand the curiosity. But if faith depends on this, it is a catastrophe. If faith depends on this exciting discovery, it's the end of faith, and it also transforms science into something suspect. We might be excited, I would be excited too, but I would try to not to mix the excitement with faith.

John D. Caputo: Why do you say that you "rightly pass" (*je passe à juste titre*) for an atheist ("Circonfession," 146, 155) instead of simply stating that "I am" (*je suis*) an atheist? Is this because you have some doubts about whether you really are an atheist? Or because you have some doubts about the distinction between atheism and belief in God? One might be tempted to construe this expression as follows: "I am to all appearances an atheist, but appearances can be deceiving, so don't be too sure; perhaps I am not."

Jacques Derrida: I am not simply the one who says "I." Also, I think we may have some doubts about the distinction between atheism and belief in God. If belief in God is not also a culture of atheism, if it does not go through a number of atheistic steps, one does not believe in God. There must be a critique of idolatry, of all sorts of images in prayer, especially prayer, there must be a critique of onto-theology—the reappropriation of God in metaphysics—-which, as Heidegger says, doesn't know anything about prayer or sacrifice. True believers know they run the risk of being radical atheists. Even Lévinas says that in certain ways he is an atheist, because he doesn't understand God. He doesn't interpret God as an existing being. God is not an absolute being. Negative theology, prophetic philosophical criticism, deconstruction: if you don't go through these in the direction of atheism, the belief in God is naïve, totally inauthentic. In order to be authentic—this is a word I almost never use—the belief in God must be exposed to absolute doubt. I know that the great mystics experience this. They experience the death of God, the disappearance of God, the nonexistence of God, or God as being that is called NonExistence: "I pray to someone who doesn't exist in the strict, metaphysical meaning of existence, that is, to the present as an essence or a substance."

Think of the *epekeina tes ousias* of Plato, or of Heidegger's being beyond beings. If I believe in what is beyond being, then I believe as an atheist, in a certain way. However paradoxical it may sound, believing implies some atheism; and I am sure that true believers know this better than others, that they experience atheism all the time. It is a part of their belief. It is in the *epoché*, in the suspension of belief, the suspension of the position of God as a thesis, that faith appears. The only possibility of faith is in the *epoché*. When I say *je passe à juste titre*, I rightly pass for an atheist; I know that I've given a number of signs of my being a nonbeliever in God in a certain way, of being an atheist. Nevertheless, although I confirm that it is right to say that I am an atheist, I can't say, myself, "I am an atheist." It's not a *position*. I cannot say, "I *know* what I am: I am this and nothing else." I wouldn't say, "I am an atheist" and I wouldn't say, "I am a believer" either. I find the statement absolutely ridiculous. Who can say, "I am a believer?" Who *knows* that? Who can affirm and confirm that he or she *is* a believer? And who can say, "I am an atheist?"

Kevin Hart: In some of your first writings you argued that the notion of God has been leagued with presence, whether understood epistemologically, ontically, or ontologically. You also pointed out that this metaphysics of presence is not in itself theological and thereby hinted that one could think God outside the metaphysics of presence. Over the years it has struck me that, even though you indicate that the Christian God has been co-opted by the metaphysics of presence, you have always responded to more or less overt philosophical framings of the Christian God. Whether for lack of expertise, religious commitment, time, or interest, you have not attended to theological understandings of the Christian God. And yet it is here that one could perhaps find the most interesting resources for thinking of God both deconstructively and in a Christian manner. Now thinking God in a Christian manner is my concern, not yours; all the same, I would be interested in your response to the following question: Is difference not at work in the doctrine of the Trinity and the doctrine of the Christ? To be sure, the unity of God is upheld in all orthodox theologies, but at the same time the triune nature of that unity is also affirmed. Theologies of the Trinity will figure the threefold nature of the deity in their own ways, but there will always be a difference to be examined: a perichoresis of the three personae. Similarly, the central christological claim that Jesus is fully human and fully divine does not erase difference. The two natures are neither fused nor dialectically related. Are there coercive reasons for regarding these differences as metaphysical, in your sense of the word? Or would it be possible for a Christian theologian to work out those doctrines both theologically and deconstructively?

Jacques Derrida: Obviously, if there is an answer to this question, it must be yours! [*Laughter*] As you say, "thinking God in a Christian manner is my concern, not yours." If you are sure of that, then you can tell me how to do it.

Ah, you are right. All the reasons why I didn't pay attention to what you call "theological understandings of the Christian God" had to do with my culture, my lack of culture, or my lack of expertise. But it is difficult simply to remove all the signs of presence in the interpretation of the Christian God. If you insist only on difference that is without presence or that is prior to presence, you would have to erase a lot of things in the Christian corpus. I assume that you are ready to do that, and I would be interested to follow you. What I am totally unable to do, because of my lack of expertise, is address the questions of Christ and the Trinity, the theology of the Trinity. You know better than I do that to do that you would you have to study the history of Pelagianism, the negation of the divinity of Jesus. You would have to study modalism and subordinationism, and I'm not competent to do that. You assume that these things are in the past, that they have lost the war, and that the dogma of the Trinity has won …

Kevin Hart: I would not say "in the past," since these things keep returning, but I would say that the doctrine of the Trinity has been established.

Jacques Derrida: Now even if we assume that this is true, that there is a reliable doctrine of the Trinitarian essence of God, do you think that it's enough to think the difference in God? The strategy of your argument is that we just give up on presence and pay attention to difference in the Trinity. But it's not enough to think of difference, to avoid what you call the philosophical framing. This is not my project, but I think someone might be tempted to refer to the difference of the persons in God and then reframe the whole thing philosophically … unless, of course, one thinks this difference in a very different way, a way that hasn't been achieved. My knowledge of this is very limited. If I am wrong, you will tell me. But if I follow what you want to do, to work out those doctrines both theologically and deconstructively, well, this will transform them in a very interesting way. Perhaps that is what is happening here today. Perhaps this is what is changing the ground of theology today. Perhaps this is what causes anxiety in some theological circles. And I would be interested in following what is happening.

Yvonne Sherwood: You have written a great deal about "woman," not so much as a feminist, but as one who is wary of the perils of transcendentalism and empiricism that beset feminism. What would you want to say to those feminists and womanists who work in the field of—and this is a phrase in which the "and" does a lot of work—"women and religion?" Or, to put it more poetically, in the beautiful words of Hélène Cixous, what would you say to those who are attempting to scamper up Mount Sinai like mice (even though they know that a mouse is not a prophet) or trying to speak with a "burning bush" [that] doesn't usually "speak to women"?

Jacques Derrida: You are asking me what I would say to these women? I would say "Yes, continue to do that." And that's the hope, the only hope. I referred to life a moment ago, and I would refer to it again and again. Today, all over the world, if these women were strong enough to go in this direction, things would radically change. We know that in the three Abrahamic religions, differently in each one of them, women have been repressed, excluded from power, interpretation, priesthood, and so on. We know that today the more fundamentalist a religion is—this is more true for Islam, but it is also true for Judaism and Christianity—women are repressed according to religious dogmas. The more that women will reinterpret the tradition of religions and the institution of the churches and religious communities, the more women will free themselves from this repression. Again, let me say that they are different in each context, in each culture, but they share something, these three religions of the book.

I know that there are a lot of women who are struggling in Muslim countries, in Jewish communities, and in Christian communities. They are struggling differently. And when the day comes that they have succeeded, if that day comes, I'm sure that geopolitics will change. This is not the only reason for the struggle, but it is an important one. Hélène Cixous' reference to Mount Sinai is symbolically very decisive. She refers to a mouse, an animal. If I had time, I would associate the question of politics and what is at stake today in Mount Sinai, in Jerusalem, in the Middle East, in Babylon, and Iraq, to the terms of animality and the beast. I am currently giving a seminar entitled "The Beast and the Sovereign." It is under that title that I would reinterpret or interpret what you have said about women and religion, what Cixous says about those who are attempting to scamper up Mount Sinai like mice or trying to speak with a burning bush. That is why my answer would be "Yes."

References

1. "Circonfession" in Geoffrey Bennington and Jacques Derrida, *Jacques Derrida* (Paris: Editions du Seuil, 1991), pp. 175–176, 188.
2. The text of the will of Muhammad Atta (last updated April 11, 1996), found in Atta's luggage, was published by the FBI and *Der Spiegel* on October 1, 2001, and on October 4 by ABC News. It is a different document to the hijacker's instruction document also quoted, differently, by various news agencies. Despite their brief existence in the public domain both documents already have complex textual histories and seem to exist in several recensions [YS].
3. The ossuary, or ancient burial box, emerged from the depths of the antiquities black market (allegedly it had turned up in someone's kitchen) in 2002. It was inscribed with the words, in Aramaic, "James, Son of Joseph, Brother of Jesus." It could, scholars told us, be reliably dated to the first century CE, and statistically there was a less than 1% chance that there would have been another James with a brother named Jesus. This box was the other special guest at the Toronto meeting besides Jacques Derrida, though due to bad handling in transit

it arrived with two major cracks, one actually running through the inscription and the name of Jesus. Unfortunately, as one of my colleagues quipped, there were no bones in the box, and so no possibility of cloning James and bringing about a second (sibling) coming. The authenticity of the ossuary has since been entirely discredited [YS].

SECTION II
Hostipitality

CHAPTER **3**

Autochthony and Welcome: Discourses of Exile in Lévinas and Derrida

EDITH WYSCHOGROD

Is hospitality not a solicitation to its addressee, "Viens, all that I have, all that I am, is at your disposal?" Is hospitality, as Emmanuel Lévinas writes, "an incessant alienation of the ego … by the guest entrusted to it … being torn from oneself for another in giving to the other the bread from one's mouth," a one for the other that fissures the ego, hospitality that does not expect reciprocity and witholds nothing from the guest?[1] Or is there, as Derrida observes, an ineliminable tension between an unconditional offer to another and the juridical, political, and economic conditions that actually constitute the offer and without which the extending of hospitality is meaningless? Does this tension inhere in Abraham's proffering of bread and refreshment to the three strangers who arrive after God appears to him at Mamre (Genesis 18:4–5), an offer generally adduced as a paradigmatic instance of biblical hospitality?

Because the invitation to the other, "Viens," issues from a corporeal subject to another corporeal subject who must traverse a space to a site to which that other is invited, it would seem that hospitality is bound up with distance and contiguity. But the awareness of the "to and fro" of this traversal is, for Lévinas, a theoretical apprehension of space that is contingent upon a prior relation to the other, not one of perception but of proximity. In Lévinas's terms in *Otherwise than Being or Beyond Essence*:

53

> As a subject that approaches, I am not in the approach called to
> play the role of a perceiver that reflects or welcomes ... Proximity is
> not a state, a repose, but a restlessness, null site, outside of the place
> of rest. It overwhelms the calm of the non-ubiquity of a being
> which becomes a rest on a site. No site then is ever sufficiently a
> proximity ...[2]

Prior to representation or reflection, the subject who approaches in
proximity, the one who is nigh (near), the neighbor, is caught up in the
relation to the other, in what Lévinas calls fraternity, itself a primordial act
of signifying. It would seem that meaning is born in and as hospitality
thus understood.

Yet if, as Lévinas also concedes, ontological significations cannot be
disengaged from their empirical conditions, the relation with the Other
may call the world into question but is not produced outside the world.
Thus in *Totality and Infinity*, Lévinas maintains that human relationships
must not remain "a beatific contemplation of the other" which would (on
his view) constitute idolatry. In contrast to his later account of hospitality
in *Otherwise than Being* as occurring at a "null site," that of a proximity
that cannot be measured, the earlier work acknowledges the necessity for
habitation. For there to be hospitality there must be a home: "Recollection
in a home open to the other [is] hospitality."[3] The home is a site that
allows for self-enclosure, the shutting in of oneself that constitutes
individuation, yet is also open to the other. To be sure, the home founds
possession or ownership but is not itself owned in the same way as are
moveable goods; it is possessed because "it already ... is hospitable for its
proprietor."[4] Yet the home is "the very opposite of a root. It indicates a
disengagement, a wandering that has made it possible."[5] Is Abraham, the
biblical paradigm of hospitality, not described as "A wandering Aramean"?
(Deuteronomy 26:5)

The Problem of Autochthony: Abraham and Lot

The other who can be seen on the one hand as the neighbor can also for
Lévinas be encountered as a magisterial presence. It is the presence of the
other as a human face that binds me in fraternity, an other that is encountered as asymmetrical and higher than myself. Does Abraham in Genesis
18:2 not run from the entrance of his tent and "bow down to the ground"
in a primal gesture of hospitality as subservience to the other, to the
strangers in recognition of their alterity and of the elsewhere from which
they come? Derrida sees this event as an exemplary instance of hospitality
in the Abrahamic religions,[6] an account that would support Lévinas's

contention that "the relation with the other is accomplished as service and hospitality."[7]

The biblical narrative continues with Abraham's intervention on behalf of the righteous in the sinful city of Sodom, Genesis 18:16–23. This plea is followed by Lot's serving as host to the strangers and his effort to protect them from the sexual desires of the citizens of Sodom by offering them his virgin daughters in their stead. The alarming implications of the proposed trade with respect to the status of daughters requires extended analysis that cannot be undertaken here. Relevant in the present context is the sacrifice, the becoming hostage of that which is held dear. For Lévinas, the primordial act of expiation is the willingness to substitute for the other.[8] Is this acceptance of being hostage for the other not also the very law of hospitality?

These brief comments on Genesis 18:1–9 and Genesis 19:1–11 lie within the disclosive conditions of a Lévinasian biblical hermeneutic but, it can be argued, the aporias of the Abrahamic narrative require further exploration. If one invites another to one's home is not the precondition of this hospitality a certain agency and a certain belonging to a site on the part of the host? Do these conditions not presuppose that the host is justified in soliciting the other in that the host can lay claim to the site? Thus, the right to invite would seem to be intrinsic to the act of invitation. If however the other is absolutely other, descriptively unspecifiable, the host can only offer the other in his/her unspecifiability a nonsite. And, if so, has the host not abandoned the power of agency required in order to fulfill the responsibility to offer food and shelter? The difficulty is compounded when we see that the face of the other that in its vulnerability solicits hospitality always already relates one to a third party:

> [The other] moves into the form of the We, aspires to a State, institutions, laws, which are the source of a universality. But politics bears a tyranny within itself; it deforms the I and the other who have given rise to it, for it judges them according to universal rules …[9]

Still, it is not enough to define the stranger in terms of ethos, family, civil society, or the state as did Hegel.[10] Today, as Derrida reminds us, states attempt to regulate the boundaries between public and private, to control the technological channels of communication thereby altering these boundaries. The state is an outside that is inside so that being at home (*chez soi*) in an inviolable domain is no longer possible.[11] Derrida points to current ethnic, national, and religious reactions against anonymous technologies. It must also be added that the rationality of the infoculture, what Dominique Janicaud calls technodiscourse, exerts a power of its own.[12]

To be sure, the rationality of technodiscourse can contest the space of the site but the latter does not disappear. If the site persists, the paradox of hospitality, in Derrida's terms "the unconditional or the hyperbolic on the one hand, and the juridico-political ... on the other", is ineliminable.[13] The ethical then extends between the two, the one governed by the absolute gift, the other by the rules of economy, between hospitality of the proper name, "Peter, come," or the absence of the name, "Whoever you are, you are welcome. As my interlocutor you are absolutely strange to me, the stranger par excellence."[14] If this tension is to be maintained, the nameless subject of ethics must be deterritorialized so that he/she emanates from a null-site. Still, it must be recalled that, for Lévinas, it is impossible to become detached from empirical conditions, as though significations could be produced from outside the world. Yet is the other as signifiying, as the subject of approach and proximity, not decorporealized, dispossessed of its empiricity in the interest of this deterritorialization? Lévinas describes the subject as a self in the accusative, passive in its exposure to being, an offering of itself that is a suffering. "The subject is in the accusative, expelled from being, outside of being."[15] If so, must it not be conceded that the one who suffers, who is not a gnostic subject but an incarnate someone, be somewhere?

I cannot enter into the details of Lévinas's critique of an autochthony that he sees as grounding Heidegger's philosophy. However, insofar as the relation of hospitality to alterity and to a certain politics of the site are at issue in the present context, it is necessary to consider, however briefly, Heidegger's account of dwelling. For Heidegger, on Lévinas's view, being at home is inextricably tied to autochthony: to dwell is to be rooted in the earth. To be, *Ich bin*, is linked to the word *bauen*, to build, so that the manner in which one exists is as one who dwells.[16] For Heidegger, it is poetry both as a measuring of that which cannot be measured, the Godhead, and as a kind of building that opens the possibility of dwelling. Significant in the present context is the claim that authentic poetry exists as long as there is kindness, understood not as a welcoming of the other in her alterity but as "the pure, [that comes] to the dwelling being of man ... as the claim and appeal of the measure to the heart."[17]

In *Totality and Infinity*, the hospitable subject is, as already noted, localized, inhabiting a site from which food and shelter are offered and, as such, having the right to invite. The home in its concreteness exists as granted to a subject by a political or an economic entity that is empowered to do so. The home is always already a place of inclusion and exclusion, of friend and enemy, a place in which the stranger may evoke distrust: is s/he friend or enemy? In an exemplary biblical instance of such suspicion, it may be recalled that the men of Sodom say of Lot, "This fellow came here as an alien, and he would play the judge" (Genesis 19:9).

Bending Etymologies

Is the friend/enemy relation not already to be discerned in the etymology of the term hospitality? It can be assumed that the Indo-European *ghosti* is the root of the Latin *hospitalitas* and of the old Norse *gestri*, a root that denotes guest and host, someone with whom one has reciprocal duties of hospitality. The term also derives from the Latin *hostis*, enemy or stranger as in "hostile".[18] Does not the German *Gastfreundlichkeit*, hospitality, not evoke its root *Geist*, spirit or ghost, so that one is reminded of the spectral possibility of the enemy in the guest? In what might be seen as a subtle correction of this picture, Carl Schmitt (admittedly a politically problematic thinker who figures in Derrida's account of hospitality) considers another etymological distinction having important semiotic implications.[19] In order to preserve the Christian injunction to love one's enemies, Schmitt distinguishes personal animus from political enmity thereby cordoning off a discursive space for the personal in which Christian love can be expressed. Derrida explains:

> In Chapter 3 of *The Concept of the Political*, [Schmitt] emphasizes … that *inimicus* is not *hostis* in Latin and *ekhthros* and *polemios* is not *poleimos* in Greek. This allows him to conclude that Christ's teaching concerns the love we must show to our private enemies, to those we might be tempted to hate through through personal or subjective passion and not to public enemies.[20]

For Schmitt, the precondition for the possibility of politics is precisely a war that does not presuppose hatred of an enemy (*hostis*). But for Derrida the reciprocal imbrication of public and personal cannot be dismissed. Turning to the text of Matthew 5:43–44, Derrida links the command to love one's enemy to the Levitical command to love one's neighbor. The neighbor, Derrida maintains, is *eo ipso* a member of the same ethnic group (*amith*) as oneself and thus always already belongs to the political in Schmitt's sense. Thus, if one loves the enemy as one loves the neighbor, Derrida concludes, "it would be difficult to keep the potential opposition between one's neighbor and one's enemy." Is the political then not already "within the sphere of the private?"[21] Do the men of Sodom not see Lot as an enemy when he assumes the role of judge because he attempts to usurp an autochthony he does not possess?

The Linguistic Turn and the Political

The etymological difference between *hostis* and *inimicus*, an aporia that brings to light what is ineliminably political in the sphere of the private, can be discerned in Lévinas's account of the rhetorical aspect of language. Consider first that, for Lévinas, hospitality arises in and as language. The relation with the other not only leads to the generality that language or the word makes possible but *is* this generality, the primordial donation or offering of the world as word. To be sure, Lévinas insists that the relation to the other is realized in and as the vocative, the language of interpellation. "The interpellated one is called upon to speak, to come to the assistance of his word."[22] Such speech is essentially a coinciding of teacher and teaching, so that true teaching is not merely drawing out of truths, (a recognizably Kierkegaardian point). Instead, "truth is made possible by relation with the other, our master" so that justice crystallizes in recognizing in the other a magisterial presence.[23] But—and this is the point—Lévinas concedes that "rhetoric, taking the position of him who approaches the neighbor with ruse ... is absent from no discourse."[24] As propaganda, diplomacy, etc., rhetoric solicits the other's agreement and is, as such, violence, injustice. If rhetoric is always already intrinsic to language must it not also infiltrate hospitality? Referring to Carl Schmitt, Derrida writes, "War has its own rules and perspectives, its strategies and tactics but they presuppose a political decision ... naming who is the enemy."[25]

In addition, it is crucial to note that for Lévinas the relation to another is not that of two monadic individuals but ineliminably plural. The other is imbricated in social existence, thus already reflecting a third person who opens the possibility for justice. The relation to the other is not one of intimacy, an *à deux*, but one in which "the third party looks [out] at me in the eyes of the Other—language is justice ... the epiphany of the face qua face opens humanity."[26] The meaning of "third in the eyes of the other" is a matter of considerable complexity. The other is both destitute and an equal. "His equality within this essential poverty consists in referring to the third party ... whom the other already serves ... He comes to join me in service."[27]

Once hospitality and justice are linked, the category of the political cannot be bypassed.

In this regard, it is helpful to elaborate further upon Derrida's reading of Carl Schmitt's "polemical use of the concept of the political" and Schmitt's rendering of the friend/enemy relation.[28] For Schmitt, Derrida argues, key concepts are already presupposed in the analyses intended to establish them. Thus, "concepts of the polemical are never implemented ... except in a polemical field [and] have a strictly polemical use."[29] This question-begging as it were is intrinsic to the "logical matrix" of Schmitt's vision of the political. Thus Derrida:

> The State presupposes the political, to be sure logically distinguished from it; but the analysis of the political ... its irreducible core, the friend/enemy configuration, can only privilege ... as its sole guiding thread, the State form of this configuration—the friend or enemy qua citizen.[30]

One must of course decide who is to count as the friend. There are, Derrida maintains, three logical possibilities in determining the meaning of this crucial relation. First, there is no friend without the possibility of killing, a possibility that establishes a political or non-natural community that is contingent upon the mortality of all parties, so that the parties are in a sense "dead for one another." Second, what is true of the enemy, his mortality, suspends or annuls friendship. The same possibility, mortality, is true of both friend and enemy and yet altogether different in relation to the friend. The interdiction against killing in the case of the friend both expresses and forbids this possibility. Third, Derrida asks whether there may be a politics of friendship beyond that of killing, whether *polis* and *filia* can be associated differently. We are, Derrida says, at the crossroads of an "undecidable triviality." Are we in pondering this tension returned to Aristotle's apothegm: "My friend there is no friend?"[31]

Are we, in applying comparable logical strategies to hospitality, compelled to say to a putative host, "There is no hospitality?" Like the bestowing of a gift, hospitality consists in an act of donation, in giving something to someone in an act which is, as Derrida points out, conditional when the gratitude of the guest is expected but unconditional if no reciprocity is anticipated. When conditional, the mastery of the host is asserted in that it is he who invites, whose house, city, and nation control the relation to the guest. When hospitality is unconditional no invitation is issued. The other, his coming a pure surprise, simply arrives and is welcomed with no thought given to the possible consequences. "For unconditional hospitality to take place you have to accept the risk of the other coming and destroying the place ... stealing everything or killing everyone."[32]

Lévinasian hospitality can be seen to exhibit a similar tension: one invites another to one's home thereby implicitly expressing proprietery rights while, at the same time, the other who arrives exerts an unconditional ethical demand. In response to the other who has come one must be willing unconditionally to offer oneself as hostage for that other so that self-donation is, in its pure form, the gift of death. For Derrida, the risk of "wild war and terrible aggression" renders the question of pure hospitality's existence undecidable. Can it then be said that the apothegm "My friend there is no friend," rearises spectrally in Derrida's claim with respect to hospitality, "There may be no such thing?"[33]

In/Conclusion

The inquiry into the private and the political, into the meaning of friend and enemy, is not an excursus in the analysis of hospitality but exposes the risks and paradoxes built into the discussions of hospitality in the works of Lévinas and Derrida. The personal is shown to remain personal yet is, at the same time, already demonstrably political; autochthony persists while engaging in its own deterritorialization. As Derrida argues, "[a]bsolute hospitality requires that I risk opening my home to the stranger ... to the absolutely unknown, [who remains] anonymous ... [so that the other can] have a place in the place that I offer him."[34] Still, it must be asked, is hospitality not also rendered to one who is named as well as to the nameless subject? If I am host is there not already a collusion between hospitality and power? Even if, as host, I may be willing to risk inviting the enemy into my home, does not the fact that I speak from a site implicate me in the *polemos* of the political? Private or family law is always already mediated by public or state law that can be both repressive and protective in keeping with Schmitt's model of friend and enemy as grounding political power. Is this configuration of power not attested in the failure to extend the privileges of inhabitants to the resident alien as exemplified in the men of Sodom's questioning of Lot's right to extend hospitality to the stranger?

Although the absence of physical boundaries in the virtual spaces of the new communication technologies radically alters biblical accounts of the home, one does not feed the hungry and shelter the destitute from the nowhere of a website. Virtual space is infiltrated by an ethical subject who is always already corporeal. To say this is not to confuse the corporeality of the ethical subject with a state of nature, as it were, but rather to see the subject in his/her bodily vulnerability as contesting political power grounded in the friend/enemy distinction wherever it is to be found.

References

1. Emmanuel Lévinas, *Otherwise than Being or Beyond Essence*, trans. Alphonso Lingis (The Hague: Martinus Nijhoff, 1981), p. 79.
2. Lévinas, *Otherwise than Being or Beyond Essence*, p. 82.
3. Emmanuel Lévinas, *Totality and Infinity: An Essay on Exteriority*, trans. Alphonos Lingis (Pittsburgh: Duquesne University Press, 1969), p. 172.
4. Lévinas, *Totality and Infinity*, p. 157.
5. Lévinas, *Totality and Infinity*, p. 172.
6. Jacques Derrida, *Anne Dufourmantelle invite Jacques Derrida à répondre: De l'hospitalité* (Paris: Calmann-Levy, 1997), p. 135. Translations of direct citations from this work are mine.

7. Lévinas, *Totality and Inifinity*, p. 300.
8. In *Otherwise than Being*, Lévinas writes: "In responsibility for another, subjectivity is only [the] unlimited passivity of an accusative ... [reducible] to the passivity of a self only as a persecution ... that turns into an expiation" (p. 112). He goes on to say that "the self of this passivity ... is a hostage" (p. 114).
9. Lévinas, *Totality and Infinity*, p. 300.
10. Derrida, *De l'hospitalité*, pp. 44–45.
11. Derrida, *De l'hospitalité*, pp. 47ff.
12. Dominique Janicaud, *Powers of the Rational: Science, Technology and the Future of Thought*, trans. Peg Birmingham and Elizabeth Birmingham (Bloomington, Indiana University Press, 1994). See esp. chap. 3, pp. 59–75.
13. Derrida, *On Hospitality*, p. 119.
14. The latter position is that of Lévinas, *Totality and Infinity*, p. 73.
15. Lévinas, *Otherwise than Being or Beyond Essence*, p. 110.
16. Martin Heidegger, "Building, Dwelling, Thinking," in *Poetry, Language, Thought*, trans. Albert Hofstadter (New York: Harper and Row, 1971), p. 147.
17. "...Poetically Man Dwells...," Ibid., pp. 228–229.
18. *American Heritage Dictionary of the English Language*, ed. William Morris (Boston: Houghton Mifflin Company, 1981), p. 1518. See also Derrida's play on the ambiguity of his coined word *hostipitalité* expressing both welcome and hostility in *De l'hospitalité*, p. 45.
19. A brief account of Schmitt's membership in the Nazi party and for a certain time his articulation of juridical principles in consonance with its doctrines can be found in George Schwab, *The Challenge of the Exception* (Berlin: Duncker and Humblot, 1970). See esp. Part II, "Schmitt and National Socialism 1933–1936." For recent engagement with Schmitt in a theological vein, see Jacob Taubes, *Ad Carl Schmitt Gegenstrebige Fugung* (Berlin: Merve Verlag Berlin, 1987).
20. Jacques Derrida, *The Gift of Death*, trans. David Wills (Chicago: University of Chicago Press, 1995), p. 103.
21. Derrida, *The Gift of Death*, p. 104.
22. Lévinas, *Totality and Infinity*, p. 69.
23. Lévinas, *Totality and Infinity*, p. 72.
24. Lévinas, *Totality and Infinity*, p. 70.
25. Jacques Derrida, *The Politics of Friendship*, trans. George Collins (London: Verso, 1997), p. 126.
26. Lévinas, *Totality and Infinity*, p. 213.
27. Lévinas, *Totality and Infinity*, p. 213.
28. Derrida, *The Politics of Friendship*, pp. 116–117.
29. Derrida, *The Politics of Friendship*, p. 116.
30. Derrida, *The Politics of Friendship*, p. 120.
31. Derrida, *The Politics of Friendship*, pp. 122–123.
32. Jacques Derrida, *Hospitality, Justice and Responsibility in Questioning Ethics: Contemporary Debates in Philosophy* (London: Routledge, 1999), p. 70.
33. Derrida, *Hospitality, Justice and Responsibility*, p. 70.
34. Derrida, *De l'hospitalité*, p. 29.

GIL ANIDJAR

A brother is always exemplary, and this is why there is war.

—Jacques Derrida

The event of literature, to which Derrida attends in "La littérature au secret," is the taking-place of secrets and of crypts that bind God, Abraham, and "the secret which we are calling literature, the secret *of* literature and the secret *in* literature."[2] Literature, Derrida goes on to explain, is "the site of these secrets without secret, of all these crypts without depth, without another depth or bottom than the abyss of the call or address, without another law than the singularity of the event."[3] Derrida then reads the biblical event constituted by an instant and in an instant, the only instant in which "autonomy and heteronomy make no more than One," when "they no longer are but One" ("À cet instant, mais depuis ce seul instant, l'autonomie et l'hétéronomie ne font plus qu'Un, oui, plus qu'Un").[4] This instant falls under the law of iterability, repeatable from the first, repeatable as the first, in a narcissistic structure which Derrida earlier describes as forgiveness begged, begged by God and of God, asked by God of himself—for of whom else could God ask for forgiveness? This

---

*"Hosting" by Gil Anidjar is adapted from Gil Anidjar, *The Jew, The Arab, A History of the Enemy*, © 2003 by the Board of Trustees of the Leland Stanford Jr. University. All rights reserved. Used by permission of Stanford University Press.

"narcissistic reflexivity, *réflexivité narcissique*" befell the French language, which constitutes the forgivable as a kind of self-forgiving.[5] The expression "cette faute se pardonne" translates, Derrida explains, "it is forgivable."[6] God would thus be the name of a certain narcissism, a narcissism where the many narcissisms would be no more than one, no longer but one. Here, God would be "the other name of self-forgiveness, of forgiving-one-self, *autre nom du pardon à soi, du se-pardonner.*"[7] Literature, always besides itself, finite by virtue of a precarious "right to say everything and to hide everything," the right not to mean or want to say anything,[8] secret without secret—literature, then, asks for forgiveness, from the beginning, for "in the beginning, there was forgiveness," from the very first and the very first word.[9] Literature would thus always be the story or a story, a history of God: *Histoire de "Dieu."*

Narcissistic reflexivity reappears around the time of the flood, a time at which God—this is his story—repents, that is to say (if one *could* say it), God repents himself. As Derrida quotes one French translation, "Dieu se repent, *vayinachem yahweh*" (Genesis 6:6), he is "sorry" (NSRV) and he "regrets" (Jerusalem Bible) what he has done. And yet, it is as if God could not forgive himself, as if—and Derrida insists on the importance of the "as if, *comme si,*" for we are reading literature in its becoming—it is as if God "did not forgive himself for the misdeed, the evil done of or by his creation."[10] God punishes his creation for the evil it has done, which is to say, for the evil *he* has done, "having created men who have evil in their heart."[11] The punishment—but is it, then, self-punishment?—entails God's decision "to exterminate the human race and to erase all trace of life from the surface of the earth."[12] This "genocidal annihilation, *anéantisse-ment génocidaire*"—once again first in a series of iterable, if also untraceable, events—will extend to all species of life, all forms of living, and all creatures, save the well-known exceptions gathered in Noah's ark. This, then, is the history of God in its becoming-literature, the history of a narcissistic reflexivity that will culminate in God's oath, at the instant I recalled earlier in which "autonomy and heteronomy make no more than One," when they no longer are but One. Much as he promised after the flood never to do it again, God now swears to himself, before and only before himself.[13] To Abraham, whom he calls, God swears, but he does so by himself and only to himself for how, Derrida asks again, could he do otherwise? "Could he mean or want to say anything else but this tautology, which does not mean, does not want to say anything? *Pourrait-il vouloir dire autre chose que cette tautologie qui ne veut rien dire?*"[14] "By myself I have sworn, *bi nishba'ti,*" God says to Abraham—or in the translation of the Jerusalem Bible, "I swear by my own self" that your descendants—those who will proclaim and swear to themselves and others that they are your descendants—your descendants, then, will become occupiers and settlers, they will gain possession and inherit the gate of their enemies, *va-yirash zar'akha et sha'ar oyivav*" (Genesys 22:15–17).[15] Narcissistic reflexivity would thus have marked the beginnings of literature—the story of God as becoming-literature—from the first; the always already first forgiveness begged; the first oath to oneself; the first promise of occupation as inheritance; and, possibly, the first self-punishing genocidal annihilation. These are no longer such well-kept secrets, and it is no wonder, therefore, that the enemy is at the occupied gate, in the occupied towns. This is the story of God, and at this point, it is also the story of Abraham. And if what Derrida gives us to read is the secret as becoming-literature, he also reminds us that this becoming has everything to do with war, and with the enemy. "Enemies" is in fact the last word, and the last word cited, in "La littérature au secret."[16] All the parties involved with Mount Moriah and, beginning with God, are implicated in a war that is, daily and horridly, not just a war of occupation but a fight to the death. It is to this fight, to one of the beginnings of this story—the story of God and the story of Abraham—that I want to now turn in order to engage a becoming that, following Derrida's powerful coinage of "hostipitality," could be called here "hosting." With this term, what would be taking place is a becoming-enemy of and by Abraham, or more precisely, the becoming-enemy of the Abrahamic.

In the story of Abraham, as it is found in Genesis, there is a passage which, although strange, seems to have remained, as it were, secret—marginal to the concerns of the canonical Jewish commentators. It is a passage that is so dissonant with the general image of Abraham that the eminent biblical critic Claus Westermann writes about it that it "has nothing more in common with the patriarchal stories than the names Abraham and Lot."[17] It is important to take note of this dissonance not only because of what it signals regarding all perceptions of Abraham, but also because in spite of the violence that surrounds him, Abraham is mostly known for his passivity. Competing with Isaac, Abraham repeatedly assents and acquiesces. He listens to and obeys his wife, God, and country, agreeing to exile, to sparing his life on his wife's account (twice), to surrogate motherhood and unexpected pregnancies, the banishment of slave and kin, bodily markings and mutilations, the sacrifice of child and animal, wavering only on collective punishment (Abraham appears to interrogate divine wisdom only when it seeks to destroy the entire population of Sodom and Gomorrah; cf. Genesis 18:22ff). Abraham submits. He is marked by, he is the very image of, passivity. And indeed, instances of an active role-taking on Abraham's part are rare and would therefore seem to be worthy of attention. The passage that will occupy us here, Genesis 14, is unique in that here only does one find Abram—it is still his name at the moment—engaged in a situation of pursuit, engaged in a military operation. Were one to follow Erich Auerbach, reading the binding of Isaac as the Hebrew equivalent of the *Odyssey*, one could then read Genesis 14, which Susan Niditch describes as "the first war text of the Hebrew Scriptures," as the Hebrew equivalent of the *Illiad*.[18] Genesis 14 has everything to do with war, even with holy war according to some, and it also has everything to do with names, as Westermann's assertion makes clear. Indeed, the chapter has everything to do with the names of Lotand Abraham. It would therefore direct us toward a reading of the names of Abraham, toward a reading of what Fethi Benslama has called "the Abrahamic origins" that could or should become accessible to deconstruction.

It is time to make one more step, no more than one step by once again turning, as if for the first time, toward the Abrahamic, toward yet another Abrahamic sibling, a brother, who has perhaps been read but whom we will have to read anew. One would still have to begin here, and to begin again, in order to elaborate upon the Abrahamic toward which Derrida engages his own readings and where dissociation is rethought out of hostility and friendship. The importance of the brother, the figure of the brother who sustains, as Derrida demonstrates, the entire edifice of Western politics—even in, and perhaps beginning with hostility—demands something else than a genealogy, an approach and a reading that, perhaps impossible, would nonetheless interrogate the ways in which the Abrahamic constitutes the "ground" of these politics. Such an elaboration, such a reading of the Abrahamic would have to be done by way of another brother, another Abrahamic brother, and another cause for war. "Where, then," Derrida asks—reinscribing the matter of obscurity and of the *vouloir-dire*, the matter, therefore, of literature:

> Where, then, is the question? Here it is: I have never stopped asking myself, I request that it be asked, what it means when one says "brother," when someone is called "brother"... I have wondered, and I ask, what one wants to say whereas one *does not want* to say, *je me demande ce qu'on veut dire alors qu'on ne veut pas dire*, one knows that one should not say, because one knows, through so much obscurity, whence it comes and where this profoundly obscure language has led in the past. *Up until now.* I am wondering, that's all, and request that it be asked, what the implicit politics of this language is. For always, and today more than ever, *depuis toujours et aujourd'hui plus que jamais*. What is the political impact and range

of this chosen word, among other possible words, even—and especially—if the choice is not deliberate?[19]

Did Abraham, that little known brother, have a politics? Was he and did he have a brother? A brother that he called, that was called, "brother?" Let us pursue these questions, and try to engage the way they are traversed by the Abrahamic, by a reading of the Abrahamic as it takes place in its becoming-literature; as it occurs from the biblical text on; and, most particularly, from a strange passage that articulates itself around the interrogation raised by Derrida, putting on stage an Abraham that could perhaps be called other.

Onto the first war, then. It is a remarkable war, not to say that it is *the* war, the true mother of all wars, the first war of the world, of the biblical world at least, and thus the First World War. As I have said, it is not only the first war narrated by the Bible (where already "the entire state is under arms and is torn from its domestic life at home to fight abroad, the war of defense turns into a war of conquest" in Hegel's words),[20] it is also the first occasion for Abraham's "conquest of the Land" ("Abram conquiert la terre" is the title that the French translator, André Chouraqui, gives to this section). The first war is thus also a war for land, the war of Abraham for the land. It is the first holy war, the first Abrahamic explosion.

The biblical narrative reports that numerous kings, including the kings of Sodom and Gomorrah who are apparently on the losing side, that "these kings made war, *'asu milchama* (Genesis 14:1)." Here is an all too familiar situation, all too familiar today, a situation where it is already the case that the winner takes all, already the winner took all:

> And they took all the goods of Sodom and Gomorrah, and all their victuals, and went their way. And they took Lot, Abram's brother's son, *ben achi abram*, who dwelt in Sodom, and his goods, and departed. And there came one who had escaped, and told Abram the Hebrew—now he dwelt by the terebinths of Mamre the Amorite, brother of Eshcol, and brother of Aner; and these were confederate with Abram. And when Abram heard that his brother was captive, *vayishma'abram ki nishbah achiv*, he led forth his trained men, born in his house, three hundred and eighteen, and pursued as far as Dan (Genesis 14:11–14).

In what follows, Abram is victorious, "he brought back all the goods, and also brought back his brother Lot, *ve-gam et lot achiv*" (Genesis 14:16). The first Abrahamic war is thus clearly a family matter. It is, more precisely, a matter of brothers.

As I have said, Genesis 14 drew little attention on the part of the great Jewish commentators. Given the problems it has occasioned for modern biblical scholarship, this is in itself noteworthy. Yet, it is all the more strange because the second century Aramaic translation of Onkelos does seem to signal that there is something troubling with this text, more precisely something troubling with the brothers in this text. Onkelos is famous for his "corrections" to the biblical text, and it is indicative, indeed, symptomatic of his troubles, that he offers such correction here. When Abram hears the rumor that brings him to war, Onkelos translates in a straightforward way: "Abram heard that his brother was taken captive, *ushma'abram ishtevei achuhi.*" Two verses later, however, namely, "he brought back his brother Lot," Onkelos "corrects," if one can say so, and translates, "he brought back Lot, the *son* of his brother, *Lot* bar *achuhi.*" As long as it was a rumor ("Abram heard") the semantic slide between "son of his brother" and "his brother" was not significant to Onkelos. So what if what he heard was that his brother rather than the son of his brother was taken captive? Yet, rather than see the second instance of the phrase "Lot, his brother" as a performative effect, as the production of Lot *as* brother insofar as he cared for and saved as a brother, insofar as he is the cause of Abraham's war—rather than see in the phrase the biblical affirmation and approval of Lot's fraternal character—Onkelos chooses to correct the biblical text by restoring the "proper" kinship relations.

For this is what is important here, namely the cause and reason that the biblical text offers regarding Abraham's involvement in a war that did not concern him. War, here the war of conquest, begins for what is, after all, a simple reason. Abraham, says the text, went to war, went in pursuit of his enemies because of—but precisely, because of whom? For his nephew? For the son of his brother, as the text calls him at first? Or does he go to war for his brother, as the text also calls him? The rumor—for it is a rumor that reaches Abraham's ears—informs him that his brother has been captured. And it is because of this rumor, because of what it tells him about his brother, that Abraham sets out in pursuit, sets out to make war, a war which will turn out to be a war of conquest.

But let us return to the word "brother"—in Hebrew, *ach.* One must take into account the semantic field of that word that enables the descriptions we have read so far and that does not therefore necessitate correction. *Ach* is the brother, but it is also the family member, kin or relative, neighbor, and *prochain. Ach* is, finally, even the friend. And yet, within the space of two very proximate verses, the biblical text itself introduced the distinction between "son of his brother" and "his brother," thus demanding interpretation. It is after all not the first time that we encounter Lot and we already know that he is the son of Abraham's brother. Aside from the apparent uselessness of the text's recalling again this kinship relation, it is the way in which the text does so, speaking two verses later only of the brother, that may evoke surprise. It has long been a commonplace of biblical interpretation that any additional or repetitive information in the case of a text that is otherwise so sparse and concise must itself signify, minimally, that it requires some consideration. All the more reason to be surprised at the lack of interest that seems to have been felt by the major Jewish commentators. Onkelos' manifest anxiety could have set off an exegetical conversation. It did not.

There is, as far as I could find, one exception, and it is an important one for what it reveals about the term "brother" and which thus provides for an alternative space of intelligibility. In the eighteenth-century commentary called *Or ha-Chayyim*, the Moroccan kabbalist Chayyim Ibn 'Attar writes the following:

> "*That his brother was captive*": This indicates that someone was taken captive and that [the captors] knew that he was Abraham's brother. With this word, it is revealed that they were the enemies of Abraham, *u-beze gilu ki oyieve Avraham hem*. And that is the reason for his pursuing them.

What the Bible indicates by using the word "brother," Ibn 'Attar explains, is the declaration, by the captors and by the biblical text, that they are enemies.[21] The use of that specific word thus conveys crucial information about the reasons for the war: because the word "brother" indicates that they are enemies, it provides the reason for Abraham's going to war. Abraham went to war for his brother, because through the brother, through the word "brother," his enemies were revealed as enemies. The text, therefore, did call for some attention. That such was given as late as the eighteenth century in the commentary of an Arab Jewish interpreter does not diminish the originary tension, indeed, the explosiveness of an act of war.

The cause of this act of war is, therefore, the brother. More precisely, what the text effectuates within the space of two verses, between the two descriptions of Lot, is the production, the becoming-brother of Lot insofar as he is the cause of the Abrahamic war. With this becoming, the brother also becomes an effect of the war, a consequence of the Abrahamic war. The pursuit of Abraham, his entering the war, is both condition and effect of this becoming. But this becoming is also the becoming of the Abrahamic, term of war and term at war, an explosive term if there is one, and which, since its illegible or at least unread beginnings, since the First

World War, engaged divided brothers, brothers separated by and in a war, by and in the Abrahamic. From its double theologico-political source, as a doubled and redoubled source, the Abrahamic did demand another reading, another reading of the name of Abraham and Ibrahim. With the Abrahamic, it is in the pursuit of this name and of this war, toward and in the sole Abrahamic pursuit documented by the biblical text, that Derrida's texts carry us. The pursuit of Abraham is the pursuit of a name that works the texts and that raises while renewing it the question of the rapport of religion to politics, the question of the theologico-political. This question is the Abrahamic, which worries and unsettles the hyphen of the Judeo-Christian in its positive and negative incarnations, which worries and unsettles, at least since the biblical Abraham, the being-Christian and the being-political of Europe, as well as the meaning of the words "Judaism, Christianity, Islam." Among the names that are deployed by the Abrahamic, "the Jew, the Arab" situates the insistence and the importance of a reading of the three religions, a reading that would not gather them in an illusory unity. To the contrary, such reading demands that history—our history—be rethought, a history that is all too sedimented in the manifest progression of the Abrahamic as the history of "Western" religions, in order of appearance: from Judaism to Christianity, from Christianity to Islam. The Abrahamic is also what desediments that history.

References

1. This paper is a revised version of a section in my *The Jew, the Arab: A History of the Enemy* (Stanford: Stanford University Press, 2003).
2. Jacques Derrida, "La littérature au secret," in *Donner la mort* (Paris: Galilée, 1999), p. 163.
3. Derrida, "La littérature," p. 206.
4. Derrida, "La littérature," p. 209.
5. Derrida, "La littérature," p. 193.
6. Derrida, "La littérature," p. 190.
7. Derrida, "La littérature," p. 193.
8. Derrida, "La littérature," p. 206.
9. Derrida, "La littérature," p. 209.
10. Derrida, "La littérature," p. 199.
11. Derrida, "La littérature," p. 199.
12. Derrida, "La littérature," p. 198.
13. Derrida, "La littérature," p. 209.
14. Derrida, "La littérature," p. 209.
15. Genesis 22:15–17. The Jerusalem Bible deviates from the Hebrew and from the NRSV by offering the gates—plural—of their enemies, explaining in a footnote that these gates are, in fact, towns.
16. Derrida, "La littérature," p. 209.
17. Claus Westermann, *The Promises to the Fathers: Studies on the Patriarchal Narratives*, trans. D.E. Green (Philadelphia: Fortress Press, 1976), p. 74.
18. Susan Niditch, *War in the Hebrew Bible: A Study in the Ethics of Violence* (New York and Oxford: Oxford University Press, 1993), p. 11.

19. Derrida, *Politics of Friendship*, trans. George Collins (New York and London: Verso, 1997), 305 / *Politiques de l'amitié* (Paris: Galilée, 1994), p. 339.

20. G.W.F. Hegel, *Philosophy of Right*, trans. T.M. Knox (London and Oxford: Oxford University Press, 1967), p. 211.

21. Ibn 'Attar could be said to follow the lines drawn by the Zohar. In its commentary on Genesis 14, the Zohar locates the episode under the sign of enmity, as an intertext to Psalms 83 ("See how your enemies are stirring, see how those who hate you rear their heads," Psalms 83:2) and to Exodus 15 ("Your right hand, Yahweh, shatters the enemy," Exodus 15:6). The Zohar insists that none other than Abraham was the real target of the attack, accounting for the value of Lot based on his resemblance with Abraham: "Lot closely resembled Abram, so that thinking they had Abram, they went off." For the Zohar, Abram is the cause of enmity, the cause of the first war: "The reason of their war to Abram was Abram himself, *de-kol ha-hu qrava begineih hava*, for this whole war was because of him" (*Zohar* I: 86b, ed. R. Margaliot [Jerusalem: Mosad ha-Rav Kook, 1984], p. 289).

CHAPTER **5**

Mary, Maternity, and Abrahamic Hospitality in Derrida's Reading of Massignon

CLEO MCNELLY KEARNS

… Where guest meets ghost
to time's utmost.

—Ezra Pound

At the opening of his talk for the colloquium on the isle of Capri that would eventually be published as "La Réligion," Derrida noted that there were no Muslims among the speakers there gathered, no representatives of "other cults" (he meant, presumably, other than Judaic or Christian) and "not a single woman!" He deplored these absences, and said they ought to be taken into account, even if that reckoning occurred only indirectly, by proxy or substitution. Someone ought to speak for these invisible interlocutors, these "mute witnesses," he argued, because their lack of representation was bound to have serious consequences in the long run.[1]

In making these remarks, Derrida was drawing attention, as he would again on many occasions, to a systematic problem in Judaism, Christianity, and Islam, a set of internal and external exclusions with respect to one another, to gender and to other spiritual stances and traditions that amounts, as he would put it, to a massive failure of hospitality. Although it might be argued that in that colloquium at Capri he spoke only in order to *avoid* speaking, Derrida clearly found and continues to find the exclusions in question problematic not only vis-à-vis Islam, but vis-à-vis other forms of difference both within and without the boundaries of what are sometimes called the three Abrahamic faiths. In other words, Derrida here raises the issue of the evident necessity for and at the same time the apparent impossibility of hospitality toward the "other" in these faiths, whether the otherness in question be one of belief, gender, or ethnicity.

Both the necessity for and the impossibility of inclusive hospitality are, of course, always much at issue on such occasions and indeed on those like the annual meeting of the American Academy of Religion and Society of Biblical Literature that generated these essays. The very term Abrahamic invokes the mandate to hospitality, for the Abraham of Genesis is legendary for his welcome, even to angels unawares. And yet this hospitality is qualified from the beginning, not only toward outsiders but toward his own kith and kin. Hagar and Ishmael are denied the protection of his home, and could it not be argued that his extreme hospitality to the voice of God puts his own son at risk? Abrahamic hospitality, it seems, is a two-edged sword from the start.

The shadow of this double-edged sword falls not only over the Abrahamic religious project per se, but over its extensions and attenuations as well. Forums and colloquia like the one at Capri, for instance, have claims to wide embrace—religion is surely a broad enough topic, even if tacitly limited to "Western" religion—but they often fall short of realizing these claims. There are of course good reasons for this, some practical, some theoretical. Well might the speakers have regretted the absence of Muslims and/or of women at the table at Capri, but surely the presence of such interlocutors would have created its own stresses and strains, at the very least the strain of accommodation in terms of time and space. As for representatives of other religions, these are even less easy to envisage.

And yet each of these forms of difference has its own claim to a place at the table, even if these claims are not all absolutely equal. Hinduism, for instance, could surely contribute to such a discussion, if only on the basis of its offer to provide a template for all religious discourses, and so could Buddhism, though on slightly different terms. But could not such claims be developed and proffered for other traditions, for Confucianism, for instance, or Shinto, or Bon? And returning to the issues signaled by "woman," surely representation of the points of view of what we might call "other genders," would be a desideratum, especially given the long record of difficulty with various sexual orientations in many of the religions in question.

The further one pursues the project of inclusion along these lines, however, the more a kind of reductio ad absurdam sets in. So studied and categorical an effort toward justice, however well-intentioned, builds all too often only on an enumeration of *ressentiments*. Choices must be made, and yet in finding a basis on which to make them, the organizers of such events are all too often responding only to tactical or strategic concerns or to merely quantitative measures. Hovering in the background here are many fruitless arguments as to whose disenfranchisement is more problematic, whose suffering more acute, whose positions more unfair, rather than serious evaluations of potential contribution to debate.

Furthermore, it is by no means clear under what rubric or by what logic a fully inclusive, fully hospitable series of speakers for such occasions might be constructed. The organizers at Capri chose the generic term "religion" as the heading under which they drew together primarily Christian and Judaic spiritual discourses. But the term religion, as scholars have long argued, generates at least as much blindness as it does insight. Many now—myself included—use the qualifier "Abrahamic" when they wish to bind Judaism, Christianity, and Islam into a common paradigm. But it must be noted that this term indicates a point of origin not only patriarchal, both in the literal and the extended sense, but based on a figure construed differently and with varying degrees of intensity in each of these three faith traditions in question. "Before Abraham was I am," Jesus is said to have said (John 8:57–59),[2] and the Abraham of the Qur'an is less a primordial founder in the sense given him by the nation of Israel than primus inter pares of a number of individual men of faith stretching back to Adam.

There are similar difficulties with several proposed groupings and rubrics. To speak of the three "monotheisms," for instance, would do well were it not for that this term takes as self-evident a theology never quite as monolithic as has often been presumed. The term monotheism also generates a number of potentially misleading and often invidious oppositions vis-à-vis other cults: "monotheistic–polytheistic" or "mono-theistic–pagan" to name only two. So, too, even with the apparently more neutral and more descriptive rubric "religions of the book." For while it is true that Judaism, Christianity, and Islam all have "Bibles" of a sort, the Torah, the gospels and the Qur'an have neither the same religious func-tion nor the same theological status in each, and the implication that no other world religion is based on a revealed text is relevant only in a very limited sense.

Given these problems, it is as difficult to avoid the failures of inclusion on such occasions as the discussion of religion at Capri as it is necessary to keep on trying to do so. Lest I seem to be offering only a counsel of despair, however, let me say from the outset that I think there are more resources for analysis and development of hospitality, inclusion, and communication in the theological and philosophical discourses around Judaism, Christianity, and Islam than perhaps might meet the eye. One such resource, I will be arguing here, and one that might usefully supplement the usual emphasis on Abraham, is the figure of the Virgin Mary, a figure that traces both the fault lines in and among the three Abrahamic traditions and the potential points of contact between and among them.

This figure may seem an odd one to introduce to an already over-burdened agenda, but there are potential advantages to doing so. For one thing, Mary is not only at the theological and narrative heart of the founding of Christianity, but she is also prominent in the Qur'an, where she is the only woman mentioned by name. It can even be argued that she plays a role in rabbinic Judaism, if only by denegation, for it is to some extent in the crucible of rejection of the claims made for her and her son that this faith tradition was forged. In all three of these discourses, furthermore, Mary's gender is not an accident, but a major issue, whether in terms of her virginity, her motherhood, or her ambivalent role as a female in an emerging male-oriented religious paradigm. She is then a marker of sexual difference in more than a token way, and she indicates both the extent and the limitations of the Abrahamic hospitality offered by Judaism, Christianity, and Islam to women, to one another and to a wider world.

The figure of Mary is, furthermore, not as absent as it might seem from considerations of hospitality in a Derridean context. When, in another venue than Capri, Derrida turns seriously to the problem of hospitality, he does so primarily with respect to the figure of Abraham, but even here Mary and her controversial maternity are in fact no stranger to his discourse, though the specific allusions occur there, as we shall see, largely by proxy. In his teaching seminar on hospitality, translated with notes by Gil Anidjar in his *Jacques Derrida: Acts of Religion*, Derrida offers an extended reflection on the paradoxes and challenges of genuine welcome to the other.[3] In approaching hospitality, he draws upon a number of formulations from his own work, ranging from the aporetic nature of classic religious values—faith, love, the gift, forgiveness, etc.—to the ambiguous functions of representation, substitution and exemplarity involved in reckoning with or taking account of such values and their underlying messianic structure. As a part of his exploration, he raises the example of maternity in its generic sense (though not without glancing allusions both to Sarah and to his own mother) as a form of and perhaps even a template for hospitality.

To understand why maternity comes to mind for Derrida in this context, we must remember that hospitality for him is very much like a difficult pregnancy, that is to say an experience fraught with expectations, perils, and contradictions. Welcomes to babies, like welcomes to strangers, are ambivalent, at once necessary and disconcerting, for by a progression of intensification hard to contain, they often involve both violence and vulnerability; they fracture existing relationships and often call for self-abnegation or sacrifice, if only the abnegation of sheltering another within. The mother is both host and hostage to her unborn child; the child is both her honored guest and an uneasy ghost of past parents, past lineages, past experiences. Thus too with hospitality, it is everywhere seen as a form of gestation of the messianic kingdom of universal peace, and yet it is a risky form, for the special status accorded the visitor is accorded with respect as much to his dangerous difference as to his potential for assimilation into the new family.

Benign outcomes of practices of welcoming and hosting are thus, for Derrida, not merely a matter of good intention or of willed desire or even of elaborate preparations and protocols. Indeed, the latter can be counter-productive. As he points out, any merely programmatic approach to encounters with the other runs the risk of abstraction and reduction that undercut the project from the start. Such programs indicate often a mere arithmetical and political calculation rather than a gesture toward genuinely inclusive and peaceful ethical order.

However well intentioned, invitations on such a basis quickly turn their recipients into mere tokens, substitutes, in the most impoverished sense, for one another. The member of a group becomes an integer, and persons are reduced to things. As Derrida puts it, while "a substitution worthy of the name would not be of something with something but of someone with someone," yet the very act of substitution itself suggests equivocation, "as if substituting someone with someone always amounted to contaminating the logic of the who with the logic of the what."[4]

Among the first conditions of true hospitality or self-sacrifice, then, is an emphasis on the demonstrable, the effective singularity or ipseity or what we might render in English as sensibility not only of the strangers, but of those who wish to host them, to see them as honorary insiders, as well. The true host, Derrida argues, cannot be a replaceable part, a cipher or a mere automaton any more than the guest can be. He or she must be aware but also self-aware; it is necessary "qu'il sente and se sente."[5] It is this awareness or sensibility that distinguishes the free and yet responsible subject from the merely animate one and makes representation, hospitality, and sacrificial substitution possible. In other words, we differ from animals or machines, and indeed from any kind of being that we would define as other, precisely and only in our capacity to enter consciously and with empathy into that being's otherness without conflation, and to entertain its welfare as if it were our own.

To this condition that a good host be "aware and self-aware," Derrida adds a call for attention to a quality hard to define, a certain combination of passive vulnerability and active engagement, the ability to put one's self, fully sensible of one's own unique and irreplaceable singularity, in the place of the other, respecting his or her singularity and sovereignty, even to the point of becoming a hostage to that other for his or her own safety or good.[6] Derrida seems almost at a loss for words, but he is trying to specify that this is not the passivity without agency of "an effect in which an inert thing would be submitted," and it is based not on a mere "mechanical or biotechnical reproduction" or phantasmatic cloning of one term to replace another.[7] It is rather "another [kind of] passivity," a practice of representation, of speaking on behalf of, of sacrifice that requires not only good intention, but the prior establishment of a genuine, gifted and differentiated selfhood, a selfhood able to empty itself to receive the other from a position of liberty and strength outside of any obligation.

It follows that any act of true welcome will be in a sense both generic and unique. For in sacrificial hospitality, as Derrida puts it,

> [A]n absolutely singular and irreplaceable existence ... in a free act, substitutes itself for another, makes itself responsible for another, expiates for another, sacrifices itself for another outside of any homogeneous series.[8]

True substitution, the putting of oneself in another's place, is indeed not "the indifferent replacement of an equal thing by an equal or identical thing [or token, or clone]." Such representations can only be made in the name of strong and established identities, of what Derrida calls "exceptional, elected existences that make themselves or expose themselves of themselves ... in their absolute singularity and as absolutely responsible."[9]

As I have already suggested, maternity is an important figuration for this sacrificial, self-aware, and singular and yet problematic hospitality, in part because it captures something of the ambiguity, the combination of desire, risk, promise, and messianic expectation inherent in entertaining another within the self and in part because it is a discourse and an experience deeply imbricated in questions of selfhood and differentiation. Motherhood is always at once generic—the most common perhaps, of human experiences—and unique. It is always about mothers and children in general and *this* mother and *this* child in particular, this child who represents his or her species precisely by being irreplaceable.

At first look, the values here seem quite secure: what could be more hospitable than a mother's welcome of another being within her own body? And yet that welcome involves danger, danger not only physical (to mother and child alike), but to an established set of erotic, familial and social relationships. All children have the potential for a disruptive, even at times a monstrous function vis-à-vis the old order, as well as of a messianic mission toward peace, and maternity and childbirth function as figures not only for individual hosts and guests but, as in Paul's letter to the Romans, for the ways in which the whole creation "groans" in the throes of labor pains the outcome of which is promised but unsure ("For we know that the whole creation groans and suffers the pains of childbirth together until now," Romans 8:22).

The use of maternity as metaphor for hospitality is everywhere evident in the text of Derrida's seminar, for reasons inherent both in his own thought and in the nature of his material. Indeed, that text is shot through with references to conception, labor, pregnancy, and biological and social reproduction, and it entrains specific instances of motherhood from the maternity of Sarah to a set of indirect allusions to the memory of Derrida's own mother, whose dying, recounted in "Circumfession," caused him such pain.[10] Maternal reproduction is important to Derrida in part because of its extreme sacrifice, even to the risk of death, and in part because of his concern for the kinds of degradation and reduction entailed in cloning, or mere replication of the species as opposed to true self-abnegating welcome of the genuinely other. Metaphors of maternity and maternal reproduction operate then as templates of a certain disposition toward that other and toward a practice of sacrificial or sacred hospitality, a mode of approach to that other involving high risk and high self-awareness, and extending, under pressure, even to self-annihilation.

As might be expected, a disposition toward motherhood in this extended sense can neither be taken for granted nor be unproblematic in its realization. At the opening of the seminar, Derrida suggests that hospitality is much like a difficult, a "belabored" pregnancy, in this case like Sarah's pregnancy with Isaac:

> What belabors hospitality at its core, what works it like a labor, like a pregnancy, like a promise as much as a threat, what settles in it, within it, like a Trojan horse, the enemy as much as the *avenir*, intestine hostility, is indeed a contradictory conception, a thwarted [*contrariée*] conception, or a contraception of awaiting, a contradiction of welcoming itself. And something that binds, perhaps, as in Isaac's pregnancy [*la grossesse d'Isaac*], the laughter at pregnancy, at the

announcement of childbirth. Abraham, of whom we will speak a lot today, laughs, like Sarah, at the announcement of Isaac's birth.[11]

Elsewhere in the seminar Derrida even invites his auditors to speculate —perhaps even psychoanalytically—on why when he begins to reflect on the theme of hospitality and substitution it is the example of child substitution that comes first to his mind, as in old tales where a child is stolen and placed in another family. (He is then struck with the uncanny coincidence that this is precisely the example of the term offered when he turns, as is his habit, to look up the word in *Littré*, as if child substitution were the instance of substitution par excellence.) From one point of view, this form of substitution is a violence, a disruption of the natural order; from another point of view, the point of view of the adoptive family, it is an ultimate act of hospitality. Furthermore, as Derrida goes on to remark, there is no such thing as a natural and immediate affiliation; we are all substitutes in some sense (*tout enfant est substitut substitué*). Just so with the self-sacrifice which puts one person at risk for the sake of another; it is neither natural nor to be expected nor generic, so to speak, but it is also not mechanical or programmatic; it is the substitution of one singularity with another.[12]

Although hospitality is a classic instance of a Derridean "impossible," based as it is on an aporia between what is defined as strange and what is defined as familiar, and although it is as difficult to realize in the present as any other value, Derrida is not content to leave his analysis at that. Rather, he seeks examples that can at least approximate what is desired. He finds one such instance in the work and life of the extraordinary scholar of Islam, Louis Massignon, whose conscious practice of hospitality and of what he called "substitution" was both engaged and self-reflective, and whose sometimes quixotic and often controversial interventions trace both the potentials and limitations of that practice. It is through this figure (and also through the better known philosophy of Lévinas) that Derrida explores the practice and theory of sacrificial hospitality, and it is in the context of this exploration, and through Derrida's extraordinary and highly self-conscious practice of citation and his running awareness of the subvocal implications of his writing, that the figure of Mary enters the seminar, so to speak.

Derrida treats Massignon in tandem with Lévinas because the two are not only roughly contemporary, but share a vocabulary and a kind of engagement that mark them out; indeed, they may have known one another. Each of these interlocutors is steeped in at least two of the discourses of the monotheisms, Lévinas in rabbinic Judaism and the Christianity of his milieu, and Massignon in Roman Catholicism and the Islam of his extensive travel and scholarship. And each of them can viably claim, or rather Derrida can claim on their behalf, a kind of primal Abrahamic hospitality to at least one of the others. It is Massignon, however, who occupies the more significant position in the seminar, and his work and life are clearly Derrida's primary exemplum both for the practice of hospitality and for the strengths and limitations of the terms in which it is conceived.

Massignon is a major source for Derrida's somewhat unusual deployment of the terms substitution, hospitality, and representation in the seminar and a major source as well for its network of metaphors of maternity and for what might almost be called its Marian subtext. For Massignon is a remarkable, perhaps unique example of the fully engaged, fully committed scholar—engaged both in the sense of being actively committed to his discipline and equally actively committed to the social and political practices it seemed to him to require—who is at the same time remarkably self-reflective and critical about the implications of his own discourse. Massignon's extraordinary biography, his *courbe de vie*, as he called it, is thus vital to Derrida's discussion, and it demonstrates a number of features—indeed a number of striking paradoxes—that provide him with a fecund source of insight and analysis.

Massignon, who died at the age of seventy-nine in 1962 after a period of intense political engagement against the Algerian War and on behalf of poor Muslims in France, was among the foremost orientalists of his generation; member of the Collège de France and professor at the Ecole des Hautes Etudes, he was for over thirty years France's greatest authority on Islam and Islamic society. He was deeply influenced by, among others, Paul Claudel, the poet; Charles de Foucauld, the Christian mystic and martyr; and J. K. Huysmans, the novelist and convert to Catholicism. He became, through an ecstatic "conversion," a serious and influential Roman Catholic, and also, again through mystical connection, an impassioned expositor of the life and thought of the Islamic mystic and martyr Al-Hallaj, to whom he felt linked by transtemporal, transcultural, and quasi-mystical ties.

He brought the full weight of this passion not only to his scholarly work but to his life in the public domain, where he campaigned vigorously for an honorable policy toward the Arabic world and for the rights of Muslims in France. Toward the later part of his life, he cast these campaigns explicitly in the mold of Gandhi, and though his temperament was fiery and his anger at the hypocrisies of church and state intense, he remained committed not only to a formal nonviolence but to an appreciation of the full humanity of all parties to a dispute.

The aspects of Massignon's life that are hardest to grasp for an Anglophone audience are the order and quality of his scholarship, its methodological inventiveness, and the position of prestige and authority with respect to political and cultural events in the Arabic world his intellectual achievements gave him. As Mary Louise Gude, his biographer in English, makes clear, Massignon did not simply master Arabic; he defined and decoded for a quite different civilization the particular discourse and technical language of Islamic philosophy and theology. He did so by immersing himself not only in the language but in the material and spiritual culture of his Islamic hosts, whom at points he even helped reconnect with their own lost past. For Massignon crossed and criss-crossed the Middle East, visiting almost every site associated with the figures of Abraham and Al-Hallaj, not only in archaeology and in the more sober accounts of their lives but in the wide dissemination of their legacies through legend and popular piety as well, and as he went he both taught and learned within the cultural institutions of his hosts.[13]

With respect to Al-Hallaj, the subject of his masterwork, Massignon made himself almost the channel of a personality, a spirituality and a theology not his own, but for which he had the utmost respect. Indeed, he offered to Al-Hallaj and by extension to Islam an unusual tribute, the reverence without conversion that the extremely generous and extremely centered seeker may feel toward a profound religious paradigm not his own. Massignon found Islam in general and the life of Al-Hallaj in particular attractive for cultural, psychological, and theological reasons, and he also clearly had what Christians would call a vocation for their study and exegesis, but he never became a Muslim in the formal sense. So intense was Massignon's spiritual experience and so immersed in Arabic language and culture his scholarship, however, that many Muslims interpreted his conversion, Christian in its official allegiance, as a turn toward a deep form of Islam.

Massignon was deeply affected by the faith of many Muslims and in particular by that of the family who first hosted him in the Muslim world of Baghdad. The head of that family, Hajj 'Ali Alussy, gave him an example of profound Islamic belief and tactful hospitality, offering support without attempting to convert him. At first the family had been somewhat concerned about his motives for wishing to live among Muslims. Indeed, suspicion of Massignon's liaisons with young men was a problem for the Alussys before they realized he would not abuse their hospitality by gaining a dubious reputation in this way. After that, however, their generosity was evident. As Massignon himself recalls of his host,

I had come and perched on the corner of his roof, like a bizarre bird from somewhere. Well, he did not try to tame me. But he nourished me at a time when there was no other place where I could drink something very pure, which was the Muslim doctrine, the way he understood it with all his heart.[14]

Massignon married and had several children, but his life was marked "in a way that is both intense and tragic," as Derrida puts it, by homosexuality.[15] It can be argued that homosexual experience was, for Massignon, an aspect of both the untameable wildness and the deep humanity of his passion for Islam, and a broken but prophetic refraction and anticipation of what became his mature spiritual and social practice. Massignon had homoerotic friendships in his life of great depth and concern, often closely associated with Islamic culture and sensibility. The most intense of these, as he himself made clear and as many who knew him testify, was his friendship with the Spanish scholar of Islam Luis de Cuadra, a tie that caused him confusion and pain throughout his life. De Cuadra had chosen to leave his Catholic upbringing and embrace Islam, where the approach to same-sex eros was in some ways more hospitable and the homes of strangers were more open to gay and bisexual men than in the Christianity of his origins.[16]

His own agnosticism forbade Massignon this recourse of conversion to Islam before 1908 and his understanding of his religious experience, during which he had felt the intervention on his behalf not only of Al-Hallaj but among others of Huysmans and Foucauld, precluded it thereafter. With his renewed Christian faith, he forwent any moral latitude vis-à-vis irregular sexual relationships (indeed, at the time of his first confession after his conversion, canon law stated that a legal conviction for homosexuality required referral to a bishop to dispense remission of sin, and his confessor stipulated that referral in Massignon's case).[17] What he saw as his failures in living up to this new standard caused him stress for many years.

However, his Christian identification and his complex relationship to his sexual orientation did not lead him into a crude condemnation of same-sex experience. In discussing his erotic life, about which he was never particularly reticent or embarrassed, though he never trivialized it either, he remarked,

The problem for me was that I was using the language of my sins, the language of the hopeless life I had led, in the homes of strangers, in search of something I did not know, that I had found in the shared agony of observing sacred hospitality.[18]

In general, he seems to have been able to regard homosexuality "without either unhealthy curiosity or hypocritical disdain," as he elsewhere put it, and in his own case as a form—however misguided—of seeking after the kind of extreme hospitality, extreme reverence for and extreme welcome of the other, that was and remained for him the highest value of the spiritual life.

As Derrida demonstrates, the figure of Abraham was central both to Massignon's erotic concerns, his scholarship, and to his spiritual life, not least because of its emphasis on hospitality and its association with the story of Sodom. Massignon traced the events of Abraham's life across the terrain of the Middle East, including a visit to Mamre, which he believed to have been the site of his prayer for the Sodomites, as well as to Jerusalem and Mecca. "I went to Mamre," Massignon writes,

> [W]here he [Abraham] asks for the forgiving of Sodom … and finally to Jerusalem. There I understood that he was the Father of all faiths, that he was the pilgrim, the gêr [the stranger, the *hôte*], the one who left his own, who made a pact of friendship with the foreign countries where he came as a pilgrim, that the Holy Land was not the monopoly of one race, but the Land promised to all pilgrims like him.[19]

Massignon referred often in his work to the three solemn prayers of Abraham before the messenger of God in Genesis, "the prayer of Sodom, the exile of Ishmael and the sacrifice of Isaac." He interpreted Sodom as symbolic not of the sin of homosexuality per se, but of the real sin, which is self love. Sodom was, he pointed out, a place defined less by unnatural practices (whatever those may be), than by its failures of hospitality, whether to the visitations of angels, guests, or strangers. Abrahamic prayer, particularly around these themes of hospitality, sacrifice, and exile, was for Massignon the precise inversion of this failure, in itself a reassertion of sacred hospitality in exactly the place where it had been violated, and in offering that prayer Abraham signaled for his entire tradition the necessity for ultimate acceptance of otherness at the heart of what is regarded as proper to one's self.

Derrida comments on this and other interpretations of the Abraham story, noting that they were not "a neutral and expert discourse of exegetical knowledge" on Massignon's part, but rather testimonial confessions, confessions of the burning martyrdom of his eros and of the spiritual intensity with which he approached the texts of his scholarship.[20] The fruit of this Abrahamic prayer and of this scholarly and spiritual hospitality in Massignon's life was not only a proliferation of writings (all in a bizarre, sometimes rambling and convoluted but intensely stimulating prose style) but a deep intercession for and an active life of social engagement on behalf of the poor, the exiled, and above all the Islamic brother.

These commitments also led Massignon to one of his stranger enterprises, an attempt to found a spiritual community based on a mission to pray for the opportunity to testify, sacrificially, to Christian truth within Islam. Massignon called this prayer community the Badaliya, a word that means "substitute" in Arabic. "We are trying to find," Massignon wrote of this project,

> [T]he living sources of these waters [of grace] for this people who were excluded, cut off long ago from the promise of the Messiah as children of Hagar, for, in their Muslim, imperfect, tradition, they preciously keep something like an imprint of the sacred face of Christ whom we adore, of "Issa Ibn Maryam" [Jesus born of Mary] whom we want them to rediscover in themselves, in their heart.[21]

This quixotic, perhaps impossible, project of the Badaliya was of course fraught with dangers, among them dangers of affronting precisely those whom it meant to embrace, and of excluding others just as worthy. Did Massignon really think that Muslims would welcome a description of their tradition as "imperfect," "cut off?" Of course he would no doubt have argued that it could equally be said of Christianity that it was also an "imperfect" reflection of the absolute hospitality called for by its founder. Nevertheless, such a formulation would surely offend. And what about women, or "other cults?" As Derrida notes, though with extreme and exemplary generosity and circumspection, Massignon's hospitality was never as freely extended to Jews as to Muslims,[22] and although women were welcome in the Badaliya (one of its cofounders, Mary Kahil, was a woman and a close associate of Massignon's in his later years), he seemed content to live, for the most part, in a male world.

Nevertheless, in his defense, it may be noted that Massignon's intent here, as he said explicitly, was not the conversion of Islam, at least not in any simple way, but a prayer for the recognition of the messianic role of Christ within its own terms. "Salvation does not necessarily mean external conversion," he wrote, "It is already a lot to obtain that a greater number belong to the soul of the Church, that they live and die in a state of grace."[23] The theological objections to this formulation would have been legion on both sides, for the Church still interpreted the formulation of the Council of Trent, *extra ecclesiam nulla sallus est,* rather literally in Massignon's day, and Islamic sensibility tends to distrust the concept of grace itself as detracting from the essential decision of each individual to submit his or her will to God. In its tradition, submission alone is the austere and unrelenting but necessary and sufficient condition of salvation. Still, Massignon was departing far from a simple missionary brief in distancing himself from conversion, and the nobility of his project was recognized by many, including Cardinal Montini, the future Pope Paul VI, who became a member of the Badaliya and helped to foster a more hospitable approach to Islam during Vatican II.[24]

In general, as his formulations make clear, Massignon sought in place of conversion, which he found an unnecessary and inhospitable condition to lay upon the friendship between two peoples or two faiths, rather the nonviolent inculcation or inculturation of the vision of Jesus Christ as the son of God within the religious discourse of Islam—at the level of personal and communal devotions if not of theology proper. In a sense, he was advocating here, however aporetically, what his own life and spiritual practice were already seeking to demonstrate, a full recognition of the other within the orbit of the self, but without violation of the integrity of either. This strange enterprise, in all its impossibility at both the level of human psychology and of systematic theology, made his life and his mission mirror images of one another.

Such were the obvious problems, theological, psycho-spiritual, and practical, of this vision of unconventional and unconverted hospitality, however, that Massignon was forced to make clear that only a complete form of self-abnegating witness, a sacrificial substitution of the insider for the outsider, perhaps even what Derrida would call a "gift of death," would address the extremity of the case. Indeed, Massignon was clearly petitioning, through the Badaliya, for the grace for Christians to give up, in an act of supreme sacrifice, what might be said to have accrued to them as their greatest good, their earnest of salvation: recognition as legitimate and orthodox children of God through incorporation in the one, true Church. The offering up of that recognition on behalf of Muslims so that the grace might be accounted to these others would thus redeem the Islamic brother and fulfill the Christian mandate at the same time.

With this end in view, Massignon actually prayed and prayed intensely that he and his colleagues on the "Christian-Islamic prayer front," as he called it, might suffer as witnesses and friends in their place whatever fate Muslims were due at the hands of the human or the divine. The Badaliya was in part founded to prepare himself and others to undergo this martyrdom, imploring God for the gift or grace of sacrificial substitution for and within Islam. In this way, Massignon thought that he would be taking up the unfulfilled challenge The Prophet himself once offered, it is said, to a vocal but ultimately defaulting group of Christian witnesses: that they might put themselves in harm's way in order to testify convincingly, by ordeal, to the truth of which they spoke.[25] It was the grace of this imaginative and singular vision that led Massignon not only to many demonstrations of social protest, but to pray that his own Christian faith might be reckoned to his Islamic brothers and sisters—though not, or not quite so graciously, as has been remarked, to his Jewish ones.

At the center of Massignon's thought and practice of Abrahamic hospitality were the figure of Mary and the practice of prayer and meditation. What initiated that practice was the experience of psychic breakdown and spiritual reorientation that he endured in the spring of 1908 and that changed both his beliefs and his mode of life. In his late years, reflecting back, he called it a "mental, Copernican decentering." "Before the Lord who has struck the blow," he wrote of this experience,

> [T]he soul … starts only to commemorate in secret this Annunciation, viaticum of hope, that she has conceived in order to give birth to the immortal. This frail Guest [Hôte] that she carries in her womb determines thereafter all of her conduct. It is not a made-up idea that she develops as she pleases according to her nature, but a mysterious Stranger whom she adores and who guides her: she devotes herself to Him … Her soul sanctifies herself to protect her Sacred Guest … She does not speak about her Guest "didactically"… but rather "testimonially," waiting for the moment when He suggests to her that she invoke Him, making her progress in experiential knowledge through compassion.[26]

Massignon himself always described the spiritual presences he felt during that period of transformation in the language of hospitality, of host and guest, and yet as a memory of psycho-spiritual trauma that, as Derrida notes, "fractured" his identity.[27] The centrality of Mary to the life that emerged from this crucible is evident in Massignon's subsequent devotions. Derrida cites a passage from Massignon's letters, a ruminative passage he imagines as uttered in kneeling prostration. It goes:

> To bring oneself to the divine presence and to invoke it from the bottom of one's heart. To compose a space for the "fiat," kneeling in front of Mary. To consider her trusting humility, her maternal intercession in our poor lives as sinners. To beg her to say for us, for all of us, sinners "fil badaliya," this humble, divine word of all vocation: "fiat."[28]

As he indicates in the seminar, Derrida is fascinated by such passages and the mode of prayer they encode; indeed, he makes of their citation a quasi-prayer practice in itself. (Elsewhere in the seminar, for instance, he quotes the entire text of the Lord's Prayer, though he is quite content to refer to other passages in the Bible as if they needed no textual citation.) Such prayers, he finds, are not restricted to those with explicit faith commitments, but are rather widespread, a running subconscious invocation of what he calls the subvocal prayer for mercy, the *miséricorde* that arises "even from the unbeliever" when caught in the aporiae of values such as hospitality. His citations themselves have just such a subvocal dimension, for they appear as if hostage to the analytical discourse in which they are embedded. They act at once as exemplum of a given discursive point, of course, but also as something more, a demonstration of what it might be like, under other conditions, to speak, as Massignon puts it, testimonially rather than didactically.

The centrality of Mary to Massignon's practice of Abrahamic hospitality is understandable, for Mary exemplifies in many ways exactly the practice of extreme embrace of the other both he and Derrida are trying to specify and understand. Though a comparatively minor figure in the gospels, Mary is vital, of course, to Christian self-understanding, and she is the only woman mentioned by proper name in the Qur'an. In both of these contexts, Christian and Muslim, her Israelite heritage and her connections with Abraham, her "father in faith" are clear. Clear also, are the profound differences in the way in which she is construed by theologians, especially with respect to her relationship to her divine child, a figure seen as the Son of the Father in Christianity, and as exemplary but not uniquely bound to the Creator by special filiation in Islam. Rabbinic Judaism is of course largely silent on the subject of Mary, who is either a fiction or an embarrassment—and later a threat—to the law. Marian discourse thus throws into sharp relief, both positively and negatively, the hospitality, or lack thereof, between the monotheisms, constituted as they are so relentlessly with respect to one another, and it bears as well on issues of kinship, gender, messianic discourse and the establishment of new religious orders, concerns that, as Derrida has demonstrated, are never far away when these religions intersect.

At the practical level, devotion to Mary is hospitable, as Massignon recognizes, because it is a discourse shared by Muslims and Christians; both concelebrate and weave into their prayers the primal faith of her great Magnificat, the prayer she uttered at the annunciation. Massignon quotes this prayer in its Qur'anic form in Arabic transliteration to make the point. Citing a friend's baptism, he says that with it the man "renews his consecration to the father of all believers, to whom Mary shouted her joy on the day of the 'Magnificat.' *Tou'azzimou nafsia erreb*, my soul glorifies the Lord."[29] The ambivalence in Massignon's prose here (as to whether "whom" refers, as it should, textually speaking, to God the father or whether it refers, as it should grammatically, to Father Abraham) is typical of his fractured and suggestive prose, where incoherence and insight vie with one another.

The figure of Mary is an apt one to the project of Abrahamic hospitality in Derrida's terms as well, though he does not make the connection explicit. Mary carries Derridean themes, however, in many ways. She does so first through what might be called her generic maternity, her function as the exemplum par excellence (and with all the paradoxes of exemplarity to which Derrida has drawn attention) of what might be called absolute motherhood or motherhood degree zero, and through her singular motherhood and unique subject position with respect to her own identity, her relationship to her messianic child, and her role in the several religious contexts in which she is depicted as operating. For Mary's maternity involves not only the generic assent of any animate being to any form of life; it indicates also the commitment of a unique and individual self-awareness and self-rapport to a unique and individual person or child.

In this case, furthermore, the valence of these qualities is intensified, for her generic maternity is hyperbolic and her singularity equally so. She is for Catholics, Mother not only of Jesus but of all the Church, and even, as twentieth century piety would like to have it, of "all nations." She is also, however, "alone of all her sex," unique in her conception as well as in her generativity, born without sin and a virgin mother, the sole biological parent of her son. These paradoxical qualities raise the symbolic value of her identity and maternity to a new power, and her hospitality becomes correspondingly more extensive, more intense.

Furthermore, Mary extends the embrace of her hospitality to gender, for this figure foregrounds, if only by contrast, the unrelenting masculinity of much of the discourse of monotheism, and the problem of the limping analogy with various conventional forms of familial and erotic love through which it has approached the divine. Daughter of her own son, theologically speaking, Mary fractures those analogies and conventions, revealing their fissures and preventing literal reductions of sex and gender rhetoric. By adding a fourth to what Isak Dinesen liked to call that "masculine club, the Trinity," Mary frames both the binary and the Trinitarian models in a classic example of the Derridean supplement, and opens them to a wider discourse.

Much of the double and doubly intense quality of Marian maternity along with a number of Derridean values is encoded in the most famous of Marian texts, the unexpected, utterly messianic annunciation of the angel

Gabriel that she is to bear a child and call his name Emmanuel and in the hymn, the Magnificat, with which she later responds to this news. To the angel's message she responds first with a question, "How shall this be?" and then with her great, affirming yes, *fiat mihi*, "And Mary said, Behold the bondmaid of [the] Lord; be it to me according to thy word" (Luke 1:26–38). Here Mary offers a welcome to the other in the form of the child whom she harbors in her body, but it is a welcome shot through and through with an element of surprise and danger.

This text insists on emphasizing Mary's conscious assent, her full understanding of the terms of the faith, and what Derrida might call her self-rapport, even in the midst of her receptivity, her passiveness, her sense of having been chosen before she chooses. The angel, for instance, recognizes her singularity by using her name, "Fear not, Mary" (Luke 1:30). Her reaction to the announcement of her pregnancy shows an exemplary presence of mind and self command; her response, while not unwelcoming to the other, is neither automatic nor unquestioning. She is not slow to ask her question, how shall this be? And it precedes her fiat.

The assent that follows, is, moreover, not, as I have remarked on other occasions, a blank check, an unlimited submission, but an assent that stipulates, as it were, the terms of a covenant of which she has some, though not a complete, understanding.[30] Her response to the angel, "be it to me according to thy word," refers immediately to the message she has just heard, but echoes also the history of promises and agreements between the people of Israel and their God, and these resound as well through the Magnificat, the prayer of thanksgiving she then utters. We even hear that Mary "treasured up" these events and "pondered them in her heart" (Luke 2:19). Even Eve did not ponder quite like this, much less, to turn to the classics, the utterly hospitable but utterly un-self-aware Nausicaea, whose welcome to the stranger Ulysses, charming in its girlish naiveté, forms an instructive counter-text.

Her responses thus place Mary directly in the context of her Abrahamic heritage; indeed, she becomes here as much the New Abraham as, in a more familiar typology, the New Eve. Like Abraham, Mary is called from a life of relative anonymity onto the stage of world religious history, and like him she answers that call affirmatively, with her own version of Abraham's famous response, "hineni," "here I am." Like her father in faith, her *yes* entails, as events unfold, the miraculous birth of an unexpected and in some ways irregular child in whose name a new religious order will be founded, and later that *yes* will entail that she endure, perhaps even countenance, the sacrifice of that child in the service of the God whose call she first answered. As in the case of Sarah, we do not hear her assent, if assent may be presumed, to this even more austere existential demand as we do Abraham's: Mary's attitude toward Jesus's arrest and conviction are not recorded, though she is depicted as taking her place at the foot of the cross. In any case, whatever she may have assumed from her presumptive knowledge of Torah (for Mary is depicted in tradition as literate in the religion of her people), no saving angel seems to appear for her son to avert catastrophe—not at least until the resurrection.[31]

But New Testament texts and hermeneutic tradition presume Mary's faith that her son would prevail, and they certainly attest Mary's continued presence in the believing community around Jesus after his death, a community that awaited his coming again. Like Abraham's, then, her faith is upheld by the substitution and representation of her divine son as token of all humanity before the divine and also by a messianic promise, opening up a future as yet unknown. Her *yes* to the stranger within her own body opens the way to an event, a future, an *avenir* in the Derridean sense that she could neither have predicted nor, from any merely human point of view, have unequivocally welcomed. The impulse toward inclusion of such a figure in conversations about the Abrahamic religions is then indeed a gesture of hospitality toward the other, at least in terms of gender, but it does not take us far from their terms of reference.

In many ways, then, Mary's maternity offers a metaphor of hospitality at its most sacrificial and fecundating. At the same time, this is not a hospitality without limits or conditions nor, alas, without the capacity for violence. "And a sword will pierce your own soul too" warns the prophet Simeon when she comes to present her child in the temple, foretelling the divisions that his life will initiate (Luke 2:35). Indeed Mary is both host and hostage to her son and he to her in a double identity that will drive a sharp wedge between the faith of her fathers and that of the monotheisms to come. For Mary is not only a sign of universal human motherhood, but a sign of the particular orthodoxies of the Christian church. Each of these roles has its own logic, though they are intertwined, and each is illustrative of an important point in Derrida's analysis of hospitality, which itself hinges very closely, as we have seen, on the aporiae at the heart of issues of reproduction, of replication, of substitution, of singularity, and of what he calls *messianicité*.

The issue of *messianicité* opens at a single stroke a breach within and among these religions. In terms of Judaism, Mary's pregnancy is, of course, a scandal. Her child is not the messiah; he is either a myth or fiction and/or a blasphemer, and is therefore by definition the issue of an illegitimate liaison—perhaps, as some early rabbinic sources like to suggest, of a Roman centurion, or, as Robert Graves argued in a book as remarkable for its crude euhemerizm as for its queasy fascination, of Herod himself. In terms of Islam, the case is more complicated. As Massignon recognizes, Mary is adored in Islam as the immaculate mother of a great prophet, but neither she nor her son are singular in their ties to divinity. As he puts it in one of the strange texts describing a form of prayer in which impossibility is braided into possibility, disavowal into avowal:

> Waiting for this hour, we pray for them and with Him during the Three Angelus of the day, affirming, through Mary's "Fiat," the mystery of divine Incarnation that the Muslims wish to deny: at the same hours the call to prayer of the Muezzin gathers the hearts in the same adoration of the One God of Abraham.[32]

In these distinct but interlocking and in many ways mutually constitutive contexts, Mary—who would be Miriam in Hebrew and Maryam in Arabic—thus appears as a key figure in the delineation of both the extent and limitations of various forms of Abrahamic hospitality, external and internal. This hospitality is deeply linked, as it is in all cultures, to questions of kinship and affiliation, and also, in this case, to the specificity of several different kinds of messianic promise. In any case, it is the singular, sacrificial and self-aware hospitality offered by Mary at once to the God of Israel and Ishmael and to her own divine son that makes her an important interlocutor for the consideration of the Abrahamic faiths in this context, and it is in part the limitations of that hospitality, at least at the programmatic level, that make her a compelling and controversial figure.

Like death, the gift, and hospitality itself, maternity and Marian discourse are shot through with paradoxes and problems, and they provide a highly cathected set of texts and subtexts both for Derrida's seminar and the work of Massignon on which it draws. The seminar ends on a relatively unresolved note, a note of postponement, even of anxiety, as Derrida considers the dangers of mechanical reproduction and human replication without the saving difference of self-aware hospitality, not to mention the endless capacity for internecine violence in the Abrahamic monotheisms. As his reflections lead the reader out into what T. S. Eliot called a wilderness of mirrors, it may be useful to return to the figure of Mary for a less closed and determinate apprehension of the possible bases for a realization of monotheistic obligation to the other.

The book of Revelation provides a possible text here, for in it Mary may be seen as moving into that ambiguous territory Derrida described by the Greek term *khôra*, a vast zone outside the pale of determinate identities, credal affirmations, and prepackaged labels where mobile identities wander and merge, always in the expectation of an order, a pattern, a messianic justice that does not quite manifest itself. In the last book of the New Testament, for instance, we find the figure referred to only as the Woman Clothed by the Sun, giving birth, and then exiled like Hagar into the desert, and awaiting in this exile the infinitely promised, infinitely postponed return of her unnamed divine son (Revelation 12:1–6). Catholic hermeneutics has always identified this figure as Mary, but she remains a Mary so to speak *sous râture,* an anonymous Mary whose true nature and function has not yet been revealed. This indeterminacy and openness to an unknown future are crucial factors in hospitality, as Derrida has long argued and as Massignon's life testifies, and it is perhaps by focusing on this Marian vanishing point at the horizon of orthodox formulations and predetermined meanings that the Abrahamic faiths can open more deeply to one another and to "other cults" as well.

References

1. Cf. Jacques Derrida and Gianni Vattimo, *Religion* (Stanford: Stanford University Press, 1996), p. 5.
2. All biblical citations are from the New International Version of the Bible.
3. Jacques Derrida, *Acts of Religion*, ed. Gil Anidjar (New York: Routledge, 2002), pp. 358–420.
4. Derrida, *Acts of Religion*, p. 411, emphasis added.
5. Derrida, *Acts of Religion*, p. 420.
6. This receptivity is perhaps what the poet Keats was attempting to indicate when he coined the term "negative capability."
7. Derrida, *Acts of Religion*, p. 417.
8. Derrida, *Acts of Religion*, p. 417.
9. Derrida, *Acts of Religion*, p. 417. To digress for a moment to a corollary of this analysis and to a larger problem within Derrida's discourse, Derrida notes that the question of hospitality toward concepts, as well as persons, follows the same paradigm. He speaks, in the seminar, of the way in which concepts can be "hospitable" or not to one another. Very often, Derrida's intensely labile and hospitable mind leads him to entertain numerous ramifying series of terms, issues, and categories, and many times the potentially infinite and yet impossible extension of these to embrace the sum of all hopes and fears leads him to a rhetorical and practical impasse. He writes, for instance, not only, as we have seen, of Islam, woman, and "other cults" but of hospitality, justice, the gift, forgiveness, "etc." or more comically of logocentrism, phallogocentrism, latinophallogocentrism, and carnephallogocentrism as if he feared slighting anyone in his invitations to the dance. These lists are not by any means random, but they are often dismaying, and never more so than when they are marked by such mechanical rhetorical devices as "and so forth" and "et cetera."
10. Compare Derrida, *Acts of Religion*, p. 407, with Derrida's running commentary on his mother's illness in "Circumfession," in *Jacques Derrida*, Geoffrey Bennington and Jacques Derrida, (Chicago: University of Chicago Press, 1993), pp. 3–325.
11. Derrida, *Acts of Religion*, p. 359.
12. Derrida, *Acts of Religion*, p. 410.
13. Cf. Mary Louise Gude, *Louis Massignon: The Crucible of Compassion* (Notre Dame: Notre Dame Press, 1996).
14. Gude, *Louis Massignon*, p. 30.
15. Derrida, *Acts of Religion*, p. 378.
16. I do not wish to imply that the Islam of Massignon's experience was free from homophobia. Indeed, Massignon experienced ridicule and even danger on account of his sexual orientation; see Gude, *Louis Massignon*, p. 29, and elsewhere. The theology and structure of Islam, however, do not institutionalize homophobia in quite the way that Catholicism does.

17. Gude, *Louis Massignon*, p. 50.
18. Cited by Derrida, *Acts of Religion*, p. 375, from *Massignon,* Charles Destremau and Jean Moncelon (Paris: Plonm, 1994).
19. "*Les trois prières d'Abraham père de tous les croyants,*" in Louis Massignon, *Parole donnée* (Paris: Seuil, 1983), pp. 257–272; trans. Allan Cutler in *Testimonies and Reflections: Essays of Louis Massingon,* ed. Herbert Mason (Notre Dame: University of Notre Dame Press, 1989), pp. 3-20; cited by Derrida, *Acts of Religion,* p. 372.
20. Derrida, *Acts of Religion,* p. 374.
21. Derrida, *Acts of Religion,* p. 377.
22. Derrida mentions as a digression "the active silence" with which the Badaliya "chokes all fraternity" with the Jews and adduces, beyond "some probability of anti-Semitism, one that would be vaguely sociological and atmospheric" were it not for two letters in which Massignon actually mentions both his fear of the influence of Jewish refugees in France and the resulting "crisis of anti-Semitism" which, he says, created conflict between himself and his friends the Maritains and Georges Cattawi (*Acts of Religion,* pp. 418–419).
23. Derrida, *Acts of Religion,* p. 379.
24. Gude, *Louis Massignon*, p. 124.
25. Derrida, *Acts of Religion,* p. 378.
26. Cited by Derrida, *Acts of Religion,* p. 374, from Massignon, "The Three Prayers of Abraham," pp. 7–10.
27. Derrida, *Acts of Religion,* p. 374.
28. Quoted in Louis Massignon, *L'hospitalité sacrée* (Paris: Nouvelle Cité, 1987), p. 30, n.26; cited in *Acts of Religion,* Derrida, p. 389.
29. Cited by Derrida, *Acts of Religion,* p. 372, from Massignon, *L'hospitalité sacrée,* pp. 253–256.
30. See Cleo M. Kearns, "The Scandals of the Sign: The Virgin Mary as Supplement in the Religions of the Book," in *Questioning God,* eds. John D. Caputo, Mark Dooley, and Michael Scanlon (Bloomfield: Indiana University Press, 2001), pp. 318–341.
31. This key point represents a gap, or tear, or silent disruption of the logic of sacrifice that governs this Abrahamic-Marian parallel and opens up a line of inquiry beyond what can be pursued here.
32. Derrida, *Acts of Religion,* p. 379.

SECTION III
The Christian, The Jew (The Hyphen)

CHAPTER 6

Rosenzweig and Derrida at Yom Kippur[1]

DAVID DAULT

> How can one say and how can one know, with a certainty that is at one with oneself, that one shall never inhabit the language of the other, the other language, when it is the only language that one speaks, and speaks in a monolingual obstinacy, in a jealously and severely idiomatic way, without, however, being ever at home in it?

—Jacques Derrida[2]

This paper is based upon a fanciful premise: that somewhere, at some undisclosed location and in some as-yet-to-be-determined year, there is a meeting. The meeting is a peculiar one—a surprise, perhaps. Imagine it occurs at the door of a synagogue. (Which synagogue? There are several choices—that question will be left open.) Imagine, moreover, that it is occurring in the context of the High Holy Days, on the eve of Yom Kippur. The meeting is a bumping-into, really, as one might find at a doorway when one is entering while another is leaving. Standing at a distance, we might then regard this moment in its passing, and make a comment or two. Such, at least, is the intention here: to make a comment or two on this fanciful passing—the meeting of two figures who never really meet—the "meeting" of one Jacques Derrida and one Franz Rosenzweig. To observe and comment upon what such a "meeting" might entail, here in this briefest of interactions.

1.

Perhaps we should begin with a word or two about *Yom Kippur* itself—the context in which it occurs, and the context it provides to those meeting to observe it. Yom Kippur is often called the "day of atonement," an at-one-ment that entails many levels at once. It is a day focused on confession, gathering, and most importantly repentance. There is a word in Hebrew that speaks to this array of foci, the word *teshuvah*. The words of Ehud Luz will help us in placing this word:

> The Hebrew word for repentance, *teshuvah*, has two distinct meanings. The first derives from the verb "to return"; when used in this sense, it signifies going back to one's point of origin, returning to the straight path, coming back home after a period of absence. The second derives from the verb "to reply," and denotes response to a question that has come from without. The Jewish idea of *teshuvah* embraces both these meanings: It is a movement of return to one's source, to the original paradigm of human—or national—life, and also, simultaneously, a response to a divine call. The act of returning to one's original self is thus in and of itself a return to God and his teaching; and this is true on both the individual and the national levels.[3]

Luz goes on to tell us that *teshuvah* "is a central concept in Jewish religious literature, and [it] may be said to express the essence of the religious and ethical ideal of Judaism."[4] *Teshuvah* is a *tissue-veil*: a weaving of concepts that hold together in the locus of Yom Kippur. This gossamer tissue-veil of the *teshuvah* will similarly be the silent backdrop of our proceedings here: the question of "return" and "reply" to a call of identity.

On a number of levels, the Jewish people in Diaspora—be it ancient or contemporary—live in constant awareness of alterity, of their otherness, even as they live within the language and culture of a host nation. This alterity manifests, as we might observe, both as an indelible mark and an active participation. However, this "otherness" of the Jew—this marking, this cadence—has been acutely and horrendously problematized by the events of the twentieth century. For the Jew to be other *as a Jew* has inextricable complications now (speaking post-Shoah) for any questions of identity—particularly in postwar Europe. In examining such complications, it can be seen how the tropes of indelible marking and participation in cadences of alterity are co-opted by lethality.

Even though he wrote in the early twentieth century, indelibility and alterity—the question of the Jewish people living in land(guage)s not their own—were aspects highlighted by Jewish philosopher Franz Rosenzweig.[5] Such difference is problematic: Rosenzweig recognized the simultaneity of this difference manifesting (1) as preservation of the Jewish people in foreign cultures and (2) that such difference historically has been cited as a "cause" for the Jewish people to become the target for radical assimilation or radical annihilation.

Moreover, post-Shoah, we find those who engage the question of Jewish "difference" in an altogether different manner; they themselves profess the intention to erase the indelible mark, to opt out of the identifying cadence of alterity. We may then ask how a refusal to be otherwise, or perhaps an insistence that one's identity is otherwise from the otherwise, might manifest itself, both in terms of interiorized, self-experienced identity and outward, self-expressed participation in sign, cadence, and liturgy.

Rosenzweig is a particularly apt interlocutor for Derrida on the question of Jewish identity. Both Rosenzweig and Derrida make biographical allusions to events they "experienced" on Yom Kippur and the effect these events had on their respective identities as Jews.[6] Like Rosenzweig (and again, but more significantly for Derrida, like Heidegger)[7] Derrida engages terms etymologically to underscore his arguments. Specifically here, Derrida makes much of the "parting" he finds in the root word of the *Kippour*—in his words, "the cut with Kippour, the noncircumcision of the sons."[8] By connecting the Day of Atonement—the day of response, return, reconciliation—to its opposite, to a parting, he ironically alludes (with awareness of the polyvalence of all such statements made by Derrida) to his "loss" of Judaism.

We turn then to Jacques Derrida—born a Jew, in the French colony of Algeria, writing after the Shoah. His *Monolingualism of the Other* explicitly, albeit briefly, addresses the works of Rosenzweig.[9] Moreover, his other works (in particular here both *Circumfession* and *Of Grammatology*) are, like Rosenzweig's works, concerned both with language in general, and with how one forms an identity within a given language that is (not) one's own. Finally, Derrida is engaged in a project through these works (as is perhaps best implied by the title "*Circumfession*,"[10] which is at once an "autobiography," a playful exploration of Augustine's *Confessions*, and a polemic—or perhaps a circumvention—against being "read" or "anticipated") that weaves together the theoretical (linguistic, philosophical) and the personal (psychoanalytic, confessional).

2.

It is improper to say that Derrida simply wished to abandon Jewishness. Even the casual reader of Derrida is aware that he has a certain *attachment* to Jewishness—be it reference to the Shoah or to his own experiences of anti-Semitism as a child. This attachment is a source, then, but it has also been a source of pain (of trembling—perhaps in the full Kierkegaardian sense)[11] from which he understandably would wish to distance himself. Thus by his accounting, at Yom Kippur he attempts to circumcise his circumcision; he *kippours*; he cuts.

That this cut can be simultaneously the loss of Judaism as the *indelible mark* and Judaism of *embraced cadence* is evident from Derrida's interplay and interuse of these tropes throughout both *Monolingualism* and "Circumfession." But breaking from these for Derrida is problematic; it involves acknowledging that his motives for the break might reflect still a fundamental compromise of his autonomy as a self (e.g., "and if I say that I am losing my life at this moment, that curiously comes down to the same thing, my life is that other that 'I lose'...")[12] What otherwise might be passed off as youthful rebellion against a mere "going through the (Jewish) motions" is unflinchingly interrogated by Derrida, and at its core he finds a contamination—meaning his drive to lose his circumcision may not be a pure drive of self, but may itself be a marking that comes from outside.

Thus Derrida, recalling for us his rebellion, speaks of it first of all as a mere parting with Judaism of ritual and sign, an *exterior* Judaism—the repetition of cadences we have been discussing ("I was dealing with a Judaism of 'external signs,'" he says)[13] But this attempt to assert himself autonomously against these motions reveals to him the (literally) deeper implications of his act:

> I could not rebel—and believe me, I was rebelling against what I took to be gesticulations, particularly on the feast days in the synagogues—I could not lose my temper, *except from what was already an insidious Christian contamination*: the respectful belief in inwardness, the preference for intention.[14]

In other words, Derrida's attempt to dispense with the exterior trappings of faith revealed to him that he was yet implicated in a form of marking, one that he perceived as coming from the culture around him; a distinctly *Christian* culture. With his exteriorized Judaism lost, Derrida, years later, makes the curious claim, "I became an *interior* Jew. A *Christian*, one could say; in other words, *a Protestant*."[15]

On one level, this can be read in light of Rosenzweig's own assertion that "the Jew between the Crucifixion and the Second Coming can only have a *negative* meaning in Christian theology";[16] the Jew (in this initial reading) is the constant other to the Christian, and the dynamic between them is not an equal one. If the Jew is negative and the Christian positive, there is the constant risk that any slippage of identity will result in instant assimilation, a negation of the "negative"—a double-negative that reduces difference to sameness. Read this way, the sublimation ("interiorization") of Derrida's Judaism is thus a *de facto* acceptance of a Christian identity.

This is a curious play of words—alluding as it does to Paul's Epistle to the Galatians (the "Christianized" Gentile, seemingly co-opting the promises of Torah covenant but no longer needing to physically submit to Torah law—most particularly [important for Derrida here], the circumcision—for everything is now a matter of *interiors*). It could also be read as an allusion to Derrida's own protest and abandonment of Judaism. Such word play need not, however, be heard to confess that Derrida is now a "convert" to Christianity (in the vulgar, a "completed" Jew). His contention should be read, rather, as a complex attempt to work out his identity in light of his discovery of these interior implications.

First of all, as an *incomplete* Jew (i.e., as one who has been "incompleted"—circumcised) he therefore has been bound—before his act of will could be exercised—to a community (whether ultimately Christian or Jewish is a question worth suspending for the moment). Thus Derrida finds himself always needing the community to be made "complete," as his incompleteness had been always already marked (circumcised) onto/into his very body by that community. He is not able, simply (or simply not able) to willfully step outside the double binds[17] placed on him by that community, even when he may claim to be an atheist.[18]

As such, the binary of polarized Christian/Jewish identities is further problematized: even though Derrida may not go through the "motions" of Christianity (and indeed, Derrida does not), the assumed "positivity" of Christian culture may well "assume" him, regardless.[19] Therefore, by attempting to be "nothing" (an "atheist" or, perhaps more properly here: a "*nay*-theist") on the outside, Derrida's Jewishness (again, with Jew as negative other to the assumed given of the Christian culture) is thus, in this second reading, reinscribed in him: "interiorized," but not lost.[20]

It is this double-bind of identity—that one can never escape being a Jew once one has been circumcised, but that one can become affected (or perhaps it is more proper to say *in*fected) by a sort of Christian "contamination"[21]—that Derrida attempts to write himself out of through the creation of an "unreadable text" in the guise of his "Circumfession."[22] This rhetorical act of unreadability is his countermove against God, specifically against "God weeping in me, turning around me, reappropriating my languages, dispersing their meaning in all directions ... as I [Derrida] am someOne that the One God never stops de-circumcising."[23] This rhetorical act of unreadability is an attempt to break all connections with one's inscribed community—to mark oneself, finally, as a *someOne* whose "root word" is exactly the someOne of whom Derrida is attempting to write (unreadably). Derrida is attempting through this writing (finally) to *speak for himself*, as someOne who cannot be read (fixed, marked, circumcised) by another. This self-marking intends to be an *arche*-text (a condition that both Rosenzweig and Derrida recognize as a construction of difference that occurs before the act of writing/speech); it comes as close as Derrida ever has to an ontological assertion of his own identity. Thus, when *spoken*, the root word Derrida utters is "*I*."[24]

Uttered as such, this "I" is an attempt rhetorically to (re)claim this someOne as the root of discourse, over and against the "we" of the normative community or the "you" of the call. The rhetorical intent of this "I" is to negate. As Rosenzweig puts it, "'I' is always a Nay become audible. 'I' always involves a contradiction, it is always underlined, always empha-sized, always an 'I, however.'"[25]

This radical I—spoken both against God and against the (Jewish/inscribing) community (which confesses as a people its relationship to God) returns Derrida to a confession of the *Cartesian* self, a *cogito*, a self of radical doubt.[26] This self, in other words, is a soul that (in the words of Rosenzweig) "disregarded the world in order to gain, instead, the soul and only the soul, the solitary soul, the soul of the individual *sans* all the world."[27]

Derrida's intention, then, is to write himself out of the circumcising relationship with God by writing himself out of the *cult*. He thus writes himself out of both the rituals and the community (and, by Rosenzweig's etymological extension, we might even say out of the world). But in doing so, he succeeds in writing himself back *into* the problem of Hegelian modernism[28]—he claims a radical, autonomous self-consciousness to the negation and exclusion of the world. This will to exclusivity—this attempt to *universalize* the self to exclusion of all others (and root that self as the starting point for discourse), does not solve the dilemma of modernism; it *is* the dilemma of modernism.

Such a result remains inescapable for Derrida (or anyone), as long as the atonement—the making-one-ness—is equated with the collapse of differ-ence into same-ness. Treated in this way, atonement becomes a hegemonic act; equivalent to the Hegelian *aufhebung* that assumes antitheses into a sin-gularity. Derrida's appeal to the "someOne" (what I am terming the "radi-cal I") is evidence of his implication in the Hegelian/Cartesian grammar. Derrida has a strong reaction against being "read" (in "Circumfession" par-ticularly, but also in the *oeuvre* of deconstruction itself). For Derrida being inscribed by *any* community—be it Jewish, Christian, or literary (as in the case of Geoffrey Bennington's *Derridabase*)—is tantamount to being eradicated as a self.[29] Derrida's written (self)/(un)circumcision—whether it occurs through the absorption (Hegel) or negation (Descartes) of the "other" (the world)—is a self-consciousness that must assert its liminal boundaries at all costs. Hence the *circumfessed* Derrida of Yom Kippur is a grammatical isolate; unmarked, unreadable, untranslatable.

3.

"Rosenzweig was never far from becoming a Christian," Derrida once wrote/said.[30] In one sense this was true. Rosenzweig attended his own formative Yom Kippur with the very real possibility of it being a crossing-over point for him into Christianity, and he remained in close affiliation throughout his life with Christians such as Eugen Rosenstock-Heussey and Hans Ehrenberg. Throughout his life he maintained that Christianity and Judaism were the "two valid religions of revelation."[31] However, it is a significant point of contrast with Derrida that, at Yom Kippur, Rosenzweig *did not* cross over to Christianity, but renewed his ties with Judaism.[32] Where Derrida appeals to the "radical I," placing self against world in (Hegelian/Cartesian) "atonement," we find Rosenzweig in atonement embracing religious community, placing self alongside world. In the place of Derrida's self-marking individual we find instead Rosenzweig as an other-marked (perhaps he would prefer to say "called") member of "an individual people ... a people *among others*."[33]

When voiced, then, this utterance of identity for Rosenzweig transcends the "Nay become audible"—the sole word of the "radical I"—and opens to

> [B]ecome *a sentence* which must be spoken simultaneously from both sides—really *in two voices*. Thus this I *cannot remain* I. Man and world must be able to sing it in one breath. Only God himself was able to pronounce the divine I. Its place must be taken by the divine name that man and the world too can carry in their heart. And it must be said: he is good ... This is the root sentence of redemption, the roof over the house of language. It is the sentence true in itself. It remains true regardless of how intended or by what mouth uttered.[34]

In working out his own Jewish commitments through language, Rosenzweig opens for us the possibility of an identity, which does not fall into the hegemony of the modernist self (the Cartesian *cogito*, Hegel's "Master," or Derrida's "someOne") but remains dialogically open to the

Other. In this model, atonement does not collapse to sameness, but opens to alterity, becoming the inseparable togetherness of irreducibly differentiated Others.

4.

Eugen Rosenstock once began a letter in his voluminous correspondence to Rosenzweig with the greeting, "Dear Fellow (Jew + post-Christum natum + post-Hegel mortuum)!"[35] In our considerations here, such an apt turn of phrase applied to Rosenzweig by Rosenstock well suits. Rosenzweig was a man of multiple investments. A Jew, yes, but aware and respectful of Christianity. He was also aware of his place in the German community—a community that had a distinct philosophical history. All of these parts are *wholly* Rosenzweig, but also wholly distinct. Separated by plus signs but contained in the brackets of a grammatical unit—a parenthetical statement: an aside; a voice of "otherwise." These aspects of the man are irreducibly, indissolubly combined.

Rosenzweig was wholly Jew: It was essential to the man that Judaism not be an affectation or something "added on" to one's life, but that one's life instead be a fully committed recognition of the Jewish reality—*if one is a Jew*. Rosenzweig's embrace of Judaism might be misleading when seen out of the context of the man's life and thought, and might lead one to assert, as did Yudit Kornberg Greenberg, that "Rosenzweig's unapologetic celebration of Jewish myths, symbols, and rituals *is indicative of his break* from his assimilated German Jewish culture, as well as his break with and profound critique of traditional philosophy."[36]

But was Rosenzweig's stance that of a break? Was it simply a matter of his own "nay" becoming audible, divesting him of connection with these other aspects of his intellectual and cultural life? Hardly. To hold such a view belies the nuance of both Rosenzweig's life and thought. The implication of Greenberg's reading of Rosenzweig is that all that was non-Jewish became inconsequential, or perhaps that all that was of consequence *became* Jewish for Rosenzweig.

It is Rosenzweig himself who warns against just such a reading. True, it is Rosenzweig who claims "Nothing Jewish is alien to [him],"[37] but he is also careful to put limits on the extent to which such a statement is to be viewed as a totalizing claim:

> It would be necessary [for the person who has succeeded in saying 'nothing Jewish is alien to me'] to free himself from those stupid claims that would impose 'Juda-ism' on him as a canon of definite, circumscribed 'Jewish duties' (vulgar orthodoxy), or 'Jewish tasks'

(vulgar Zionism), or—God forbid—"Jewish ideas" (vulgar liberal-ism).[38]

Rosenzweig is Jew, but always as a *Jew plus* … Rosenzweig's identity is not a monistic (or monolingual) reduction to one or another single voice. One might even claim that precisely *because* Rosenzweig was wholly Jew, he was always aware of the polyphony of irreducible voices within him—as well as the voices of others "outside" himself:

> Let us remember that Judaism leaves its own inner core open, protecting it from the kind of "positivity" that assumes idolatrous powers. In Cohenian terms, the openness of that "inner core" of Israel is ideally an openness toward self-criticism, providing room for the "voice that differs" and instilling into our souls an absolute concern with human suffering. And let us remain aware that that when talking about a "pluralistic hermeneutics" or a "polyphony of voices" we are indebted to Rosenzweig's theoretical preoccupation with Cohen's "method of origin," which Rosenzweig advances toward a theory of intersubjectivity in which an "infinity of origins"—that is, an infinite number of particular faces—indicate the limits of the self (myself).[39]

So the self for Rosenzweig—and indeed, Rosenzweig's self—is defined both in its interior and its exterior by its ability to coexist with otherness. This otherness calls for a return and demands a response. Rosenzweig's vision allowed for the radical notion that "[t]he Pharisees walking away from Jesus and the disciples walking with him are both on God-ordained paths," and that such divergent paths remain true in their respective integrities.[40] For Rosenzweig the proper role of identity is that which is able to comprehend and evaluate otherness in a nontotalizing way, and remain bound to this otherness in a (comm)unity.

5.

Rosenzweig's self, then, is a self constantly in translation. Wholly itself, it is yet inextricably bound up and dependent upon its other(s) for integrity and identity, and it must *confess* itself and be confessed with these others.[41] Rosenzweig *is* the German; Rosenzweig *is* the Jew; Rosenzweig *is* the man who deeply respected—and almost converted to—Christianity. These otherings are each fully formed in Rosenzweig, and yet none of them must be allowed to tell the whole story. Not one of them can form a totality. Each, though whole, is incomplete by itself.

Derrida's self—at least the self he chooses to present in "Circumfession," the "someOne" self of the radical "I"—can, in contrast, never be whole. It wanders, "inhabiting what remains": of Judaism, of place, of common language.[42] Where Rosenzweig embraces, Derrida resists—perhaps with good reason. Abandoning the cut that inscribes, Derrida writes himself out of pain—perhaps? Perhaps. But to do so he must "write to alienate,"[43] and create a hermetic place, where he can finally say, "I do not know anyone, I have not met anyone, I have had in the history of humanity no idea of anyone …"[44]

And yet: here: in the midst of this pulling back, this sealing off, this decircumcising—at the height of the *Cartesian* impulse—there is—perhaps? Perhaps—a meeting. "I think therefore I am" softens … *opens*? Perhaps. Derrida's "I" opens, opening "one eye then the other"—opening to "overrun this discourse on castration and its supposed substrate, that old concept of narcissism," to become—perhaps?—like "those circumcised ones."[45] The *cogito* reverses: "I am … I think." Softening, opening against the hard closure of "I think … I am" is the *reversal* of the radical "I." And we *read* (Derrida? Perhaps) *someOne* who writes: "I am. I think. I gather my spirits, *for there are more than one of them sharing my body* … multiplying in me the counterexamples and countertruths that I am …"[46]

The dialogue does not end. On the Day of Atonement Rosenzweig and Derrida "meet" and "part" at the synagogue, "meet" and "part" with themselves, and "meet" and "part" with this hanging question—this call to return and to respond. They speak—for the moment, through an interpreter—aware of the ghost of a common tongue that eludes them. They are warm in their greeting and leaving, however, and one might catch the faint hope in the voice of one or the other as they ask—In French? In German?

"… Next year … perhaps …?"

References

1. This chance meeting between Derrida and Rosenzweig at the door of the synagogue has been placed in the doorway between the "Hostipitality" section and "The Jew, The Christian, The Hyphen," for reasons that will become clear (YS and KH).
2. Jacques Derrida, *Monolingualism of the Other OR the Prosthesis of Origin*, trans. Patrick Mensah (Stanford: Stanford University Press, 1998), p. 57. This is one of several works in which Derrida deals with his (endlessly problematized) "Jewishness," (of which we will say more in a moment).
3. Ehud Luz, "Repentance," in *Contemporary Jewish Religious Thought*, ed. Arthur A. Cohen and Paul Mendes-Flohr (New York: Scribners, 1987), p. 785.
4. Luz, "Repentance," p. 785.
5. I am deeply indebted to Oona Eisenstadt for her insights on Rosenzweig, language, and national identity. Her work on Rosenzweig was especially timely and helpful in the writing of the initial drafts of this paper. See in particular Oona Eisenstadt, "Making Room for the

Hebrew: Luther, Dialectics and the Shoah," *Journal of the American Academy of Religion* (September 2001): pp. 551–575.

6. I will follow Rosenzweig's contention that all holy days in the Jewish Liturgical calendar (and thus all Kippurs) are a prefiguration of eternity, to frame this "event"—separated by place and time but unified in eternity and central to each in their self-making acts of narrative. Thus Yom Kippur will serve as a meeting place of sorts between these two thinkers, though they are separated by a lifetime of years and the deathtime of Shoah.

7. For Derrida's indebtedness to Heidegger, see Jacques Derrida, *Positions* (Chicago: University of Chicago Press, 1982), pp. 9–10. He sometimes claims that all he writes is observed (or haunted) by a sort of ghost-like Heideggerian interlocutor (he did so, for example, in public remarks at the Villanova conference on Augustine's *Confessions*, September 28, 2001).

8. Derrida, "Circumfession," in *Jacques Derrida*, Geoffrey Bennington and Jacques Derrida (Chicago: University of Chicago Press, 1993), p. 202. Much of what I write about Derrida here will hinge upon my "reading" of the passage from which this statement comes.

9. In a conversation with Derrida I asked him what effect, if any, Rosenzweig had had on his work. He admitted regret that he had never had the time to do extensive work on Rosenzweig, and mentioned the footnote to *Monolingualism* as his most comprehensive engagement with Rosenzweig to date (see *Monolingualism*, pp. 79–84). He stated that it was his hope to undertake a more extensive reading of Rosenzweig at some point in the future, should time allow it (Jacques Derrida, private conversation with author, Villanova conference on Augustine's *Confessions*, September 28, 2001).

10. The sheer finesse with which Derrida has concatenated this term *circumfession* out of *confession*, *circumcision*, *circumscription* (the drawing of boundaries, limits), *cum* (the French *with* and also a vulgar reference to *dissemination*) etc. is breathtaking. I hope to interplay all of its concomitant meanings in my use here.

11. I direct the reader particularly to *Jacques Derrida*, "Circumfession," pp. 309–10, where in one sentence Derrida strings together circumcision, the almost-sacrifice of Isaac by Abraham (hence my allusion to Kierkegaard), the Final Solution of the Shoah, and his own experiences of trembling (again, Kierkegaard).

12. *Jacques Derrida*, "Circumfession," pp. 202–03.

13. Derrida, *Monolingualism of the Other*, p. 54.

14. Derrida, *Monolingualism of the Other*, p. 54, emphasis mine.

15. This was a comment made by Derrida at the conference on Augustine's *Confessions*; Jacques Derrida, unpublished remarks, Villanova conference on Augustine's *Confessions*, September 28, 2001.

16. Franz Rosenzweig, quoted in *Judaism Despite Christianity*, ed. Eugen Rosenstock-Huessy (Birmingham: University of Alabama Press, 1969), p. 99, emphasis mine.

17. My use of this term is a dual-pointer, first acknowledging Derrida's frequent use of this term, as well as pointing to the work of R.D. Laing on the genesis of schizophrenia in a *double-bind* situation. In Laing's typology, a double-bind is a "schizophrenogenic" situation, one in which an individual is conformed by social pressure to "live in" two equally powerful, non-negotiable and mutually exclusive realities at once with no opportunity to articulate the anxiety this necessarily causes, resulting in dissociative behavior. See for example R.D. Laing, *The Divided Self* (New York: Penguin Books, 1979).

This is a useful psychoanalytic model, perhaps, but is psychoanalysis itself a model that can illuminate theology, particularly *Jewish* theology? Many would argue against such parallels. However, I find myself agreeing here with Walter Brueggemann, who avers:

> It is suggested in many quarters that Sigmund Freud's theory of psychoanalysis is a thoroughly Jewish enterprise and is much informed by Midrashic practice. Freud's assumption is that a surface articulation or representation of reality is to be treated with great suspicion and not to be taken at face value. When Freud is understood as a social critic and not simply as a therapist (in any popular sense of the term), it is clear that Freud's interest is in *a theory of repression that constitutes a practice of pervasive deception*. (Walter Brueggemann, *Theology of the Old Testament* [Minneapolis: Fortress Press, 1997], p. 327, emphasis mine.)

Curiously, in Laing's writing, an acknowledged double-bind can be a path to healing the psyche, but a bind that is not allowed to be honestly confronted may very well drive one to madness. For further explanation of this phenomenon, I highly recommend two of Laing's most thought-provoking works, *The Divided Self* and *The Politics of Experience* (New York: Random House, 1983).

18. Derrida made this claim publicly at the Villanova conference, and again at a keynote session of the 2002 American Academy of Religion/Society of Biblical Literature conference in Toronto (collected in this volume; see below). However, Derrida should not be seen as closing off religious questions in his project. That is not, I think, what he is implying in his remarks. Rather, I believe what Derrida refers to as atheism is what most would term a form of agnosticism—a manner of keeping questions about the divine undecided, quite intentionally (Jacques Derrida, "Epoché and Faith: An Interview with Jacques Derrida").

19. This was a circumstance of which Rosenzweig was acutely aware. In an early letter to his parents, during his phase of contemplating "conversion" to Christianity, Rosenzweig asserted, "We are Christians in all things, we live in a Christian state, go to Christian schools, read Christian books, our whole culture is based on a Christian foundation" (quoted in Rüdiger Lux, "Franz Rosenzweig 1886–1929," published online at http://www.jcrelations.net/articl1/lux.htm).

20. "Derrida's treatment of circumcision as the inescapable sign of particularism of Jewish manhood reproduces that the debates of the Enlightenment in which Jews, in particular, were understood to be particularistic—especially as evidenced by the intransigence of *that* sign ... And like the parents we happen to have, however fortunate we may be in this accident of our birth, and like death, circumcision also is not understood as freely chosen. It is confronted after the fact. Indeed, Derrida writes as if his Jewishness were determined by the very fact of his having been circumcised" (see Steven Kepnes et al., *Reasoning After Revelation: Dialogues in Postmodern Jewish Philosophy* [Boulder: Westview Press, 1998], p. 81).

21. Derrida, *Monoligualism of the Other*, p. 54.

22. Geoffrey Bennington, in commenting upon "Circumfession" at the Villanova conference, declared it a text he "could not read" (Geoffrey Bennington, unpublished remarks, Villanova conference on Augustine's *Confessions*, September 28, 2001).

23. Jacques Derrida, "Circumfession," p. 224.

24. Franz Rosenzweig, *The Star of Redemption* (Notre Dame: Notre Dame Press, 1985), p. 173. My intention here is to point to Rosenzweig's discussion of the "inner conversion" which also figures so prominently in our discussion of Derrida. In attempting to "write himself out" of both Jewish practice and Jewish interiority, I see Derrida writing himself into a type of secular modernism, which Rosenzweig rightly terms here "Interior Paganism" (see also Rosenzweig, *Star*, pp. 172, 280).

25. Rosenzweig, *Star*, 173.

26. Derrida does not make such a confession explicitly. In fact, much of his extended project through the years has been calculated to undermine just this sort of radical "I". In a very Derridean manner, however, we may venture that we find, when he is pushed to the very core question of his *identity,* he implicitly (reflexively?) resorts to rhetorical structures he has elsewhere explicitly sought to deconstruct (in this instance, the present and located self).

Curiously, this predicament replays moves Derrida has made against other authors—notable for us here is Derrida's critique of Rousseau and *his* version of the *Confessions*—whereby he has shown that the Rousseau's intention is undermined by the very language the author uses. Numerous examples of Derrida's method on this front are readily available; the one mentioned here has a central place in his early work *Of Grammatology* (Baltimore: Johns Hopkins University Press, 1977), but there are many others.

As such, in my reading of the statement "I am someOne that the One God never stops de-circumcising" this someOne is seen as a radical (attempt at) *self*-definition, equivalent perhaps to "I think, therefore I am." Interestingly, by the very act of *de*-circumcision, the "One God" referred to here *negates* the covenant—and therefore negates itself as the True God—and replaces itself with a false god: the "I" of paganism, which no longer appeals to God nor world for its (self) readability, taking as it does *itself* for the root of discourse.

27. Rosenzweig, *Star*, p. 281.

28. For a brief discussion of these matters by Derrida himself, the reader is directed to Jacques Derrida, *Dissemination* (Chicago: University of Chicago Press, 1983), p. 194.

29. On this point I am in basic agreement with Walter Brueggemann's statement that, against being "known in advance," Derrida "protests in the name of unexpected possibility" (*Theology*

of the Old Testament, p. 330). Moreover, Brueggemann's analysis is confirmed by the "contract" made by J.D. and G.B. and spoken of at the outset of *Derridabase/"Circumfession."* (If we may assume for the moment that J.D. is Jacques Derrida and G.B. Geoffrey Bennington, then it can be explained that it was Bennington's intention to create a seeming "Derrida-machine"—one that would always already inscribe the "real"(?) Derrida's possibilities—and that Derrida "responded" to by undertaking to write the "unreadable" "Circumfession".)

Brueggemann goes on to claim, however, that Derrida's protest is "a thoroughly Jewish enterprise" (*Theology of the Old Testament*, p. 330). I must respectfully disagree. What Derrida utilizes in his practice of deconstruction certainly has a family resemblance to Midrash—but a "Midrash" stripped of all divine commitments. A Midrash so stripped is not and cannot be *Midrash*. To deny the power of the divine is to divorce oneself from the *derash* (which admits to spiritual-theological, and not merely literary, possibilities in a given text) at the heart of Midrash.

Rosenzweig's model of a difficult—but ultimately necessary—*self-translation* with the other is a sharp contrast to Derrida's attempt at radical unreadability. Derrida's very unreadability writes him out of the possibility of Judaism being the source of his project. Derrida denies/ cuts off/ uncuts/ decircumcises his connections to Judaism, to God, and therefore to any true Midrash ("thoroughly Jewish" or otherwise).

30. Derrida, *Monolingualism of the Other*, p. 83.
31. Ronald H. Miller, *Dialogue and Disagreement: Franz Rosenzweig's Relevance to Contemporary Jewish–Christian Understanding* (Lanham: University Press of America, 1989), p. 83.
32. To cite but one example, Rosenzweig writes: "We are wholly agreed as to what Christ and his Church mean to the world: no one can reach the Father save through him. No one can reach the Father! But the situation is quite different for one who does not have to reach the Father because he is already with him. And this is true of the people of Israel (though not of individual Jews)" (quoted in *Dialogue and Disagreement*, p. 5).
33. Rosenzweig, *Star*, p. 305, emphasis mine.
34. Rosenzweig, *Star*, p. 231.
35. September 13, 1916: "Dear Fellow (Jew after Christ's birth and the death of Hegel)!" *Judaism Despite Christianity*, p. 94.
36. Kepnes, *Reasoning After Revelation*, p. 69, emphasis mine.
37. From Rosenzweig's "On Being a Jewish Person," quoted in *Understanding the Sick and the Healthy*, Franz Rosenzweig, (Cambridge: Harvard University Press, 1999), p. 15.
38. Rosenzweig, from "On Being a Jewish Person," quoted in *Understanding the Sick and the Healthy*, p. 16.
39. Kepnes, *Reasoning After Revelation*, p. 118.
40. Miller, *Dialogue and Disagreement*, p. 115.
41. Kepnes, *Reasoning After Revelation*, p. 39.
42. Jacques Derrida, "Circumfession," p. 303.
43. Derrida, "Circumfession," p. 274.
44. Derrida, "Circumfession," p. 268.
45. Derrida, "Circumfession," p. 313.
46. Derrida, "Circumfession," p. 254, emphasis mine.

CHAPTER 7

Christianity and Anti-Judaism

WALTER LOWE

I write as one whose primary vocation is theological but who has been, for some number of years, in conversation with Derrida. Let me begin with a passage from Theodore Adorno's marvelous essay, "Reason and Revelation." Adorno writes, "The excision of the objective element from religion is no less harmful to it than the reification that aims to impose dogma ... inflexibly and antirationally upon the subject."[1] The excision of the "objective" element is no less harmful than fideistic reification. Now I am aware that for many, the notion of there being an objective element to religion, and of its falling into the hands of the theologians, is a prospect to be regarded with twofold alarm. If it be any assurance, my own assumption is that insofar as there is such an element, it will demonstrate its objectivity by its independence of the theologian. But that said, I do wish to argue, in agreement with Adorno, that the antidote to reification is not, as is often urged, a disavowal of any objective element.

In the first section I criticize what I take to be a common but misguided conception of postmodernism, its disingenuous relation to an aspect of modernity often neglected by religionists, namely Romanticism. The second section sketches a view of this neglected topic, noting with the help of deconstruction certain apocalyptic elements within Romanticism that are, whether intentionally or unintentionally, anti-Judaic. Yet these same elements derive from apocalyptic convictions within the New Testament

111

that are, I suggest, essential to the "objective element" in Christianity. The final section briefly considers this apocalyptic knot.

Prima Facie Postmodernism

Any espousal of "postmodernism" trades, of course, upon some specific construal of the modern. Unfortunately, a significant part of contemporary postmodernism proceeds by collapsing modernity into the Enlightenment, and then collapsing the Enlightenment into the Newtonian worldview—all the while professing sensitivity to difference. This convenient reductionism is disingenuous at best. "Western Civ. 101" suffices to remind one that any delineation of modern culture must encompass not only Enlightenment but Romanticism as well. By this act of suppression, it becomes apparent that certain postmodernists who would critique all notions of identity are simultaneously defending a spurious uniqueness or self-identity. For while it is easy enough to argue that postmodernism represents a break from Newton, it is more difficult to show that postmodernism represents a break, let alone an epochal disjunction, from Romanticism.

Clearly these observations do not encompass all of postmodernism but only an uncritical element within it. The point is that whatever the extent of this oppositionalist rejection of the Enlightenment, it does not include Derrida, who writes that an "absence of univocal definitions is not 'obscurantist,' it respectfully pays homage to a new, very new *Aufklärung*. This, in my eyes, is a very good sign."[2] Derrida is no enemy of the Enlightenment.

To return to matters of religion, if we ourselves resist the notion of an objective element therein, it is perhaps because a residual Romanticism in our own thinking disposes us to assign religion to the side of the subject. In fact, the challenge before us is less to overcome a purported subject-object split than to surmount the Enlightenment-Romanticism split; for the very notion of a subject-object split is itself a product of Romanticism. In a society that is indeed dominated by an impoverished calculative form of reason bent on domination (i.e., instrumental reason), "countless people project the suffering imposed upon them by society onto reason as such."[3] Too often Christian theology, under the press of social suffering, encourages this obscurantism by associating religion more or less exclusively with some other "human faculty" such as feeling or imagination.[4] But it is precisely through a fusion of critical Enlightenment and visionary Romanticism that social criticism is possible.

The Legacy of Romanticism

Leo Baeck, a survivor of Theresienstadt, distinguishes between "classic" and "Romantic" religion. For the Romantic believer, "Experiences with their many echoes and their billows stand higher in his estimation than life with its tasks; for tasks always establish a bond with harsh reality. And from this he is in flight."[5] Baeck believed that the inward orientation of Christianity was evidence of its Romantic character and illumined its failings. We will return to Baeck's indictment in the final section. At present our task is to understand something of Romanticism from within.

In the Enlightenment, poetry tended to be didactic, at the service of rationalism. With Romanticism poetry shed its secondary status; now it was the poet who saw the larger truth. The great impetus for this reversal was of course a concrete historical event, the French Revolution, which seemed in one gesture to have thrown open the full range of human possibility. Given its revolutionary birthright, early Romanticism was prone to portray its age in quasi-apocalyptic terms: a New Day was dawning and Romanticism was its herald.

The emergence of the Reign of Terror compelled the Romantics to rethink their relation to the history in which they had found their emphatic validation. But in the process, it should be emphasized, apocalyptic was not so much rejected as sublated; it became an apocalyptic *vision* that was now more explicitly spiritualized. Better yet, the vision itself *became* the apocalypse. The moment when the poem or the poet "speaks" became itself the moment of *apo-kalypsis* or "uncovering." From this point it is not difficult to trace a line eventuating in Heidegger's conception of truth as *a-leithia*, "unveiling."

Now when a New Age, itself an apocalyptic notion, is announced through a poetics of *apo-kalypsis*, a certain logic comes into play. For if the New Day, the definitive daybreak, is now, then all that went before is—with perhaps a few, selective exceptions (Jesus in William Blake, the presocratics in Heidegger)—thrown into shadow or outer darkness. In short, the rhetoric of *apo-kalypsis* promotes blindness regarding what went before. Such polemical distortion was already at work in the Renaissance-Enlightenment, which regarded itself as a new dawn in contrast to the preceding "Dark Ages." Then, when Romanticism in turn proclaimed its revolution, a polemical stance toward reason emerged and Enlightenment itself was made to darken. All in all, this polemical sequence, this internecine struggle within modernity, amply confirms Heidegger's cautionary dictum that every revealing is simultaneously a concealing. If Derrida, for his part, has got beyond Heidegger, it is perhaps because he embraced the insight more fully than did the master himself.

Two prints by William Blake, artist and poet, dramatize the Romantic vision. In *Glad Day*, a young man stands naked, his arms gesturing

Fig. 7.1 *Glad Day*, 1794, Copyright The British Museum.

expansively (see Figure 7.1). The orange and yellow of dawn radiate from behind him as if he himself were the source. This luminous presence, bringer of a New Day, is Romanticism's peculiar achievement, the fusion of poet and prophet. For those who are concerned, as so many of us are, to break free of the constraints of religious reification, the figure of the poet-prophet can be virtually irresistible. The philosopher Alain Badiou writes that "since Nietzsche, all philosophers claim to be poets, they all *envy* poets, they are all wishful poets or approximate poets ..."[6] So too perhaps with some religionists and theologians. For my part, I know that when confronted with a skeptical audience, my first impulse is to seek to ingratiate myself by taking a few cheap shots at the role of technology and quantification in our society, and then to speak of religion in tones that suggest that I myself have something of the subversive poet about me.

In a quite different print, Blake portrays the god of patriarchy, bearded, glowering and stonelike, seated upon a fiery throne (see Figure 7.2). His outstretched arm holds a rod before which an armless human figure mutely bows. The image reminds us that the Romantics could be highly theological, if for no other reason than that they saw in traditional religion

Fig. 7.2 *God Judging Adam*, 1795, formerly known as *Elijah in the Chariot of Fire*, Copyright Tate, London, 2003.

a reification of true deity, a sullen usurper hiding behind the rod of judgment. Blake named this glowering god "Urizen" to suggest "your reason," but also to recall perhaps the Greek verb *ourizein*, to limit. Urizen, God of limit and law, is the toxic distillate of all that oppresses true humanity: benighted reason, religious reification, economic exploitation—and bad art.

Romanticism is a call to dethrone Urizen. The summons to a spiritual warfare, a struggle even unto death, becomes its guiding mythos, whereby what we may call "Life-1" plus "Death-1" pass through conflict and tragedy into life raised to a higher power: LIFE. From early sentimentalism to late existentialism, this vitalistic dialectic drives Romanticism's off-again, on-again alliance with religion. Through it all, the message of the poet-prophet is constant, a relentless denunciation of anything that bears a suggestion of religious reification. And what are the marks of reification? They are: a credulous penchant for the literal; attachment to the dead letter, refusal to hear the living Word; adherence to form and institution; resistance to the spirit, subservience to the law. It is a familiar and effective polemic. But within it reside the essential elements of anti-Judaism.

The Pertinence of Derrida

The purpose of beginning these reflections not with Derrida but with certain penchants and perplexities indigenous to modern Christian theology has been to arrive at Derrida's pertinence for theology in an inductive manner. I have leaned heavily on the legacy of Romanticism and its entwinement with religious thought in order now to announce with a certain dramatic flourish that this poetic-religious legacy is precisely what Derrida means by "logocentrism."

The Romantic gesture, which posits itself as a radical break with the past, is, in light of Derrida's critique of logocentrism, less a break from an errant past than a repetition and intensification of the very error. It is a programmatic assertion of the quintessence of Western metaphysics, namely the dominance of speech over writing, the "living word" over the inscribed letter. Now this is disconcerting. We are drawn to deconstruction as a means of critiquing the idols, dissolving religious reification. But Derrida, it seems, cannot be so readily assimilated to that predetermined program. He tells us that some of our central tropes for doing idolatry critique, such as the contrast of Spirit and letter, are profoundly flawed.

A first step in rethinking these matters is to recognize that there can be a metaphysic of life. Anticipating the ploy we observed in an uncritical postmodernism, Romanticism associated metaphysics with a mechanistic worldview. But the predictability with which LIFE arises from Life-1 and

Death-1 makes clear that one metaphysic has simply been replaced by another. Stepping back and painting with a broad historical brush, we might say that while the eighteenth century was governed by a mechanistic trope and the nineteenth by an organic, vitalistic trope, the twentieth century was shaped by what many have called the linguistic turn. We could then propose that Heidegger, who presided over the turn in Europe, still retained through his imagery of earth and word, decadence and decline, a certain dependence upon the vitalistic metaphysic. That lingering attachment might provide some fragmentary clue to Heidegger's assent to Nazism.[7] If there is something to this account, one can appreciate Derrida's achievement in disengaging the linguistic from the metaphysical by naming the bias of logocentrism.[8]

In theological terms, the metanarrative of Life, Death, and LIFE amounts to a temporalization of immortality, notwithstanding Hegel's belief that he had captured therein the inner meaning of Christian resurrection. That Christian resurrection is not interchangeable with immortality is the thrust of Kierkegaard's debunking of the Hegelian dialectic. But this means, as Kierkegaard knew, that there is something in Christianity that cuts across life, cuts across "the aesthetic," and is not sublated within it.

The Apocalyptic Knot

Having traced a certain apocalyptic blindness in modern culture and having linked it to the logocentrism of Western culture at large, we must now consider, however briefly, the role of Christianity in all this. For it is Christianity that opened Pandora's box, channeling apocalyptic into the mainstream of Western culture and endorsing the revolutionary/triumphalist rhetoric of a New Age.

Two issues of the utmost importance converge here. One is the question raised at the outset regarding a possible "objective element" in Christianity. The other, darker issue is one that has been implicit in much of the foregoing, namely Christian anti-Judaism. The terrifying fact, it seems to me, is that the two of these lie so perilously close together. Specifically, both are profoundly apocalyptic.

Without attempting to delineate in this paper what the objective element might be, one can hypothesize that, whatever it is, it has to do with the coexistence in the synoptic narratives of (1) a message of nonviolent freedom and love associated with the imminent apocalyptic Kingdom of God; (2) an apocalyptic rhetoric of life, death, decision, and judgment which, if dissociated from nonviolent love, becomes insidiously violent; and (3) the crucifixion, God's taking violence upon God's self, which can be regarded restrospectively as an—or indeed as the—apocalyptic event.

Certainly one can imagine that the interaction of these three together might generate an objective element—one might even call it "the gospel"—that would be objective in the specific sense that it would exceed the grasp of the theologian. But one can also see that by being so demanding and uncontrollable, this apocalyptic excess would be disconcerting, threatening, thus eliciting defensive efforts at reification and control.

About Christian anti-Judaism I hesitate to speak at all. It exists. It is perhaps the originative sin of Christianity. My suggestion regarding what Christian theology needs to do now runs the risk of being distortive and self-indulgent, but I will venture it anyway. There comes a moment in Rolf Hochuth's play *The Deputy* when the emissary priest realizes that he will not succeed in persuading the pope to act against the deportation of Jews. At that point the priest does the one thing that remains for him to do. He pins the yellow star to his own chest to share the fate of the despised.

I have an imagination of Christian theology doing something analogous. It is an imagination of Christianity taking upon itself the invectives of a vitalistic triumphalism, drawing the poison from them, and pinning them to its own chest in solidarity, thus affirming thereby that no letter is dead; that we ourselves are inscribed in a text we do not control; and that there is a living law that cuts across our dreams of unbridled freedom, and blesses us in so doing.

References

1. Theodor W. Adorno, *Critical Models: Interventions and Catchwords* (New York: Columbia University Press, 1998), p. 140.
2. Jacques Derrida, *Limited Inc.* (Evanston: Northwestern University Press, 1988), p. 141.
3. Adorno, *op. cit.*, p. 137.
4. See Lowe, *Theology and Difference: The Wound of Reason* (Bloomington: Indiana University Press, 1993).
5. Leo Baeck, *Judaism and Christianity* (Cleveland: World Publishing Co., 1958), p. 193.
6. Alain Badiou, *Manifesto for Philosophy* (Albany: State University of New York Press, 1999), p. 70; emphasis Badiou's.
7. Cf. Jean-Francois Lyotard, *Heidegger and "the jews"* (Minneapolis: University of Minnesota Press, 1990), pp. 81–82 and *passim*.
8. See also Derrida, *Of Spirit: Heidegger and the Question* (Chicago: University of Chicago Press, 1989); and *Of Derrida, Heidegger and Spirit*, ed. David Wood (Evanston: Northwestern University Press, 1993).

CHAPTER **8**

Messianic Epistemology

ROBERT GIBBS

In most contexts, my title is a puzzle, almost humorous, but amongst readers of Derrida it has, I believe, a clearer referent. I wish to jump directly to the key question that concerns not only religious readers of Derrida, but also many other readers: the relation between the formalism of his thinking and the concrete contexts and instances for his thought. At the American Academy of Religion and the Society for Biblical Literature that means: What is the relation of his reflections on religion, on forgiveness, and so on to specific religions, especially to Judaism, and perhaps as especially, to Christianity?[1] In other contexts, the question is the relation to the literary texts he interprets, or to specific bodies of law, or to national philosophical schools, and so on. As Philosopher, Derrida has reexamined and recharged the question of the relation of the particular to the concept. Let me collect all of his reflections about concrete contexts under the question of the example and the logic of exemplarity—a logic that I cannot redevelop adequately here. At the end of the paper, I will suggest that engagement with scripture need not be governed by that logic, and indeed, that the particularity encountered in historical research can help disrupt the specific identity of the people who engage in that inquiry, disrupting the temptation to make ourselves an example.

The task would be to make a thick rope, but I will only offer you two strands, strands that will intertwine here, but will have to stand in for the rest. The first strand is the messianic assignment to become historians. In order to await and even to hurry the messianic future we must examine and explore the past, and indeed, the past as not only what did not *have to be*, but as having been what it should not. The second strand is the question of how we would interpret a specific Jewish history and whether the specificity of that history can be abandoned in favor of a formal logic. What I will NOT answer here is the question: How Jewish is Derrida?

I have been working on a book called *Messianic Epistemology*. It examines a family of Jewish thinkers in the twentieth century: Hermann Cohen, Franz Rosenzweig, Martin Buber, Walter Benjamin, Gershom Scholem, Ernst Bloch, Emmanuel Lévinas, and Jacques Derrida. I do not examine their interaction particularly, but the claims I make come in a straightforward form:

1. Truth is in the (messianic) future.
2. The present is not true nor just.
3. The past was not true, not the way it had to be nor the way it should have been.
4. Messianic hope makes us criticize the present and the past.
5. The study of the past, therefore, exposes the falsity of the present, and in particular, the false sense of limitations for change, for the chance of justice.

Historiography, even more than some history telling the story of messianism, is a messianic enterprise, according to these thinkers, and it bears, as Benjamin says, "a weak messianic force"[2] to change the present, the past, and especially the future. I realize that for historians this is a radical and disturbing claim. For readers of Derrida, however, the nature of these claims is familiar, even if one hesitates to acquiesce on the question of their validity. We might easily enough observe that what is at stake with this radical futurity could be parsed either as *différance*, a deferral and distinction that never is fully present. We might also see this as a rejection of the incarnation of God in Christ—that the messianic is always a promise, and that the world is profoundly unredeemed. Whether Christian theologians want or are able to think this deferral (say under the sign of the Christ to come, the second coming), or not is clearly beyond my task. Is the saturated phenomenon, one wonders, like a Eucharist, a full presence, or even over full, or indeed, present, or is it still waiting?

The Archive (Strand #1)

My first strand begins with Derrida's reflection on the task of historiography, and in particular with the role of the archive. Derrida explores how the archive as a preserve of past events exists for the sake of the future, and indeed, for an opening of the future. Historical research is not about the past but about the future. Consider this text from *Archive Fever:*

> …[T]he question of the archive is not, we repeat, a question of the past. It is not the question of a concept that we can dispose or not dispose of *already,* a subject *of the past, an archivable concept of the archive.* It is a question of the future, the question of the future itself, the question of a response, of a promise and of a responsibility for tomorrow. The archive, if we want to know what we will have wanted to say, we will only be able to know that in times to come. Perhaps. Not tomorrow, but in times to come, right away, or perhaps never. A spectral messianicity works in the concept of the archive and ties it, like religion, like history, like science itself, to a very singular experience of the promise.[3]

To engage in historical research, to "have" or to "use" an archive is to relate to the future, to a promise, to a responsibility. That future might happen right now ("today") or never—it is not the future that we expect, the future that is located at the end of the story we tell. The research into the past is not for the sake of a straight line from past to present to future (where it ends), but rather about the break between the past and the present, and in that break a presentiment of the break of the future into the present. Messianicity is at work in historiography, but then also in religion, science, and so forth. It is at work in all knowing, and especially in historiography and in the work of remembering. This text, by noting the messianicity at work, is a clear articulation of messianic epistemology.

Messianic without Messianism (Strand #2)

The second strand of this paper begins with another thematic statement about the messianic, this time from "Faith and Knowledge." Here is Derrida's clearest claim to abstain from any relation to specific religious traditions, including Judaism.

> First, the *messianic,* or messianicity without messianism. This would be the opening to the future or the coming of the other *as* the advent of justice, but without horizon of expectation, without prophetic prefiguration. The coming of the other can only arise as a singular event where no anticipation *sees it coming,* where the other and death—and radical evil—can surprise at any moment. Possibilities that at the same time open and perhaps always interrupt history, or

at least the *ordinary* course of history.... It concerns a "general structure of experience." This messianic dimension does not depend on any messianism. It does not follow any determinate revelation. It does not belong properly to any Abrahamic religion (even if I may here continue "entre nous" for essential reasons of language and of place, of culture, and of provisional rhetorical and historical strategy of which I will speak later, to give to it the names inscribed by the Abrahamic religions).[4]

We might read this text as a transcendental reflection: that what is universalizable (the messianic) is formal and is logically independent of every example (messianisms), or every instance. It logically requires no determinate revelation. Or we might read this as a temporal radicalization of the transcendental: that the futurity, the unanticipatable quality of the messianic stands for a kind of narrative rupture, that hovers at the horizons of our synthetic temporal unity of experience. Not merely prior as a condition for thinking religion, but prior in that radical sense of coming from so far beyond our language, our experience, our cultures—that "eye hath not seen." However we read this claim for the messianic without messianism, we cannot miss the emphatic exclusion of the determinate revelations. This is a future so radical that no religion (or group of religions) can claim it, can even claim to have a particular insight or vision of it. The parenthetic that excuses the lingering vocabulary of the Abrahamic religions "(even if I may here continue 'entre nous' for essential reasons of language and of place, of culture, and of provisional rhetorical and historical strategy of which I will speak later, to give to it the names inscribed by the Abrahamic religions)" requires some deeper attention. What is the relation to the "here," to the place in which this thought is thought, written, or spoken? Does one dwell and depart simultaneously, and if so, then should it not be better to say that the messianisms are part of the messianic?

Particularity without Messianism (Strand #1)

The more familiar interpretation of the historian's work is a descendent of the nineteenth century interpretation of particularity. Ethnic, or better, national historians devoted themselves to delivering to the future the specificity of a people or a nation. Their logic was often one of exemplarity: that our particular nation is the best way for everyone to be. ("Everyone wants to be an American, to celebrate the freedoms of the marketplace, of the press, of religion, of the right to bear arms, and so forth"). The specific events are not to be ignored, but they do serve as the model for all others. Scientific Jewish historiography sometimes shared in this mentality, and in a shocking and fascinating way, Derrida interrogates one of the great historians of our time, Yosef Yerushalmi, who in a specific way suspended the Judaism in Jewish history in the case of Freud by focusing on his Jewishness. Derrida questions the possibility that the messianic historiographic task could be located in a formalism that was found only in the people without a messianism as Judaism, as religion.

> As if Yerushalmi were ready to renounce everything that is in Judaism (terminable) that was not jewishness (interminable), everything, the belief in the existence of God, the religion, the culture, etc. except for his archived trait which would be something that *resembles* at least election, even if it is not to be confused with it: the absolute privilege, the absolute uniqueness in the experience of the promise (the future) and the injunction or the law is already presented and *inscribed* in the historical memory as an injunction of memory, with or without support, the two absolute privileges are bound one to the other. As if God only inscribed one thing in the memory of a *single people* and of a *whole people*: **in the future, remember to remember the future.** As if the word "people" in this phrase, could be thought only from the unheard of uniqueness of this injunction of the archive.[5]

Here is the formal claim: in the future, remember to remember the future. What Yerushalmi claims, according to Derrida, is that even without any messianism, without the Jewish God, religion, and so forth, there is the experience of an inscription, a prescription, to be historical ("remember" as think about the past) in the future, and such prescribed remembering should be precisely to hold open the future. This sounds like the messianic prescription for historiography, and Derrida continues to explore just how Yerushalmi defines Jewishness around this kind of remembering (which Yerushalmi himself distinguishes from the modern historian's act). For Derrida such a claim that Jewishness is being historiographic (even messianically historiographic) is utterly contestable, particularly in its exemplarity. Just as someone might have said that Jews have a genius for ethics, and another might have said for historiography—but removed from the Judaism, from the religion and the relations with God, removed from the claim for a covenant, for commandments, and so forth.

Derrida himself in many ways supports the formal claim. It is, I would suggest, the core of messianic epistemology, including Derrida's version of it. But identifying this abstraction from religion as ethnicity disturbs

Derrida. And so if Derrida wants the formal claim, he will have to decontextualize it from the Jewish people, as a privilege or a prize.

Judaism and Historiography (Strand #2 and #1)

In place of the Jewishness of the non-Jewish Jew, and the failure there to achieve what Derrida considers messianicity, I wish to turn back to Judaism, to ways of interpreting the history of the relation of Jews and God. I now accentuate the second strand, precisely to think more emphatically about the messianic exigency to explore Jewish texts, and Jewish tradition. A first step is to notice that the religious tradition is best understood as a history of discontinuity. Derrida himself explores this by "deconstructing" the event of revelation at Mt. Sinai. Studying this history is discerning the disruption and discontinuity of God's relation to the Jews.

Derrida presents this interpretation of revelation in a few places but most clearly in *Adieu to Emmanuel Lévinas:*

> In a time that is already hard to hold as *one* and to bend to the homogeneity of a story without internal rupture, the name (of) *Sinai* cannot not signify, of course, both the place of the given Torah and the oil of consecrated messianity, and the ark of witness, and the Tables of the witness written by the hand of God, then the Tables given by God after he had changed his mind from the evil with which he had threatened the stiff-necked people (first rupture or interruption), then the broken Tables (other interruption), then the carved Tables anew after God in some way had again interrupted all theophany in prohibiting in the passing of his glory, the sight of his face, face-to-face, then the place of the covenant renewed, then the veiling and unveiling of Moses' face. So many interruptions *of itself,* so many discontinuities in history; so many ruptures of the ordinary course of time, caesuras nonetheless as historicity itself of history.[6]

The question is how to interpret the ongoing revelation of God to the Jews. The primary narrative of the revelation at Sinai is itself utterly discontinuous, with God breaking off the discourse, and even Moses breaking up the revelatory stone tables. Such an event, or story, is hard to hold as a single event. Leaving aside the question of whether there is a generic or formal accounting of which this is somehow a specification, we find, instead the key moment in the last sentence: that time and history are repeatedly ruptured here. What makes history historical? For Derrida, this "narrative" of Sinai is itself so internally ruptured, so broken up and into, and out of, that historiography becomes impossible. The history of the revelation, of the event that seems to stand above all other events, is a history of interruptions and discontinuities. The "deconstruction" of the event happens in the biblical text, and is the very production of the historiography that characterizes a messianic task.

But let me contrast that with two other accounts of specifically Jewish historiography. First with Hermann Cohen:

> Jewish history however, understood as history, that is insofar as it displays ethical ideas, is an ongoing chain of human, of national misery. The servants of God were always despised and pierced, cut off from the land of life. And despite the astonishment at the continuation of this oddity amongst the people, it remains always true, what was so characteristically expressed in the original text: "And in its age, *who thought on it?*" (Isaiah 53.8). The messianic people suffers as representative for human suffering. This perspective is no exaggeration of Israel's mission, if the messianic realization of monotheism is the historical task of the Jewish religion.[7]

Derrida has insight into discontinuity as it marks the disruption of revelation; Cohen has insight into suffering, and the constancy of misery. It has been, for some years, unfashionable to characterize Jewish history as a lachrymose tale, and so the historians may even be more aghast at this claim than theologians would be with Derrida's deconstruction of the revelation at Sinai. Historiography is governed by "ethical ideas," for Cohen, and such ideas are incapable of supporting the claim of exceptional virtue by the Jews. Rather, such ideas in Cohen require an extremity of moral duty, and a keen sense of the present as unredeemed, unjust. For Cohen being Jewish is not yet achieved: it is a task, an ideal that is critical of the people who wish they could just claim already to be Jewish. Notice that Cohen claims that the Jewish mission is messianic, that to live messianically is to participate as the one that suffers as representative for others. Here, by the way, is the central contrasting logic to Derrida's interpretation of exemplarity—for to be not-yet oneself by taking on others' suffering is quite different from being the paradigm for human excellence. At least it comes at quite a cost. Cohen's rational rigor and moral strictness cannot allow a claim that Jews are somehow better, or even that the Jews have lived up to the ideal of this messianic mission. Not only is this history not triumphal (we have been winning all along), it is not complacent (we today are the righteous sufferers, the messianic).

But consider then a third option, perhaps even stronger than Cohen's, this time from an essay by Buber written in 1933:

> For this is what the Bible understands as history: a dialogue in which human beings, the people, is addressed and refuses [*versagt*] and in refusing always rises up again and tries to answer; the history of God's disappointments, but a history of disappointments, which is a way, so that the way, the way of the people, the way of human beings, yes the way of God, His way through humanity leads from disappointment to disappointment, beyond all of them.[8]

While Derrida found discontinuity, Buber finds disappointment. And serial disappointments, a history of failures, a history of refusals. Buber confronts the biblical historians and claims that neither a history of events nor one of literary sources is adequate for understanding the biblical text. Instead, he proposes a history of religions approach, to see the texts as testimony to different modes of relations between God and human beings. Unfortunately, the biblical accounts are of the sort where God calls and people do not answer, they refuse the call. While Derrida's discontinuity disrupted the notion of a clear and ongoing steady communication from God, Buber's disappointments disrupt the notion of a clear I-thou, a kind of ongoing relation with God.

We are at the point where the two strands must wind more tightly together. Buber's claim about biblical history promises a profound disruption of what we might have expected. If we had learned to expect some idea of discontinuity, we still would not expect the relations to fail, repeatedly. And we cannot help but wonder how such a historiography contributes to our present, and even awaits a future. To return to the first strand: triumphal historiography and much positivist historiography interpret the past as the cause of the present, and interpret that present as causing the future, often with some sense of causal necessity. The task of historiography, however, is to hold open the future, but that means that the relation from the present to the future is unforeseeable, that it allows for a radical change, a marked gap. The relations in the past, from earlier to later, then model just these sort of discontinuities, these gaps. To free the future from a fated destiny (as things seem these days), to see war as not inevitable; hatred, terror, oppression, all as not necessary, as not the logical consequence of today, we must turn to the past and look. And what do we see? Not the happy story of a fabled golden age of just society and love of God. On the contrary, we see the past under the sign of discontinuity, of suffering, indeed, disappointment. The failures of the past are a sign that the present and our expectable outcomes are in fact neither obvious nor unavoidable.

But that might work to break up the timeline, provided we only needed discontinuity. But the biblical text requires an interpretation of our failures, of our miseries. We discern the refusals to respond as our own, almost like an inversion of the heroic mythology in which we become the patriots of yore. We borrow from the past failures and misery for the sake of self-criticism. The "identification" with sinners of the past is a process of opening up the future, and destabilizing our own sense of who we are now. But now we emerge into the second strand more emphatically: while one could negate the present in a merely formal way, the specific opening for the future requires a disruption of the "this," of the very indexed sign. A formal structure of the future of the past does not transform us and charges us to hold open the future. Rather, the future interrupts by means of our negotiation with our own past, a past that is not a single theme, not a unified story, but is rather a rhythmic reiteration of specific failures, even as Derrida himself notices that the interruptions at Sinai are a series constructed in differences.

Thus the historiographic task is in relation to God, to the commandments, to religion, as well as to all of the "essential reasons of place and of culture," and to language perhaps most of all of those. Although I might not be able to indicate here the formal structure of temporality and historiography, the ethical demands for disruption, the epistemological shift to the future—I can present these as a philosopher.

But, can those important changes occur without a recursion to the specific textual and theological tradition that singles me out? Are not the "essential reasons of place, etc." the ones that require us to engage a historiography that implicates me in the self-critical examination of what I held as my past—for the sake of the future?

Resurrection from the Torah

Let me end, if briefly, with a key text from the Mishnah (*Sanhedrin*, *Perek Helek* XI:1):

> All Israel have a portion in the world to come. As it is said: "Your people shall be righteous. They shall inherit the land forever. They shall be the branch of my planting, the work of my hands to be adorned" (Isaiah 60:21).

> And these do not have a portion in the world to come: the one who says, "there is no resurrection of the dead from the Torah," "there is no Torah from Heaven," and the *apikoros*.

The text juxtaposes two concepts of "the afterlife": the world to come, as a new time, and the resurrection of the dead—that at some point all of Israel (and that will include others as well) will be raised and reembodied. I, like many others, have read this text as trying to justify the idea that the world to come, indeed, the resurrection of the dead, were based on scripture. That is, it might be a fine idea, but if it could not be located within the Jewish tradition, then one could not accept it. But perhaps the claim needs a different reading. The argument that the resurrection of the dead can be found in the Torah (and I should admit that the hermeneutic pyrotechnics needed to achieve that discovery are impressive) does not serve to ground the claim on the Torah. On the contrary, the task is to reread the Torah, to engage in just such a hermeneutic activity. Resurrection, the world to come, the messianic, these are terms that recharge the biblical text, and the task of discovering them is a negotiation with discontinuity and even disappointment in and with the biblical text. We are not saving the doctrine (the concept) by finding a text for it; rather, we save the text by interrogating it with this concept. But the rescue of the Torah, the discovery of its new life, is itself a way of thinking messianically. And at the same time, this inquiry is also a critique of our own ideas about the Torah, of our own identification with a Torah that lacks the messianic, that lacks redemption. We are reinterpreting not only the text, but also our own past, and in that practice disrupting our own present, for the sake of the future. Rabbinic Judaism retains a practice of reinterpretation that in a reiterated movement cites and displaces its own present. For a present requires a specific take or view of the past, a somehow past that belongs to this current moment. The task of the historian and the goal of the archive, is to disrupt that connection of specific past to specific view of the present—because only in disrupting that connection does the future open beyond a similarly bound construct of our present moment. Rabbinic rereading is a practice of this disruption, and in finding resurrection of the dead in the Torah it confronts the specific interpretation of the past in its time. Only in reinterpreting the past traditions that constitute our present, in addressing the specificity of Jewish texts, of Christian texts, of Muslim texts and of others, only then can we exert our weak messianic force, opening a path for a messianic entrance.

References

1. This paper was delivered in Toronto in 2002 at the conference of those two societies. The particular section for this paper was under the banner of Theology and Continental Philosophy. Because of these contexts, there were diverse listeners, including those who were concerned with Derrida and religion, those who were ignorant of Derrida's works and were interested in religion and biblical literature, and others who were well-read in Derrida but

unfamiliar with theology and with biblical literature. To welcome all, I accompanied my paper with a handout of the texts upon which I comment below. All translations are mine, and I cite the original with the available English as well.

2. Walter Benjamin, "Über den Begriff der Geschichte," in the *Gesammelte Schriften* vol. I.2, eds. Rolf Tiedemann and Hermann Schweppenhäuser (Frankfurt: Suhrkamp, 1974), p. 694; trans. Harry Zohn as "Theses on the Philosophy of History," in *Illuminations* (New York: Schocken, 1969), p. 254.

3. Jacques Derrida, *Mal d'Archive* (Paris: Éditions Galilée, 1995), p. 60; trans. Eric Prenowitz as *Archive Fever* (Chicago: University of Chicago Press, 1996), p. 36.

4. Jacques Derrida, "Foi et Savoir," in *La Réligion*, eds. Jacques Derrida and Gianni Vattimo (Paris: Éditions du Seuil, 1996), pp. 27–28; trans. Samuel Weber as "Faith and Knowledge," in *Religion* (Stanford: Stanford University Press, 1998), p. 18.

5. Derrida, *Mal d'Archive*, pp. 120–121; *Archive Fever*, pp. 75–76.

6. Jacques Derrida, *Adieu à Emmanuel Lévinas* (Paris: Éditions Galilée, 1997), p. 117; trans. Pascale-Anne Brault and Michael Naas as *Adieu to Emmanuel Lévinas* (Stanford: Stanford University Press, 1999), pp. 63–64.

7. Hermann Cohen, *Religion der Vernunft aus den Quellen des Judentums*, reprint of 2nd ed., 1928 (Wiesbaden: Fourier Verlag, 1988), p. 312; trans. Simon Kaplan as *Religion of Reason Out of the Sources of Judaism* (New York: Frederick Ungar Publishing Co., 1971), p. 267.

8. Martin Buber, *Werke*. 3 vols. (Munich: Kosel-Verlag, 1962), vol. II, p. 910; translated as "Biblical Leadership," in *On the Bible*, Nachum N. Glatzer (ed.), (New York: Schocken, 1982), p. 144.

CHAPTER **9**

Midrash and the "Magic Language": Reading without Logocentrism

DANIEL BOYARIN

Interpretation is the dominant mode of commentary in a culture within which value is expressed in terms of an abstract, universal, and in itself substance-free standard: the coin, the Phallus, the father, the Logos. By interpretation I mean virtually all of our methods of formal response to texts by which the text is taken to mean something, by which meaning is extractable from a text and presentable, even if incompletely and not exactly, in paraphrase. Even the most extremely antiparaphrastic of western interpretative methods, for instance the poem-interpretation of the New Critics, still is infinitely more paraphrastic than midrash, which simply refuses to take even the text as verbal icon, preferring almost to read each word, and sometimes each letter, and sometimes the shape of the letter or even its serifs, as a virtual icon in itself. One way to bring this point home would be to insist that even according to those who would argue that "a poem must not mean but be," the poem remains at least partially translatable. With the modes of linguistic operation that are characteristic of early midrash in place, the text is simply untranslatable (something on the order of the untranslatability of *Finnegan's Wake*). Too many of the features upon which midrash founds its meanings are simply artifacts of the materiality of the language in its Hebrew concreteness. Midrash is the dominant mode of commentary in a signifying economy without the "universal equivalent." Famous by now is the moment in talmudic legend when God himself seeks to intervene in midrashic interpretation and is informed that he has no status whatsoever since the

131

majority of the sages disagree with his interpretation. In commentary, at any rate, for the Rabbis, even the deity is not the measure of all things.[2]

It is fairly well accepted by now that midrash does not intend to give an *interpretation* of the text, interpretation being understood here as a particular kind of commentary; it does certainly function as the most serious kind of reading and commentary on the most authoritative and holy text that Judaism knows. As Simon Goldhill has remarked,[1] any practice of commentary implies a theory of language. The apparent eccentricity of midrash, its frequent seeming extreme incoherence from the point of view of what counts as commentary in our culture, has to be explained, therefore, via a theory of language. Language itself is embedded in whole systems of signifying practices.

These signifying practices through which rabbinic culture differs all involve a denial of platonistic splits between the material and the ideal. Marxian classicist, George Thomson, has proposed a direction for thinking about this issue in remarking the novelty of the platonic revolution in consciousness (although carefully avoiding, correctly, assigning this revolution to the person of Plato himself):

> As Plato says, the soul is by rights the ruler and master, the body its subject and its slave. This dichotomy of human nature, which through Parmenides and Plato became the basis of idealist philosophy, was something new in Greek thought. To the scientists of Miletos, as to the Achaean chiefs and to the primitive savage, the soul was simply that in virtue of which we breathe and move and live; and although, the laws of motion being imperfectly understood, no clear distinction was drawn between organic and inorganic matter, the basis of this conception is essentially materialist. The worlds of Milesian cosmology are described as gods because they move, but they are no less material. Nowhere in Milesian philosophy, nor in the Homeric poems, is there anything that corresponds to this Orphic conception of the soul as generically different from the body, the one pure, the other corrupt, the one divine, the other earthly. So fundamental a revolution in human consciousness only becomes intelligible when it is related to a change equally profound in the constitution of human society.[2]

It is this revolution in consciousness that also enabled the idea that meaning is abstractable from the matter of text, that the words are bodies and the meanings, souls. The Rabbis, it could be said, in the end developed out of their powerful rejection and renunciation of Logos theology a consciousness more similar to that of the "scientists of Miletos [Thales and

Anaximander]" than to that of Parmenides, Plato, and most of European thought in their wake. We might refer to their activity, then, as a counter-revolution in consciousness.[3]

My hypothesis is that midrash came about within rabbinic culture as the product of a complex politics of resistance to logocentric thinking, owing in large part to the Rabbis' efforts to define themselves over-against the growing hegemony of orthodox Christianity.[4] As logos theology grew into Christology and as "Israel" became a signifier whose signified was not the historical people of Israel, the Rabbis deferred the logos and undid, as it were, the Parmenidean revolution with enormous cultural consequences.[5]

Froma Zeitlin has clarified that the very foundations of philosophy, as a specifically European practice (analogous, of course, but not identical to practices in other human cultures), are grounded in:

> ...bring[ing] together phallus and head...for the ending of the [*Oresteia*] is also concerned with a shift in modes and behavior, as it charts a progression from darkness to light, from obscurity to clarity. Representation of symbolic signs perceived as a form of female activity gives way to the triumph of the male *Logos*. Representation and lyric incantation yield to dialectic and speech, and magic to science. Even more, this "turning away from the mother to the father," as Freud observed, "signifies a victory of intellectuality over the senses."[6]

Zeitlin proceeds to provide an extensive list of the ontological oppositions grounded in the primary opposition of male as Apollo and female as Erinyes that grow from this "turning" or "victory"[7] and that are characteristic of Greek philosophy from some pre-Socratics to Plato and Aristotle. Freud, however, quite mistakenly assigned this "turning" to biblical culture.[8] Biblical culture, however, did not make this move toward idealism, toward what Jean-Joseph Goux has called, quite brilliantly, paterialism, and rabbinic culture was to shake it off.[9] Both remained as materialistic at least as the Milesian scientists. Biblical and the classic form of rabbinic culture (as manifested in the Babylonian Talmud) resists the abstraction of the male body and the veiling of the penis that produces the phallus, and forms, accordingly, a subdominant fiction within the cultural space of the dominant fiction.[10] This subdominant fiction is no less oppressive than the dominant.[11]

No Logos, no Phallus:

> But the truth psychoanalysis tells us about the logic of truth, and thus about philosophy, is "that *the feminine occurs only within models and laws devised by male subjects*," that this model "is a *phallic*

one, [which] shares the values promulgated by patriarchal society and culture, values inscribed in the philosophical corpus: property, production, order, form, unity, visibility…and erection."[12]

Neither in hermeneutical strategies nor in the production of philosophical (as opposed to mythical) documents do the texts of the classical rabbinic period indicate "the passage from mythology to philosophy."[13] No one would characterize rabbinic culture as being one in which "order, form, and unity" are dominating values, and there is, as I have already emphasized, no philosophical corpus at all.

The identification of Logos with Phallus is not an artefact of a modern attack on the "west."[14] Neoplatonic texts are unabashed about this equation. Plutarch writes:

> And that is the reason why they make the older Hermae without hands, or feet, but with their private parts stiff, indicating figuratively that there is no need whatsoever of old men who are active by their body's use, if they keep their mind [or their power of reason, *Logos energon*], as it should be, active and fertile.[15]

For Plutarch, as for the later Plotinus, it was so obvious that the stiff private parts of the Herm were not related to the "body's use" that he didn't even have to argue the point; he could assume that his readers would understand it implicitly. Plutarch doesn't need to tell us that the phallus is the logos or why this should be so; he can assume that we already understand this and then applies this assumption to the interpretation of the Hermae. In other words, Plutarch's rhetoric here suggests that this association had become virtually commonplace by his time. He may be innovating in his interpretation of the Hermae, but he can't be with respect to the meaning of the phallus, or his very comment would have been incoherent or even laughable to his readers. The stiff Phallus of the Herm simply *is* the Logos![16] This would be an absurd statement for a talmudic Rabbi. Theories of signification are thus deeply imbricated with and implicated in theories of sexual difference.

No Logos, no Phallus, no father. The symbolic role of the father had also not been fully realized within rabbinic Judaism. As Pietro Pucci has well summed up a virtual topos:

> The father comes into being not by sowing his seeds, but with the Logos: for only humans have a father, though animals are often begotten like humans. A father is a figure that, within the strategies

of the Logos, acquires a set of meanings and functions ... In a word, he may be equated to a sort of transcendental signified.[17]

The father simply does not have that transcendental status in early Jewish culture.[18] Although the father had power over the mother, and is distinctly marked as more important socially, the difference between father and mother functions with respect to the child is not marked symbolically within rabbinic culture. Both have the same ontological status vis-à-vis the child; in short, the father-function is not removed from the system of "commodities" of kinship relations. On the other hand, it must be emphasized that since such "transcendental status" did remain the prerogative of the distinctly male deity (only God, one might say, has the phallus),[19] without the possibilities of transcendence of gender that Platonism and Christianity offered to both men and women, the lack of phallus certainly did not issue in a rabbinic Judaism less male-dominant and androcentric in its social and cultural discourses.

As Goux, once more, has perspicaciously phrased it: "Western civilization is not patriarchal in the sense in which certain societies have been or still are patriarchal. It is pervaded by the abstraction of the Father."[20] Among these "certain societies" is surely classical rabbinic Judaism, an ideal-type, in this sense, precisely of a patriarchy, because the father was not an abstraction. The abstract "father" in the western civilization is an exact parallel to the abstract phallus. The father for the Rabbis is not a transcendental signified (for all his power and privilege) but a physical genitor exactly like the mother, just as the penis in that culture (for all its socioreligious significance) is no less an organ and a part of a body than is the vulva. Rabbinic Judaism, I suggest, is not pervaded by the abstraction or the Name-of-the-Father; rabbinic Jewish society was undoubtedly pervaded by the power of fathers.

Of course, rabbinic interpretation, as all reading, was constrained and produced by rabbinic ideology and the struggle for hegemony and exclusion of many voices from the community; it, nevertheless, remains the case that certain characteristics of rabbinic textuality can best be described, on my hypothesis, by seeing rabbinic thought as nonlogocentric (this is not in any way to be taken as celebratory, nor, of course, as pejorative, but hopefully as usefully descriptive). The Rabbis might indeed be designated by that ancient heresiological label, the "Alogi." By a kind of theological askesis, the Rabbis, in their nativism and their rejection of Christian platonism, denied themselves virtually all of the forms of abstraction that enable the production of philosophical texts and of interpretation in the senses in which we understand those terms. The point is not that only Rabbis make midrash—we have seen and will see more that that is not the case—but rather that the Rabbis don't make philosophy, don't make allegory, and don't make paraphrastic interpretation. In a situation in which midrash is the only form of response to Holy Writ it has a different function and a different significance from a system in which other modes of commentary function alongside of it. Similarly in a system of signification within which narrative (viz, the Gospels and Acts of various types) appears alongside of other types of writings (the Epistles, apologetic literature, systematic theology), narrative will have a different significance than in a system such as the Talmud within which only narrative signifies religious (and other) ideas.

The late Babylonian Rabbis seem to be articulating and acting out an hermeneutic practice of dissemination of meaning and fracturing of textual organicity: the shattering of the Logos, like the breaking of the atom, I suggest, released an enormous stockpile of hermeneutical energy, the sparks of the Logos. That practice can certainly be better apprehended by us in the light of the denaturalization of metaphysics of language which Derrida has endeavored to perform, and provides a kind of model for a nonlogocentric reading practice. Through one of the accidents of history, it is perhaps this odd confluence that has given a possibility for a renewed (but critical) recovery of Jewish *différance* in our own time.

A useful philosophical description of the condition of midrash (without necessarily claiming that the Rabbis would or could have articulated it in this fashion) can perhaps be hazarded using the terms of Samuel Wheeler who has directly addressed this issue. In his work, Wheeler articulates the undertaking of a (surprising) joint project in the philosophy of language between Jacques Derrida and the American analytical philosopher, Donald Davidson:

> The fundamental point of agreement between Derrida and Davidson, as well as other thinkers in the analytic tradition, such as Quine and Wittgenstein, is their denial of what I call the "magic language." This is the language of *nous*, a language that is, in Wittgenstein's terms, self-interpreting. The magic language is the language in which we know what we mean, think our thoughts, and form intentions. There is no question of interpreting sentences in the magic language, since the magic language is what interpretation is interpretation into. Furthermore, there is no question of discovering what the terms of the magic language mean, since the terms of the magic language are nothing but the meanings expressed by words of natural languages.[21]

In discussing Derrida here, Wheeler is referring to several different early Derridean texts in which these ideas have been articulated and have proved formative for the (post)modern study of midrash. These ideas go back to the very foundational moments of Derrida's work as early as his *Speech and Phenomena*.[22] In that work, he elaborated his crucial concept of iterability. The linguistic sign, by virtue of being a sign, is necessarily repeatable in other contexts and thus of having other meanings. While, as Wheeler points out, "On an occasion of utterance, of course, the intention would clarify the meaning of the utterance," intentions themselves are something languagelike (as Wheeler puts it) or simply language (as I would prefer).[23] The only possibility for intention, and thus interpretation, to be fixed would be to imagine a perfect language of *nous*, such as that which virtually all philosophers from Parmenides, through Plato and Aristotle, and the entire tradition have explicitly posited. That perfect language, which Derrida calls by one of its names, Logos (the name that Parmenides gives it), is precisely the "magic language" (in Wheeler's terminology) that Derrida's grammatological work has set out to displace philosophically. In the classic works of his early writings, *Of Grammatology* and *Writing and Difference*, Derrida has further pursued and worked out the details and implications of such a nonlogocentric account of language and texts.

Having dispensed, I think, with apologetic, celebratory accounts of rabbinic Judaism as proto-deconstruction (or proto-analytic philosophy!), I can assert that the denial of a "magic language" that attended the late rabbinic construction of a religious community defined by its alogocentricity gives us an example of what commentary without such a "magic language" might look like and thus an important way of desublimating Derridean theory via the close study of an actual historical practice, analogous perhaps to the benefit that would accrue if somewhere we could find people who actually construct their perceptions of the universe on non-Euclidean interpretations of geometry. Pursuing this investigation further is one of the major goals of my current research.

References

1. Simon Goldhill, "Wipe Your Glosses." *Aporemata: Kritische Studien Zur Philologiegeschichte.* ed. Glenn W. Most. (Göttingen: Vandenhoeck & Ruprecht, 1999), pp. 380–425.
2. George Thomson, *Aeschylus and Athens: A Study in the Social Origins of Drama* (London: Lawrence and Wishart, 1973, 1941), p. 147; *The First Philosophers* (London: Lawrence and Wishart, 1955), vol. II of *Studies in Ancient Greek Society*, p. 239.
3. See Daniel Boyarin, *Carnal Israel: Reading Sex in Talmudic Culture*, The New Historicism: Studies in Cultural Poetics 25 (Berkeley and Los Angeles: University of California Press, 1993), pp. 5–6 for further elaboration of this point on the anthropological level. Cf. also Boyarin, "The Bartered Word: Midrash and Symbolic Economy," *Aporemata: Kritische Studien zur Geschichte der Philologie* 4 (2000): 19–65, but cum grano salis. This is an area that I hope to further illuminate in a work that I am just beginning now, tentatively titled, *Sophisticated Rabbis*.

4. Cf. Thomson, *The First Philosophers*, p. 100 on the unique set of circumstances that produced the biblical prophets.

5. It needs to be said that this formulation requires much more specification and detail, since, as Virginia Burrus has impressed on me, Nicene Christianity constitutes just as much a rejection of Logos theology. In my forthcoming *Border Lines: The Idea of Orthodoxy and the Partitioning of Judaeo-Christianity*, Divinations: Rereading Late Ancient Religions (Philadelphia: University of Pennsylvania Press, 2004), I hope to provide a much more nuanced account.

6. Froma Zeitlin, "The Dynamics of Misogyny: Myth and Mythmaking in Aeschylus's *Oresteia*," in *Playing the Other; Gender and Society in Classical Greek Literature*, Women in Culture and Society (Chicago: University of Chicago Press, 1996), pp. 87–119 (111).

7. Zeitlin, "The Dynamics of Misogyny," p. 112.

8. As Zeitlin remarks, "Freud's view of the female as a mutilated male lies squarely within the Aristotelian doctrine of the woman as a 'deformity in nature'" ("The Dynamics of Misogyny," p. 111, n. 49), and see continuation there. See also Daniel Boyarin, "'An Imaginary and Desirable Converse': *Moses and Monotheism* as Family Romance," in *Reading Bibles, Writing Bodies: Identity and the Book*, Biblical Limits (London and New York: Routledge, 1997), pp. 184–204. Charles Shepherdson has contributed another valuable insight for this discussion: "Indeed, when Freud speaks of 'the force of an idea' in order to explain the basic distinction between psychoanalysis and organic medicine, every reader of Heidegger will note that this ambiguity characterizes a long philosophical tradition, and is internal to the very term *idea:* as many commentaries on Greek philosophy have pointed out, the classical term *eidos* means both the 'concept' or 'idea' and something 'seen.' Seeing and knowing are thus constitutively linked, and easily confused, but this should not conceal the fact that the logic of the concept has a very different structure from the logic of the image, understood as a supposedly immediate, 'physiological' perception. Where the image provides us with an illusion of immediacy and presence, … the symbolic confronts us with a play of presence and absence, a function of negativity by which the purportedly 'immediate' reality (the 'natural' world) is restructured. This is the difficulty Lacan takes up with the concepts of the imaginary and the symbolic, thus rendering the ambiguity less of a mystery" (Charles Shepherdson, "The Role of Gender and the Imperative of Sex," in *Supposing the Subject*, ed. Joan Copjec [London: Verso, 1994], pp. 158–184 (166). The mysterious ambiguity, however, that this paper is dealing with is the historical origin of the logic of the concept.

9. "The rabbis had evinced little interest in philosophical speculation" (David Winston, *Logos and Mystical Theology in Philo of Alexandria* [Cincinnati: Hebrew Union College Press, 1985], p. 9).

10. By referring to rabbinic Jewish culture here as the "subdominant fiction," I immediately disarm any reading of my work—finally, after much internal and external struggle—that would interpret the presentation of rabbinic gender "theory" as more "true" or less mystified than that of the dominant fiction. Also, by using the term subdominant fiction, as I do here, I clearly indicate that rabbinic Jewish culture is not separate from the cultures of which it is a part but forms a complexly related subculture, at the same time avoiding, as well, the romanticism and claims for privilege that a term like subaltern (which I have used previously) would levy.

11. Daniel Boyarin, *Unheroic Conduct: The Rise of Heterosexuality and the Invention of the Jewish Man*, Contraversions: Studies in Jewish Literature, Culture, and Society (Berkeley and Los Angeles: University of California Press, 1997), pp. 51–85; Daniel Boyarin, "Women's Bodies and the Rise of the Rabbis: The Case of Sotah," *Studies in Contemporary Jewry: Jews and Gender, the Challenge to Hierarchy* XVI (2001): 88–100.

12. Dianne Chisholm, "Irigaray's Hysteria," in *Engaging with Irigaray: Feminist Philosophy and Modern European Thought*, eds. Carolyn Burke, Naomi Schor, and Margaret Whitford, Gender and Culture (New York: Columbia University Press, 1994), pp. 263–283 (271) citing Luce Irigaray, *Speculum of the Other Woman*, trans. Gillian C. Gill (Ithaca: Cornell University Press, 1985). It should be unnecessary by now to point out that by describing rabbinic culture as nonphallocentric, one is not in the slightest denying the sharp male dominance to which the culture was heir. In fact, as I have argued extensively elsewhere, there are ways in which the absence of the spiritualizing move to a phallus inscribes male dominance all the

more literally. See Daniel Boyarin, "Gender," in *Critical Terms for the Study of Religion*, ed. Mark C. Taylor (Chicago: University of Chicago Press, 1998), pp. 117–135.

13. Jean-Joseph Goux, *Symbolic Economies: After Marx and Freud*, trans. Jennifer Curtis Cage (Ithaca: Cornell University Press, 1990), p. 93.

14. Jean-Joseph Goux, "The Phallus: Masculine Identity and the 'Exchange of Women,'" trans. Maria Amuchastegui, Caroline Benforado, Amy Hendrix, and Eleanor Kaufman, *Differences* 4.1 (Spring 1992): 40–75.

15. Plutarch, "*Moralia 797F*," in *Moralia X*, trans. Harold North Fowler (Cambridge: Harvard University Press, 1936), 10:153. See also Goux, "The Phallus," p. 49.

16. Plotinus, *Enneads*, trans. A. H. Armstrong (Cambridge: Harvard University Press, 1987), vol. 5 of *Enneads*. Loeb Library, p. 287.

17. Pietro Pucci, *Oedipus and the Fabrication of the Father: Oedipus Tyrannus in Modern Criticism and Philosophy* (Baltimore: Johns Hopkins University Press, 1992), p. 3.

18. God is, of course, a sort of transcendental signified in early Jewish culture, and it is not trivial that Godhead is most often (but not only) imagined as a father. However, as Howard Eilberg-Schwartz has elegantly argued, the disproportion between divine and human father is as relevant as the homology (Howard Eilberg-Schwartz, *God's Phallus and Other Problems for Men and Monotheism* [Boston: Beacon Press, 1994]).

19. Eilberg-Schwartz, *God's Phallus*.

20. Jean-Joseph Goux, *Oedipus Philosopher*, trans. Catherine Porter, Meridian: Crossing Aesthetics (Stanford: Stanford University Press, 1993), p. 204.

21. Samuel C. Wheeler, *Deconstruction as Analytic Philosophy*, Cultural Memory in the Present (Stanford: Stanford University Press, 2000), p. 177.

22. Jacques Derrida, *"Speech and Phenomena" and Other Essays on Husser's Phenomenology*, trans. David Allison (Evanston: Northwestern University Press, 1973).

23. Wheeler, p. 24.

CHAPTER 10

Creatio Ex Libidine: Reading Ancient Logos Différantly[1]

VIRGINIA BURRUS

It is the kind of desire that is set in motion when God is dead—that is, when God cannot be personified or fully characterized in understandable terms but is rather called "boundless," an unfathomable something that constantly eludes human categories and defies "objective" language that would distance the maker from what is made. The "boundless" cannot be captured ... but it can be imagined.

—Patricia Cox Miller
The Poetry of Thought in Late Antiquity

In the Beginning

I am beginning this essay, but the page is already full. More than that: it is overflowing. I write over the overflowing page. I write the page over.

Why not leave it alone, or make a clean start? Why begin again? *Because I want to.* (A child's answer—or a god's.) I write first about writing, next about wanting. (But the wanting was always there, in the writing, in the wanting to write.) I write about *poiesis*, about *eros*, about the desire to create, about the desire at the heart of creation. The text is layered and shifty.

Still, it is the same *logos* as before, and by then it was already ancient. Full—overflowing. Perfect—a perfect mess.

Try again. Keep trying again. Do it over. If I have to, I will make a mockery of this *logos*, of the very act of writing, of the inexplicable desire to make something out of these words. There is no way to give a straight account of desire, which is always perverse, least of all divine desire, the ultimate perversity.

Here is my question: Why should an eternal and immutable god begin again? Begin anything at all? *Because the god wants to.* What? How can a god—*the God*—be found *wanting*?

Not a Blank Page: Word as Writing

Jacques Derrida both writes and unwrites a history of textuality. It is his reading of Plato's *Phaedrus* that initially draws my attention. Therein the philosopher discovers an instructive scene that is also a scene of instruction regarding the the priority of speech over writing, in which speech—*logos*—is aligned with the presence, transparency, or graspability of meaning, writing—*graphein*—with meaning's absence, occlusion, deferral. Gazing at the Platonic text over Derrida's shoulder, I see the prototypical scene extended—and seemingly indefinitely suspended—in a chain of iteration: the *Phaedrus* itself already claims to revoice an Egyptian myth, while at the same time it appears to agree in advance with "that other, Judaeo-Christian account of God's creating word and the power of the *logos* to manifest itself direct in thought-made-deed"[2]—as one commentator boldly interpolates the Derridean text. The so-called "Judaeo-Christian account" seemingly so uncannily prefigured is presented by Derrida himself as the "all of philosophy, which is as such constituted" in the Platonic gesture of writing's repudiation.[3] (Here, as so often, he leaves the critique of theology merely implicit.) The perduring Platonic pattern tracked by Derrida across centuries of western intellectual habit encounters epochal shifts as it is "re-edited" in the writings of Rousseau and Saussure, both of whom inaugurate new "'eras' in the repetition of Platonism."[4]

If a long history of Platonic logocentrism—silently intersecting with "the Judeo-Christian account"—is the problem, what is the solution? It begins—but does not end—with a strategic reversal: in Derrida's works, "speech is presented, explained, as a form of writing."[5] "The alleged derivativeness of writing, however real and massive, was possible only on one condition: that the 'original,' 'natural,' etc. language had never existed, never been intact or untouched by writing, that it had itself always been a writing," proposes Derrida. "An archi-writing ..."[6] A new practice of reading—dubbed "deconstruction"—thus disrupts the Platonic history of writing as a late (and lamentable) arrival. Derrida not only *embraces* the "fall" from speech into writing (thereby inverting the Platonic binary) but also *erases* the pre-lapsarian era of pure orality (effectively collapsing the binary). Now we learn that speech is always already "fallen," marked by writing, marked as writing. "Discontinuity, delay, heterogeneity, and alterity already were working upon the voice, producing it from its first breath as a system of differential traces, that is, as writing before the letter," asserts Derrida.[7] Logocentrism itself turns out not to have a history but to perpetuate a fiction, through a practice of reading that continually reinscribes a false origin—that reinstates the fallacy of originality.

It is, however, a useful fiction, not least for deconstructionists. ("It is necessary ... to accede to the virtue of the lie.")[8] If it is tempting—albeit manifestly false—to imagine that Derrida has simply evacuated the interiority of the Platonic myth of the Logos (a.k.a. "the Judaeo-Christian account"), it is more difficult to position him purely on the outside of the Jewish question of the Book, as we encounter him, for example in his meditative reading of Edmond Jabès's *The Book of Questions*:

> God separated himself from himself in order to let us speak, in order to astonish and to interrogate us. He did so not by speaking but by keeping still, by letting silence interrupt his voice and his signs, by letting the Tables be broken

writes Derrida between the lines and in the margins of Jabès's text.

> In Exodus God repented and said so at least twice, before the first and before the new Tables, between original speech and writing and, within Scripture, between the origin and repetition (Exodus 32:14, 33:17). Writing is, thus, originally hermetic and secondary. Our writing, certainly but already His, which starts with the stifling of his voice and the dissimulation of his Face. This difference, this negativity in God is our freedom ...[9]

Here we see clearly that the aim for deconstruction can never be to *annihilate* the myth of logocentrism that funds the hierarchical dualisms of the western ontotheological tradition so as to inscribe a new theory of language *ex nihilo*. Rather, deconstruction uses the posited primacy of a speaking God to articulate what is otherwise virtually inarticulable, namely the self-silencing of God and the "original secondariness" of all language. One might say that the deconstructive process necessarily inscribes a narrative of origins—promotes a fallacy of originality—that it subsequently overwrites, thereby locating itself in the almost unlocatable (and impossibly fertile) space "between the origin and the repetition."

Once we understand that Derrida is not writing history after all (but rather engaging in an interpretive practice that continually both mimes and undermines narratives of origin and fall, presence and exile),[10] *we are able to see that he is a surprisingly faithful interpreter of the "Judaeo-Christian" tradition of Logos theology.* By this, I mean that his move to deconstruct logocentrism by subverting the binary of writing and word repeats a dynamic already subtly at work "in the beginning," "before the letter"—before Christianity and Judaism (Logos and Book) had hardened into opposing (or even "opposite") identities.[11] For the ancients, as for Derrida, Word is always already Writing, "hermetic and secondary." Or, in Derrida's own somewhat more abstract terms: "The name of the relation is the same as that of one of its terms. The *pharmakon*[12] is *comprehended* in the structure of *logos*."[13]

Am I now writing history over Derrida's erasure? Perhaps (though my "history" is therefore inevitably tainted with the memory and thus the anticipation of its own undoing). *Historically speaking*, the figure of Logos is more a product of scriptural interpretation than of Platonic speculation—a "fact" that is most frequently overlooked or even deliberately obscured, swallowed by the chasm forcefully (falsely?) wedged open between Logos and Book. The divinized or hypostasized Logos that reappears in Derrida's texts is collaboratively invented in antiquity by writers who are (with a few minor exceptions) readers of Genesis 1 and Proverbs 8,[14] ma'ny (but not all) of whom also happen to be readers of Plato and other philosophers. From the Gospel of John to the Gospel of Truth, from the Tripartite Tractate to Clement's Alexandrian trilogy of the Word, from Philo to Justin to Origen, Logos emerges in the dialogical play of scriptural interpretation. More intriguing still, the figure is paralleled in (if not anticipated by) the Aramaic exegesis of the Hebrew "memra" ("word")—it is thus not only almost always a "Jewish" but sometimes also a non-Greek invention.[15] I might broaden the point further and say that Logos, first and foremost a product of scriptural exegesis, is also a product of a particular style of self-consciously intertextual reading that *makes* Scripture Scripture. (For Scripture does not preexist its interpretation but emerges as an effect of interpretation.)

Reinscribing the Page: Creation as Desire

Contemporary historical theologians find reason to critique the "logocentrism" of pre-Nicene theology, but their concerns are diametrically opposed to those of deconstructionists. "To speak of the Logos as 'coming forth' from God, and so as 'becoming Son of God' seems to suggest some kind of change in the Logos himself," objects Alasdair Heron. "The ambivalence of the Logos concept, with its double reference to 'mind' and 'word,' partly conceals this suggestion, but it cannot eliminate it, for the suggestion flows from that very ambivalence," he observes astutely, going on to comment further on the ontological instability of the pre-Nicene Logos (and its concommitant tendency to destabilize ontology):

> By the same token, the nature of the continuity between the two stages in the history of the Logos remains problematic, and for the same reasons. Similarly, to link his "being begotten" with the creation of the universe does indeed serve the purpose of connecting him with God the Creator, and of subordinating the existence of all other reality to his being; but it also ties him in his status as Logos/Son to the whole of created reality as its arche, as the mediating principle between God and everything else.[16]

Like it or not (and Heron doesn't much like it), Logos is neither sheerly internal nor sheerly external in relation to either God or God's creation. It is ambivalent, doubled, and from that ambivalence flow other troubling suggestions. Indeed, Logos as both God's primal product and the agent of all subsequent creation, is situated at the most unstable place, not only ontologically but narratively as well. For *why*, and indeed *how*, should a God who is one, indivisible and unchanging, create anything at all? Is creation not the *"fall" of God*? Is a creative God not *always already "fallen"*—thinking the thought, uttering the word, desiring the world, opening up the gap, the fecund void, in which wholeness is ever exceeding itself, oneness ever shattering into multiplicity? The very concept of a "pre-lapsarian" deity who is independent of and prior to creation may be, for Platonic and scriptural traditions, and above all for those traditions that are both Platonic and scriptural, *a necessary and productive fiction that invites its own deconstruction*—not unlike the myth, both Platonic and Derridean, of an original logocentrism. The focal figure—the conceptual node—of that theological deconstruction (of that deconstructive theology) is Logos itself.

Cosmologically framed, Logos is both the interval of separation and the agent of mediation between God and creation, as Heron points out. I am here suggesting that one might push this point just a bit further and say that Logos is the binary itself—the One-Many—as well as its inevitable subversion, both revealing and reveiling the instability inhering in the unchanging, the multiplicity harbored within the unity, the difference with which sameness is impregnated—that Logos is thus yet another term in "the chain...of non-synonomous substitutions" for the Derridean *pharmakos*, "archi-writing," *différance*.[17] Like the Pythagorean Monad-Dyad, or the still more unstable co-presence "in the beginning" of Demiurge, Forms, and Receptacle depicted in the *Timaeus* (diversely interpreted by later Platonists), Logos contains and also exposes the excessiveness and deficiency of a perfect monotheism. Where limitless divine outpouring (plenitude and then some) spills into the yawning abyss of infinite potentiality (leaving the cosmos itself always less than complete), the posited dichotomy of a holy wholeness (pure being) and an unholy deficiency (absolute nothingness) collapses, and "creation" is reframed as "a flow at the heart of things, rather than a creator set over against a thing created."[18] As we shall see, it is above all by exposing desire as the font of divine creativity that Logos undermines the absolute alterity claimed for a transcendent God.

It is "gnostic" texts that are most attuned to the generative ambivalence of Logos. Forcefully asserting the radical otherness and incomprehensibility of the invisible Spirit who is "more than a god," these works also subtly subvert both the epistemological and the ontological foundations of such a theology:

> And his thought performed a deed and she came forth, namely she who had appeared before him in the shine of his light. This is the first power which was before all of them and which came forth from his mind. She is the forethought of the All—her light shines like his light—the perfect power which is the image of the invisible, virginal Spirit who is perfect... This is the first thought, his image; she became the womb of everything... (NH II 1, 4–5).[19]

Thus the Sethian *Apocryphon of John* regarding its Logos-figure, Barbelo, from which "womb" the "fullness"—*pleroma*—of divine perfection proceeds. Already, one might say, the pristine Spirit is in trouble, exceeding the bounds of its Oneness (as if caught in an embarrassing pregnancy). Already the text reveals (even as it tries to cover its own messy tracks) that divine "thought" is the site of a dangerous excessiveness, the point at which God's "fullness" is marked as a self-transgressive process, defying any limit that might be implied by "wholeness." (Indeed, when limit is eventually inscribed, it comes as both a concession to and a confession of the deficiency of divinity that is at the same time the font of divine plenitude.)

Enacting such excess through the explosive proliferation of names ("the Mother-Father, the first man, the holy Spirit, the thrice-male, the thrice-powerful, the thrice-named androgynous one") as well as aeonic offspring (foreknowledge, indestructibility, eternal life, truth) (NH II 1, 5–6), the Barbelo Logos-figure continues to transgress limits by subsequently (and not for the last time) duplicating itself, with the introduction of another divinely womblike persona—who both is and is not "the same," in this strangely postcolonial text-world of fractured, overlapped, hybridized identities.[20] "And the Sophia of the Epinoia, being an aeon, conceived a thought from herself and the conception of the invisible Spirit and foreknowledge." Here, the creative desire is explicitly marked as excessive—indeed excessively marked as such, marked with the sign of the "fall."

> She wanted to bring forth a likeness out of herself without the consent of the Spirit—he had not approved—and without her consort, and without his consideration. And though the person of her maleness had not approved and she had not found her agreement, and she had thought without the consent of the Spirit, and the knowledge of her agreement, yet she brought forth. And because of the invincible power which is in her, her thought did not remain idle and something came out of her which was imperfect and different from her appearance (NH II 1, 9–10).

To cut a long story short: the "something" that Sophia conceives illegitimately (out of her desire) turns out to be the "God" of Genesis 1–2, and thus Sophia—not father to an only-begotten word but mother to a misbegotten creator—gives rise to the arrogant pseudo-deity and his cosmos (itself a perverse replica of the divine pleroma) as "the consequences of her desire" (NH II 1, 10). This explicit act of *creatio ex libidine* is so ambivalent that Sophia herself is fractured in her repentance, broken off from herself, taken up into the ninth heaven and also dispersed and also sent to the dispersion to correct her deficiency—a split subject indeed, parody of perfection, both savior and the one, the many to be saved.[21]

The gnostic myth thus equates the fall of an intermediate—and not inconsequentially "feminine"—divine entity with the creation of the material universe, an identification that has earned gnosticism a robust reputation for "cosmic dualism." We should note, however, that this "dualism" is based at least as much on imitation and iteration—on *resemblance*—as on negation. Taking the specific form of mimicry, gnostic cosmology exposes the deficiency of the material world and/or its political regime by situating it as a "bad copy" of a divine original. The myth thereby devours the totalizing claims of the Creator God Ialdabaoth and his imperial henchmen in the maw of an even more totalizing, directly oppositional metanarrative, as Karen King has argued persuasively.[22] As Patricia Cox Miller has pointed out, the gnostic critique is aimed not merely at "creation" as we know it but at the very concept of

God *as "Creator"*—or, more precisely, at a demiurgic theology that implies an "artistic or plastic model of creating." For the gnostic, as for a Platonist like Porphyry, "to be enlightened ... involves coming to terms with metaphors of divine making," suggests Miller. Specifically, enlightenment involves excavating "the erotic foundations of creating," rejecting as false the notion that "the maker...is related to the objects that he has forged from nothing by power rather than by nature" and recognizing instead that "the 'first reality' is a flow, not the work of a potter."[23]

Less frequently remarked is that the mimetic and repetitious patterning of gnostic cosmology does more than mock the derivativeness and consequent inauthenticity or imperfection of "the world." Like the forms of mimicry analyzed by postcolonial theorist Homi Bhabha, the gnostic myth also undermines the very concept of "originality" and thus disturbs the serene stasis of the perfect "One." It is here, in the (delicate and ambivalent) mockery of theology itself, that I would locate the ancient concept of creativity that Miller describes as "*making* under the banner of ... the kind of desire that is set in motion when God is dead."[24] Although there is a sense in which the Logos qua "writing" is "patricidal,"[25] the point for the reader of the gnostic text is not so much to kill the Father or even triumphantly to announce "his" death, as to attempt to glimpse what cannot quite be seen, namely, the always already dying or withdrawing that is God—"the stifling of his voice and dissimulation of his Face," as Derrida also puts it—which is merely the shadowed side of the always already desiring or outpouring that is also God. Sophia—re-presenting, intensifying, and partly revising Logos-Barbelo as First Thought and Womb of All, *but also re-presenting the invisible Spirit* (as Barbelo herself already re-presents it)—becomes a hermeneutical key releasing the abysmal secret of creativity as the dying/desiring of God, a "flow at the heart of things." The self-contained transcendence of the invisible Spirit and the self-transgressing womb of divine fecundity; the safety of a controlling will and the danger of uncontrolled desire; the One that perfectly encompasses all possibilities and its fracturing into the never-perfected, ever-extending Fullness of the Many—such distinctions are *not* simply eradicated but they *are* significantly confounded, provisionally reversed, persistently interrogated (in short, deconstructed) in the interpretive cycle of mimesis and mimicry.

The multiplicity of mythical "versions"—merely accentuated by the dogged attempts of heresiologists, ancient and modern, to mark them all as "the same" gnosticism—itself offers oblique witness to the fluency and fluidity of the divine conceived as (and in) abysmal and plenitudinous creativity. The heavily philosophical Valentinian treatise known as the *Tripartite Tractate* represents an especially interesting variant that partly bridges the (at most points, already very slender) gap between "gnostic" and "anti-gnostic" Christian texts. In the *Tripartite Tractate*, the name of the split, ambivalent figure of divine desire is not Barbelo or Sophia but Logos itself. "His" intentions were good, we are assured in advance (an overt and even somewhat abrupt apologetic, absent in accounts of Sophia and thereby confirming the suspicion that the ancient texts love prodigal sons better than hysterical daughters).[26] The continued defensiveness of the *Tractate*, however, intensifies rather than mitigates the ambivalence of the Logos: "When he had come forth, he gave glory to the Father, even if it led to something beyond possibility, since he had wanted to bring forth one who is perfection, from an agreement in which he had not been, and without having the command ..." Although, like his analog Sophia, this youngest sib of the divine litter clearly harbors an inappropriate desire: "he acted, magnanimously, from an abundant love," the text insists, "Therefore, it is not fitting to criticize the movement which is the Logos, but it is fitting that we should say about the movement of the Logos that it is a cause of an organization which has been destined to come about." Despite his good intentions and providential role, "those whom he wished to take hold of firmly he begot in shadows and copies and likenesses. For he was not able to bear the sight of the light, but he looked into the depth and he doubted. Out of this there was a division—he became deeply troubled—and a turning away because of his self-doubt and division, forgetfulness and ignorance of himself and of that which is." Divided by doubt, his deficiency may seem to degrade him, even as his love exalts him. He "brought forth little weaklings," a runt of a creation that makes a mockery of the divine Fullness—"likenesses, copies, shadows and phantasms" (NH I 5, 76–78). Yet in the repentence that arises out of self-doubt, deficiency is at least partly filled. "The Logos established himself at first, when he beautified the Totalities, as a basic principle and cause and ruler of the things which came to be, like the Father, the one who was the cause of the establishment ..." (NH I 5, 96).

The text can't quite come to rest around this unsettling figure. Simultaneously accusing and defending the Logos, the *Tripartite Tractate* attempts to come to terms with a complex model of creativity and creation that is irreducibly dynamic and erotic—an "organization" or "establishment" always (re)emerging from the depths (and thus, troublingly, both excessive and deficient in relation to what has already seen the light of day), escaping the clutches of "originality" by "opening up the possibility of the double, the copy, the imitation, the simulacrum."[27] As John Kenney observes, "In describing the method of generation employed by the Logos, the language becomes more that of agency than of contem-plative emanation."[28] This is in marked contrast to the *Tractate*'s initial representation of the divine pleroma, which addresses the problem of how divinity can be both creative and unchanging by positing the inherent or essential generativity of a God depicted in an eternal process of self-contemplation. The subsequent account of Logos thus surfaces what is suppressed (indeed seemingly actively refused) in this first account of creation, namely, the paradox of desire at the heart of divine generativity, now articulated via the invocation of a dyadic tradition of first principles.[29] The Logos's desire transgresses "the limit to speech set in the Pleroma" (NH I 5, 75), a limit established by the Father's own will, or rather by his *active withholding* of his will: having "his power, which is his will" (i.e., his will to be known), "in silence he himself holds back, he who is the great one, who is the cause of bringing the Totalities into their eternal being" (NH I 5, 55). The distinction between nature and will, between the generative modes of Father and Logos, thus finally does not hold, for the activity of self-contemplation that defines the Father's nature is also the expression of his desire. Desiring to know himself, the Father generates thought (figured successively as Son, Church, aeons) that is at once identical and alien to him—"a trace of him" (NH I 5, 66). The plenitudinous fecundity that is the product of his own self-extention, or "stretching out," is at the same time the effect of his willful withdrawal as an object of knowledge. As Miller puts it, "no language can convey him; it would seem that the other side of linguistic plenitude is silence and inadequacy."[30] The Totalities name the glory of the one who remains incomprehensible; their existence has its foundation in such inevitably imperfect "naming" (NH I 5, 65). If Logos transgresses the limits of possibility by seeking perfect knowledge without constraint (thereby becoming the demiurgic maker of an inferior subpleromatic cosmos), his actions nonetheless give expression to the inevitable frustration of words that always fall short of comprehending the one who is established beyond comprehensibility. Logos "personifies and so brings to attention the disseminative plight of all the aeon-words that dwell in the depths of language," notes Miller.[31] Such frustration can be converted to joy when deficiency is recognized as the source of limitless plenitude. Learning humility, ceasing to grasp while continuing to seek, Logos may rejoin the doxological chorus of the divine fullness. His desire—his fall—is also the Father's desire: it was "destined to come about."

From here it is but a short jump to the thought-world of Origen of Alexandria. Less overtly ambivalent but no less complex, Origen's Logos—the perfect image of God—is also the site at which the One shatters into the "many differences and varieties," the "dispersion and division" of materiality (de princ. 1.6.2,4), where the temporal finitude of creation (the seeds of which are always already borne in the Word's womb) intersects with the eternity of divine generation. In an early and highly theoretical work titled *On First Principles*, Origen meditates on the only-begotten Son of God, who "is called by many different names" (1.2.1).[32] It is under the label of Sophia that the creatureliness as well as the creative power of the Son is emphasized. "Now this Son was begotten of the Father's will, for he is the 'image of the invisible God' [cf. Colossians 1:15] and the 'effulgence of his glory and the impress of his substance' [Hebrews 1:3], 'the firstborn of all creation' [cf. Colossians 1:15], a thing created [*ktisma*], Wisdom. For Wisdom herself says: 'God created me in the beginning of his ways for his works' (Proverbs 8:22)," recites Origen (4.4.1). Eternally generated ("a flow at the heart of things"), this incorporeal *ktisma* is also, as Miller reminds us, identified by Origen as one whose "desire was by means of this very emptying [cf. Philippians 2:6,7] to display to us the fullness of the godhead" (1.2.8). "What, then, is the invisible Wisdom, whose emptying reveals a pleroma?" asks Miller. Pointing out that *ktisma* can mean not only "creature" but also "foundation" or "building," she suggests that for Origen the Son who is both Logos and Sophia is "God's binding structure in which all things are made new."[33] In Sophia, "there was implicit every capacity and form of the creation that was to be …; she contains within herself both the beginnings and causes and species of the whole creation," writes Origen (1.2.2). "In this Sophia … the creation was always present in form and outline" (1.4.4). Not made of "stuff," either intellectual or bodily, but rather constituting the something-else that underlies corporeal existence, the Son/Sophia "provides a kind of intermediate, or mediating, structure within which *nous* and *soma* are associated in varying degrees."[34]

It is at this point that Origen's curious doctrine of the fall—both repeating and resisting the gnostic account—fruitfully complicates his scheme. Origen suggests that the differentiated mingling of intellect with body that constitutes the creation of the material universe occurs as a result of the fall of souls that were originally created as pure and undifferentiated intellect. Starting from one beginning, these souls "were drawn in various directions by their own individual impulses and were distributed throughout the different ranks of existence in accordance with their merit" (1.4.2). Thus, oddly enough, "the beginnings and causes and species of the whole creation" that are said to be always already contained in Sophia are *also* attributed to a lapse in creation itself—a lapse not located, as in the gnostic myth, in the inexplicable surge of divine desire in Sophia/Logos but rather in its even more mysterious cessation in human souls (whether due to negligence or to satiety or some other cause, Origen cannot say for sure [1.3.8, 1.4.1]). Whatever their differences, both Origen's *On First Principles* and the gnostic texts situate transgressive desire and the withdrawal of God in the beginning of a creativity that results—that is eternally resulting?—in a universe marked by multiplicity, flux, and difference. Regardless of whether the "fall" into materiality is assigned to an errant aeon within the divine pleroma or to the disembodied spirits of a prematerial creation, it doubles (and therein both reveals and reveils) the scandal of the "original" lapse that gives the lie to originality—*namely, the eternal "falling" that is the Logos as the mark of divine desire—that is, in other words, the trace of God in the world and of the world in God.*

Writing it over, beginning again with creation, am I not also still writing about writing? Logos as *poiesis*—as divinely erotic *making*—is also *the trace of the world in the text and of the text in the world.* For Origen (as for the gnostics, albeit differently), writing is the privileged site of the materialization ("re-incarnation") of the Logos, who is also, as we have seen, the womb of the material creation itself. Thus, there is a deep linking of cosmic and scriptural "makings" that profoundly complicates (though it by no means renders irrelevant) understandings of the pursuit of truth and of the role of desire, imagination, and interpretation in constituting reality.[35]

Beginning (Yet) Again

Abandoned by Jews in the effort to distinguish themselves from Christians, Logos theology is likewise eclipsed in Christian discourse by Nicene trinitarian theology. By the fourth century, the one God may claim to encompass multiplicity, indeed to be constituted out of the "flow," the "process," "relationality" itself—while at the same time remaining untainted by a materiality more absolutely than ever distanced from divinity, through the reassertion of the distinction between erotic and technological "making," between the "begetting" at the heart of the flow of Divinity and the "creating" that decisively separates Maker from Made. This separation is, paradoxically, emphasized in the simultaneous reassertion of the doctrine of creation *ex nihilo*: materiality is now not merely different from Being Itself but rather its opposite—nothing at all. (The new model is, fortunately, no more stable than the old, but it *is* effectively shrouded in mystery).[36] Trinitarian theology—the scandal of "Jewish monotheism"—accompanies the rise of a "monologic" writing culture simultaneously liturgical, credal, and polemical, frequently positioned in binary opposition to the emergent "dialogical" rabbinic culture of writing.

As Daniel Boyarin has argued, two competing textualities emerge with the birth of two distinct "religions"—one now rejecting the heritage of Greece, the other claiming it, one easily aligned on the side of a more sheerly material ("carnal") textuality, the other seeking transcendent truth (one that can be claimed for Derrida, the other by "radically orthodox" Christians).[37] But, as Boyarin also argues, each is still implicated in the other (not least in their constitutive mutual resistance), linked by a common heritage and shared suppression of the Logos—the speech that is text, the one that is many, the transcendent desire that is always already materializing in creation.[38]

Eternally Beginning?

Writing, and rewriting, the never-blank page, have my own repeated beginnings of meditations on beginnings inadvertently reinscribed a shifting ground of "origin"[39] for an erotic creativity that is always already both divine and human, in which materiality and transcendence can never be fully distinguished? (Which is thus, nonetheless, some kind of "god?" even some kind of god-as-*logos*?) Perhaps. And if this is (my) desire, it is not, cannot ever be, finished. Write it again, keep writing it over, make it something new—don't stop!

References

1. Not mentioned below—and thus all the more meriting acknowledgment up front—are my colleagues Catherine Keller and Stephen Moore. To a great extent, their thoughts provide my point of departure in this essay. In particular, my own positing of a theology of *creatio ex libidine* is much indebted to the *creatio ex profundis* articulated by Keller in her *The Face of the Deep: A Theology of Becoming* (London: Routledge, 2003).
2. Christopher Norris, *Derrida* (Cambridge: Harvard University Press, 1987), p. 31.
3. Jacques Derrida, *Dissemination*, trans. and ed. Barbara Johnson (Chicago: University of Chicago Press, 1981), p. 109.
4. Derrida, *Dissemination*, p. 158.
5. Jonathan Culler, *On Deconstruction: Theory and Criticism After Structuralism* (Ithaca: Cornell University Press, 1982), p. 101.
6. Jacques Derrida, *Of Grammatology*, trans. Gayatri Chakravorty Spivak (Baltimore and London: The Johns Hopkins Univerisity Press, 1974), p. 56.
7. Jacques Derrida, *Margins of Philosophy*, trans. Alan Bass (Chicago: University of Chicago Press, 1982), p. 291.
8. Jacques Derrida, *Writing and Difference*, trans. Alan Bass (Chicago: University of Chicago Press, 1978), p. 68.
9. Derrida, *Writing and Difference*, p. 67.
10. Cf. Paul de Man's suggestion that Derrida's narration of the logocentric fallacy "as a historical, consecutive process" is a "fiction" that should not be taken literally: "his historical scheme is merely a narrative convention" (*Blindness and Insight: Essays in the Rhetoric of Contemporary Criticism*, 2nd ed. revised [Minneapolis: University of Minnesota Press, 1983], pp. 137–138).

11. The term "Judaeo-Christian" is, of course, hugely problematic in its supersessionism. For my purposes here, however, what is still more problematic is the tendency to harden the boundaries between "Judaism" and "Christianity" by too rigid an alignment of logocentrism, Platonism, Christianity, on the one hand, and deconstruction and Judaism, on the other. I hasten to add that this alignment is not without its insightful defenders; see, for example, Susan Handelmann, *The Slayers of Moses: The Emergence of Rabbinic Interpretation in Modern Literary Theory* (Albany: SUNY Press, 1982). Daniel Boyarin has argued that "Judaeo-Christianity" may be reappropriated for the purposes of deconstructing the very binary that it has frequently served to reinstate, as for example in Norris's seemingly uncritical use of the term. "Instead of two defined entities, Judaism and Christianity, I would suggest that for the second and probably third century, we should still be thinking of a complex religious system, Judaeo-Christianity (not in its modern sense of common heritage and lowest common denominator!) in which there are only borderlands, and no-man's lands, a web-site in which the very borders and rules for admission and citizenship are still under-construction by heresiologists on one side, Rabbis on the other. 'Jewish Christianity' is a name for the third term, as it were, that deconstructs the binary opposition of two ostensibly mutually exclusive entities, as well as the social continuum that maintains the possibility of constant 'contamination' between them on the ground." (Daniel Boyarin, "Justin Martyr Invents Judaism," *Church History* 70, no. 3 [2001]: pp. 427–461).

12. Derrida, *Dissemination*, p. 96, n.43, remarks that "with a few precautions, one could say that *pharmakon* plays a role *analogous*, in this reading of Plato, to that of *supplément* in the reading of Rousseau." He augments the list in *Margins of Philosophy*, p. 12: "différance," "reserve," "archi-writing," "archi-trace," "spacing," "hymen," "margin-mark-march."

13. Derrida, *Dissemination*, p. 117.

14. This fact leads John Dillon, who is unable to consider scriptural interpreters "Platonists," to the awkward conclusion that there is "only one real Platonist before Plotinus [who] can be identified as making use of the concept of the Logos, and that is Plutarch ..." He goes on to confess, however, that "even with Plutarch, the evidence is somewhat controversial, since a Logos-figure only appears in one treatise, that *On Isis and Osiris*, in the guise of the Egyptian god Osiris ..." ("Logos and Trinity: Patterns of Platonist Influence on Early Christiantiy," in Godfrey Vesey (ed.) *The Philosophy in Christianity* (Cambridge: Cambridge University Press, 1989), pp. 1–13(4). In Mark Edwards's decisive framing, "There is no such intermediary as the Logos to be met with in the writings of the Gentile Platonists" (*Origen Against Plato*, Ashgate Studies in Philosophy and Theology in Late Antiquity [Aldershot: Ashgate, 2002], p. 66).

15. Daniel Boyarin, "The Gospel of the Memra: Jewish Binitarianism and the Prologue to John," *Harvard Theological Review* 94, no. 3 (2001): 243–284. Other recent studies also relevant to the exegetical origins of Logos theory include Mark J. Edwards, "Justin's Logos and the Word of God," *Journal of Early Christian Studies* 3, no. 3 (1995): 261–280, and Nicola Frances Denzy, "Genesis Traditions in Conflict? The Use of Some Exegtical Traditions in the Trimorphic Portennoia and the Johannine Prologue," *Vigiliae Christianae* 55, no. 1 (2001): 20–44.

16. Alasdair Heron, "'Logos, Image, Son': Some Models and Paradigms in Early Christology," in *Creation, Christ, and Culture*, R. McKinney, ed. (Poole: T&T Clark, 1976), pp. 52–53.

17. Derrida, *Margins of Philosophy*, p. 12.

18. Patricia Cox Miller, *The Poetry of Thought in Late Antiquity: Essays in Imagination and Religion* (Aldershot: Ashgate, 2001), p. 115.

19. English translations of the "gnostic" treatises preserved in the codices discovered at Nag Hammadi may be found in *The Nag Hammadi Library in English*, 3rd ed., ed. James M. Robinson (San Francisco: Harper and Row, 1988).

20. Karen King has argued persuasively that gnostic texts should be read through the lens of the contemporary critique of colonialism, on the grounds that the cosmic "alienation" so frequently attributed to the texts is a disguised articulation of political alienation experienced under the Roman Empire (Karen L. King, "Translating History: Reframing Gnosticism in Postmodernity," in *Tradition und Translation: Zum Problem der Interkulterellen Übersetzbarkeit Religiöser Phänomene. Estschrift für Carsten Colpe zum 65. Geburtstag*, Christoph Essas [Berlin, New York: Walter de Gruyter, 1994], pp. 264–277). I find Homi Bhabha's (Derridean) postcolonial theory particularly relevant to such a reading, not least because it

is strikingly resonant with gnostic theory itself. "The colonial presence is always ambivalent, split between its appearance as original and authoritative and its articulation as repetition and difference," notes Bhabha. "Colonial specularity, doubly inscribed, does not produce a mirror where the self apprehends itself; it is always the split screen of the self and its doubling, the hybrid ... The display of hybridity—its peculiar 'replication'—terrorizes authority with the *ruse* of recognition, its mimicry, its mockery. Such a reading of the hybridity of colonial authority profoundly unsettles the demand that figures at the centre of the originary myth of colonialist power" (Homi K. Bhabha, *The Location of Culture* [London: Routledge, 1994], pp. 107, 114, 115).

21. Cf. Miller, *Poetry of Thought*, p. 110, in reference to the particular multiplication of *feminine* figures in gnostic texts: "The feminine dimension of reality not only appears, but is intensified, underscored, by its multiplied form, setting the masculine world of Ialdabaoth atremble."

22. Karen L. King, "The Politics of Syncretism and the Problem of Defining Gnosticism," *Historical Reflections/Reflexions Historiques* 27, no. 3 (2001): 473–77. Also relevant is the earlier work of Elaine Pagels on the "political" implictions of gnostic cosmology; see especially "'The Demiurge and His Archons'—a Gnostic View of the Bishop and Presbyters," *Harvard Theological Review* 69 (1976): 301–324.

23. Miller, *Poetry of Thought*, pp. 110–111.

24. Miller, *Poetry of Thought*, p. 112.

25. Derrida, *Dissemination*, p. 77.

26. Paula Fredriksen, "Hysteria and the Gnostic Myths of Creation," *Vigiliae Christianae* 33 (1979): 287–290, calls attention to the linguistic and narrative parallels between the gnostic Sophia and the figure of the "wandering womb" as represented in medical discussions of "hysteria." But perhaps we should not overemphasize the difference between hysterics and younger sons. Cf. Derrida's designation of writing as "the lost son" for whom the father is absent, as opposed to the "elder brother" speech (or alternatively, "good writing"). "One, writing, is a lost trace, a nonviable seed, everything in sperm that overflows wastefully, a force wandering outside the domain of life, incapable of engendering anything, of picking itself up, of regenerating itself. On the opposite side, living speech makes its capital bear fruit and does not divert its seminal potency toward indulgence in pleasures without paternity." (Derrida, *Dissemination*, p. 152).

27. Derrida, *Dissemination*, p. 157.

28. John Peter Kenney, "The Platonism of the Tripartite Tractate (NH I, 5)," in *Neoplatonism and Gnosticism*, ed. R. T. Wallis (Albany: SUNY Press, 1992), p. 198.

29. Kenney, "The Platonism of the Tripartite Tractate," p. 189. See also Einar Thomassen, "The Structure of the Transcendent World in the Tripartite Tractate (NHC I, 5)," *Vigiliae Christianae* 34 (1980): 363, on the contrast between the contemplative generativity of the Father and the demiurgic activity of the logos.

30. Miller, *Poetry of Thought*, p. 248.

31. Miller, *Poetry of Thought*, p. 250.

32. An English translation of Origen's *On First Principles* may be found in *Anti-Nicene Fathers*, vol. 4, eds. Alexander Roberts and James Donaldson (Peabody: Hendrikson, 1994).

33. Miller, *Poetry of Thought*, p. 183.

34. Miller, *Poetry of Thought*, p. 184.

35. These are concerns that are threaded through the essays now collected in Miller, *Poetry of Thought*. I have tried to record some of my debts to Miller, whose interest in the intersections of desire, creativity, and writing strongly coincides with my own. I must also acknowledge the influence of Rebecca Lyman; see her fine treatment of Origen's cosmology in J. Rebecca Lyman, *Christology and Cosmology: Models of Divine Activity in Origen, Eusebius, and Athanasius*, Oxford Theological Monographs (Oxford: Clarendon Press, 1993), pp. 38–81.

36. I have tried to explore some of its more fertile instabilities in my *"Begotten, not Made": Conceiving Manhood in Late Antiquity*, Figurae: Reading Medieval Culture (Stanford: Stanford University Press, 2000).

37. See, for example, Catherine Pickstock, *After Writing: On the Liturgical Consummation of Philosophy* (Oxford: Blackwell, 1997). In close debate with Derrida, Pickstock celebrates the Graeco-Christian and the "logocentric," for which she claims the honor of a linguistic materiality and fecundity that Derrida reserves for "writing," and from which she receives the mantle of authority for a "radically orthodox" theology taking place "after modernity."

38. Boyarin's interest in rabbinic textuality and its comparison with hellenistic textuality threads throughout many of his publications; it is a topic he is revisiting in his *Border Lines: Hybrids, Heretics, and the Partition of Judaeo-Christianity*, Divinations: Reading Religion in Late Antiquity (Philadelphia: University of Pennsylvania Press, 2004).
39. Cf. Derrida, *Margins of Philosophy*, p. 11: "*Différance* is the non-full, non-simple, structured and differentiating origin of differences. Thus, the name 'origin' no longer suits it."

Reading a Page of Scripture with a Little Help from Derrida

Other Eyes: Reading and Not Reading the Hebrew Scriptures/Old Testament with a Little Help from Derrida and Cixous

HUGH S. PYPER

Dear M. Derrida,

I understand from the program book of the American Academy of Religion and the Society of Biblical Literature that you may be able to help me to read a page of scripture. I have a particular question to put to you. I am paid a reasonable if not excessive salary by a university in Britain to teach the Hebrew Scriptures but here is the rub: I am not sure if I have ever read even a page of them. Don't get me wrong—I have learned Hebrew, up to a point, and possess multiple copies of the relevant texts and translations which I sit and pore over. But can I, as a non-Jew, a gentile, read, let alone teach, the Hebrew Scriptures? This is not a moral question—ought I as a gentile to give myself out as doing this?—but an entirely practical one. As a product of a Christian and post-Christian culture, can I read anything but the Old Testament? I would appreciate your advice as otherwise I may have to resign my job (only joking!). In an attempt to help myself, I have been reading your works, and especially *Voiles*, where you touch on Paul's serious play with Moses' veil in Exodus chapter 34.[1] Paul writes that there is now a veil on the hearts of the sons of Israel when Moses is read, a veil removed by turning to the Lord. On the other hand, the Zohar tells me that only the circumcised can read clearly.[2] Either way, does this mean I cannot see what Jewish readers see even if I want to?

Yours sincerely,

Hugh S. Pyper

***

Dear Dr. Pyper,

If you have read *La carte postale*,[3] and as I am, if Foucault is correct, simply your device to rein in the claims of my texts, you will understand that I take it as high testimony to the post office that your letter has in fact found me. And what is the force of that "I?" Who am I if you write me? Can you look me in the eye and tell me? I and the eye—a *jeu* of *je* and *les yeux* would, I suppose, be the nearest French approximation to a fascinating structure of assonance in English, one Shakespeare's Juliet knew too.[4] See what Cixous and I do with "dieu" in *Voiles*. Diachronically, of course, there is just an accidental crossing of two lines of phonetic evolution. Synchronically, though, what effect does that have on your English-speaking sense of the self as spectator? I read because the eye reads—but no eye can read of itself. It is not the eye that reads but I who read with the eye, I who eye you, who eye the text.

Dear Dr. Pyper, have you ever read *anything*? I'm not just referring to a lack of general culture—one becomes wearily used to that—but to a broader question. What would it be—to *have read* something? Some kind of act of memory, of enlargement of the archive of your identity perhaps, but can one ever say that one *has read* something? There is always another reading—that is what iteration entails. Reach the final page, return to the beginning, and you read—a different book? The same book but with new eyes, a new I? I am what I have read, but I have never finally read anything. I shall be what I shall have read, perhaps, when yet another impossible condition is met. But what I have—or haven't—read and what you have or haven't read are not the same, even if the books were the same, which they are not and cannot be—and will never be again. The readings that intersect to constitute me are not yours.

So, dear Dr. Pyper, I am not sure I recognize this voice—these voices—you have written me. I even detect an unaccustomed tetchiness in my tone which may say more about your relationship to your elders and betters than it does about me. It is surely more than a coincidence that the answers I give and the questions I ask are those which best further your own idea, such as it is, of where this exchange is heading. Don't you risk doing what Plato—or was it Socrates?—did to Socrates' conversation partners, where their part in the conversation often reduces to "Nothing could indeed be clearer, my dear Socrates?" And you may have the advantage of me in making me speak English. Furthermore, Dr. Pyper, perhaps you should really write your paper in your own voice instead of borrowing or inventing mine.

This letter is, of course, unsigned,

J. Derrida.

***

Dear M. Derrida,

Well, yes indeed, nothing could be clearer—and from now on, I write my own voice. But that is my problem. If I have given you a voice, then is that not the problem of reading—the voice I give you, the voice you give Paul, the voice Paul gives Moses or Jesus—all constructed and all to be reconstructed—how do I read your reading of Paul's reading of Moses, let alone Paul's reading, if I cannot read? Nothing could be clearer—is that as clear as it could be? Clarity, it seems, is the problem. Paul in 2 Corinthians is clear, but not clear: there is a veil which moves from Moses to the faces of his Jewish readers but which is done away with in Christ. You take him to task for this in *Voiles*.[5]

But what is it we see when the veil is removed? How clear is the Exodus text? Is Moses in fact veiled, or is it that he is masked? Does his face *shine*, or is it *horned*? Does he unveil once he has spoken, or while he speaks? What would we see beneath the veil?[6]

Let's try a picture, one I would like to send you as a postcard (Figure 11.1). It comes from the Farfa bible, written and illustrated in Catalonia in the eleventh century. Ruth Mellinkoff, from long study of medieval depictions of Moses, regards it as a unique portrayal.[7]

Depicting Moses veiled is not something many painters have tried. How would we check the likeness? Here, however, Moses is double-faced. We see his face in three quarter view, both his eyes towards us, but looking to the right, where, attached to his head in profile is another face, its one visible eye gazing at the Israelites gathered to hear the reading of the law, we presume. In one hand Moses holds aloft the book. In the other, the left, he holds a stylus. What is puzzling, however, is that one of the Israelites is reaching forward and has his hand on the stylus too.

Fig. 11.1 Farfa Bible. Copyright Apostolica Vaticana. Used with permission. "Two-faced" Moses is in the center.

This picture is not a meeting of Socrates and Plato, but a meeting of Picasso and Roland Barthes. Who holds the pen—Moses in his white hand (Origen said this white leprous hand represents the failure of the works of the law) or his hearer, his reader? What are they writing? Is it Paul the Israelite who wrests the pen from Moses, or who guides his hand as he writes? Who is writing whom? Who is listening, who is reading? Who can see Moses, or Moses' eyes?

> First we feel. Then I write. This act of writing engenders the author. I write the genesis that occurs before the author. How does one write the genesis [or Genesis]? Just before? I write on writing. I turn on the other light.[8]

That is Hélène Cixous in "Writing Blind"—could that be *her* portrait in the Catalan Bible? The one who writes for Moses by another light? Or is that Paul? What of Paul's eyes? The same Paul (the *same* Paul?) who speaks of clarity in 2 Corinthians speaks of unclarity in 1 Corinthians 13, of seeing in a glass darkly. The same Paul—or is this Luke's Paul (although here he is Saul)?—is himself blinded by the light on the road to Damascus. Acts 9:8: "Saul arose from the ground; and when his eyes were opened, he could see nothing; so they led him by the hand and brought him into Damascus." The same Paul (the *same* Paul?) writes to the Galatians, "See what large letters I am writing to you with my own hand" (Galatians 6:11): large letters betokening a failing eye/I? The blind eye sees through blinding and then falls blind again.

Paul, the apostle of the clear vision, was once—perhaps—blinded Saul, if Luke is to believed. Do you remember *Memoirs of the Blind*?

> Each time a divine punishment is cast down upon sight in order to signify the mystery of election, the blind become witnesses to faith.

An inner conversion at first seems to transfigure light itself. Conversion of the inside, conversion on the inside: in order to enlighten the spiritual sky on the inside, the divine light creates darkness in the earthly sky outside. This veil between two lights is the experience of bedazzlement, the very bedazzlement that for example knocks Paul to the ground on the road to Damascus.[9]

Too much light.

In that moment, bedazzled Saul becomes a Jew, just as surely as he becomes Christian, though in fact neither occurs except in memory, and in Luke's memory at that. The Jewish Saul of Paul's memory is not the Jew Saul thought he was, however. Saul becomes the-Jew-seen-through-Christian-eyes. Saul is rent in two. Scales form on his eyes and fall from the light that blinds him so that he sees too clearly. Remember, you wrote:

> Sunflower [*tournesol*: turning to the sun] blindness, a conversion that twists the light and turns it upon itself to the point of dizziness, the blacking out of the one bedazzled, who sees himself go from brightness and clarity to even more clarity, perhaps to too much sun. This clairvoyance of the all-too-evident is Paul's madness. And one blames it on books, in other words, on the visibility of the invisible word: Festus cries, "You are out of your mind, Paul! Books [*grammata*] are driving you mad!"[10]

Too much light—too much reading.

Paul is one who has been blind but now sees or reads well—or all too well. In *Savoir*, her contribution to *Voiles*, Cixous tells the story of a woman, a Hélène Cixous, who once could hardly see, but now sees again—too well? "She had been born with the veil in her eye," she writes.[11] *Savoir* reveals an epistemology of the myopic. Unable to distinguish boundaries, only able to see clearly what is close, the myope is subject to what she calls "the reign of an eternal uncertainty that no prosthesis can dissipate," or in another way of putting it, "everything was perhaps" or "Do I see what I see?"[12] A blurring, a need to have the courage to approach the other close enough to see her, the danger of mistaking a stranger for one's own mother, of not recognizing one's own son, a sense of borders always dissolving into one another.

To move from myopia to clear-sightedness, she tells us, is one of the few truly unique moments a life can hold. In ten minutes, she moves from *being* a myope to *having had* myopia—a defining condition becomes a past accident, something that can be lost. She is no longer a myope, no longer able to not-see. Borders crystallize. Something is lost, something that may not have been visible before. In "Writing Blind," she writes: "I owe a large part of my writing to my nearsightedness. I am a woman. But before I am a woman I am a myope ... I belong to the Masonic Order of Myopes."[13] No longer.

There are remarkable parallels here to *The Eye*, a recently released Chinese film by the Pang Brothers.[14] A young woman, Mun, who has been blind since the age of two, has her sight restored by a corneal implant. The film develops as a deeply unsettling exploration of the way in which she tries to make sense of a world gradually coming into focus. Through the use of imaginative camera techniques, it becomes a vivid enactment for the spectators of the epistemology of the myope, of the way things look through eyes that will not focus.

As Mun's eyesight improves, she finds she has exchanged the problem of blindness for the problem of seeing too much. She begins to realize that among the resolving blurs she is seeing not just the living but the dead and that others around her are blind to them. She also sees shadowy figures who appear before death and accompany the dying to the next life. Mun's loss of blindness brings with it other painful losses. She loses not only her sense of security but also her community. A devoted member of an orchestra of the blind, she is now not allowed to take part in the gala performance for which she has been practicing. Her social status has changed. She is "no-longer-blind."

Italo Calvino's "The Adventure of a Near-Sighted Man" resonates here.[15] A young Italian man gets new spectacles. The world becomes new to him and he recovers a delight in just looking, to the extent that he has to relearn what is worth looking at. But this also changes his identity. He becomes a "man who wears glasses." The fact that such a detail becomes the first thing that people use to identify him makes his identity seem arbitrary and estranged: "If he inadvertently caught sight of himself in the mirror with his glasses on, he felt a keen dislike for his face, as if it were the typical face of a category of person alien to him."[16] When he returns to his native city and encounters his old love, he is caught in the paradox that when he wears his glasses she does not recognize him, but without them he cannot recognize her. "The eyeglasses that made the rest of the world visible to him ... made him invisible."[17]

Mirrors figure in Mun's story too, where they also threaten identity. As her vision continues to improve and she can decipher reflections, she realizes that the face she sees when she looks into mirrors is not her own. Terrified, she retreats back into a world of the dark, but the psychologist assigned to help her adjust to her new vision intervenes—she is now more than a patient to him. They decide to track down the donor of her corneas,

Ling, to get to the root of the problem and travel to Ling's home village. There they find her family. It turns out that from childhood Ling could see the dead and their shadowy companions and repeatedly tried to warn her neighbors of impending deaths that then took place. The villagers grew to hate her as a witch who was the cause of these deaths. Ling's long tragedy of rejection culminates in the aftermath of a disastrous fire in the village. As always, her frantic warnings of impending deaths are met with revilement. Many people die in the fire and she is blamed. She hangs herself in response to this rejection, not just because of her situation as an outcast but because the burden of what she sees is unbearable. Ling's mother, who defended her throughout her life, is embittered by her daughter's failure in giving up on herself and refuses to forgive her suicide. In Chinese belief, Ling is condemned every day to reenact her death until she is released. Mun alone can see Ling hang herself every evening. Mun's ability to see literally with Ling's eyes is able to bring the girl's mother to do the same and to forgive.

On their return to Hong Kong, Mun and her boyfriend are stuck in a huge traffic jam caused by a tanker accident. Mun sees crowds of shadow figures streaming to the scene and realizes that, like Ling, she is foreseeing a devastating fire and, like her, frantically but unavailingly tries to warn those around. In the ensuing explosion, hundreds are killed and Mun is blinded again, this time permanently, by flying debris. At the end of the film, she is resigned to her blindness, because she has seen the most beautiful things the world could offer. The last frames show her smiling as she meets up with the young psychologist. A story of two blindnesses, with only too much to be seen between.

If this resonates with Cixous, it also resonates with Paul. What, for Cixous and for Paul, corrects (corrects?) the eye is light. The operation, the removal of the veil, is an action of light: of the laser. As you write, M. Derrida,

> In the amplifying cave, or in the resonating cavity that engenders this radiance, there'll already have been need of two reflecting surfaces, two mirrors, parallel to each other and perpendicular to the rays. Two mirrors echo each other in parallel, an echo of light, in parallel, one next to the other, before there be light, before the luminous beam is projected and powerful enough, with a view to cutting, for example, they will have needed, like in nature, this double mirror with two voices ...[18]

Two voices: two voices in *Un ver de soie*; two characters, Ling and Mun, in *The Eye*; two writers in the Farfa illumination; Cixous and Derrida in *Voiles*; male and female, old and new: two testaments in parallel, perpendicular to the light, neither the source of light. What is a Laser, you ask? l.a.s.e.r—Light Amplification by Stimulated Emission of … Readings? A blinding light that gives sight. "And when I could not see because of the brightness of that light, I was led by the hand by those who were with me, and came to Damascus": Paul's testimony to the people of Jerusalem in Acts 22, Paul who was Saul.

Luke's Paul is not just the blinded one who now sees. He also blinds—or has blinded. In Acts 13 he is the agent by which the magician Elymas loses his sight "for a time." But more than sight is lost—or gained. Until this chapter, the man we have read in Acts is Saul. After this chapter, the name Saul only occurs in Paul's reports of others' speech to him when he recounts the incident of his own blindness and its healing (see Acts 22:7, 13; 26:14). This chapter is also the first time in the New Testament that the name Paul appears. The single, quite explicit, acknowledgment of this paradox of difference and identity is the phrase "Saul, who is also called Paul" [literally, even more compressed: "Saul, the also Paul," *Saulos de ho kai Paulos*] (Acts 13:9), the only biblical verse that brings these two names together. But the two names echo further. In this same chapter is the only reminiscence in the entire New Testament of the other Saul, Saul son of Kish, characterized as the king who is removed in David's favor (Acts 13:21). Not only do we have an after-echo of Saul, but the name Paul is pre-echoed in Acts 13:7 where the Roman proconsul in Paphos, Sergius *Paulus*, is introduced: Sergius Paulus whom Acts describes as a "believer." Paul's sermon in Acts 13:16–41 reiterates the theme of those who are genuinely chosen by God only to be supplanted—Samuel by a king, Saul by David, John by Jesus—Moses and the Jerusalem élite by Paul's message.

Saul takes on his new name, which is a Roman's name, not when he is blinded or when he has his sight restored, not at the point of illumination or healing, but when he becomes the agent, filled with the Holy Spirit, by whom another Jew is blinded. That act brings the first Paul, the gentile Sergius Paulus, to believe. Paul the myope—one of the Masonic order, but no longer. Does it take the moment of blindness and revelation for Paul to see Saul the Jew, and so what Paul the Jew might be?[19] With sight lost and then restored, who is that Saul—or Paul—sees in the mirror—Elymas the magician or Christ?

Arthur Miller's *Focus*, a novel which has startling echoes of the issues raised by Cixous, Calvino, and *The Eye*, develops a parable around Laurence Newman, an unremarkable and unreflectively anti-Semitic man, who is told to get glasses by his boss because he has given a job in the company to a visibly Jewish girl. He takes them home and tries them on in the bathroom. Miller records his experience as follows:

In the mirror in his bathroom, the bathroom he had used for nearly seven years, he was looking at what might very properly be called the face of a Jew. A Jew, in effect, had gotten into his bathroom. The glasses did just what he had feared that they would do to his face, but this was worse because this was real. … now with the lenses magnifying his eyeballs, the bags being colourless, lost prominence and the eyes fairly popped, glared. The frames seemed to draw his flat, shiny-haired skull lower and set off his nose, so that where it had once appeared a trifle sharp it now beaked forward from the nosepiece. He took the glasses off and slowly put them on again to observe the distortion.[20]

Not only Newman but also the other characters in the story read his new appearance as Jewish. In particular, there is a scene where Miller explores Newman's reactions to another woman being interviewed for a job, a woman who stirs his lust:

She was taking him for a Jew … She must not do that with her eyes! … He was sitting there in the guilt of the fact that the evil nature of the Jews and their numberless deceits, especially their sensuous lust for women—of which fact he had daily proof in the dark folds of their eyes and their swarthy skin—all were the reflections of his own desires with which he had invested them. For this moment he knew it and perhaps never again, for *in this moment her eyes had made a Jew of him*; and his monstrous desire was holding back his denial.[21]

Miller here is playing seriously with the idea that there is a Jewish appearance, a Jewish eye, a Jewish gaze, something that Sandor Gilman alludes to in *The Jew's Body*.[22] He cites, among other evidence of this, Francis Galton's composite picture of Jewish boys where Galton picked out the "cold scanning gaze" of the Jew as an essence of not just Jewish physiognomy but also of Jewish nature. "It is in the Jew's gaze that the pathology can be found," Gilman writes.[23]

Gilman refers to the dilemma of the Jewish healer, especially the psychoanalyst:

When the Jewish physician looks into the mirror he sees the person at risk, he sees the Jew; he also sees the physician, the healer. How can the image of the healer be the same as the image of the patient? How can the gaze which is pathological also be the gaze which diagnoses in order to cure?[24]

Can Jew and Christian read with each other's eyes? Is not the loss of Paul's coming to see through his blindness, the loss of Saul's Jewish eyes, the loss of not being able to see, or of being able not to see? How can the Jewish Saul/Paul be the healer for both the Jewish and the gentile blindness that he diagnoses—Saul/Paul, the blinded and restored who writes in "such large letters [*grammata*]?"

The patriarchs face blindness as they age: their eyes dim—Isaac, Jacob, and Joseph, among others. Moses' veiled eye, says Deuteronomy as it recounts his impending death (Deuteronomy 34:7), does not dim, nor, if we translate literally, "lose its moistness." The eye, as you write so movingly at the end of *Memoirs*, M. Derrida, is the instrument not so much of sight as of tears, blinded by the tears which clarity of vision brings.

Moses' eye remains moist. In a remarkable exposition from Rabbi Shimon in the Zohar on why God says he "appeared" rather than "spoke" to Abraham, Isaac, and Jacob, the rabbi reflects on the invisible colors above of which the patriarchs were aware but which only Moses has seen:

> The secret is: the eye closed and open.
> Closed, it sees the mirror that shines.
> Opened, it sees the mirror that does not shine.
> So, "I appeared" in the mirror that does not shine,
> which is open and revealed.
> This is described as seeing.
> But the mirror that shines, which is concealed—
> This is described as knowing, as it is written:
> "I was not known."[25]

It is Moses who sees with the closed eye, in this passage, a closed eye that no other could see with. Another veiling. Another place of tension with the biblical tradition. "An eyelid, a membrane, separates two kingdoms," writes Cixous.[26]

There are many veils—the veil in the eye, the veil over the face, the veil between the temples that is torn. "The messiah, the man-God and the Two Resurrections, voilà the great unveiler," you write in *Voiles*. "Perhaps it's because of that that at his death the veil of the temple tore."[27] The tearing of the veil and the breaking of the tablets, of what Paul calls "the dispensation of death," But for Paul, death is no condemnation of the law, it is the gift that resurrection demands. "When the law came, sin sprang to life, and I died" (Romans 7:9). Remarkable syntax of the I—if I, Paul, died, who speaks? Who sees? Who reads?

And is the veil, then, the veil of the law? Slavoj Žižek almost suggests so:

The first paradox to note is that the vicious dialectic of Law and its transgression elaborated by Saint Paul is the invisible third term, the "vanishing mediator" between the Jewish religion and Christianity—its spectre haunts both of them, although neither of the two religious positions actually occupies its place. On the one hand, the Jews are *not yet* there, that is, they treat the law as the written Real which does not engage them in the vicious superego cycle of guilt: on the other, as Saint Paul makes clear, the basic point of Christianity proper is precisely to *break out* of the vicious superego cycle of the Law and its transgression via Love.[28]

This may raise as many questions as it answers, (and should I mention Žižek to you, M. Derrida?) but it does rephrase the question we have raised. There is a point, an impossible point, an invisible point of transition between Christian and Jew, between Paul and Saul, a point where none can live, with too much light to see. We might want to rephrase Žižek's implications of supersession in which Christians have broken out of the law which Jews and have not reached. This Sauline/Pauline point might be one which Jews have had the sense not to venture towards, and which Christians have fallen away from. Between Saul and Paul is the slash (/), the interruption from outside which tears the fabric of the text.[29] Either way, the point of vision, the impossible blinding light, is a point at which one cannot stay.

Rabbi Marc-Alain Ouaknin, in his astonishing work *The Burnt Book*, tells us that "The breaking of the tables is not the destruction of the law; it is on the contrary the gift of the law in the form of its breaking ... Moses does not pass on, at first the Law, but its shattering; its impossibility of being an idol, the place of perfection."[30] For Ouaknin the coming of a man who "fulfils" scripture is itself idolatry. He quotes Daniel Sibony who writes that the New Testament is "an order of writings entirely organized around quotations; at each gaping in the text, when the thread that bears it is pierced, immediately a quotation comes along like a stitch that sews it up and acts as a basis."[31]

The New Testament fills in the holes in the Old Testament. The main upheaval brought by Christ "is not so much that he embodies the word, but that he identifies himself with that which is missing in the word, is left in suspense, and which Christ comes to fill in, plug, or rather identify with his person, to bring an end to that which is missing in any word, to that which disappoints in that which speaks when speech is uttered."[32]

For Ouaknin, "The Hebrew text and its Hebrew reader realize what could be called an anti-Christic coup. By introducing 'blanks' even where there are none, he makes time enter into the word to give it the chance of remaining in the planning stage, open to its impossible completion."[33]

That's what is needed. Let's repeat:

> Two mirrors echo each other in parallel, an echo of light, *in parallel*, one next to the other. Before there be light, before the luminous beam is projected and powerful enough, with a view to cutting, for example, they will have needed, like in nature, this double mirror with two voices ...[34]

The two mirrors cannot be the Christian Old and New Testament because there the veil is rent, and one is aligned with the other. They are not in parallel, which would mean that they can walk together but will not meet. The Christian testaments and the Jewish bible, the bible that is Tanakh and Talmud—they do stand in parallel. The two mirrors, one which reveals the holes that the other reveils. Revelatum: in Latin both revealed, and reveiled. Unveiling reveals the hidden, but not the invisible. The invisible needs the veil to make it seen, just as the visible may disappear behind the veil.

In her remarkable meditation addressed to you as that seeming oxymoron "a young Jewish saint," Cixous gives us another point on which we as biblical readers cannot rest: the summit, the crest:

> Now, look how having been poised for several weeks on the point of the word Jew, I have just noticed for the first time the oldest characters in my mythological imagination are those who also were manifested in face on a mountain, at the height of their solitude. Of their unbelievable solitude. I think of those two Separated Ones, by whom I have entered into a profound and tormented relationship with the bible. Separated by belief. In belief. I think of Moses, the sublime doubter, the one who goes out and does not enter. The sentence said, you shall not enter. I think of Abraham, the sublime non-doubter. The one who knew the threat of the promise. The sentence says: you shall do it. All three, beings of the summit, place without extent, crest without sides, pure elevation where speaks the word without a face. Being of the summit I say, absolutely far from the cemetery which he fears, he who, if he knew it, is chosen for the summit without a third.[35] A witness is necessary.

How many times have I reread the bible to follow them, in following them. And by dint of not understanding and of not understanding, and of asking why, how I've ended up by falling silent and accepting the unacceptable. For everything that passes us by passes through the spectres of scripture its ellipses, its *asyndeta*, its dazzling juxtaposition, there is no passage way, there has never existed a dictionary between the language of God, or rather God-the-sentence (he talks curtly in sentences) and the language of mortals. But it is necessary to read the whole of Genesis on one's knees on its pebbles to approach this Abraham of Nothing-saying. God says. It's done. One must approach by means of scripture while cutting the means of scripture. As the philosophers of the heart, of Kierkegaard and Jacques Derrida, have proved, it is there that there is an unimpartable secret. But one can feel its waves and tremble because of them.[36]

Dear M. Derrida, thank you. Perhaps you help me to read by showing me how *not to have read* a page of scripture, not to worry because my eyes are veiled and not to strive to clear away that veiling, to read clearly. You teach me how not to see what would blind me, or how my blindness comes from seeing. You speak beautifully of the weaving and the embroidering of the veils, the stitches that are added, but Rabbi Ouaknin makes me ask what I can do now. What are those after Paul, coming to the text from outside the Jewish fold, to do with a torn veil, letting through a light too bright to read by? Do we embroider it, or, as a strange slip of the fingers indicated to me in writing this paper, is what we have to do not to embroider it but to darn it, to sew it up, so that the holes show? The patient thrifty task of darning, in French *raccomodage*, which also means "reconciliation." Revealed is reveiled, not with another veil, but with a patched veil always tearing and always stitched back together from its torn fragments, with its seams/seems showing: a darned veil that makes the invisible the hidden.[37]

If once again I may take your name in vain, and paraphrase you, I hold to the words that end *Mémoires d'aveugle*: "Je ne sais pas, il faut croire. (…)"[38] Can I read this as "*I* do not know, *he* must believe?" Can "he" be—you? Or can here the Christian and the Jew address each other across the hiatus, across the tear, across the abyss? "I do not know—he must believe?" Or perhaps even more distortedly, "Je ne sais pas: il faut lire … une page d'écriture?"

References

1. Hélène Cixous and Jacques Derrida, *Voiles* (Paris: Galilée, 1998), pp. 71–74; trans. Geoffrey Bennington, *Veils* (Stanford: Stanford University Press, 2001), pp. 75–78.
2. On this point see Elliot Wolfson, "Circumcision, Vision of God and Textual Interpretation: From Midrashic Trope to Mystical Symbol," *History of Religions* 27 (1987): 289–315, esp. 210–215 where *Zohar* 3:72b–73a is cited and expounded.
3. Jacques Derrida, *La carte postale: De Socrate à Freud et au-delà* (Paris: Flammarion, 1980).
4. See *Romeo and Juliet* Act 3 Scene 2, lines 45–49:

Say thou but "I"
And that bare vowel I shall poison more
Than the death-darting eye of cockatrice.
I am not I if there be such an "I";
Or those eyes shut that make thee answer "I".

Fuller study of the significance of this pun throughout the play would repay the effort.

5. Cixous and Derrida, *Voiles*, p. 74; *Veils*, p.77.
6. For recent discussions of these exegetical points, see Thomas B. Dozeman, "Masking Moses and Mosaic Authority in Torah," *Journal of Biblical Literature* 119 (2000): 21–45 and John Van Seters, *The Life of Moses: The Yahwist as Historian in Exodus–Numbers* (Louisville: Westminster/John Knox Press, 1994), pp. 356–360. The uncertainties derive from the ambiguity of the rare verb *qaran*, which Jerome translates as "horned" but the Septuagint takes as "shining," and the use of unique word *masweh*, which may be etymologically linked to a verb for "covering," but which could be either a mask or a veil. These are combined with the unparalleled nature of the episode where the understanding of the context is in fact the point at the issue, not an aid to interpretation.
7. This illumination is discussed in Ruth Mellinkoff, *The Horned Moses in Medieval Art and Thought* (Berkeley: University of California Press, 1970), pp. 7–8 and is reproduced as fig. 11 on p. 111. Mellinkoff herself makes the allusion to Picasso, but not to Barthes. The original manuscript is held in the Vatican Library, catalog number 5729, folio 6v.
8. Hélène Cixous, "Writing Blind: Conversation with the Donkey," in *Stigmata: Escaping Texts* (London: Routledge, 1998), pp. 139–152 (143).
9. Jacques Derrida, *Memoirs of the Blind: The Self-Portrait and Other Ruins*, trans. Pascale-Anne Brault and Michael Naas (Chicago: University of Chicago Press, 1993), p. 112. The original edition is *Mémoires d'aveugle: L'autoportrait et autres ruines* (Éditions de la réunion des musées nationaux, 1990).
10. Derrida, *Memoirs*, p. 117. Translation slightly modified: in Derrida's French original, Festus cries: 'Tu es fou, Paul. Les livres [*grammata*] te rendent fou' (*Mémoires*, p. 119), rendered by Brault and Naas, presumably under the influence of, e.g., the RSV translation of Acts 26:24 as "Too much learning is driving you mad."
11. Derrida and Cixous, *Veils*, p. 6.
12. Derrida and Cixous, *Veils*, p. 6.
13. Cixous, "Writing Blind," p. 140.
14. *The Eye*, Hong Kong, 2002.
15. The story is part of Calvino's collection *Difficult Loves* (London: Vintage, 1999) [original Turin: Giulio Enaudi ed. s.p.a., 1957; English trans. William Weaver, 1983], pp. 82–90.
16. Calvino, *Difficult Loves*, p. 85.
17. Calvino, *Difficult Loves*, p. 88.
18. Derrida and Cixous, *Veils*, p. 49.
19. An earlier insight into the crucial nature of this moment of Paul's identity in Acts is to be found in F.C. Synge, "Acts 13.9: Saul, who is also Paul," *Theology* 63 (1960): 199–200. The implications of this dual naming and dual identity are also explored in Dieter Hildebrandt, *Saul/Paul: Ein Doppelleben* (Munich: Carl Hauser Verlag, 1968).
20. Arthur Miller, *Focus* (London: Methuen, 2002; original edition New York: Reynal and Hitchcock, 1945), p. 24; my emphasis.
21. Miller, *Focus*, p. 33.
22. Sandor Gilman, *The Jew's Body* (New York: Routledge, 1991).
23. Gilman, *The Jew's Body*, p. 68.
24. Gilman, *The Jew's Body*, p. 71.
25. Daniel Chanan Matt, *Zohar: The Book of Enlightenment* (Mahwah: Paulist Press, 1983), p. 109.
26. Cixous, "Writing Blind," p. 140.
27. Cixous and Derrida, *Veils*, p. 78.
28. Slavoj Žižek, *The Fragile Absolute: or, Why is the Christian Legacy Worth Fighting For?* (London: Verso, 2000), p. 145.

29. See here the wonderfully interwoven tapestry of text and commentary that Robert Gibbs provides in his *Why Ethics: Signs of Responsibilities* (Princeton: Princeton University Press, 2000), especially in the chapter "Why Read?" (pp. 86–113) where he knits and knots threads from Derrida and Lévinas on the trope of text as fabric. All readings reknot the threads of the text broken by the interruption, so the knotting becomes the trace of the interruption itself. In particular, Gibbs draws attention to Derrida's 'En ce moment même dans cet ouvrage me voici' in *Textes pour Emmanuel Lévinas*, ed. F. Laruelle (Paris: Jean-Michel Place, 1980), pp. 21–60 (trans. "At This Very Moment in This Work Here I Am," by Ruben Berezdivin, in *Re-reading Lévinas*, eds. Robert Bernasconi and Simon Critchley [Bloomington: Indiana University Press, 1991], pp. 11–48) where Derrida responds in kind to the pervasive metaphors of tearing, weaving, and knotting in Lévinas's discussion of text and reading in *Otherwise than Being*. The naming of Christ as interruption could, or maybe did, start or unravel a whole new thread of text, reading and discourse. Here, it must remain a loose end.
30. Marc-Alain Ouaknin, *The Burnt Book: Reading the Talmud*; trans. Llewellyn Brown (Princeton: Princeton University Press, 1995), p. 300.
31. Ouaknin, *The Burnt Book*, p. 300; quoting Daniel Sibony, *La Juive: Une transmission d'inconscient* (Paris: Grasset, 1983), p. 170.
32. Ouaknin, *The Burnt Book*, p. 301.
33. Ouaknin, *The Burnt Book*, p. 301.
34. Cixous and Derrida, *Veils*, p. 49.
35. The text here is shot through with puns in French between *cime* [height], *tiers* [third], and *cimetière* [cemetery].
36. Hélène Cixous, *Portrait de Jacques Derrida en Jeune Saint Juif* (Paris: Galilée, 2001), p. 112 (my translation).
37. See again note 29.
38. Derrida, *Mémoires*, p. 130.

CHAPTER 12
To Love the Tallith More Than God

TIMOTHY K. BEAL AND TOD LINAFELT

The Question of This Trip

The history of truth, which is a short way of saying the history of faith in a truth hoped for but not seen, is a history of veils, a history of separation: truth as the anticipated unveiling of that which is concealed, or truth as ultimate agreement or adequation between the representation and the thing being represented (that is, the removal of the veil of language that separates the word from the thing).

The veil: separation from what it leads us to believe lies behind it: the truth, the thing itself, the beloved, the light of revelation.

As such, the idea of the veil inaugurates the very possibility of revelation, as *revealability*. Without the veil, there could be no idea of unveiling, no faithful expectation of a final revelation of an otherwise never fully known other, no assurance of things hoped for, no conviction of things not seen.[1] Revelation, and faith in its coming, is predicated on the veil. Without the veil there is no revelation. It goes without saying. So there's no getting away from the veil, no Morpheus with a red pill to lift the veil, pull you through to the other side and show you the truth beyond the veil of *The Matrix*. "You take the blue pill and the story ends. You wake in your bed and believe whatever you want to believe. You take the red pill and you stay in Wonderland and I show you how deep the rabbit hole goes. Remember that all I am offering is the truth."[2] Truth is, the matrix and the truth of it all are all caught up in the logic of the veil, including Morpheus

175

and his blue and red pills. Once you're on the veil or in its folds, there's no way off.

If your taste in epigrams runs more to the high than to the low, consider Milton's "Sonnet 19":

> Methought I saw my late espoused saint
> Brought to me like Alcestis from the grave,
> Whom Jove's great son to her glad husband gave,
> Rescued from death by force though pale and faint.
> Mine as whom washed from spot of childbed taint,
> Purification in the old law did save,
> And such, as yet once more I trust to have
> Full sight of her in heaven without restraint,
> Came vested all in white, pure as her mind:
> Her face was veiled, yet to my fancied sight,
> Love, sweetness, goodness in her person shined
> So clear, as in no face with more delight.
> But O as to embrace me she inclined
> I waked, she fled, and day brought back my night.[3]

Milton wrote this poem after having been blind for many years, and after the death of his wife Katharine (*katharos*, the pure one), a wife he never saw in the flesh owing to his blindness. Despite the fact that her face remains veiled in the poem, there is a proximate revelation ("Love, sweetness, goodness in her person shined/So clear, as in no face with more delight"), which promises a fuller, more permanent unveiling to come ("And such, as yet once more I trust to have/Full sight of her in heaven without restraint"). So the veil remains, even in the poet's "fancied sight," and even in heaven, if only by dint of being lifted.

For Milton as for Morpheus, the desire to lift the veil depends on a veil being there in the first place. It's a hope for, indeed a faith in, an unveiling, a revelation, an apocalypse. It's an affirmation of faith as a reaffirmation of the veil. Such faith is caught in the logic of the veil.

Of course, none of this is any great revelation for Jacques Derrida. He has written enough, or too much, on and about the veil and its "baffling economy of seduction."[4] He himself admits as much in "A Silkworm of One's Own," the response to Hélène Cixous's "Savoir." He's utterly weary of veils, of thinking and writing about "the truth as a history of veils."[5]

> If you only knew how fatigued I feel at these revelations and unveilings, … weary of the opposition that is not an opposition, of revelation as veiling, vice versa … I no longer want to write about

the veil, do you hear, right on the veil or on the subject of the veil, around it or in its folds, under its authority or under its law ... With other *Schleiermachers* of all sorts, I have used and abused truth—as untruth of course, come come, *et passim*, and of revelation and unveiling as veiling, of course, in so many languages. Go and see if I'm lying.[6]

Yet it seems there's no way off. "You poor thing," he tells himself, "you poor thing: finishing with the veil will always have been the very movement of the veil: an un-veiling, unveiling oneself, reaffirming the veil in unveiling ... You'll end up in immanence—and the un-veiling will still remain a movement of the veil."[7]

He's weary of these travails on the veil: "Fed up with veils and sails." Odysseus waylaid, on layover with Calypso (whose name in Greek means "I hide," "I cover," "I veil"). "On what footing to make a fresh start, that's the question of this trip."[8] How to leave behind the veils and their promises of revelation, the Calypsos and their promises of *apocalypsis*? How, when even the possibility of getting away from Calypso is predicated on Calypso, the covering, the veiling, being there, standing between him and something other?

There's something about what Derrida calls "today's revelation" by his close friend Hélène Cixous that intimates a possible way away. Something about her intimate revelation to him of a veil—her secret myopia—that had always been there, until just before she revealed it to him. "I know Hélène Cixous, I have known her ... for more than thirty-three years, but since forever without knowing," *sans savoir*, that is, without knowing this intimate secret, this veil over her eyes, and without knowing her new text, *Savoir*, which he's reading while on this trip.

> I have known her forever without ever knowing what she confides here in *Savoir*, i.e.—and this would be, feeble hypothesis, today's revelation, the revolution of an avowal at last disarmed—that she could not see: all this time she will have been short-sighted, in truth almost blind. Blind to the naked eye up to the day she had an operation—yesterday.[9]

There's something about her revelation of this veil "in her eye" and "in her soul," now removed, which turned out to be no great revelation, which left her longing for the old veil, her old myopic faith in things not seen. Something about all that seems to provoke his weariness concerning his own numerous "still penelopean works" of weaving and unweaving on the veil. Something about all that seems to call to mind, call to memory, something likewise disarmingly intimate about himself, something in which or with which he might be able to escape the logic of the veil: namely, his first "reference cloth," his *tallith*, his Jewish prayer shawl, which refers back instead of ahead, which looks forward to no revelation but rather calls to mind an event that has already taken place in all its fullness: the giving of the law.

Scenario for a Soap

Somewhere in one of the numerous "introductions" to Derrida's thought (we can't recall which at this point, perhaps in Norris or Culler) there is the statement that Derrida entertains "no nostalgia for lost presence." That never seemed quite correct. We could go back for example to the essay on Jabès from *Writing and Difference*: "God no longer speaks to us; he has interrupted himself: we must take words upon ourselves. We must be separated from life and communities, and must entrust ourselves to traces, must become people of vision because we have ceased hearing the voice from within the immediate proximity of the garden."[10] A necessary absence, yet a felt absence nonetheless. Or more recently from *Cinders*: "In this sentence I see the tomb of a tomb, the monument of an impossible tomb—forbidden, like the memory of a cenotaph, deprived of the patience of mourning."[11] Memory may be two steps removed, mourning may be deprived, but there is nonetheless a haunting. And yet, in "A Silkworm of One's Own," it is revealed that to the extent that Jacques Derrida *did* exhibit no nostalgia for lost presence, it may well be because presence was never lost—it was, rather, safely tucked away in a bag.

> For after all: before the experience of what remains to be seen, my reference cloth was neither a veil nor a canvas [*une toile*], but a shawl. A prayer shawl I like to touch more than to see, to caress every day, to kiss without even opening my eyes or even when it remains wrapped in a paper bag into which I stick my hand at night, eyes closed.[12]

Derrida continues:

> It was given to me by my mother's father, Moses … I no longer wear it. I simply place my fingers or lips on it, almost every evening, except when I'm traveling to the ends of the earth, because like an animal it waits for me, well hidden in its hiding place, at home, it never travels. I touch it without knowing what I am doing or asking in so doing.[13]

Even the "always already" of deconstruction—that cliche that one feels one has always already heard—seems not to apply to the *tallith*:

> *Before* hiding from sight like an opaque veil,
> *before* letting light through like a translucent veil
> *before* showing the thing like a transparent veil
> *before* hinting to sight like a veil that lets one make out, through the diaphanous light, the thing and the forms it is embracing,
> *before* all else, my *tallith* touches itself.[14]

The prayer shawl represents, like prayer itself, the event which precedes all representation of it, which precedes all memory of it, which precedes, quite simply, *all.*

> You don't keep a prayer waiting, what's more it never lets itself be waited for, it comes before everything, before the order, before the question, before the reply, before dialogue, before knowledge, before the "this is" or the "what is…?"[15]

good

Derrida goes into no little amount of detail in describing both his own *tallith* in particular—given to him by his mother's father Moses, borrowed for a few years by his own father after whose death Derrida "inherited it a second time" —and the nature of the *tallith* in general. He notes the biblical origin in Numbers 15 of the *tzitzit*, or fringes, that adorn the *tallith*. "You have the fringe so that, when you see it, you will remember all the commandments of the Lord and do them" (15:39). Derrida applies what is said about the *tzitzit* to the *tallith* as a whole: "It is worn in memory of the Law."[16] And again later, "This *tallith* depends on the One of the unique, the singular event whose repetition repeats only, and that's history, the 'once only' of the Law given."[17]

It is this singularity of the event, this "irreducible reference to the One," Derrida avers, that distinguishes the logic of the *tallith* from the logic of the veil. Such emphasis on irreducibility, on something outside or before discourse, is somewhat puzzling coming from Jacques Derrida. Indeed, as one of the countervoices in "A Silkworm of One's Own" puts it:

> It looks so unlike you, you look so unlike yourself, it looks so unlike the image of you that circulates in these regions. It's as though you were talking about the scenario for a soap in which (as happens) you have to change a character because the actor died or broke his contract.[18]

You have to love that image. It's as though the voice-over comes on, informing us that "the role of philosopher of deconstruction will be played by John R. Searle." The response Derrida offers to the above objection is telling: "You mustn't believe in images." The veil has fundamentally to do with seeing, with seeing more fully. Even when the veil is in place, obstructing full vision, it implies that there can be a lifting, an unveiling, a revelation at which point everything will be seen in all its glory. But of course, the fringes of the shawl have also to do with vision: "When you *see* them, you will remember all the commandments of the Lord ..." However, it is not a seeing that becomes a "vision" of what was hidden, a vision of glory, but rather a seeing that evokes loss by invoking memory—one cannot remember what has not been forgotten. The logic of veiling and unveiling is future-oriented, apocalyptic according to the popular meaning of the word—oriented toward the end of time—as well as in the more literal meaning of uncovering; whereas the logic of the *tallith* (and the fringes that adorn it) is past-oriented, looking back to the giving of the law and the subsequent forgetting of it. "It veils or hides nothing," Derrida writes, "it shows or announces no Thing, it promises the intuition of nothing. Before seeing or knowing, before fore-seeing or fore-knowing, it is worn in memory of the law."[19] And it is telling that Derrida moves quickly from the fringes on the corners of the shawl, which one sees and in the seeing is reminded of the law, to the shawl itself, which is less seen than it is felt. One wears the shawl, wraps oneself in it, or, in the case of Derrida, touches it while it waits in its bag.

Paul Moses

As Derrida works to set apart the logic of the *tallith* from the logic of the veil, he comes, not surprisingly, to Paul's treatment in 2 Corinthians 3 of the "veil" (Greek *kalumma*, "covering"; Latin Vulgate *velamen*) that separates the mind from divine glory for those not turned to Christ. Paul's scriptural basis for this theologic of the veil is the story of Moses' "veil" in Exodus 34:29–35. In that story, when Moses returned from the mountain (for the second time) with the tablets of the law, his face radiated light (Greek Septuagint *dedoxastai*, "glorified") and terrified the Israelite people. After instructing them in the law and before returning to the tent to speak further with God, he would cover his face with a "veil" (Hebrew *masveh*, "cover" or "sheath"; Greek Septuagint *kalumma*, "covering"; Latin Vulgate *velum*). According to Paul in 2 Corinthians 3, a similar veil now covers the minds of those Jews who continue to follow the letter of the law, the old covenant of Moses, which he calls the "ministry of death" (*diakonia tou thanatou*; also called *diakonia tes katakriseos*, "ministry of condemnation"). "Whenever Moses is read," Paul declares, a *kalumma* is drawn over their minds, separating them from the full revelation of divine glory (*doxa*) in Christ.[20] But for those who turn to Christ, living according to the new covenant of justification by faith that Paul calls the "ministry of spirit" (*diakonia tou pneumatos,* also called *diakonia tes dikaiosunes,* "ministry of righteousness" or "justification"), the veil has been lifted and full glory has been revealed.[21]

In Paul's realized eschatology, then, the apocalypse (*apo-kalupsis*) has already happened for those who have turned to Christ. The *kalumma* has been removed and followers of Christ are living in the full glory of apocalypse.

But by declaring that the apocalypse has already happened, is happening, for the faithful, by lifting the veil and ushering them over to its other side, Paul is also reaffirming the presence of the veil. It needs to remain there, for it serves another purpose in his theological rhetoric: namely, as a veil of separation between the old covenant and the new, and especially between Jews who continue to adhere to that old covenant and those Jews and Gentiles who have turned to Christ. For Paul, then, the veil remains as a memory of the law quite different from Derrida's *tallith.*[22] To see it is to remember the old covenant, separating those turned to Christ from those whose minds remain captive behind it. Likewise for so many post-Pauline Christianities, in which Paul's supersessionist theologic of the veil has been reinforced and embellished without ceasing.[23]

For Paul, then, the veil exists in order to be removed, to reveal, for those with eyes to see, the full glory of God. Indeed, for those who turn to Christ, it has already been removed. But does the same hold true regarding Moses' "veil" in the Exodus story on which Paul draws? Is it, too, beholden to the logic of the veil? Is the giving of the Torah, the memory of which the *tallith* and its fringes bear witness, a revelation according to Paul's logic of the veil? Or might it be in fact something closer to the logic of the *tallith?* Let's see.

The key passages are in Exodus 33 and 34, in which, for the second time, God gives Moses the commandments to be inscribed on the tablets of the covenant. (Recall that Moses smashed the previous tablets in a rage when he descended the mountain to find the people dancing and reveling—"running wild"—in the presence of the golden calf.) Before God gives the commandments, Moses makes a request: "Show me your glory [Hebrew *kabod*]" (33:18).

> And he said, "I will make all my goodness pass before you, and will proclaim before you the name, 'The Lord,' and I will be gracious to whom I will be gracious, and will show mercy on whom I will

show mercy. But," he said, "you cannot see my face; for no one shall see me and live." And the Lord continued, "See, there is a place by me where you shall stand on the rock; and while my glory passes by I will put you in a cleft of the rock, and I will cover you with my hand until I have passed by; then I will take away my hand, and you shall see my back; but my face shall not be seen" (Exodus 34:19–23; NRSV translation).

Chapter 34 then gives us the content of the renewed covenant, along with the information that Moses spent forty days and forty nights "there with the LORD" on the mountain. Then, *déjà vu*, we see Moses once again coming down the mountain, tablets in hand:

> Moses came down from Mount Sinai. As he came down from the mountain with the two tablets of the covenant in his hand, Moses did not know that the skin of his face shone [Hebrew *qaran 'or*; translated into the Greek Septuagint as *dedoxastai*, "glorified"] because he had been talking with God. When Aaron and all the Israelites saw Moses, the skin of his face was shining, and they were afraid to come near him. But Moses called to them; and Aaron and all the leaders of the congregation returned to him, and Moses spoke with them. Afterward all the Israelites came near, and he gave them in commandment all that the Lord had spoken with him on Mount Sinai. When Moses had finished speaking with them, he put a masveh on his face [*masveh* translated into the Greek as *kalumma*; Latin Vulgate as *velum*; "veil" in most English translations]; but whenever Moses went in before the Lord to speak with him, he would take the *masveh* off, until he came out; and when he came out and told the Israelites what he had been commanded, the Israelites would see the face of Moses, that the skin of his face was shining; and Moses would put the *masveh* on his face again, until he went in to speak with him (Exodus 34:29–35; NRSV modified).

The "veil" (*masveh*) in this text hides nothing. Notice the difference between what Exodus says about Moses' veil and what Paul says about it. Paul states that the children of Israel "could not gaze at Moses' face because of the glory of his face," and that Moses "put a veil over his face in order to keep the people from gazing." But Exodus 34 states that although the people were afraid (at least initially) when they saw the skin of his face shining, nevertheless they beheld it and came near to Moses when he called to them, and they listened as he spoke all that God had commanded him. Only after he *finished* speaking with them did he don the *masveh*. Then he removed it again upon entering the tent of meeting to speak with God. In Exodus 34, the *masveh* doesn't veil or hide or otherwise separate off glory from the people. Rather its function is to mark Moses' new primary role (now that liberation from Egypt has been completed) as the transmitter of tradition, of the Law—in other words, as a learner and a teacher. The veil is removed when he learns Torah from God and when he teaches Torah to Israel. The unveiled face of Moses in Exodus 34 is not the theophanic face of divine presence, as it is in Paul's text, but the face of dialogue, of hearing and speaking. "The shining face is characterized by language."[24] It is not outside time or at the end of time, but firmly embedded in the day-to-day and the here-and-now. The imperfect Hebrew verbs in the passage imply ongoing action, that is, from this point on Moses will be continually repeating this action of veiling and unveiling. This is hardly a final revelation.

But if the Exodus passage does not operate by the same logic of the veil that Derrida has critiqued in Paul and elsewhere, how might it relate to the logic of the *tallith*? There is, after all, no explicit mention of the *tallith* here. Surely not. But consider the following comment from Rashi in which he provides this version of God's response to Moses' request to see God's glory:

> The time has come for you to see My glory, as much as I permit you to see. For I want and will to teach you the order of prayer ... of mercy pleas, so that even if the merit of the patriarchs is exhausted, teach Israel to do as you now see Me doing, wrapped in a *tallith* and proclaiming the Thirteen Attributes ...[25]

The image of God wrapped in a *tallith* is striking. And since Rashi reads 33:19 as "I shall call on the name of God in your presence," the idea is that God is praying to God. But beyond this paradox, what is Rashi doing here? He is filling out what it means for Moses to have seen God's back, what it means to have a revelation that does not really reveal. In fact, he takes the scene of revelation and turns it into a scene of teaching and learning: God models prayer for Moses, who will then model it for Israel in turn. Notice, moreover, that here, at the heart of the revelation, it is the *future absence* of God's full presence that is emphasized: there will be a time when Israel will need to pray, and here is how to do it. The story reminds us that the *tallith* is not just a shawl but a *prayer* shawl, even if, as in Derrida's case, it is no longer worn in order to pray. And prayer, unlike revelation which depends on the "desire for a total vision, without history, without development,"[26] implies both language and time. The point then could not be more different from Paul's point in 2 Corinthians. Avivah Zornberg notes the poignancy of the scene in Exodus 33 where the people gaze at *Moses'* back as he enters the tent of meeting to speak with God: "The hungry gaze of the people is not hypnotized by a presence, but provoked by an absence."[27] Paul, on the other hand, gives us almost precisely the image of being hypnotized by a presence: "And all of us, with unveiled faces, seeing the glory of the Lord as though reflected in a mirror, are being transformed into the same image from one degree of glory to another" (2 Corinthians 3:18). Time ceases to exist, language is useless, memory irrelevant; there is only glory, and more glory.

In Times New Roman

"But *we are already speaking in Latin,*" Derrida reminds us in "Faith and Knowledge," reflecting on a conference on the topic of religion which took place in Capri, Italy in 1994.

> For the Capri meeting, the "theme" I believed myself constrained to propose, religion, was named in Latin, let us never forget. Does not "the question of *religio*," however, quite simply merge, one could say, with the question of Latin? By which should be understood, beyond a "question of language and culture," the strange phenomenon of Latinity and of its globalization ... For everything that touches religion in particular, for everything that speaks "religion," for whoever speaks religiously or about religion, Anglo-American remains Latin. *Religion* circulates in the world, one might say, like an *English* word [*comme un mot anglais*] that has been to Rome and taken a detour to the United States. Well beyond its strictly capitalist or politico-military figures, a hyper-imperialist appropriation has been underway now for centuries ... From here on, the word "religion" is calmly (and violently) applied to things which have always been and remain foreign to what this word names and arrests in its history. The same remark could apply to many other words, for the entire "religious vocabulary" beginning with "cult," "faith," "belief," "sacred," "holy," "saved," "unscathed" (*heilig*).[28]

And, of course, "revelation." Indeed, in *Veils* and "Faith and Knowledge" and elsewhere, one central question is whether there's any way to talk about religion that isn't already fundamentally Christian, specifically Roman-Anglo-American Christian. Perhaps that's why he published the first half of "Faith and Knowledge" (the part he presented at the Capri meeting) in *italics*, sloping away from the upright *Roman* type. *Italic*, after all, has sometimes meant those regions of Italy apart from Rome. On the other hand, it has also been used to refer to the *Vetus Italia*, the old Italic Latin version of the Bible before Jerome's Vulgate translation. Indeed, one question we hear him asking is whether a "non-Christian" discourse on religion is possible in these New Roman Times. To want such a discourse is understandable for many reasons, not least among them being the fact that the logic of veils and revelations is itself caught up in the insidious anti-Jewish logic of Christian supercessionism, as we have seen in Paul and Augustine, and as we can easily imagine in Luther, Calvin, *etc.*

To make matters more complicated, Judaism itself is also caught up in the logic of the veil on various levels and in various folds. Indeed, in many relatively early texts, there is an unmistakably revelatory warp being woven into biblical Hebrew designs for curtains. For example, the Merkevah mystical text of 3 Enoch (45:1), among others, describes a heavenly curtain or veil (*pargod*) that separates the immediate presence of God from the rest of heaven, simultaneously protecting angelic beings from divine glare and hiding divine mystery.[29] Earlier in 3 Enoch 17, and in several other ancient rabbinic texts (apparently of Babylonian origin), the first and lowest of the seven heavens is described as a veil called *Wilon*, a Latin loanword deriving from *velum.* "Like a curtain drawn across a doorway, … those within can see those without, but those without cannot see those within."[30]

To be sure, the *tallith* offers at least a partial alternative to Latinspeak about "religion" and "religious vocabularies," including, above all, the vocabulary of revelation. As a reference cloth for a fresh start, it shows (dare we say) promise. Yet it, too, appears to have a few snags that are easily twisted into the logic of the veil. Even in Rashi, where the *tallith* functions as a symbol of prayer it also serves to cover God's glory. God's demonstration, revelation, of how to pray, must have been something to see, and can we imagine Moses the student not hoping for a peek under the *tallith* of this most unusual teacher? Derrida recalls briefly a childhood scene from Yom Kippur, the Day of Atonement: a father holding his *tallith* over two sons, who are "stifling a little under the solemn protection."[31] The scene is undoubtedly the *birkat kohanim* (the "priests' blessing"), and tradition has it that the custom of the father drawing his tallith over the heads of himself and his sons originates in the biblical prohibition from Exodus 33:20 against seeing the face of God, since God's presence is thought to be manifest at the spot where the priests are standing. Tradition apparently also has it—as perhaps Derrida knows?—that whoever looks directly at the priests during the blessing will go blind. And in some communities it is reported that the first look results in blindness, and the second in death; which of course raises the wonderfully paradoxical question, "If you go blind the first time, how can you look a second time?"[32] The *tallith* would seem to function here as a veil, a covering that protects one from overexposure to divinity; and if the *tallith* is meant to protect one from blindness, blindness is meant to protect one from death. Blindness as a veil: we are back then to Cixous.

It appears that the history of the *tallith* has not escaped the logic of the veil unscathed. And that as well should be no great revelation to Derrida, who writes of how, "by ineluctable contagion, no semantic cell can remain alien ... 'unscathed,' in this apparently borderless process [of globalatinization]," which is "essentially Christian, to be sure."[33] Essentially Christian perhaps but clearly not solely Christian. It is too late to separate Paul and Moses completely, to separate memory from anticipation, the veil from the *tallith*. Indeed, in a parenthetical aside that reminds us of the intimate nature of this confessional essay, Derrida notes, "my young dead brother, dead before my birth, was also called Paul, Paul Moses."[34] The late Paul Moses, whom Derrida arrived to late to know, haunts the essay beyond this parenthetical aside. "So late have I loved thee," Derrida quotes Augustine earlier in the essay. "'Late' evaluates, desires, regrets, accuses, complains—and sighs for the verdict, so late, very late, late, quite simply (*atkenos*), always comes the time for loving. You were with me and I was not with you."[35] Paul Moses is with Jacques, inevitably, in a way that Jacques never was with him.

So too are Paul and Moses with us inevitably, we who are late compared to them. Yet each of them was, in turn, late. Moses we are told in Exodus (32:1) was late in coming down from the mountain, and it was this lateness that led to the peoples' demand for tangible gods before which they could dance. And that other Paul was aware not only of his lateness as an apostle ("Last of all, as to one untimely born, he appeared also to me" [1 Corinthians 15]), but also, he thought, the lateness of the time: "I mean, brothers and sisters, the appointed time has grown short" (1 Corinthians 7:9). And yet the *parousia* that Paul so fervently expected to see was late in coming, is late in coming. And we, of course, are too late for either Moses or Paul, too late to accept either without question, and too late to pretend to do without them. Too late, finally, to separate the veil from the shawl. And perhaps that's okay. Perhaps one need not give up the mystical longing to see the face of God, to experience fully, even for an instant, glory—divine or otherwise—in order to value the tangible shawl. The woven, wooly shawl mostly reminds us of a past that is truly past rather than a glorious future soon to come. It is in any case too late for this future to come "soon." We know too much; we have forgotten too much; we have *seen* too much.

One can love the *tallith* more than God, and yet, if the opportunity arose, still want to have a peek underneath it.

References

1. Now faith is the assurance of things hoped for, the conviction of things not seen … By faith we understand that the worlds were prepared by the word of God, so that what is seen was made from things that are not visible … All of these that died in faith without having received the promises, but from a distance they saw and greeted them. They confessed that they were strangers and foreigners on earth, for people who speak in this way make it clear that they are seeking a homeland. If they had been thinking of the land that they had left behind, they would have had opportunity to return. But as it is, they desire a better country, that is, a heavenly one. Therefore God is not ashamed to be called their God; indeed, he has prepared a city for them (Hebrews 11:1, 3, 13–16).
2. *The Matrix*, dir. Andy Wachowski and Larry Wachowski, Warner Bros., 1999.
3. John Milton, "Sonnet 19," *Selected Poetry*, eds. Jonathan Goldberg and Stephen Orgel (Oxford and New York: Oxford University Press, 1997), p. 58.
4. From the last page of the first part of Jacques Derrida's "The Double Session," *Dissemination*, trans. Barbara Johnson (Chicago: University of Chicago Press, 1981), p. 226. This first part was first presented on February 26, 1969, and was first published in *Tel Quel*, 41 (1970). "Enough! or too much" closes William Blake's "Proverbs of Hell" in *The Marriage of Heaven and Hell* (c. 1793).
5. Jacques Derrida, "A Silkworm of One's Own: Points of View Stitched on the Other Veil," Hélène Cixous and Jacques Derrida, *Veils*, trans. Geoffrey Bennington (Stanford: Stanford University Press, 2001), p. 38.
6. Cixous and Derrida, *Veils*, p. 39. Schleiermacher, the name of the German theologian, translates literally as "veil-maker."
7. Cixous and Derrida, *Veils*, pp. 24–25.
8. Cixous and Derrida, *Veils*, p. 98, note 18.
9. Cixous and Derrida, *Veils*, p. 34.
10. Jacques Derrida, "Edmund Jabès and the Question of the Book," *Writing and Difference*, trans. Alan Bass (Chicago: University of Chicago Press, 1978), p. 68.
11. Jacques Derrida, *Cinders*, trans. Ned Lukacher (Lincoln: University of Nebraska Press, 1991), p. 53.
12. Cixous and Derrida, *Veils*, pp. 42–43.
13. Cixous and Derrida, *Veils*, pp. 44–45.
14. Cixous and Derrida, *Veils*, p. 64.
15. Cixous and Derrida, *Veils*, p. 67.
16. Cixous and Derrida, *Veils*, p. 43.
17. Cixous and Derrida, *Veils*, p. 64.
18. Cixous and Derrida, *Veils*, p. 79.
19. Cixous and Derrida, *Veils*, p. 43.
20. Paul is reading the Septuagint, or something like it, as he follows its translation of key Hebrew terms. Hebrew *masveh*, "sheath" or "covering" (like a hood?) is translated into Greek as *kalumma*. And *qaran*, probably "radiate" or "shine," is translated into Greek in terms of *doxa*, "glory," thereby making it much more than a story about terrifying brightness. Now it's about the need to veil/cover/separate from divine glory.

    The Septuagint translates the curtain separating the Holy of Holies (Exodus 26 *et passim*) into Greek as *katapetasma*, not *kalumma*, thus keeping the two coverings distinct (likewise, the Greek New Testament gospel stories of the tearing of the curtain use the term *katapetasma*). But the Latin Vulgate translates both the curtain separating the Holy of Holies and Moses' face covering (in relevant Old and New Testament texts) as *velum*, "veil," separating divine *gloria*. Thus the Vulgate, perhaps taking its lead from Pauline theology, treats both the curtain before the Holy of Holies and the covering over Moses' face as veils that separate the people of God from the fully revealed presence of divine glory.

21. Compare Romans 1:17: "For God's righteousness [*dikaiosune*] is revealed [*apokalyptetai;* un-covered] in it [the gospel]."
22. In 1 Corinthians 11, the *kalumma* becomes a memory of the law in another sense, imposed by Paul as a means of separating men from women in their respective relations to divine glory. Derrida (*Veils,* pp. 76–78) notes the irony of this insistence on separation by Paul, who elsewhere attacks the circumcision of the flesh in favor of the circumcision of the heart.
23. Augustine, for example, in a sermon on Psalm 46, reads Paul's veil into Gideon's fleece: "[T]he nation of the Jews hath just so remained as a fleece dry upon the ground. For this, ye know, happened in a certain miracle, the ground was dry, the fleece only was wet, yet rain in the fleece appeared not. So also the mystery of the New Testament appeared not in the nation of the Jews. What there was the fleece, is here the veil. For in the fleece was veiled the mystery. But on the ground, in all the nations open lieth Christ's Gospel; the rain is manifest, the Grace of Christ is bare, for it is not covered with a veil. But that the rain might come out of it, the fleece was pressed. For by pressure they from themselves excluded Christ, and the Lord now from His clouds raineth on the ground, the fleece hath remained dry. But of them then 'the Most High gave His Voice,' out of those clouds; by which Voice the kingdoms were bowed and worshipped."
24. Avivah Gottlieb Zornberg, *The Particulars of Rapture: Reflections on Exodus* (New York: Doubleday, 2001), p. 447.
25. Cited and translated in Zornberg, *The Particulars of Rapture,* p. 441.
26. Zornberg, *The Particulars of Rapture,* p. 422.
27. Zornberg, *The Particulars of Rapture,* p. 440.
28. Jacques Derrida, "Faith and Knowledge: the Two Sources of 'Religion' at the Limits of Reason Alone," *Religion,* eds. Jacques Derrida and Gianni Vattimo (Stanford: Stanford University Press, 1998), p. 29.
29. In 3 Enoch 45, the heavenly *pargod* is printed with all the generations of the world and all their deeds, and Metatron teaches Ishmael how to read it "like a father teaching his son the letters of the Torah." Thus this veil, too, in some sense, may be a memory of the law as well as a veiling of divine mystery.

    Pargod is a Persian loanword, related to Hebrew *paroket,* the name in Exodus 26 and elsewhere in the Torah for the elaborately decorated curtain which serves as a partition in the Tabernacle between the *haqqodesh* and the *qodesh haqqodesh,* the "holy" and "holy of holies" (Exodus 26:31-35, 27:21, 30:6, 35:12, 36:35, 38:27, 39:34, 40:3, 21-26; Leviticus 4, 16, 21:23, 24:3; Numbers 4:5, 18:7). The *paroket* is consistently translated into the Greek Septuagint as *katapetasma,* thus eliding potential associations of it with Moses' *masveh* ("cover" or "sheath"; Greek *kalumma,* "covering") in Exodus 34. But the Vulgate translates both the Tabernacle's *paroket* and Moses' *masveh* into Latin as *velum.*
30. *Midrash Aseret Hadibrot,* in *Bet HaMidrash,* vol. 1, 63f.
31. Derrida, "Faith and Knowledge," p. 47.
32. The customs are reported in Rabbi Joseph Telushkin, *Jewish Literacy,* pp. 658–659.
33. Derrida, "Faith and Knowledge," pp. 29–30.
34. Derrida, "Faith and Knowledge," p. 76.
35. Derrida, "Faith and Knowledge," p. 33.

CHAPTER 13
Derridapocalypse

CATHERINE KELLER AND STEPHEN D. MOORE

Catherine Keller: As nothing like a philosopher or a biblical scholar, but something like a theologian, I perch at this table with fear and trembling. But then theology is always trembling. It oscillates between bible and philosophy, between a ghostly apocalypse of conjurations and the discipline of the reasonable doubt. Theologians have been embarrassed by the oscillations, we have (unlike biblical scholars) tended to disavow the apocalypse and the doubt. So no wonder some of us are grateful for the mysterious resonances of deconstruction with our own lost irony, with our haunting uncertainty, and more recently, with our politico-messianic hopes. But beyond this table, among most theologians, such appreciation of Derrida sounds at best like gratitude for crumbs—crumbs from the banquet of high theory for the hungry dogs. (Not that there is any shame in the posture of the Syrophoenician woman, the grief-stricken mother who for that moment healed Jesus of his Abrahamic chauvinism [Mark 7:24–30].)

In the light of Derrida's coming, it would at any rate be inhospitable not to risk admitting this gratitude. But the risk is double-edged, like the Messiah's tongue. Gratitude in the present context may be the inhospitable itself. As it has been said: "When a gift is given, first of all, no gratitude can be proportionate to it … As soon as I say 'thank you' for a gift, I start canceling the gift, I start destroying the gift, by proposing an equivalence, that is, a circle which encircles the gift in a movement of reappropriation."[1] So without saying thank you, without fantasizing equality or proportionality, without preaching a Sunday school poststructuralism—shall we risk an appropriation in order to avert a destruction? Shall we risk apocalypse in order to defer it? Doesn't *he*?

Stephen D. Moore: As it *is* a Sunday,[2] and as "poststructuralism" (however we define the term or be ourselves defined by it) is, let's face it, the only thing, other than "religion" (no more amenable to definition, no less amenable to deformation), that brings us together around this table, the notion of a Sunday school poststructuralism might not, after all, be such a fanciful conceit. What we preach on Sunday, indeed (those of us who do), we practice throughout the week—or so Jacques Derrida has recently been teaching us.

Derrida, who has confessed, indeed circumfessed, that he "quite rightly pass[es] for an atheist,"[3] has, paradoxically, also declared himself *for faith*, albeit a faith that is "not religious" per se but is instead "absolutely universal."[4] Faith is what enables any and every address to the other, for to address the other, any other, is always to ask to be believed. This request, this *demand*, for faith—utterly quotidian and ordinarily implicit—is, as such, the structural *a priori* of any address whatsoever. (The elucidation *of* Derrida *to* Derrida, in the *presence* of Derrida[5]—whatever that expression might mean *after* Derrida—is a somewhat bizarre public ritual, a ritual of torture at times, no doubt, to which Derrida has repeatedly been subjected over the years. And it is not without a certain dismay—but, if I may say so, also not without a certain pleasure—that I now find myself charged with turning the screws.)

If the demand for faith is to be regarded as the structural *a priori* of any address whatsoever, what then are we to say about the extended epistolary address that is the Apocalypse of John? Twenty years or so ago, Derrida, in the course of a dual analysis of the Apocalypse and an antiapocalyptic essay by Kant, argued that the former reveals, in exemplary fashion, "a transcendental condition of all discourse, of all experience even …"[6] It seems to me, however, that Derrida has succeeded in making a better case for that contention in his more recent work on faith—even though the Apocalypse is not, as far as I can see, mentioned by name in that work. (Derrida's most incisive commentary on biblical texts, however, often occurs when his attention is directed elsewhere.) "In testimony, truth is promised beyond all proof," Derrida argues near the end of his extended meditation on faith and knowledge. And again: "The act of faith demanded in bearing witness exceeds, through its structure, all intuition and all proof …"[7] *On the one hand* (to employ a formulation long familiar to readers of Derrida, the corresponding "on the other hand" being deferred until long after the amnesiac reader has forgotten that there ever was an "on the one hand"), the Apocalypse amounts to the provision of "proof" of the truth of that to which Christian witness testifies, announcing: "These words are trustworthy and true [*houtoi hoi logoi pistoi kai alēthinoi*], for the Lord ... has sent his angel to show his servants what must soon take place" (Revelation 22:6; cf. 1:1–2).[8] Now, faith, for Derrida, is inextricably bound up with blindness, and as such with an eclipsing of the ordinarily privileged sense of sight and the entire attendant epistemology of vision.[9] Indeed, "faith, in the moment proper to it, *is* blind," as he remarks. "It sacrifices sight, even if it does so with an eye to seeing at last."[10] The Apocalypse, however, does not sacrifice sight; it is an affair, not even so much of seeing at last, but of seeing from first to last. It testifies not to the unseen but to the seen. Pushing impatiently against the opaque barriers of faith, of testimony, of witness, it attempts to surmount them by dissolving them in revelatory radiance. Being "blind," in the Apocalypse, in consequence, is explicitly equated with being "wretched," "pitiable," "poor," and "naked" (3:17).[11] *On the other hand*, the Apocalypse assaults the barriers of testimony precisely *through* an act of testimony: it testifies to what it claims to have seen, in order to elicit faith from the other—thereby embracing the very terms of the structure it strives to contest. And yet the Apocalypse is no ordinary demand for faith. The testamentary structure of everyday speech acts amounts, Derrida suggests, to declaring: "Believe what I say as one believes in a miracle."[12] But the testamentary structure of the Apocalypse amounts to a still more audacious declaration (and demand): "Believe what I say, because I testify to a miracle." As such, the Apocalypse might indeed be said to exemplify the quasi-transcendental structure of any and every speech act: it makes manifest (or *reveals*, to use the Apocalypse's own idiom) the structural conditions of the speech act as such (even while chafing at the operational restrictions of those conditions, as we have seen). The Apocalypse, any apocalypse, would thus be a privileged instance of what Derrida has termed "pure attestation" ("if there is such a thing"),[13] which is precisely attestation to the miraculous, demanding a response of "pure faith."

Now, faith, in the Derridean sense (or, perhaps, in any sense), might be said to bear a privileged relationship to the *secret*. The secret subtends my address to the other—any and every address, to any and every other—insofar as my address, as testimony and appeal for blind faith, inevitably gestures to that which is always already veiled from the other. The secret that most preoccupies Derrida, however—what he has termed the "absolute secret"[14]—is not something subject to provisional concealment, and that could, in consequence and in principle, be made manifest under different conditions. The absolute secret—which, extrapolating a little from Derrida's own reflections on it, might be said to be the structural prerequisite of faith itself, and, hence, by extension, of each and every address to the other—does not admit of manifestation, revelation, apocalyptic uncovering, or denuding. The absolute secret is absolutely closed, absolutely clothed, but as such infinitely open.

Now, a secret *is* evoked in the opening words of the Apocalypse of John; whether or not it is the *absolute* secret remains to be seen. "The unsealed secret of Jesus Messiah, God's gift to him ...," begins the text (at least in my admittedly customized rendering of it: *Apokalypsis Iēsou Christou, hēn edōken autō ho theos...*). God's gift, then; but given where, given when? In answer, the text enjoins us to gaze, to gawk, to gawp through the gaping door of heaven itself, seductively left ajar by the divine doorkeeper (4:1)—the same one, no doubt, who earlier identified himself as he "who opens and no one shuts, who shuts and no one opens" (3:7; cf. 3:8). Thus it is that we become openly covert witnesses to the gift of the sealed scroll, the secret scroll—or perhaps it suffices to say: the secret. "Then I saw in the right hand of the one seated on the throne a scroll [*biblion*] written on the inside and on the back, sealed with seven seals ..." (5:1). The only anthropomorphic physical trait attributed to "the one seated on the throne" (other than the implied backside doing the sitting—the same one formerly paraded before Moses in response to his request for a vision of the divine glory [Exodus 33:17–23]) is this hand, and the only purpose attributed to the hand is the clutching of the scroll. Thus encircled by the divine fingers, this mystified cylindrical object looks and acts suspiciously like a phallus, and not just any phallus, but the Lacanian phallus that can only perform its function when veiled.[15] For it appears that the scroll, the secret scroll—again, it will suffice simply to say: the secret—is indeed absolute at first, indecipherable because inaccessible, and hence unpossessible and impossible: "no one in heaven or on earth or under the earth was able to open the scroll or look into it" (5:4)—that is, until the mortally wounded Lamb, who, up until this moment, has been bleeding quietly and unnoticed nearby (5:6), working earnestly but unsuccessfully, it seems, at accepting his own castration, precipitously steps forward to claim the scroll as his own, with all the phantasmatic power and pomp that possession of it automatically confers (5:7–14). But enough of this Lacanian digression, or regression.[16]

When the Lamb unzips the very first seal (6:2), the secret threatens to leap whole and entire out of the scroll—or so it seemed, at any rate, to certain patristic expositors in particular, beginning with Irenaeus, who, taking their cue from the messianic cut of the rider on the white horse thereby let loose (cf. 19:11), imagined the parousia already to have begun.[17] But the denuding of the secret has barely begun. And even when the seventh seal has been broken, and heaven itself has been plunged into suspenseful silence ("When the Lamb opened the seventh seal, there was silence in heaven for about half an hour" [8:1]), all that ensues is another series of seven—seven further deferrals of climactic disclosure. Seven trumpets are distributed to seven angels, who proceed to blow them in turn. When the sixth trumpet is blown, a further angel—anxious, perhaps, at the prospect of yet another nail-biting half hour of heavenly silence, issuing in yet another stupendous anticlimax—blusters impatiently that "There will be no further delay, but in the days when the seventh angel is to blow his trumpet, the God's secret will be fulfilled [*etelesthē to mystērion tou theou*]..." (10:6–7).

Immediately before this portentous announcement, however, the "seven thunders" (*hai hepta brontai*) have sounded—or spoken, rather (*elalēsan*), and John, pen poised, as always, to record the disclosure, is unexpectedly instructed instead to "Seal up what the seven thunders have said, and do not commit it to writing" (10:4). All of which raises the question: What if the real secret, the absolute secret, in the Apocalypse, were the secret revealed, unveiled, uncovered by the seven thunders—and then immediately reveiled, covered over, closed up again; in which case the absolute secret would, once again, have slipped surreptitiously through our grasp? The secret announced by the seven thunders remains secret in the Apocalypse even after all else has been laid bare. It is not covered (nor is it uncovered) by the closing injunction to the seer, "Do not seal up [*mē sphragisēs*] the words of the prophecy of this book" (22:10). But does the text dismiss the absolute secret even as it demarcates it? As if in refusal of the very concept of an unopenable secret, our text, following the sounding of the seven thunders, throws up an impatient angel, as we have just seen, who, raising his right hand to heaven for dramatic effect, swears that "in the days when the seventh angel is to blow his trumpet, God's secret will be fulfilled ..." (10:5–7).

So what *is* the secret that is fulfilled, or rather leaked, when the seventh angel finally blows his trumpet? First and foremost, it is a *secret empire*: "Then the seventh angel blew his trumpet, and there were loud voices in heaven, saying, 'The empire [*hē basileia*] of this world has become the empire of our Lord and his Messiah, and he will reign forever and ever'" (11:15).[18] A secret empire, then, that is also a global empire, and as such always already an open secret, administered from a heavenly throne room that, the more we peer through the door thoughtfully left ajar for our edification and instruction, seems to resemble an oval office—except when it resembles a CIA debriefing room instead, or even a Pentagon war room.[19]

But if this is the secret that the Apocalypse is only too eager to uncover, indeed to flaunt, what might be the secret that it would prefer to keep under wraps, first and foremost from itself? Here is where Derrida's earlier reading of the Apocalypse, aided and abetted by his more recent reflections on justice, proves especially illuminating, enabling us to read the Apocalypse against itself.

The testimony of the Apocalypse, of any apocalypse, to a secret conceived, not as a closed body of content, but as an absolutely open space of possibility, is, for Derrida, quintessentially encapsulated in the apocalyptic injunction, "Come!" (as in Revelation 20:17: "The Spirit and the bride say, 'Come [erchou].' And let everyone who hears say, 'Come.' And let everyone who is thirsty come"; and again in 20:20: "The one who testifies to these things says, 'Surely I am coming soon.' Amen. Come, Lord Jesus!"). By the time Derrida has finished with it, indeed, the apocalyptic "Come" shows all the signs of having become yet another nonsynonymous synonym for *différance*: "'Come,'" he declares, "could not become an object, a theme, a representation …"[20] As a radical, irruptive opening to and for the other, otherness, the future, "Come" is inextricably intertwined in turn with other recent Derridean themes or nonthemes, not least justice beyond the law, hospitality beyond reciprocity, and the gift beyond debt (up to and including the gift of death).[21] And, of course, the messianic.[22]

Derrida is enamored of a particular anecdote about the Messiah that Blanchot relates,[23] in which the Messiah appears one day at the gates of Rome, but decked out all in rags—a disguise intended to *defer* his advent, as it turns out. One of those who lays eyes on this ragged Messiah does see through his disguise—but tellingly elects to reveil rather than reveal him, putting the denegating question to him: "When will you come?" For the Messiah, in order to be the Messiah, can never actually be present, never actually have arrived, any more than justice—justice beyond the law, that is—or hospitality—hospitality beyond reciprocity—can ever simply be assumed to be present, to have arrived. To assume their arrival would be to evade their demands.

Appropriately enough, therefore, when the Messiah does finally show up in the Apocalypse (19:11ff.)—and at the shattered gates of Rome, no less (cf. 18:1-24)—the indiscretion, the inappropriateness, the scandal of the event is duly, if obliquely, marked in the text that announces his advent. His name is secret: "he has a name inscribed that no one knows but himself [*exōn onoma gegrammenon ho oudeis oiden ei mē autos*]" (19:12). He is incognito, in disguise. A thin enough disguise, to be sure. It is not as a beggar or a leper that he comes. And that, perhaps, is the problem. We dread his appearance, appropriately enough, but for all the wrong reasons.

First, the dread. The Messiah, in order to be the Messiah, is, and must be, a figure of dread, as Derrida compellingly argues:

> [W]ho has ever been sure that the expectation of the Messiah is not, from the start, by destination and invincibly, a fear, an unbearable terror—hence the hatred of what is thus awaited? And whose coming one would wish both to quicken and infinitely to retard, as the end of the future? ... [H]ow could I desire [the] coming without simultaneously fearing it, without going to all ends to prevent it from taking place? Without going to all ends to skip such a meeting? Like telepoiesis, the messianic sentence carries within it an irresistible disavowal. In the sentence, a structural contradiction converts *a priori* the called into the repressed, the desired into the undesired, the friend into the enemy.[24]

The Messiah of the Apocalypse, too, is a figure of dread no less than desire—but less because his parousia marks the impossible arrival of an absolutely unanticipatible future, oriented to justice beyond the law and hospitality beyond reciprocity, than because the Apocalypse's "Come," which impatiently holds the door open for the imminent advent of the Messiah, is an implementation of justice as slaughter on a surreal scale,[25] and an implementation of hospitality as a horrid invitation to feast upon the mangled mountains of the slain—an invitation that opens, precisely, with "Come" (although this time as *deute*, not *erchou*): "Come, assemble for God's great banquet, to eat the flesh of kings, of captains, of the mighty, of horses and of riders—the flesh of all, whether free or slave, small or great" (19:17–18). That which the Messiah establishes through the cataclysm of his coming (in a word: empire) is also that which the Messiah has come to destroy (in a word: Babylon). The Messiah builds by destroying, and destroys by rebuilding. The Apocalypse, in consequence, compulsively converts the desired into the undesired, the friend into the foe, the Christ into the Antichrist. We have long been conditioned to regard the Antichrist as a *monster*: "And I saw a beast [*thērion*] rising out of the sea, with ten horns and seven heads ..." (Revelation 13:1). But what if the Messiah, the Christ, were the true apocalyptic monster, the emblem, and revealer of a monstrous truth? Do we dread the coming of the Messiah precisely because he *is* a monster, *the* monster, the very form of monstrosity itself?

The future, when it is absolutely unanticipated and unanticipatible, assumes monstrous form, as Derrida has averred in a relatively recent interview. Actually, it is one of his oldest themes: it is sounded at the end of the subsequently famous "Structure, Sign, and Play" paper that he used to smuggle a poststructuralism *avant la lettre* into a 1966 conference at Johns Hopkins University designed to welcome French structuralism to the United States (thus turning his paper into a "gift beyond hospitality" indeed, though neither the hosts nor the guest could know it at the time).[26] He continues in the interview to reflect on "the form of the unacceptable, or even of the intolerable, of the incomprehensible, that is of a certain monstrosity." To embrace such a future would be "to welcome the monstrous arrivant, ... to accord hospitality to that which is absolutely foreign or strange."[27]

The cataclysmic future that the Apocalypse so eagerly rushes forward to embrace, however—war-ridden, famine-ridden, ecocidal—is far from unfamiliar; it can always, and all to easily, be regarded simultaneously as our present (which, of course, is how this text has managed to live on, to craftily survive the demise of Rome that, on its own account, should have ushered in the end of history). But might not the intolerability of an all too familiar present, or of an all too easily anticipated future present, be far more *monstrous*, in the end—more unsettlingly strange in its absolute familiarity, more disturbingly intimate in its absolute foreignness—than a wholly unanticipatible future? Why pretend to cage the monster in the secret structurally destined to remain forever sealed—the secret that the seven thunders have sounded—when it is an open secret that the monster is, and was, and is still to come—and then to come yet again?

Catherine Keller: Well, frankly, I would prefer not to know what is coming. Because of all those all too predictable processes, so vulgarly empirical. Like the U.S. push toward a war in the neighborhood of Israel—when as Derrida said already in 1992 "the war for the appropriation of Jerusalem is today the world war."[28] Like the boundless reach of the newly revealed American Empire; like the boundless "blowback" of terrorism; like the boundless filling of the globe and the exhaustion of the gift of the bounded earth. The finite future of the infinite drive to profit requires no prophet. Where I come from, the four horsemen star in movies, they have fans on every street. You can rap, dance, or tap your fingers to their familiar hoof-beat. It is, as Stephen D. Moore suggests, the *anticipatable* future that sends us back into the hard arms of John of Patmos. And as Derrida insists, it is in the *unknown* coming, the *avenir* in uncertainty, that hope would lie. So we turn (again) to the Derrida of what Gayatri Spivak (somewhat self-justifyingly) calls his "ethical turn."[29] Turning is already apocalypse: "then I turned to see whose voice ..." (Revelation 1:12).

So how would we read, with Derrida's help, the open secrets of apocalypse? How would we see its voices?[30] With eyes wide shut? "And I began to weep bitterly because no one in heaven or on earth or under the earth was able to open the scroll or to look into it"(5:4). But it is the messiah with seven eyes, the gory lamb, the first and last, whom John (in his "prayers and tears") inscribes as the ultimate reader—who is worthy to read the scroll of seven seals. Or might we mistake Derrida for the hyper-reader (after all his first and last names both have seven letters)? John's lamb who comes displays monstrosity from the start—with "seven horns and seven eyes, which are the seven spirits of God." So each eye *is* a spirit, an optical specter. The seven-lensed spectacles fit the lamb-messiah to read the spectacular predictions hidden behind the seven seals. No blind faith, this—but true super-vision.

Read under the supervision of these ghost-glasses, what is the Book of Revelation but a book of specters? Its angels of terror, its ghosts under the altar, its ghost riders—not to mention John as the ultimate ghostwriter for God, or is it for the spooky messiah, head and hair "white as white wool, white as snow," with red burning eyes … Does it not anticipate Derrida's *Specters of Marx*? Derrida invokes the dread, not quite dead, ghost of Marxism (which haunts the triumph of capitalism) but also the host of ghosts that haunted Marx himself. But Derrida shows that Marx failed to develop patience for ghosts—including the specters of the Jewish messianism that energizes all political eschatology. So Derrida proposes his eerily hospitable spectropoetics. In the interest not of exorcising but of discerning these spirits he writes some of his most theologically important prose:

> If there is a spirit of Marxism I will never be able to renounce, it is not only the critical idea or questioning stance … It is even more a certain emancipatory and messianic affirmation, a certain experience of the promise that one can try to liberate from any dogmatics, from any metaphysico-religious determination, from any messianism …[31]

Is it also the Messiah of the Apocalypse from whom a messianic deconstruction would liberate us? Is Derrida's democracy to come, promise, gift—that which in its vulnerability must be protected from the apocalyptic Coming? The *avenir* from the *future*? But if we "look into it," isn't such a binary too oppositional, indeed too apocalyptic, for deconstruction? It would make the messiah into the antichrist, and Derrida's messianicity into the *true* Coming.

Yet once one reads the scroll with the spectral lenses of deconstruction one recognizes how closely the monster and the messiah mimic and mock one another—right down to their display of wounds, their surplus of horns and of eyes, their coupling with an urban femininity: New Jerusalem as the Bride in one instance, the Whore of Babylon, as Rome, in the other. Such a politically charged mimicry: for the messiah has always signified the antiempire, and the whore-beast empire itself.[32] But as it turns out they both stand under the banner of the "coming": the lambmessiah is "the one who is and who was and who is coming"—*ho erchomenon*. But according to John, the beast also was and is to come.

Yet the leading eschatological thinker in twentieth century theology, Jürgen Moltmann, has theology depend upon the "coming" as the distinguishing mark of the Jewish and Christian Messiah. This politically progressive Protestant translation of eschatology into "hope" rather than "end things," and hope as the *Zukunft*, the to-come of *adventus* rather than the calculable linearity of *futurum*, parallels Derrida significantly—if not, as we will see, unproblematically.[33] But it is not just the messianic which comes! People "will be amazed when they see the beast, because it was, and is not, and is to come.[34] Amazed, perhaps, because the beast iterates, it parodies, the temporal structure of the messianic hope—but with a *différance*: one recognizes that the difference between the Messiah and the Monster comes, indeed comes down, to the copula. Both were, both will come. But only the Messiah IS.

This is the infinitesimal but infinite gap: the beast is only as an is-not, as a present of absence, whereas the messiah is the subject of a tense presence, the present tense of a "to be" that conjugates the entire alphabet of salvation history. But the copulating beast-whore couple mocks the copula itself, it haunts the alpha-omegic order of "is" with monstrous writing; the beast is "full of blasphemous names." We will have been alerted (by a certain critique of the metaphysics of presence) to the totalizing potential of this revelation of a pure present. But how would this messianic wisp of minimally hellenized ontology, in this abysmally unphilosophical text, written in an inelegantly hebrewized Greek, have caught the *ousia* virus? Or does it rather carry the precondition for the subsequent ontotheologizing of Christianity—that which Derrida calls in distinction from and as the ghostly precondition of ontology—"hauntology?" Might this precondition lie in the hope, all too human among subjects of imperial injustice then and now, for the cessation of brutality? But more, for its reciprocation, and finally—oh surely, so deservedly—for the gift of a life without suffering, without death?

The Apocalypse wants an end to mourning (at least for its own people). Yet Derrida is teaching, if I am not mistaken, that any politics that would eschew brutality, that would not replicate empire even as it revolts against empire, can never eschew the work of mourning.[35] John's ecclesia, with its ghost-martyrs crying for vengeance, its strangeangels bringing justice by way of global terror and mass death, wants no more tears. No more death. No more sea. For tears condense out of the chaos of the primal saltwaters. So immediately after 9/11 the Bush regime forced mourning toward violence; one hundred times that many children die daily, daily, from avoidable causes: and as Derrida has noted, we let them.[36] Nor can we grieve for all whom the peoples of the book daily make into ghosts.

No wonder: at the end of the *biblos*, an entire *bibliotheque* of texts rich with grief, mourning got shut down once for all. Along with messianic comfort, the apocalypse offers a merciless preemption of history: dis/closure as closure. A closing of the very space of disclosure (final revelation). We who dwell in the land of the doctrine of preemption, the land of *Ghostbusters*, must now newly grieve and resist our beastly messianism. Among us the tearless white warrior of they-are-evil-we-are-good have-a-nice-day righteousness comes hybridized with the drag queen of Babylon/Roman-hattan, she who said "I will never see grief" (Revelation 18:7). How else can we read the peculiar production of a born-again Christian (who says his favorite philosopher is Jesus) as Roman-style emperor? Not that Dubya Caesar is performing an original—there is a long history of copulation between messianism and colonialism. It was born in Western form as the crusade to Jerusalem. But now this hybrid Messiah-Caesar-complex metabolizes in the high speed global media of what Hardt and Negri have dubbed the "postmodern Empire."

Yet the medium of John's Apocalypse already seems spectropoetic. In its scrolling bombardment of images, blunt bits of the poetry of prophets kaleidoscope at an oneiric speed.[37] It prefigures what Derrida calls "techno-tele-iconicity": the medium of the media, the "techno-tele-discursivity," he says, "determines the spacing of public space, the very possibility of the *res publica* and the phenomenality of the political... [T]his element itself is neither living nor dead, present nor absent: it spectralizes."[38] Indeed the *res publica* is now *res privata*—so notes Nestor Miguez, who like most liberation theologians (all knowingly haunted by the ghost of Marx) loves John's Apocalypse for its denunciation of the globalizing greed then and now.[39] "Public things" are being privatized for profit, while what was private appears in televised public spectacles, public impeachments, and talk shows.

Indeed Derrida's "Faith and Knowledge" tracks the alliance of religion with "tele-technoscience," which he calls globalization itself. But "on the other hand," it declares war against this power that dislodges religion from "all its proper places, *in truth from place itself*, from the *taking-place* of its truth"—hence the "auto-immune reaction" within religion: "the auto-immunitary haunts the community ... like the hyberbole of its own possibility."[40] Intriguingly, this ghostly global techno-tele-iconicity, which is so effectively deployed among the apocalyptic hyperboles of Abrahamism (the so-called fundamentalisms), is specifically what provokes in *Specters* the announcement of a hauntology.

So is it too much of a stretch to suggest: the global spatiality (and what place is more global than apocalyptic space?) of the dissolution of the public and private into each other sheds light on Derrida's "taste for the secret?" Instead of reading the latter as a symptom of his crypto-bourgeois-individualism, we could recognize its protection of a space of alterity, of nonbelonging. That space characterizes not only one Franco-Algerian Jew but the ever more migratory masses of the globe: "the demand," he writes, "that everything be paraded in the public square … is a glaring sign of the totalitarianization of democracy." (We who mourn the possibility of U.S. democracy will be needing this phrase.) "In terms of political ethics: if a right to the secret is not maintained, we are in a totalitarian space."[41] In the space of the apocalyptic utopia, the displacement of space itself, darkness, ocean, and death have been eliminated. "God is the light" of the New Jerusalem, "and its lamp is the Lamb" (Revelation 21:23). A ghost-white transparency of goodness and security rule: a neon panopticon, shining through the lamb-lamp. For the seven spectral eyes do not just see but shine.

On the other hand: these city streets "transparent as glass" are lined with trees leafing "for the healing of the nations": they encode the oppression of those often inhabiting filthy streets. They yearn for "water of life as a gift" as the desert spreads, water wars loom, and the empire privatizes every public good. The book concludes with an entire riff on coming: "I am coming soon the spirit and the bride say come; everyone who hears, say 'Come' … let everyone who is thirsty, come …" (22:12a, 17). To this water, always at least literal, every other is invited along with the invitation of the utterly Other. "*Tout autre est tout autre.*"

Does John's Apocalypse dis/close—or only close—what Derrida has here and there—delicately empirical—referred to as the chaos of the gaping mouth, of thirst and hunger as well as speech? Having looked into it for all too long, I still see no closure of this undecidable scroll with the End always already in its sight. Its empire and antiempire continue to conjugate history, separated only by the negation of a presence too pure to recognize its own irony: its own *is/is not*. No end in sight of apocalypse or of empire; of the autoimmune violence of our bloody Abrahamic purities.

If this text won't close, don't we need an opening within the space of its haunted iconicity? But—within the terms of the sibling rivals of the

Abrahamic patrilineage—how would that space open—except as more desert? Derrida finds a promising chaos in that very desert, a deconstructive kenosis. But what of the rivalrous women, Sarah and Hagar, unsisterly, divided but never quite conquered? Would their ghosts settle now, after so much movement of women, for these desert patrimonies—for the messianic masculinities? For their crumbs? Unexpectedly, Hagar survived in the desert, as did the anonymous goddess of the apocalypse chased there by the first beast.[42] Then the earth opened its mouth: the very maw of chaos nonviolently swallows the vomit of the dragon, the effluvium with which he had sought to drown her. But now—would these desert women, practiced in a wide variety of open mouths, not also (re)open the watery chaos, *thalassa*, the mythic sea, the salty birthwaters—the bottomless flux or *tehom* that apocalypse nihilates along with death, night and tears?

Not a pure femininity (goddess forbid), not a feminist apocalypse, and certainly not a pure origin, a patristic *ex nihilo*—but something more like a Joycean "chaosmos of Alle?" Might *tehom* (in some dream of a divine woman) lend another "nonsynonymous substitution" to what Derrida calls, in a chaosmically clarifying paradox, the "heterogeneity of origin?" "Heterogeneity opens things up," he says.[43] Is this the very dis/closure that opens the apocalypse up, precisely there where it would shut everything down, a counterapocalypse that is no mere pro- or antiapocalypse?

Here my question becomes confessedly, though not circumfessedly, theological. If the "heterogeneity of origin" deconstructs (as I believe it must) the ex nihilo of an orthodox origin, doesn't it also call for a heterogeneity of the eschaton? But wouldn't such a heterogeneous future upset the purity, the absoluteness, the unilateral gift, of the coming? At times Derrida's messianicity seems to invoke such a purity: when he calls for the "absolutely undetermined messianic hope,"[44] or with Kierkegaard the "absolute secret," *ab-solutum*, absolved from any bond, detached, out of joint.[45] Then it is as though any moment of joining, any connectivity, would deny the time-out-of-joint; as though one is either detached or fused, as though attachment entails determination, confinement, closure; as though we might disavow the chaosmic fluidities of our interrelations for the sake of a deconstructive absolute, purified even of the possible. I realize that Derrida—at these present-transcendent moments—means to save the undetermined future from any (theological) foreclosure: "As soon as a determinate outline is given to the future, to the promise, even to the Messiah, the messianic loses its purity, and the same is true of the eschatological ..."

Still: is messianic purity the only alternative to determination? This question is posed within a tradition in which the omnipotent One,

Himself the essence of origin and end, routinely determines outcomes; in the name of opening up a transcendent future He closes down history. (O please, whoever comes fresh to religion, "turn and see" the force, the violence, the homogenizing Presence of every unhistoricized enunciation of this "He": please do not casually erase the grammatology of a few decades of fragile, feminist theology.) From this "Nobodaddy" (Blake) the indeterminate certainly needs messianic salvation.

Derrida proposes therefore a "messianic eschatology so desertic that no religion and no ontology could identify themselves with it."[46] This is an intriguing tactic: to dry the ontotheology out of eschatology, to bake the religious out of the messianic. Of course I love its negation of dogma itself, and *ipso facto* of all the dogmatisms that keep women in the role of God-dogs, licking the leavings of the religious Masters. This desert eschatology answers to his "faith without religion." But here is my worry (and let me state it without frisson of feminist fury, without for the moment the distraction of symbolic sex, without apocalyptic ambush): might this very strategy not be echoing—so inadvertently, indeed with such gentle intent—the foundation of orthodox theology? For "in the beginning"—not of Genesis but of Christian orthodoxy—the *ex nihilo* had evaporated the *tehom*, the watery abyss whose traces remain in scripture until they are vaporized in the apocalypse? The *ex nihilo* purged the Jewish and mythic residues of chaos, and at the same time established a divine sovereignty of pure power—which determines through grace the purity of faith. After all, wasn't Protestant neo-orthodoxy founded on such an opposition between the purity of faith and the heterogeneity of religion—Karl Barth's "Christian faith" vs. any, including Christian, "religion?" (Naturally enough Derrida's Christian interlocutors are understandably, but massively, Roman Catholic: Caputo, Hart, Marion, even Tracy—so I am aware that a certain problematic within Protestantism, involving the totalizing effects of Protestant versions of transcendence *sola scriptura, sola gratia, sola fides*, may for Derrida lack comparable mediation, except by way of Kierkegaard, Barth's inspiration, or Heidegger oddly, and fundamentalism repugnantly.)

Nonetheless, some of us within and between the religions depend upon Derrida to help release the infinite indeterminacy—khoric and tehomic—from the anxious grip of every orthodoxy, even the most progressive. Indeed for this bottomless indeterminism—in its democratically cosmopolitan justice as well as its meditative apophasis—some of us have come to depend upon his mysterious overflow into theology, his divine surplus.

So then one does not want some spectral afterimage, some theological ghost, of Derrida to be reinforcing the kind of paternalist dichotomy that invests even the socially responsible messianisms of theology. (Perhaps it is not he who is responsible for such Derridean specters, but those of us who interpret him theologically.)

As I noted earlier, Derrida's assertion of the pure coming, the *avenir*, over against the deteterminate *futur* structurally nearly parallels Moltmann's binary of a pure and promised *Zukunft* vs. the emergent future: coming vs. becoming. (Not only against being but against any Nietzschean or Whiteheadian immanence of becoming.) But Moltmann criticizes the Parmenidean eternal presence only to yield to a *theologia gloriae* of "lasting being in the coming presence of God": the *parousia* yields total *ousia*, in the end—after death and transience have been overcome.[47] The One who comes arrives in His [*sic*] glory, never again to suffer the *zimzum* of nonbeing. Of course, even if it comes dangerously close to mirroring the two kingdom structure of law and grace, Derrida's own binary of determinate history and absolute promise heralds no total or final coming. *Au contraire.* He presumes—with *theologically* crucial insight—that the hardening of the messianic into a messiah will produce such totalizing effects. But if the only alternatives are a determinist appropriation, on the one hand, and the gift of a separative absolute, on the other, might Derrida's own "gift" not harmonize, hauntingly, with the triumphant chorale of God's absolutely free and transcendent gift, *charis*, grace, *sola gratia*—a unilateral, pure omnipotence, whether coming from above or from the future?

This would be a spooky surplus indeed—at least for those theologies, including most feminist and ecological varieties, which for the sake of a sustainable justice and a credible faith resist the imaginary of omnipotence, indeed for those heterodoxies in which the divine morphs into the *ruach*, *Geist*, spirit of infinite indeterminacy. Can Derrida's "messianic performative" work within Christianity to gird the loins of a *deus absconditus* who absconds once again with all agency, leaving humanity enough rope to hang itself with? Or mainly, as I hope, to provoke spirited—indeed sometimes graceful—actualizations of what might not otherwise have been possible?

Instead of reestablishing the dry abyss—between the future which will come predictably from our efforts and *ho erchomenos,* that which comes despite all effort: can we not admit the Derridean heterogeneity into the gap itself? Need we understand the agency of our efforts as a linear determinism rather than as a complex, uncertain multicausality, unfolding at the edge—the *eschatos*—of chaos? I find a hint of this alternative flow of agencies enacted in Derrida's notion of the "I": "there is no 'I' that ethically makes room for the other, but rather an 'I' that I structured by the alterity within it, an 'I' that is itself in a state of self-deconstruction, of dislocation ..." And so "the other is there in any case, it will arrive if it wants, but before me, before I could have foreseen it."[48] The messianic Other—*tout autre*—as arriving before "I am" upends the linear determinism of any closed system. It counters apocalypse with dis/closure. At the same time it suggests a momentary "I" always already heterogeneous with—indeed co-constituted by—the future coming. This "I" comes-to-be as event (to borrow Whitehead's language from the 1920s, loved by Deleuze) only through its prehensions of the others which precede it. Indeed, which haunt it!

This impure "I" can never be absolved of its Other. So why impose purity onto the Other itself? Why not let the *tout autre*, whatever or whoever it will come-to-be, also appear as impure, heterogeneous, already taking account of *its* others (of me), *as* it comes? Then *ruach* is emptied of the dominological structure of *sola gratia*—though perhaps not of her tehomic grace. As to Derrida's so graceful gift to theology: he will not offer us an apocalyptic feast, *dieu merci*, but healing crumbs. In the shared spirit of an indeconstructible justice—"as indeconstructible as deconstruction itself"—he will not cease to haunt scripture and its interpreters. As we have come—to haunt him.

References

1. Jacques Derrida, "The Villanova Roundtable," in *Deconstruction in a Nutshell: A Conversation with Jacques Derrida*, ed. with a commentary by John D. Caputo (New York: Fordham University Press, 1997), p. 18.
2. Or was, at any rate, an auspicious day on which to tackle the Apocalypse of John: "I was in the spirit on the Lord's day ..." (Revelation 1:10).
3. Jacques Derrida, "Circumfession: Fifty-Nine Periods and Periphrases," in *Jacques Derrida*, Geoffrey Bennington and Jacques Derrida (Chicago: University of Chicago Press), pp. 155–156.
4. Derrida, "Roundtable," p. 22.
5. Modestly seated in the second row, as this paper unfolded.
6. Derrida arrives at this conclusion through reflection on the inaugural moments of the Apocalypse in particular, in which the revelation passes from God to the seven churches by way of a circuitous series of relays: Jesus, an angel, John, John's written testimony ... (Revelation 1:1–2). To this convoluted structure of relays—perpetually in danger of derailing—Derrida perversely (re)attaches the term "apocalypse": "as soon as one no longer knows who speaks or who writes, the text becomes apocalyptic." What apocalypse, thus reconceived, reveals is not, however, nothing, but rather "a transcendental condition of all discourse, of all experience even, of every mark or every trace." As such, apocalypse is "an exemplary revelation of this transcendental structure" (Jacques Derrida, "On a Newly Arisen Apocalyptic Tone in Philosophy," in *Raising the Tone in Philosophy: Late Essays by Immanuel Kant, Transformative Critique by Jacques Derrida*, ed. Peter Fenves, trans. John P. Leavey Jr. [Baltimore: Johns Hopkins University Press, 1993], pp. 156–57). The essay was originally published as *D'un ton apocalyptique adopté naguère en philosophie* (Paris: Galilée, 1983)—unless we count the English translation of it that somehow managed to precede the French original by a year: see *Semeia* 23 (1982): 63–97.

7. Jacques Derrida, "Faith and Knowledge: The Two Sources of 'Religion' at the Limits of Reason Alone," in idem, *Acts of Religion*, ed. Gil Anidjar (New York: Routledge, 2002), p. 98.
8. English translations of the Apocalypse follow the New Revised Standard Version, except when I veer off the path to beat the bushes for Greek nuances that NRSV conceals.
9. Cf. Jacques Derrida, *Memoirs of the Blind: The Self-Portrait and Other Ruins*, trans. Pascale Anne-Brault and Michael Naas (Chicago: University of Chicago Press, 1993), p. 12.
10. Derrida, *Memoirs*, p. 30, emphasis added.
11. "You do not realize that you are wretched, pitiable, poor, blind [*tuphlos*], and naked. Therefore I counsel you to buy from me…salve to anoint your eyes so that you may see [*hina blepēs*]" (Revelation 3:17–18).
12. Derrida, "Faith and Knowledge," p. 98.
13. Derrida, "Faith and Knowledge," p. 99.
14. Jacques Derrida, *On the Name*, ed. Thomas Dutoit, trans. John P. Leavey Jr., et al. (Stanford, CA: Stanford University Press, 1995), p. 59.
15. Jacques Lacan, "The Signification of the Phallus," in *Écrits: A Selection*, trans. Alan Sheridan (New York: Norton, 1977), pp. 281–291.
16. Especially as further pursuit of it would necessitate difficult passage through Derrida's own reading of Lacan: "Le Facteur de la vérite," in *The Post Card: From Socrates to Freud and Beyond*, trans. Alan Bass (Chicago: University of Chicago Press, 1987), pp. 411–496.
17. See David E. Aune, *Revelation 6–16* (Word Biblical Commentary, 52b; Nashville: Thomas Nelson, 1998), p. 393; G. K. Beale, *The Book of Revelation* (The New International Greek New Testament Commentary; Grand Rapids: Eerdmans, 1999), p. 375.
18. I am following Wes Howard-Brook and Anthony Gwyther in rendering the Apocalypse's *basileia* as "empire," in place of the more traditional and more anodyne "kingdom." See their *Unveiling Empire: Reading Revelation Then and Now* (Bible & Liberation; Maryknoll: Orbis Books, 1999).
19. To anticipate several of Catherine Keller's themes.
20. Derrida, "Apocalyptic Tone," p. 165. By the early 1990s (when I last had occasion to count them), the list of (non-)synonyms for *différance* already ran to some forty or fifty terms, and the non-(re)presentability of that to which they variously gestured—or which they variously performed—was a recurrent trait of Derrida's discourse on them. For a catena of relevant quotations, see my *Poststructuralism and the New Testament: Derrida and Foucault at the Foot of the Cross* (Minneapolis: Fortress Press, 1994), pp. 36–39.
21. See Jacques Derrida, "Force of Law: The 'Mystical Foundation of Authority,'" in idem, *Acts of Religion*, pp. 230–98; idem, *Of Hospitality: Anne Dufourmantelle Invites Jacques Derrida to Respond*, trans. Rachel Bowlby (Stanford: Stanford University Press, 2000); idem, "Hostipitality," in *Acts of Religion*, pp. 358–420; idem, *Given Time. 1: Counterfeit Money*, trans. Peggy Kamuf (Chicago: University of Chicago Press, 1991); idem, *The Gift of Death*, trans. David Wills (Chicago: University of Chicago Press, 1995).
22. Derrida's most considered statement on which would seem to be *Specters of Marx: The State of the Debt, the Work of Mourning, and the New International*, trans. Peggy Kamuf (New York: Routledge, 1994), pp. 166–169; Cf. p. 55.
23. Maurice Blanchot, *The Writing of the Disaster*, trans. Ann Smock (Lincoln: University of Nebraska Press, 1986), pp. 141–142. Cf. Jacques Derrida, *Politiques de l'amitié* (Paris: Galilée, 1995), p. 55n; idem, "Roundtable," pp. 24–25.
24. Jacques Derrida, *Politics of Friendship*, trans. George Collins (London: Verso, 1997), p. 174.
25. The *locus classicus* of this theme is Revelation 6:9–11, wherein "the souls of those who had been slaughtered for the word of God and for the testimony they had given [cry] out with a loud voice, 'Sovereign Lord, holy and true, how long will it be before you judge and avenge our blood [*Heōs pote…ou krineis kai ekdikeis to haima hēmōn*] on the inhabitants of the earth?'" They don't have long to wait, as it happens. I have reflected elsewhere on the violence of the Apocalypse; see my *God's Beauty Parlor: And Other Queer Spaces in and around the Bible*, Contraversions: Jews and Other Differences (Stanford, CA: Stanford University Press, 2001), pp. 173–199.
26. The paper ends with "a glance toward those who, in a society from which I do not exclude myself, turn their eyes away when faced by the as yet unnamable which is proclaiming itself and which can do so, as is necessary whenever a birth is in the offing, only under the species of the nonspecies, in the formless, mute, infant, and terrifying form of monstrosity."

"Structure, Sign, and Play in the Discourse of the Human Sciences," in *Writing and Differ-ence*, Jacques Derrida, trans. Alan Bass (Chicago: University of Chicago Press, 1978), p. 293.

27. Jacques Derrida, *Points...Interviews, 1974–1994*, ed. Elisabeth Weber, trans. Peggy Kamuf, et al. (Stanford, CA: Stanford University Press, 1995), pp. 386–387.

28. "It is happening everywhere, it is the world, it is today the singular figure of its being 'out of joint.'" If Derrida's presciently expansive "today" seems all too empirically correct, let us remember he is rereading its disjointedness by way of *Hamlet* (Derrida, *Specters*, p. 58).

29. Gayatri Chakravorty Spivak, *A Critique of Postcolonial Reason: Toward a History of the Vanishing Present* (Cambridge: Harvard, 1999), p. 431. In a posture not unfamiliar among certain theologians, she is straining toward an activist appropriation of Derrida, and yet distancing herself from the taint of a merely academic deconstruction. Hence the last sen-tence of this hefty book: "... the scholarship on Derrida's ethical turn and his relationship to Heidegger as well as on postcolonialism and deconstruction, when in the rare case it risks setting itself to work by breaking its frame, is still not identical with the setting to work of deconstruction outside the formalizing calculus specific to the academic institution."

30. Cf. "Seeing Voices" in *Apocalypse Now and Then: A Feminist Guide to the End of the World*, Catherine Keller (Boston: Beacon, 1996), 36ff. I did imagine a certain begrudging pneuma-tologial kinship with John's anti-imperial vision/audition. For a Derridean afterthought to this counterapocalypse, cf. Keller, "Eyeing the Apocalypse," in *Postmodern Interpretations of the Bible—A Reader*, ed. A.K.M. Adam (St. Louis: Chalice Press, 2001), pp. 253–277.

31. Derrida, *Specters*, p. 89.

32. I will not rehearse here the case, which is not hard to make, for the anti-imperial intentions of the book, for the millennium-long history of politically revolutionary deployments of John's Apocalypse, and the twentieth century liberation apocalypse among Christians of the so-called developing world. These are recapitulated in *Apocalypse*. Let me point only to Ernst Bloch's *Philosophy of Hope*, and less enthusiastically, Norman Cohn's *Pursuit of the Millennium*, as pivotal accounts of the political *Wirkungsgeschichte* of the text.

33. Jürgen Moltmann's *Theology of Hope* (New York: Harper & Row, 1965–67), a twentieth-century theological classic, made the key transitions: "The more Christianity became an organization for discipleship under the auspices of the Roman state religion and persistently upheld the claims of that religion, the more eschatology and its mobilizing, revolutionizing and critical effects upon history as it has now to be lived were left to fanatical sects and rev-olutonary groups." But once we read the biblical testimonies as "full to the brim with future hope of a messianic kind for the world," we realize that: "the eschatological is not one ele-ment of Christianity, but it is the medium of Christian faith as such ..." (pp. 15–16). His specific enunciation of the "coming" as *adventus/Zukunft* will be discussed below.

34. *Egō eimi to Alpha kai to Omega, legei kyrios ho theos, ho ōn kai ho ēn kai ho erchomenos, ho pantokratōr.*(1:8).
   To thērion ho eides ēn kai ouk estin, kai mellei anabainein ek tēs abyssou, kai eis apōleian hypagei; kai thaumasthēsontai hoi katoikountes epi tēs gēs, hōn ou gegraptai to onoma epi to biblion tēs zōēs apo katabolēs kosmou, blepontōn to thērion hoti en kai ouk estin kai parestai (17:8).

35. Derrida's "topology of mourning" as the "spectral spiritualization that I at work in any *techne*" may be as interminable as mourning itself, and so extends of course indefinitely beyond, if one can, the contours of the specifically political: "A mourning in fact and by right interminable, without possible normality, without reliable limit, in its reality or in its concept, between introjection and incorporation. But the same logic...responds to the injunction of a justice which, beyond right or law, rises up in the very respect owed to who-ever is not, no longer or not yet, living, presently living" (*Specters*, p. 97).

36. Cf. Derrida's Kierkegaardian meditation on responsibility, suggesting of course no ethical fix to a paradox that perhaps the invocation of "Bush" flattens—but also tests (for at what point does the inevitability of "sacrifice" enable the most vulgar collusion with brutality)? "As soon as I enter into a relation with the other, with the gaze, look, request, love, com-mand, or call of the other, I know that I can respond only by sacrificing ethics, that is, by sacrificing whatever obliges me to also respond, in the same way, in the same instant, to all the others. I offer a gift of death, I betray, I don't need to raise my knife over my son on Mount Moriah for that ... I am sacrificing and betraying at every moment all my other obligations: my obligations to the others whom I know or don't know, the billions of my

fellows (without mentioning the animals that are even more other others than my fellows), my fellows who are dying of starvation or sickness" (*Gift of Death*, pp. 68–69).

37. I discuss the breathless compression of Hebrew poetry, especially Ezekiel, in this flashing proto-MTV vision, in "Eyeing the Apocalypse" as well as *Apocalypse Now and Then*.

38. Derrida, *Specters*, p. 51.

39. For this invaluable formulation, I thank Nester O. Miguez for his unpublished keynote address for the Oxford Institute, "The Old Creation in the New, the New Creation in the Old" (August 2002).

40. Derrida, "Faith and Knowledge," p. 82.

41. Jacques Derrida & Maurizio Ferraris, *A Taste for the Secret*, trans. Giacomo Donis (Cambridge: Polity Press, 2001), p. 59.

42. "But the woman was given the two wings of the great eagle, so that she could fly from the serpent into the wilderness, to her place where she is nourished for a time, and times, and half a time. [Time out of joint indeed!] Then from his mouth the serpent poured water like a river after the woman, to sweep her away with the flood. But the earth came to the help of the woman: it opened its mouth and swallowed the river that the dragon had poured from his mouth" (Revelation 12:14–16). Amidst the many graphic oralities of the Apocalypse, the nurturing desert and the vomiting yet voracious beast invoke the scene of a burning and many orificed desire (Cf. *Apocalypse Now and Then*, pp. 70–73).

43. Derrida, *Specters*, p. 33.

44. Derrida, *Specters*, p. 65.

45. Derrida, *Gift of Death*, p. 57.

46. Derrida, *Secret*, p. 21.

47. "God's Being is in his coming, not in his becoming. If it were in his becoming, then it would also be in his passing away. But as the Coming One (*ho erchomenos*), through his promises and his Spirit (which precede his coming and announce it) God now already sets present and past in the light of his eschatological arrival ... The coming of God means the coming of a being that no longer dies and a time that no longer passes away" (Jürgen Moltmann, *The Coming of God*, trans. Margaret Koh [Minneapolis: Fortress Press, 1996], pp. 23–24).

48. Derrida, *Secret*, p. 84.

CHAPTER 14

Otobiographies,[1] Or How a Torn and Disembodied Ear Hears a Promise of Death

(A Prearranged Meeting between Yvonne Sherwood and John D. Caputo and the Book of Amos and Jacques Derrida)

YVONNE SHERWOOD AND JOHN D. CAPUTO

Within what one calls religions—Judaism, Christianity, Islam, or other religions—there are tensions, heterogeneity, disruptive volcanos, sometimes texts, especially those of the prophets, which cannot be reduced to a corpus, or a system. I want to keep the right to read these texts in a way which has to be constantly reinvented.[2]

The end is near … which does not exclude that it may already have taken place, a little as in John's Apocalypse the imminence of the end or the last judgment does not exclude a certain "You are dead. Stay awake."[3]

"If anyone has ears, let him hear" (Apocalypse of John 2:7, 11).

Death Sentence: "You Are Dead"

"You are dead. I promise you, you are dead."
Is it not a performative contradiction—a "perverformative"[4]—to pronounce, not a eulogy, in which we speak to the dead as if they were alive to praise their deeds, but the opposite, a death sentence, in which we speak to the living as if they were dead, promising them death, condemning their misdeeds? Can we tell someone who is still alive, "I have been sent to tell you, you are dead," as if their death were already given, a foregone conclusion? Can we say, "I look upon you as so many dead men walking"?

Suppose, in turn, that these words are spoken not by us but to us. Would not the very fact that we hear them mean that we are not dead, so that the words come at most, at worst, as a warning that we are in mortal danger? Even if we are told we are about to be overcome by an overwhelming force that we cannot hope to avoid, still, if we are alive enough to hear these words, would there not still be hope of escape? Does not time always insert some interval between us and death?[5] Is not some promise still held out even in this promise of our death? Is not the end that is foreseen by that very fact always already forestalled?

"The words of Amos,[6] who was among the shepherds of Tekoa" (1:1) are delivered as an irrevocable death sentence, foreseeing an absolute dead end. But how can Amos say, and how can we or anyone hear, a word of absolute death? Is not language shattered, scattered by his traumatic discourse? Do not these words push language beyond its breaking point, incinerating it, turning it to ash, consuming it in a fiery death? Does not language, rocked by an enormous shock, collapse from these terrible tremors? Can Amos, can we, can language itself, sustain this trope? Or will this discourse, under the pressure of the limit, in the intensity of this fire, be forced to turn around?

Those are the questions we are posing.

Writing over the Volcano (or the Earthquake)

The words that Amos *sees* arrive just before the earthquake, and maybe the synaesthetic confusion of seeing words is one of the seisisms of the earthquake,[7] for the book performs the trembling of the quake and sends numerous underground faults running through the theological and biblical soil. Amos says of Israel, almost three thousand years before Gershom Scholem will say it again: "This country, this land, is like a volcano, in which language boils."[8] As Scholem describes how twentieth-century Zionists "sleepwalk" on the surface of a seemingly neutralized *lashon haqodesh*[9] (holy tongue), but "shudder" at sudden irruptions of words from the "religious sphere" that "terrify" just where they were "intended to comfort,"[10] so Amos performs the domestication of religious language, and language's sweet rage. Just as modern Hebrew, for example, uses the verb *ḥazah* (to have a vision) to describe a weather-forecaster (a *ḥazai*), so Amos's contemporaries use the verb *mashiaḥ* (the verb connected with the anointing of kings and the messianic) to refer to a simple rubdown with massage oils.[11] And language takes its revenge by lighting fires in the house of language and dislocating *relation*: relation to our mother-tongue, our being-at-home, or being-among-ourselves.

Those knights of good conscience who take it upon themselves to defend the Bible from the alleged brutality and gratuitousness of deconstruction should look at the book of Amos as it orientates—or disorientates—itself around the key word and principle *hfk* (הפך; to over-throw), and spins words on the axle of pun. Language boils with the fury of a poetic justice that rips through the name of the shrine Gilgal, splinter-ing it into *Ha-gilgal galoh yigleh* ("Gilgal shall surely go into exile"), and that hollows out the name of the sanctuary *Beth-el* ("the house of God"; בת־אל) into "Beth-Al" (בת־אַל, the "house of nothing") (Amos 5:5–6). What Amos and Derrida seem to share is the desire to mobilize the forces of writing in a way that cannot be annexed to the rhetoric of human mastery and the power of the subject (the wit of the deconstructor, the intricacy of the deconstructive machine, the rhetorical accomplishment of the prophet), but that assaults the notion of the subject by evoking the "memory of some powerlessness ... reminding the other and reminding me, myself, of the limits of the power."[12] They evoke the realization that we never "have" a language or writing in the same way that we "have" other objects—that language is like a god or a body or a homeland or a house[13] in this respect—and they use writing as a way of destabilizing knowing and of opening language to its other(s), particularly at is borders and its edges. In Amos the name of this other is Yhwh, and Yhwh's role is to demolish the security of those who stretch out in Zion, and the worlds created by the cultural idioms of Zion, as easily and comfortably as they stretch out on their ivory beds (6:1, 4). Indeed, as "God" becomes the force that guarantees nothing but that every word will "hfk" into its opposite, he creeps closer to a certain caricature of the "deconstructor" than a certain Derrida. Yhwh for Amos is primarily a violent word-scatter-ing force who, to borrow Seyyed Hossein Nasr's description of the God-broken language of the Qur'an, breaks human language "into a thousand fragments like a wave scattered into drops against the rocks at sea."[14] (Nasr's metaphor, in fact, could have been custom written for the book of Amos, the book that generates bizarre idioms of horses running on rocks and sea-ploughing oxen which themselves are made from ricocheting bits of words: horses [*sussim*, סוסים] comes from *ressissim* [רסיסים, "frag-ments"] and *babeqarim* [בבקרים, "with oxen"] comes from *biq'im* [בקעים, "pieces"] [6:11–12].)

In Amos, time and logic are out of joint: the book opens with Yhwh, the warrior and storm God who is so much less placid and calm than the "first cause" of Western Metaphysics, dispensing fire in the manner of most Ancient Near Eastern deities, roaring like a lion in the manner of most Ancient Near Eastern deities, and then distinguishing himself from his Ancient Near Eastern neighbors on the basis that he turns (הוא הופך) to maul and burn his own. The book ends (or at least the book before the optimistic coda added by an editor ends) with an *anti-Exodus*: "'Are you not like the Ethiopians to me?' says the Lord. 'Did I not bring Israel up from the land of Egypt; and the Philistines from Caphtor and the Arameans from Kir?'" (9:7).[15] The Exodus—the event at the heart of Israel's most ancient creeds, the event that those who translate the Bible into German see as the core of Israel's *Heilsgeschichte*—is already, in this, the earliest of the Prophets, being mauled and mutilated into an *Unheilsgeschichte*, as Yhwh proclaims, "I sent among you a pestilence after the manner of Egypt" (4:10), and promises to make the land tremble, toss, surge and subside like the Nile (9:5; 8:8).[16] Language is already turning against its speakers, the concept is already opening itself to its opposite, and this hospitality is killing us.[17] Amos's claim that God *may be* primarily attached to the Egyptians, the Ethiopians, the Philistines, or the Arameans, and that the covenant between God and Israel may be just as unstable as the linguistic convenants between, say, Beth-El and "House of God" invokes a drastic Lévinasian shift where the world really does begin to orientate around the Other, with terrifying implications that bland discourses on "tolerance" and "universalism" have never been able to accomodate. Over and against a tolerance that presents itself as "a gift" of "Christian domesticity,"[18] over and against a "universalism" that always stumbles over its own parochialism, the book of Amos provides a glimpse of a story in which the Other no longer serves as bit-player in your narrative of Self—as God's agent in punishing your sins, for example—but in which the center of the one God's love is absolutely elsewhere.[19]

Nor is monotheism as simple for Amos as for those who praise him for his "ethical monotheism" in apostrophes that seem to assume that ethics and monotheism are simple, uncontentious things, worthy of praise. His God is not so much the *Causa Sui*, the creator of all that is, but the God of unmaking and convulsion. He marks his difference from other fertility gods by being a fertility god and an unfertility god and, without any devil (yet) to exculpate him,[20] he bears the full force of his oneness: earthquake and storm, fire and famine, are his. This God presents, or rather absents, himself not as plenitude, but as famine (a famine of God and the words of God [8:11]), and depicts himself (and think what *this* does to the "gift") as the *giver of lack*: "I gave you cleanness of teeth in all your cities and lack of bread in all your places" (4:6). In an impossible self-retraction that echoes the "I am not your I am" of Hosea 1:8, Yhwh edges close, if such a thing were possible, to *khôra*, the place of the nongift, that which ungives, emphatically not the beneficient father or mother, closer to the French *il y a* rather than *Es Gibt*. Ashes are also there (*il y a là cendres*): a vision of a basket of fruit (קַיִץ; *qayits*) given to Amos in 8:1–3 dissolves, through something far more brutal than word*play*, into *qaits* (קֵץ, the end) and a scene of "women wailing; corpses lying everywhere."[21] In Amos 3:12 the prophet says, "You, that is the body of Israel, are like two legs or *a piece of an ear retrieved from the lion's mouth* or the corner of a couch and a bed leg snatched from the mouth of the disaster," a statement that resonates with Derrida's strange "*Je suis* (I am/I follow) the last or the least of the eschatologists," or "*Je suis* (I am/I follow) the last/least of the Jews."[22] Both Amos and Derrida tamper with the image of the remnant by claiming the impossible ("I follow the last"; "You are dead") and both suggest that something very little, very qualified, and *almost* choked by qualifying clauses, lives on. But whereas Derrida is responding to a long tradition of the remnant in biblical and Jewish history, in Amos the yet embryonic idea of remnant is being aborted before it has been brought to (the status of a) full term.

Or rather, the idea of the remnant (the part that survives), is both aborted *and* survives, in part. For according to Exodus 22:12–13, bloody animal parts prove, before the law, that an animal is dead. But Amos 3:12 produces a torn and bloody remnant ear, and expects that ear, curiously, to hear …

Harsh Economics

The thing that we and all those liberation theologians who have used bits and pieces of the book of Amos most admire in Amos is the way the book earths the theological in the economic and explores the intimate covenant between economy and violence—condemning, for example, those who pile up violence (חָמָס; *ḥamas*) like so many gold coins in their vaults (3:10).[23] Like Shakespeare's *Timon of Athens*, the book casts money as that which "solders" together "impossibilities," or alchemically converts "foul" to "fair," "wrong" into "right"—or in Amos' terms turns poison into seeming-justice (6:12)—and it seems to see economy, language, and selfhood as inextricably linked to one another, as if money, as for Shelley, were somehow the "visible incarnation" of the "principle of Self."[24] Without wanting to cast Amos as a proto-Marx, proto-Engels, or proto-Derrida, there may be, just about, an early flicker of a specter of Marx here—or at least the Marx who sees the principle of buying and selling as underlying our very vocabularies of ontology, philosophy (theology?), and the self. Certainly there is something very "contemporary"-sounding about Amos' cynical exposure of the material base of the moral and theological, while the biblical cashing-out of abstract ideals in terms of grain, wine, fines, debt, and credit seems to whisper, across the centuries, to the grandiose hubris of "Operation Infinite Justice" and the accusations that the rhetoric of freedom is being used as a "semantic container for oil."[25]

Like the other biblical prophets, the book of Amos sets up a rhetorical courtroom in which God is judge, jury, and prosecuting attorney. But whereas in the other prophetic books God is also plaintif and the crime is apostasy, cast as sexual trespass against the God-husband's exclusive oneness, here Israel is by God's own acknowledgment *virgin* (Amos 5:2), the book begins with a list of war atrocities and what we might call human rights abuses, and the face of the weak, the poor, the needy is represented in the face of the Most High, the *Autrui*. Justice and Yahweh are presented as interchangeable terms if not semantically then certainly pragmatically, and (all the time wanting to guard ourselves against an alliance with a certain Protestantism that appropriated "inwardness" for itself, and used Amos to condemn the empty external rituals of Jews and the Catholics) we want to say that there is a glimpse of something here that we could justly begin to call "religion without religion."[26] Apart from occasional references to the debasement of the "holy tongue" (expressed in terms of maintaining proper exchange rates between words and preserving pure, linguistic value, uncorrupted by false semantics and economics), God seems more concerned with economic and social justice than with his own marital and sacred honor: as an aspiring Lévinasian deity he seems to interpret religion as ethics and posit "salvation and survival" entirely on the "ethical-moral dimension of life."[27] The book of Amos, in effect, presents a kind of hyper-Wisdom theology, where a hidden God is expressed in a world so finely tuned to justice that the slightest infringement (wine bought with wrongly imposed fines, a garment or pair of sandals purchased through exploitation of the needy) will trigger off the numerous sensitive mines, and trip-wires, that express the will-and-character-of-God in the world, and where the world, in response, will decoagulate, descend into chaos, and toss and surge like the waters of the Nile (9:5; 8:8).[28]

The Hebrew word for oracle is משׂא (*masa*; weight, burden, that which is lifted up) from נשׂא (*nasa*; to suffer, lift, bear), and the purpose of

Amos's burden is, as Amos 7:10 makes clear, to be the heaviest, most exorbitant, inassimilable משא possible, overrunning the container or border that is sanity, self-interest and the land.[29] Amos does not know of words like "*différance*," the "trace," or "*khôra*," but repeatedly uses tropes of fire and water—fire that burns, water that spills—to express the exorbitant nature of the prophetic word: a word which, as one of us says elsewhere, is designed to "exceed us infinitely," which is why there is no point in exposing the Prophets to a "correspondence theory of truth" or a test of "*adequatio* or of *ad literam*."[30] Like one of the hyper-ethical stories of Lévinas, the book lets us all have it, telling us that what happens everyday is a scandal; telling us that we are more obliged, more hostage to the other and more insolvent in our debts than we could ever begin to imagine; telling us, as Derrida and Lévinas in their different ways tell us, that our world is founded on the chaos of the open mouth, and that guilt is inherent in responsibility because responsibility is unequal to itself. The people are arche-guilty—guilty before the letter, before language and the law, condemned by an infinite privilege which is an infinite prerogative. Not only have they committed "three sins and four" (Amos 1:4–8) but those seven sins have been multiplied by the infinite accumulator of their (our?) chosenness.[31]

They/we exist in a particularly sensitive relation to God and his world: privilege is a gift which is not a pure gift in the Derridean sense because it has placed them/us in debt— "You only have I known of all the families of the earth; therefore I will punish you for all your iniquities" says Yahweh in Amos 3:3, which roughly translates as: "I give you a pure gift, without exchange, but whether I want this or not the gift guards itself, keeps itself, and from then on you must owe."[32] The case against the people is that they have turned justice to wormwood and poisoned the gift, and the punishment is that on the day of the Lord, which will be truly a day of reckoning, the corrupt economy of the Israelites will be trumped by a harsher and more unforgiving divine economics. In return for their oppression of the poor, Yahweh will scatter their wealth and raze their towers; for their transgressions, Amos says, Yahweh will variously send famine over the land, or pestilence, or floods, or fire, or serpents, or earthquakes, or send them all packing into exile. One good turn deserves another; one unjust turn is returned in kind. As they have turned justice into wormwood, Yahweh will practice the same kind of negative alchemy on them to their destruction: he will turn their day to night, their songs of joy into lamentations; he will make darkness appear at noon and turn their festivals into dirges (Amos 8:9–10). Amos cannot, like Nietzsche, entertain thoughts of a world in which the wicked prosper without retribution: his God must keep a watch on the "false balances" that shrink the measure and inflate the shekel (Amos 8:5; cf. Proverbs 20:23: "scales and balances of justice are the Lord's"). But Amos cannot imagine a world in which virtue is exercised for its own sake, as an intrinsic form of *arte* or excellence—he can only trust to a justice that is index-linked to self-interest, like one strand of Christian thought in Matthew 6:19–21. Toward the end of *The Gift of Death*, Derrida shows how Matthew's celestial economy runs the risk of functioning precisely like the terrestial economy by exhorting believers to accumulate stocks in heaven, beyond the reach of moth, rust, and theft; he shows how Matthew's theology makes Christian sacrifice remunerative, even as it subjects the remunerative principle to an internal critique.[33] Amos has no recourse to celestial coffers because his thought-world does not accommodate the possibility of life- or stocks-after-death, but he does still present a view of religion dangerously index-linked to the pursuit of salvation, security, shelter, food, indemnification, safety, and the pursuit of the best (or avoidance of the worst) for oneself.

If we are tempted to think that the God who gives lack to the self or who knocks down our house and gives the Ethiopian his Exodus *disrupts* the economics of salvation as self-interest or eating well for ourselves, we are mistaken, for these threats to the shelter and to the stomach are ways of appealing to our instinct for self-saving and shelter-seeking in order to bring out the best. This vision of the best may be appealing; it may seem at moments to touch the ideal of justice to the widow, the orphan, and the needy that Lévinas wanted to distil out as the true essence of Torah, but the harsh retributive economics that watches over this world makes it firmly resistant to modernist democratic sensibilities and postmodern theologies of the gift. What is at stake is, as Shalom Paul correctly says, *our* "salvation and survival": the other will matter to us because our salvation is tied to his/her well-being—indeed on his/her well-being is staked the very stability of our world and the solidity of the ground beneath our feet. The theology of Amos is no *worse*, but no *better*, than theologies of heavenly salaries or immortality as the extension of the personal ego in the world-to-come. The difference is that, without recourse to an afterlife, Amos' ethical critique of this world can only take the form of the implosion of the present.

God Is Death

The awful and incendiary logic, the traumatic and fatal grammar of Amos's oracle, is that, to plunder some words from Isaiah 28:15, the people have achieved the impossible and "made a covenant with death."[34] Your limbs can already be seen protruding from the lion's mouth, the prophet tells the

Israelites. The venom of poisonous serpents and spiders is already in your veins. You are still moving about, still talking, but there will not be enough graves to bury you; the birds of carrion are already circling above your rotting corpses, drawn by the stench. Who is Amos talking to? To dead men who can no longer hear. He does not think there is hope for them. He does not expect them to turn around. He seems even to be beyond warning them or threatening them or urging them to reform, to be simply shouting in their ears as they were being carted off to execution. The famous passage in Amos, the one that everyone quotes, fluctuates undecideably between an *exhortation*, "Let justice flow, like rivers, and righteousness like a never-ending stream," and a *prediction* "[God's] justice and righteousness will flow like a never ending stream."[35] In the first case it can be read as a call to a justice without reserve and in the second as a threat: i.e., "My justice, says the Lord, will flow like blood and like disaster spilling all over the place." "Let justice flow like water": those beautiful words that lovers of peace and justice cite again and again also mean the hills and streams of Israel will soon flow with the blood drawn by the sword of Yahweh's justice. The book of Amos resonates with the words of Johannes Climacus, who celebrated the thanato-faith of the Israelites thus: "There was a people who had a good understanding of the divine; this people believed that to see the god was death."[36] What we love about Amos—the running waters of justice for the poor—is also running blood and bloody swords and severed body parts: what we must hate.

The God of Amos, a warrior God and a wielder of swords, wrathful and vindictive, is an offense to the metaphysicians and a stumbling block to the faithful. "I am not your I am, I am death. Go tell the people of Israel that I will be death to them, that I promise them the sword and I am the one who will be true to my promise. Tell them that Yahweh spells death to Israel. For I am the Lord of hosts, the giver of life, but now I am the giver of death. 'I will kill with the sword; not one of them will flee away, not one of them will escape'" (9:1).

The God of Amos is too dark and volcanic for the concepts of the metaphysicians, too merciless and retributive for the Gift. God is justice, but a rigorous retributive justice in which injustice is repaid with death. Contrary to everything that the philosophical and theological traditions want us to think, contrary to every intuition of thought or piety, God is death, not the sublime death that comes from mystical rapture but death by the sword. God is the wholly other, not of the numinous or luminous other of the mystic but the dark alterity of death, of the blade, of hunger, or of poison.[37] His contribution to the debate about the divine names is terrifying: Yahweh is neither Being nor Love but the Sword and the Spider, the Famine and the Flood. Neither the calm Athenian unmoved mover who cuts eternal patterns in the skies, nor the Lord who will be my shepherd of the psalms, Yahweh is the one who withers their pastures (1:2).

That is the substance of the fifth and final vision (9:1–4), fifth and final tremor or volcano, the end of the pre-exilic text, and the end is absolutely dark,[38] a vision of horror, of pure death and total destruction, where no one is spared. The Lord, standing by an altar, says that though the Israelites may flee to the top of mount Carmel or the bottom of the sea or hide underneath the earth, he will seek them out and slay them, every last one of them, without exception, "not one of them shall escape" (9:1). "I will fix my eyes upon them for harm and not for good" (9:4). That is the last word of Amos: God will spell the death of the evildoers who oppress the poor. The last verse of the older text, the final word, is an inescapable death sentence. There is no longer any question of reforming Israel, of repentance and forgiveness, no possibility of a new beginning. The time of forgiveness is over; that remedy has been exhausted; this is the end. Time has run out for the Israelites. They are dead.

Darker than Søren Kierkegaard's final vision of Christendom, laced with as much irony and wit and even more prophetic black humor than Kierkegaard's blackest day, Amos's puns about death, about summer fruit and corpses, belong to a grim genre of inescapable death and the unassimilable grammar of the absolute dead-end.

The End That Is a Secret

In Amos something is coming—or rather, something that takes everything is coming—but what that something is, or will be, is a secret. It is a secret not in the sense of a content to be opened, not even in the sense of something shared in a private *tête-à-tête* between God and the prophet (as a certain secret is whispered between God and Abraham), but it is a secret kept from both the prophet and the people. Editorial inserts and addenda reassure us that "Surely the Lord does nothing without revealing his secret (*sod*) to his servants the prophets" (3:7) and a doxology proclaims "He reveals his thoughts to mortals" (4:13), but these are more by way of editorial response and correction to the original text's perceived sin of omission. It is as if the book were somehow being heard as requesting our forgiveness: "Forgive me for not having said, or wanting to have said; forgive me for not having fulfilled the requirements of revelation and for not having revealed."[39]

"For three transgressions and for four, I will not revoke 'it,'" says Yahweh, but all the book tells us about "it" is that "it" is like the operation of poetic justice: "it" is what rips through Gilgal and Beth-el turning them into "exile" and "the house of nothing"; the force of "it" is what leaves a national body as two torn-off legs and a piece of an ear and that floors the virgin daughter Israel so severely that she will never stand again (5:2). We can never see "it": we only see "its" back, as Moses sees the back of God (Exodus 33:23); we can only see people fleeing away from "it" (Amos 2:14; 5:18; 9:2) and hear the ghostly mourning songs and wailings in the aftermath of "it" (Amos 5:1–3, 16–17; 8:3). "It" is signalled by the force of linguistic irruption and volcanic eruption, around which pieces of language ricochet and time stutters. "It" is what falls somewhere between the two ostensives "thus" and "this," which seem to have no referent other than each other in Yahweh's proclamation: "Therefore, thus I will do to you, O Israel; because I will do this to you, prepare to meet your God, O Israel!" (4:12).[40] The antecedent of "it" is something for which we wait (as if we were reading a very long German sentence and waiting for the verb at the end) but that is never present to us—being somehow in the future, then, in a mere blink or *Augenblick*, in the past. The mourning songs and aftershock suggest that death is the "most tempting figure" for "it,"[41] and yet this secret, this death, seems to be something that has missed us, or that we have missed. As those who still hear/read of "it," we seem to be in the curious position of Melville's Ishmael at the end of *Moby Dick*. As Ishmael (whose name relates to hearing) alone survives to tell, we alone (?) survive to hear. And thus we take on the only role that the text, logically, leaves available to us: not so much that of the grandiose immortal, as the disembodied, but still hearing, ear.

Chorus: Come

Come, Lord God of Israel, come. May the day of the Lord come.

But in Amos we choke on our words. We cannot bring ourselves to say it, to say "it," even to whisper for "it" to "come," even in fearful, hushed tones. The word will not come. It sticks in our throats, or burns our vocal chords, rocks and shatters our powers of language. "Come" comes like a great famine or flood or fire that leaves nothing behind. Who would dare say come to a looming storm or call upon a volcano to erupt? Who would dare call for the coming of the day of the Lord if they knew what they were asking for? Who would call for the coming of a fearsome night, for a terrible day of famine, for a whirlwind and a tumult? Will we not live to regret the day we called for the day of the Lord to come? What if the stranger knocking at our door is a monster? What if he brings death? What if the coming of the *tout autre* means the coming of death? One calls for the coming of this day like a defendant awaiting a verdict, a *vere dictum* (which is, Derrida says, a good nickname for the Messiah) of a jury in a trial. The verdict lies in an unforeseeable future that befalls us like death, which means that it is a future that we are waiting for and postponing. The defendant is waiting for justice, waiting to hear the verdict, but then again, if it is going to go against him/her, s/he does not want to hear, so that s/he does not want what s/he wants. For the promise cannot be disentangled from the threat. All things are intertwined, interwoven, and you cannot separate the saving from the danger, the Messiah from the Monster.

Who is that knocking at the door?
Who will dare to say "Welcome"?

Oracles against All Domestication

In Amos, the passage of the secret is marked, obsessively, over and over again, by scenes of the decimation of the house: the destruction of the ivory house, the tearing down of the winter house and the summer house, the smashing of the great houses to bits and the little ones to pieces, and also the demolition of safety within the house—thus a man who escapes from the mouth of the disaster into his house leans against a wall and is bitten by a snake (Amos 3:15, 6:11, 5;19; cf. 6:1 and 5:11). Sheol[42] is safer than the house—scorpions lurk in the walls of the house—and Amos 6:9–10 reports an eerie scene of death in the heart/hearth of the house, that seems to be written up as if it were an ancient film treatment (so that one can almost imagine the scene directed by an ancient Israelite Ingmar Bergman or David Lynch):

> Ten people remain in one house—but they all die. Then the one who cremates bodies (or, alternatively, a grieving relative), comes to take up a corpse to bring it out of the house, and calls to someone in the innermost parts of the house, "Is anyone else with you?" The answer comes, from somewhere (but from whom, if they are all dead, and from where?) "No." The cremator (or relative) leaves, saying "Hush, we shall not mention the name of the Lord" (6:9–10).[43]

The final hush (*hass* in Hebrew),[44] and the accompanying exhortation to save or reserve the name of God seems to be neither the hush of apophasis or negative theology, nor a hush awed before a plenitude or richness that defies all language, but rather an expression of a literal fear of a God who is somehow provoked by language, a noninvocation of a God who is hurt by language and who in turn hurts language, and whose relation to language is a radical taking away. God is hush because God is the name given to the future that is monstrous—monstrous beyond all possibility of domestication, bringing home, because it makes *unheimlich* all that we mean by home, which is how we read all those allusions to crumbling and unsafe houses. As Lévinas observes, we never "have" a home in the same way that we have other objects, and perhaps the home suggests certain analogies with God or with language in this respect, in that it is a site and condition of our existence, rather than a simple adjunct to it; moreover it is a site that "is the very opposite of a root" because it "indicates a disengagement, a wandering that has made it possible."[45] Amos seems to go even further than Lévinas in dispossessing us from "our" home, estranging us from the very idea of "our" home as something we possess, that encloses us as the very grounds of "our" hospitality. The book writes of the coming of an other to whom no "I" opens the door and indeed whose coming constitutes the exile or dispossession of all that is myself and mine, the destruction of "my" house, the grounds of "my" hospitality, and the annihilation of myself as subject. (The scorpion in my house, death in the heart or hearth of all that constitutes me and my home, is a microcosmic version of the radical dispossession of Israel, enacted in the exile of the people beyond the land, the death of the people in the land, and the incoming of the Aramean/Ethiopian/Philistines into "my" narrative of Exodus.)

Except, Save, Saving (*Sauf*)

The scorching discourse of Amos ends with a surprise, like a language that, unable to sustain its own searing intensity, finally relents or burns out and begins to simmer, or loses its nerve and begins to stammer: "I will destroy it [Israel] from the face of the earth—except that I will not utterly destroy the house of Jacob, says the Lord" (9:8). All along we are being taunted, hounded by the howling cry that God is death and the death sentence inescapable, incommutable, which makes the closing coda (9:5–15) unbelievable, like a bad joke, and makes Yahweh look inconstant, even foolish. Here a logic of the "save/except" (*sauf*) is suddenly injected into the grammar of the death sentence. I will destroy everything, except for what I will not destroy. I will destroy everything save what I except. This postexilic "save/except" echoes the preexilic "perhaps," *peut-être*, of 5:15: "It may be that the Lord, the God of hosts, will be gracious to the remnant of Joseph." Perhaps, but by the end of the preexilic text it was perfectly clear that there was no chance of that, that every chance had been used up, and that God is death. But then the coda resurrects the "perhaps" out of its grave and turns everything that precedes it on its head: "On that day [of reckoning], I will raise up the booth of David that is fallen, and repair its breaches, and raise up its ruins, and rebuild it as in the days of old … I will restore the fortunes of my people Israel" (9:11, 14).

The concluding coda (9:11–15) flatly contradicts the main text,[46] not on a minor point but on its central claim, which is that no one will be spared and that there will be no exceptions. The prophet goes to gruesome lengths to burn upon our minds that the mercy of Yahweh has been tested beyond its limits, that Yahweh is not going to relent, not this time, from which the coda concludes that the wrath of God is appeased and Yahweh relents! The contradiction is resolved easily enough in the traditional manner of historical-critical exegesis: applying the logic of mutual exclusivity that governs historical criticism, J.L. Mays concludes that the coda is "hardly a saying of Amos," since it presupposes as its context the disruption that descended on Israel later. The received scholarly wisdom is that it was probably written two centuries later in the southern kingdom during the exilic period, and that it was written to express a longing for relief from the very curse that Amos was predicting during the prosperity that reigned during the rule of Jeroboam II.[47] Amos told a prosperous people that they were headed for ruin; the redactor tells a ruined people that there is hope that prosperity will return. Not long after Amos spoke these words, the northern kingdom (Israel) fell to the Assyrians, and two centuries later the southern kingdom (Judah) was sent into exile into Babylon, which is likely when the coda was composed. Amos was more than half right; he was right enough, except for the fact that they were not all dead and wiped from the face of the earth.

Far from being a mere historical curiosity, the coda—in its glaring incongruity—points to a tension internal to the structure of the writing, "sayings" and "words" of Amos, which causes the text to totter and strain. For the book turns on a death sentence, on a promise of death, which is an aporia that fissures it from within. Amos has never read about the unmoved mover of metaphysics and he has never dreamed the dream of the God of the gift, but he did not live long enough to reduce "God" or "justice" to an inexorable economy of death and retribution. Because of the structure of *écriture*, the words that Amos uses to call for death turn around and also call for life; the words he uses to say that the end is coming turn into a call for the future and for a justice beyond retribution. That is because, for reasons inhabiting the very structure of writing, as soon as he opens his mouth, the future is being promised, even if he himself is not promising it. Life is all that remains when life has become unlivable; hope is all that is left over when every hope is dashed. But while this future may be treated as a matter of theology or metaphysics or history, we are concerning ourselves with the hushed movements of *écriture*. What is fallen, rises; what is dead, lives on, from the ashes of the absolute end, a future rises—and all this by *écriture* alone.

Prophetic Stammering and the Promise of Scripture (*Écriture*)

The aporia in which the book of Amos, and its hearers, are caught is reminiscent of those curious oracles against ears in Isaiah, chapter 6. Here, God proclaims a stoppage of the people's ears so that they cannot hear anything and then strips the land back to absolute nothingness, so that there is no-thing and no-one left to hear. But then, from what should be absolute silence (what could be more silent than a deaf ear, hearing no-one?) we yet hear an oracle—an oracle about absolute annihilation, then the whisper of an addendum: even if everything is felled, a stump will yet remain and the holy seed will germinate producing new writing, *écriture* (Isaiah 6:13). Perhaps it is not, as we tend to assume, the rich *volume* of the biblical corpus that generates so much extra text, but the lack, the silence, the almost burning up of everything by fire, and the provocation of the deaf, damaged, bloody ear. Like the dry bones of Ezekiel 37, the damaged ear cries out for healing, resurrection. You remake the body of the people of God starting with the ear.

Scripture, *écriture*, is a composite archive,[48] an old-new language full of inner-biblical corrections, addenda, disputations, annotations. The book of Amos is already aborting the embryonic idea of remnant and retracting key items in the cumulative archive of biblical memory, even before they have fully crystallized out, while the corrective coda means that God effectively revises, annotates, and qualifies himself ("*Dieu ... se retracte*"; "*Dieu, comme d'habitude, se contredit.*")[49] We are interested in the volatility of the corpus and the moments when it recoils against itself or overruns its limits—for example, those editorial reminders, directed to the text's God as much as to its audience, that Yahweh should and therefore does share his secrets (3:7; 4:13); or that appendix of what biblical scholar Julius Wellhausen called "lavender and roses" taking root, so unexpectedly, in the textual scrapyard of "blood and iron."[50] We are interested in the way in which the stifling of God's voice and the dissimulation of his face (or what Amos talks of as the giving of the lack of his presence and the famine of his words) leads to more writing by Christians and Jews who fan into flame the sparks of hope incubating within the dust. We are interested in interpretative histories that stubbornly read the ashes of Amos as a sign of "what remains from what is not," and defiantly use writing as a way of "outsmart[ing] the worst ... so as to prevent it taking everything away."[51]

Amos presents a vision of God and the future that is so desertic that no religion can identify itself with it,[52] for what religion can *live* with the image of a virgin people on her knees, never to rise again, for lapses in human justice (Amos 5:2), and what religion can *live* with the statement "You are dead"? For all the Apocalypse of John's injunction against supplementing scripture, for all the cries of the so-called fundamentalists who know not what they ask for, the fact is that no religion *alive* has ever been able to truly, madly abandon itself to the principle of *Sola Scriptura* or *Sola Amos*, and have had to apply the rabbinic principle "*al tiqra*": "Do not read it (at least in the conventional, literal sense)." Christians read themselves into the textual legacy on the condition that it would be interpreted as the history of a single exhortation or imperative ("*Let* justice flow"), while Jews in exile, in the diaspora, grammatically fiddled the death sentence to wring from it not only a reprieve but a command to live again. "She has fallen and will no more rise (comma) the virgin of Israel" was adjusted to "She has fallen and will no more—Rise!"[53] The Rabbis heard the roar of Amos and the lion-God of Amos as a deliberate strategy to "break open the ear (*leshaber et ha-ozen*) in its capacity for hearing."[54] Thus they transformed a disaster for the ear into productive pain, or sacrifice, of the ear.

The Rabbis saw the pain of the ear as a means of healing—as if the ear, by being broken, would grow new life, new text, new body; they healed the ear *but did precisely the reverse to Amos's lips*. Though the biblical text contains nothing to suggest that anything at all was wrong with Amos's mouth, the Rabbis claimed that his name was really *Amus* (tongue-heavy, leaden-tongue or stammerer)[55] thus bringing him more into line with those other prophets—Moses, Jeremiah, Isaiah, and Ezekiel—who protest about their slow, stuttering, unworthy and uncircumcised mouths and lips (see, for example Exodus 4:10; Jeremiah 1:6; Isaiah 6:5). There are many ways of interpreting this doubt about the strength or virility of the mouth that characterizes the Hebrew prophet, but one way—and one prioritized in the Jewish notion of the ideal prophet—is that the stammering reflects the conflict of the prophet who speaks equally for the word and for the people who are to be consumed by that word.[56] Stammering Amos is a way of amplifying the protest that biblical Amos (the unideal prophet?) speaks only twice on behalf of the people in his plaintive cry: "O Lord God, cease, I beg you. How can Jacob stand? He is so small" (Amos 7:2, 5). Amos's "*dis*ability" becomes a way of *en*abling the text to take its call to insolvent, exorbitant empathy to its logical conclusion—the moment where the call rebounds on God and calls God to justice, justice to the virgin (that is, by implication, too young, too innocent, to-be-pitied) Israel, lying on the ground. Stammering Amos is a way of hearing the people's cry back into the text, and allowing it to come in at exactly the same frequency, and the same priority, as the word that condemns them to death, so confusing the words in Amos' mouth and jamming the transmission of the death sentence. Through stammering Amos, the hearers of Amos tell God, as a Rabbinic Abraham tells God, just before the fire and sulphur descends on Sodom and Gomorrah: "You desire the world and you desire absolute justice. Take one or the other. You cannot hold the cord at both ends at once."[57]

Living-on (*Sur-vivre*)

There is a deadly dance, a grim play of grammar, in a death sentence, a textual operation in virtue of which the phrase turns itself around. You are dead, but in your living death you live still on. Amos's terrifying prophetic logic, his nightmarish poetics, obeys what we might call the law of "survival," *sur-vivre*, living on, in Derrida. In a discussion of Blanchot's *Death Sentence (L'Arrêt de mort)*, Derrida explores the undecidability in Blanchot's use of *arrêt*, which means in French the "final judgment," the word or sentence handed down at the end of a trial, which condemns the guilty party to imprisonment or death—like the sentence handed down by Amos. But it also means an arrest in the sense of a stoppage, halt, or suspension. Hence, as Geoffrey Hartmann says, Blanchot's book could also be called *The Suspension of Death*, the arresting of death.[58] The death that the death sentence promises is for the living also arrested or commuted, delayed or deferred. That is to say, life itself is structured as an *arrêt de mort*, the "triumph of life" emerging not so much as an active victory over death as a passive suspension or deferral of death. Life is or means living on, deferring death, buying more time, so that life is not pure life, but as Augustine says a *vita mortalis* or a *mors vitalis*, a living death or a deathly life, and this because life is internally structured by the arrest of death. Life goes on, and life turns on the hope and expectation of the future, so that the "come, *oui, oui*" of the future always calls to us from the borders of life/death, which is the very structure of time itself. Pushed up against the limits of an absolute end, brought face to face with absolute death, death turns its back and language reverses course, inverts itself, subverts itself.

The death sentence subverts itself. In extremis, brought to the brink of death, face to face with the absolute end, the absolute turns its back and one finds oneself still alive. Life and time are always moving on, testifying to the impossibility of death. However fiery the terms in which Amos promises the Israelites death, he cannot burn out the future that is inscribed in language; he cannot control the ear of the other that always hears a promise if it hears at all. As soon as he pronounces the words of the death sentence, the very words he uses stir with the promise. The promise of death cannot spell the death of the promise. When he says, "You are dead, I promise you," he cannot, as a structural matter, suppress the promise. As soon as he opened his mouth, as soon as "the words of Amos" began to flow, the promise began to stir.

Even were the coda never added, some version of what the coda claims is the only possible way one can receive this text, in virtue of the very idea of *écriture*, for writing and reading are a repetition. There cannot be a last and final word, beyond which nothing. If the very idea of writing involves a work of repetition, then the reader is expected to counter-sign this text. But if the reader says, "I am dead," that means that death is all around, that I am filled with death, but as of yet death is deferred. Death is always not yet. Even if I am walking death, I am not dead, not yet. The "not yet" always stirs in writing.

There is in fact no pure and absolute death, which is the excess in the final vision of Amos, no more than there is pure life, which is the excess in the ecstatic visions of the mystics, which are always mixed with death. Pure life and pure death would be the same. There is, *il y a*, only life/death, the interweaving of the difference, the interweaving of the one with the other, in order to draw the lines of life. The death sentence always turns round into the arrest of death, not in virtue of a fortuitous change of fortune or of the heroic efforts of a knight of faith, but in virtue of the structure of writing, of the time of writing, which is a time of repetition. The promise itself is inscribed in the promise of death; the promise of death depends upon the promise of writing. The very movement of life is the movement of time, and in life there is always more time. Time keeps death at bay, keeps the future open, keeps us breathing, time being another way to describe being alive, living on. Time and writing, the time of writing, keeps the promise alive. The "words" of Amos are in virtue of their structure as words a call for a future, a call to the future, a *viens, oui, oui*. Even when we hear, "You are dead," the future is not dead. Even when we hear, "I promise you, you are dead," the promise is still alive. When Amos says "justice," "Yahweh," there are promises inscribed in those words that Amos cannot repress, try as he might, including the promise of a justice beyond retribution.

We are speaking of structural matters, not history.[59] We are speaking of the structure of writing and time, not of an Abrahamic leap of faith. Every time I open my mouth I am responding to the promise. We cannot avoid hearing the word of hope in the hopeless words of Amos; we cannot avoid hearing the future in the promise of the absolute end. That is the basis of what Derrida calls the "messianic" structure, or "messianicity" in general, which is not a matter of subjective heroics but of *écriture*. We are identifying the messianic as an operation of grammar, inasmuch as the promise is ineffaceable just so long as there is the spacing of *différance*. Messianic expectation is not a gigantic expenditure of effort by a religious hero, but something that belongs to the structure of the time of writing, to the structure of the "come." The "come" comes not so much as the doing of a valiant subject who keeps on coming, but as a function of the structure of time itself, which goes on and on, and of the time of writing, in which the promise of more time is irreducibly inscribed. The "come" issues every bit as much from the heart of time and of writing as from the human heart. Indeed, as a strictly structural matter, it is more reliable than the frailties of the human heart.

The death sentence is death deferred. Despite doing his best to promise us death, to promise that the justice of the day of Yahweh is to be visited upon us—by which he meant the avenging wrath of God, paying back the Israelites for their sinful ways—history could not help but hear the call of justice beyond retribution, the call of justice as the Gift, the call of the justice to come. For justice calls, and it calls across the ages; it flows like water across the ages from Amos to Nelson Mandela, with or without their cooperation, whatever their subjective intentions. Amos means to invoke a harsh economy of retributive justice, of flowing blood, a rigorously closed economic circle of transgression and punishment, but he cannot suppress or erase the "gift" that pulsates through his words, the hope for the least among us that breaks out of this circle, which calls for a future and for forgiveness. It is not up to Amos. Justice is not his word and he cannot command its semantics but only serve its purposes.

Warning: "It's As If They're Already Dead. We're the Only Ones in the World."[60]

Amos speaks a word of absolute terror, of inescapable death; he speaks the impossible, that which cannot be thought, like God himself. It is only because we are alive that we can hear his word of absolute death, which means he describes a step we cannot take. Had this grim oracle been simply true—had it been a constative uninfected by a performative, thwarted in its strivings to master the structures of time, the event, and the other—it would have gone unknown and unread. Everything would have been wiped away without a trace, both the oracle and the community that preserved it, and we would not have known about it. It would have remained an absolute secret. But the oracle, the writing, the text, is testimony to survival, to the impossibility of absolute death.

But the saving, safe, *sauf*, is tied up with the danger—the danger that the very opening in time and logic that overflows the text's totalizing vision becomes the means by which the text reconsolidates around a narcissistic reaffirmation of the self. The book of Amos fails to establish its totalizing vision of a world burnt up by the consequences of ethical and economic injustice, but the failure too easily becomes, by means of an instant reflex, a means of simply reestablishing that which is self-affirming and self-evident. Given that a legacy becomes a legacy when those that the text/tradition chooses choose to accept the call to chosenness,[61] it is curiously symptomatic that readers of Amos have traditionally welcomed the book on the condition that they can make a distinction (as they must, and as they wish) between the dead addressees and their living selves. They have emphatically *not* identified with the insolvent chosen, the dead ones, the ones that Yahweh loves less than the Egyptians, the Ethiopians and the Arameans, and so have only ever listened with a bit, or a piece, of an ear. A safe (logical) place of refuge from the ravages of the book's madness offered itself, short-circuiting the book's capacity to harm "us": does not the fact that we are still living not insist that this oracle applies/applied to others geographically, temporally, or theologically elsewhere? Does it not mean that we must be those who rise up after the absolute end of "it" and so are always outside, above "it," like the brand snatched from the fire of "it" (where "it" is both the disaster and the text)?

The risk—which is also the promise—of the prophetic death sentence is that no-one can hear it for/of themselves. The field of dead corpses too easily offers itself as an occasion for *Schadenfreude* and reconstitution of the self-evident truths that Amos goes to such efforts to decompose (the fact that we live on is surely the very proof of God's approval), and the logical and structural difficulty of hearing Amos's/God's "you" as an "I" or "we" automatically deflects the address to a third term, a "them." Thus a book that attempts to decompose our composure by subsuming "us" in the disaster, which is the consequence of our injustice, is remade by our interpretative self-defenses into something as fundamentally conservative as literature of the End of the World. The message becomes, as in Derrida's gloss of the overriding sentiment of the *not*-very-world-shaking world of biblical apocalyptic, "It's as if *they're* already dead. *We're* the only ones in the world."[62]

In the apocalypse, the dream of the "end" is the dream of our justification and vindication; in Amos, the impossibility of there being an absolute end as long as we live to hear tell of it all too easily becomes the crack in time and logic by which we vindicate, save, indemnify ourselves. If we look closely at the editorial layers, the sediments of different times out of joint with one another, we can imagine the Judeans who speak of the promise of the restored "booth of David" in Bethlehem (Amos 9:11–15) already separating the time of death from the time of the living, and looking out upon the waste of "Israel" from the safe vantage point of their coda, their own higher, safer, later Judean place. Later in interpretative history, the book became a means of dividing along the hyphen of the "Judeo-Christian," as Christians increasingly read this text as a condemnation of the rich, ritual-trapped Jews, locked in their horrible theological economics; then it divided along the lines of the Reformation, as the book allied itself with a dichotomy between the proto-Christian prophetic spirit and the empty rituals of the (Jew)-Catholic, in a reading abetted by the showdown between Amos, the prophet, and Amaziah, the "priest" in chapter 7. The same gesture is repeated in contemporary biblical scholarship, where commentators habitually interpret the book as the literal record of the depravity of a social group who allegedly lived like the moral grotesques of a Georg Grosz cartoon, and where the discovery of ivory inlay in the Ancient Near East is, in a crude empiricist reflex, taken to be authentification of the excess of those terrible "ivory beds."[63] Thus, as Kierkegaard observed 150 years earlier, we tend either to assume that the inhabitants of the biblical were "great," simply because they owned real estate in the prime moral property bracket of the Bible, or that "they" were personifications of levels of moral depravity over which people like "us" can only grieve.[64] This crude antithetical reflex enables us to avoid the conflict between modernity and biblical ethics (by which the "biblical" might be called to account) for these moral "monsters" surely merit their annihilation. It also enables us to circumnavigate any conflict between "us" and the God(s) and visions of the Bible, by which "we" might be called to account, and caught in the aporiae of competing and irreconcilable responsibilities.

The Danger of Twos

> Do two walk together unless they have arranged to meet?
> (Amos 3:3)

This paper performs unlikely covenants between Derrida and Amos and between a theologian and a biblical scholar—covenants at least as difficult as that between Israel/Judah and Yahweh, for, as Lévinas says, where two are involved, everything is in danger.[65] We arranged these meetings because it seems to us that current labors in the philosophical turn to religion can help biblical studies to think the questions that tend to be ignored in studies that tend to be classed as either "literary" *or* "historical" (strange antitheses, both designed to justify the secrets of religion to the luminous searchlight of the Enlightenment and the University) and because we believe that not every question worth asking can be answered by traditional archaeological or philological digs in the empirical soil of a self-enclosed "text." Biblical scholars have of course noted the way in which the divine "No" runs through the text of Amos like wildfire, destroying everything solid before it, and have generally tried to treat or ameliorate Amos' "Absolute No" through various forms of genre and text analysis. But these studies seem to us, to use Kierkegaard's words, like so many pseudoscientific nooks and crannies in which consciousness goes to take cover when compared to the existential and religious question of what it might *mean* for God to whisper in a disembodied ear, "You are dead and will not rise again."[66] Conversely, when biblical scholars turn to contemporary appeals to the biblical in philosophy and theology, they often feel, disappointedly, that the Bible is being distilled off into what Ricoeur called "anemic generalities."[67] The *difference* between religion and ethics, or theocracy and democracy is elided by seizing on what Johannes Climacus disparagingly calls scriptural "peppernuts."

Let's be clear: we certainly do not want to *celebrate*, with Kierkegaard, a hard, virile, masculine, ugly, supremely difficult Bible for which only Amos, Abraham, and all the true men have the stomach—we do not want to be coerced by the Bible into philosophizing and theologizing with a hammer—but we do want to be able to analyze and *criticize* (and not just in the euphemistic-scholarly sense of the word) the moments where the Bible theologizes with a hammer or with fire. We want to find ways of reading these texts that are not subject to the perceived imperative of *either* having to drop these fire-filled texts like a hot coal, like Spinoza, *or* being forced to convert them into a self-evident moral principle before which we can all bow down. We want to avoid harmonizing subterfuges that claim that this fire (which Derrida rightly terms "a very biblical figuration")[68] is *roughly* the same as the Enlightenment's light. We want to be able to think about difficult and dangerous scriptural legacies in ways that do not automatically take refuge in Hegelian dialectics or evolutionary theologies, turning them into at best, foetal ur-texts for *us* and *our* history of revelation; and we do not want to subordinate the deadlier parts of the canon for us, without being aware of that age-old mechanism whereby our rejection turns the text into *their* dead letter, *their* sentence of death. Nor do we want to be constrained by the assumption that the biblical is a vague deposit of Being, Faith, and Presence at the back of the philosophical and theological tradition, or to assume that there is a necessary alliance between the progress of the Euro-American human spirit and the Spirit of the Judeo-Christian God. We want to undo a certain conflation of the spirit/soul of the religious subject and the spirit/soul of the aspiring Enlightenment subjects, and the attendant alliance between monotheism and humanism, God- and man-made stories of progress, accommodated by the idea of ethical monotheism and that most slippery of philosophemes—*Geist.*

As Derrida says, "within what one calls religions—Judaism, Christianity, Islam, or other religions—there are tensions, heterogeneity, disruptive volcanos, sometimes texts, especially those of the prophets, which cannot be reduced to a corpus, or a system," which is a way of saying that everything is in the Bible, everything and the rest. He says that he wants to "keep the right" (notably not to *assert* the right, as if for the first time, as if this has never happened before) to "read these texts in a way that has to be constantly reinvented," and he suggests that "beliefs, dogmas, scriptures, institutions" need to be deconstructed, "sometimes in the name of faith."[69] To deconstruct is to take account of *différance*: *différance* between scriptures, theologies, beliefs, institutions; *différance* between Old Testament/Tanakh and Jewish and Christian response. It is to explore *différance* between the Gods of Christian and Jewish theologies and ontotheology and the Gods of scripture, as well as *différance* within the biblical (a bundle of variously singular idioms in a deceptively single binding) and *différance* within a saying (or a hearing) and the structure of time and logic itself. Attuning our ear to *différance* opens interpretation up to the risk and promise of, for example, hearing the conversation that goes on between Christians and Jews and the editors of the biblical as they hear scripture request forgiveness for the not-said; or "placing in the way of the [theologically] systematic and the programmatic, reminders of the [biblically] idiomatic";[70] or taking account precisely of those texts that emerge as "a monster, a monstrous mutation without tradition and normative precedent,"[71] on the assumption that even monsters (from *monstrum*: to show) show us something, even if they are slouching "rough beasts" to whom no Synagogue or Church in its right mind would fling open the door and say "welcome."

We are not simply restating the Lutheran/Kierkegaardian truism that the Bible can deliver shocks or wounds to Christian theology that are guaranteed to be sacrificially productive for that theology; they may also be a disaster, though some (God-as-woman, God-as-animal, or God-as-radically-incarnate [before Jesus]), may offer a certain promise through their threat.[72] We are not attempting to recall Jews and Christians back to the stable, permanent, originary letter of the Bible, in a brand of neo-fundamentalism of which, as Derrida rightly warns, there are many; nor are we advocating another version of so-called "biblical theology," that has, to date, relied on the principles of constancy and the *wil'o'the wisp* desire that the Bible will, if left long enough, decant its own theology, somehow other to Western metaphysics, somehow disentangled from all the Greek and German that has been overlaid on it.[73] Nor are we adding our voices to those who argue that we should overcome the God of ontotheology (seen, in the legacy of Pascal, as an idol, an abstraction, a marrano, a vaporization of the personal God of Abraham, Isaac, and Jacob) by returning to the arms of the Gods who came before "him." (Anyone who *reads* the Bible knows that its Gods also constitute a warning, and are certainly not only, and often not even, "personal" Gods before whom you "sing" and "dance."[74]) Even the briefest glance at the regretful, embodied, jealous, hidden, abject, wound-like, animal-like, riddling, volcanic gods of the Old Testament/Tanakh, throws into clear relief the services rendered by the philosopher's God of absolute presence, absolute transcendence, and unadulterated unity. As poor existing individuals we can see how a God who is emphatically not subject to the vacillations, calculations, injustices, and violences of the world is *infinitely* preferable to a God who provides no Archimedian point of refuge outside the world, and whose identity is intimately tied to the vacillations of time, and the time and space of *différance*. We can see how the God of metaphysics provides us with secure systems and secure outcomes and the assurance that the biblical (insofar as it *is* for us) is good (for us). We can see how the ontotheological word "God" does important work as a consolidating "word-hope," like the word "I"; and we can fully endorse—in a sense—the desire to fully equate God with the good, an equation which implicitly (and silently) *corrects* earlier Jewish and Christian gods, some of whom seem not to have heard of the Enlightenment critique of sovereignty and the injunction against cruel and unnatural violence. But the harmonizing discourses of ontotheology exonerate us from laboring, actively and critically, in the legacy of the biblical to articulate how the possibility of the very best is tied up with the risk of the very worst (indeed it implies that it is possible to decant the best from the worst, as if that were simply a possibility of choosing a canon-within-a-canon, rather than engaging with the performative promise and threat of each and every text). And it effectively *saves* us from engaging the problematic of God-in-language, God-in-time, the becoming-literature-of-God and God not as "one man only," but "the steady advance" of changing characteristics, text after text, "hour after hour."[75]

What would it mean, we wonder, to write (within) the legacy of the "biblical" as an unfinished sentence, where we do not know what precisely awaits us at the end? What would it mean to write in/of the biblical as if we did not know what will happen to us or what awaits us at the end of the sentence, neither who nor what awaits whom or what? What might it mean to live and write within this promise and this threat?[76]

The Morning After the Day of the Lord

What is coming for Amos is corpses and *khôra*, a formless and unnameable "it" that he cannot identify but only evoke with images of unidentifiable horror, like a kind of dissolution into the *tohu wa bohu*, what Lévinas calls the *il y a*, the elemental night.

All is lost, time has run out, death is all in all, this is the end.

The trigger is pulled, the shot rings out, a fiery flash and an ear shattering blast—except we are not dead. The coda reads like a man whose execution is—unknown to him—being staged by executioners firing blanks. The moment of the absolute end comes and goes and he is not dead. It reads like someone who has awakened from a horrible nightmare, the morning after (the day of the Lord), or like someone whose last memory was of being caught in a catastrophe in which he was about to be destroyed who awakens to find that he is not dead. In the coda the whole thing turns around in a way that, considered as a purely textual operation, may be viewed as a kind of self-subverting auto-deconstruction. Language swoons under the terror of absolute alterity, the threat of absolute death; it falls vertiginously into the volcano over which it had been hovering—except it awakens to find itself still alive. Living on. We always wake from the dream at the point where we are about to die. In the coda, the discourse of Amos—unable to sustain this impossible trope any longer, unable to dream its own death, unable to incinerate itself or wipe away its own trace, in short, unable to die—turns itself around. Whether or not the final coda is, from the standpoint of its content, a logical contradiction or a clumsy historical addendum, it represents from a purely textualist point of view the operation of *écriture* and the impossibility of sustaining this impossible trope. Here language awakens from the nightmare, relents and relaxes its intensity; here from sheer exhaustion the death sentence turns itself around into a deferral, the death foreseen turns into death forestalled. The textual coda marks the temporal coda, the little interval between now and death that is always added on by time and writing, the postponement in which there is always hope in a future that is not a matter of individual courage but of the very idea of time and writing.

In the end, or from the start, the sayings of Amos—whatever they may imply about the God of Metaphysics or the God of the Gift or the God of Retribution—make use of the structure of *écriture* which is why they can and do turn around. The words that Amos finds to call for death also call for life and for the justice to come and testify to the impossibility of thinking death, of saying what the words of Amos want to say. The absolute and simple end—God, like death, death, like God, God or death—being unthinkable and unsayable, turns its back on us, deflects our approach, turns us aside, and turns our words inside out.

"I will restore the fortunes of my people Israel," says the Lord God. Precisely in accord with the structure of time, of history, of the future, and of writing. The "come, *oui, oui*" is inscribed in living on, in life, which is, however unlivable, the arrest of death.

"I promise you, you are dead."
I promise you.

References

1. Our own story of the ear (or our reading of Amos's) was prompted by Derrida's "otobiography." See *The Ear of the Other: Otobiography, Transference, Translation*, trans. Peggy Kamuf, ed. Christie V. Macdonald (New York: Schocken Books, 1985).
2. Jacques Derrida, "The Villanova Roundtable: A Conversation with Jacques Derrida," in *Deconstruction in a Nutshell: A Conversation with Jacques Derrida*, ed. John D. Caputo (New York: Fordham University Press, 1997), p. 21.
3. Jacques Derrida, "Of An Apocalyptic Tone Recently Adopted in Philosophy," *Oxford Literary Review* 6:2 (1984): 3–37.
4. Jacques Derrida, *La carte postale: De Socrate à Freud et au-delà* (Paris: Flammerion, 1980), p. 148; trans. Alan Bass as *The Postcard: From Socrates to Freud and Beyond* (Chicago: University of Chicago Press, 1987), p. 136.
5. Emmanuel Lévinas, *Totality and Infinity: An Essay on Exteriority*, trans. Alphonso Lingis (Pittsburgh: Duquesne University Press, 1969), p. 165.
6. By way of convenient shorthand we will be referring to the authors of Amos collectively as "Amos," even though we want to detach ourselves from a former (Romantic) period of biblical scholarship that personified the book as the unmediated expression of a single soul, mind, heart.
7. Technically the book is set just *before* the earthquake. However, as Derrida observes in a different context, the very trembling of the text may be a "signal or symptom of something that has already taken place, as in the case of an earthquake [*tremblement de terre*]" (*The Gift of Death*, p. 53).
8. Gershom Scholem: *Dies Land ist ein Vulkan. Es behebergt die Sprache* cit. Jacques Derrida, "The Eyes of Language: The Abyss and the Volcano" in *Acts of Religion*, Jacques Derrida, ed. Gil Anidjar (New York and London: Routledge, 2002), pp. 191–227 (195).
9. Please note that all "transliterations" of Hebrew in this paper are intended only to give easily readable, and rough, approximations of the sound of the Hebrew words for non-Hebrew readers.
10. Jacques Derrida, "The Eyes of Language: The Abyss and the Volcano," in *Acts of Religion*, ed. Gil Anidjar, pp. 191–229 (202, 227).
11. Amos 6:6. Another less stark example in the same verse is the application of the word *mizraq*, "cultic vessel," to refer to everyday drinking vessels.
12. Jacques Derrida, "Passages—from Traumatism to Promise," in *Points: Interviews 1974–1994*, Jacques Derrida, ed. Elizabeth Weber (Stanford: Stanford University Press, 1995), pp. 372–395 (385), citing "A Discussion with Jacques Derrida," *Writing Instructor* 9, nos. 1–2 (Fall 1989–Winter 1990), p. 18.
13. Compare Edith Wyschogrod's comments on the home as that which can never be owned in the same sense as moveable goods (Wyschogrod, "Autochthony and Welcome," in this volume [chap. 3]; cf. Lévinas, *Totality and Infinity*, p. 172).

14. Seyyed Hossein Nasr, *Ideals and Realities of Islam* (London: Harper Collins, 1994; 1st ed. 1966), p. 47.
15. Compare the more muted "anti-Exodus"—or at least inverted Exodus—of Genesis 16 and 21, where the expulsion of Hagar at the hands of Abraham and Sarah explores, up to a point, the idea of the Egyptian as the one who suffers at the hands of the Israelite aggressor (see Phyllis Trible, *Texts of Terror: Literary-Feminist Readings of Biblical Narratives*, Overtures to Biblical Theology [Minneapolis: Fortress, 1994], pp. 9–35).
16. For Israel, who is Yahweh if not he who "brought Israel out of Egypt" (e.g., Deuteronomy 26:5–9)? Traditional theologies see the revelation of the I AM who brings Israel out of Egypt as the defining moment of a "Judeo-Christian" trajectory defined by the intersection of revelation and time (in a cross that anticipates the future incarnation of God in time and the climax of Christian revelation). Amos's story, in contrast, is not one of chronological revelation but of kairological disruption, jeopardizing any construct of religion built around concepts of salvation, the safe and sound, and the unscathed (cf. Derrida's meditations on religion in "Faith and Knowledge: The Two Sources of 'Religion' at the Limits of Reason Alone," in *Religion*, Jacques Derrida and Gianni Vattimo, trans. Sam Weber [Oxford: Polity Press, 1998], pp. 1–78).
17. On language's potential to turn against its speakers, see Scholem, cit. Derrida "The Eyes of Language," p. 210. For Derrida's observations on the contradictory, deconstructive laws of hospitality, see "Hostipitality," in *Acts of Religion*, pp. 358–420.
18. Derrida, "Faith and Knowledge," p. 22.
19. Generally speaking, the biblical others, for all their strength, are described as mere accessories in a theological economy that revolves around Israel and Judah: Assyria, the razor hired from beyond the river (Isaiah 7:20) is hired because of Israel's sin; Babylon is used as a tool of God's wrath to rinse out the unclean bowl of Judah (2 Kings 21:13); and Pharoah's heart is hardened and the Egyptians are bombarded with plagues, boils, frogs and lice so that the Israelites "may tell in the hearing of their sons and their sons' sons how Yahweh made sport of the Egyptians" (Exodus 10:2). But occasionally, perhaps when even the most credulous Israelite or Judean cannot quite believe that the national sin (and less frequently worthiness) is of such magnitude as to truly bear responsibility for the balance of world affairs, the Old Testament/Tanakh asks, "What if God is giving the Egyptians *their* Exodus; what if these events are not attributed to our sins but to God's love of the Assyrians, or Babylonians?" Working from the assumption that the one God must by definition calculate his relative responsibilities, the Old Testament/Tanakh asks, and not just in Amos, *what if* we are not always at the centre of the ledger? The whole book of Jonah, for example, asks, in an at once terrifying and jocular *what if*, what if the known world were overthrown, if God "*hofak*-ed," and started to love the Ninevites (the Assyrians) more than his own? (For discussion of how Jonah and Jewish interpretation of Jonah deals with this question, see Sherwood, *A Biblical Text and Its Afterlives: The Survival of Jonah in Western Culture* [Cambridge: Cambridge University Press, 2001], pp. 120–127 and pp. 239–287, especially pp. 244–245 and 280–287). At these crisis points, ethics and theology are inextricably entangled with *Realpolitik* and the texts confront, more in the manner of Derrida than Lévinas, the self-jeopardizing consequences of loving the stranger or "having" (or rather being dispossessed of) a God more in love with the stranger than yourself. Lévinas elides the distinction between an active subject who welcomes and a hostage-subject, subjected to the persecution and trauma of an alterity that precedes "him", and allows an uncomfortable slippage between the story of the self hollowed out and preceded by the other, and a messianic Israel that should, by rights, defend itself against the other-as-threat. But more in the manner of Derrida, these biblical crisis points open out the aporiae of self-gift, self-defense, and self-taken-before-the-consent/being-of-the-self. It would be a fascinating study (for another time and place) to ask how the biblical story of a lately come nation, whose experience is frequently described as that of being slopped from one container to another, or "gnawed," hooked, or digested by the other—indeed actually passing through the stomach of the other (Jeremiah 51:34)—relates to Lévinas's and Derrida's different visions of radical alterity.
20. On the function of the devil as the one who serves to exculpate the one God precisely by his exteriority to the one God (and the analogous role played by the Jew in the Christian

economy), see Derrida, following Freud, in *Archive Fever: A Freudian Impression*, trans. Eric Prenowitz (Chicago and London: University of Chicago Press, 1995), p. 13.

21. For a playful treatment of the fruit-corpse vision as "illustrated" by René Magritte, see Sherwood, "Of Fruit and Corpses and Wordplay Visions: Picturing Amos 8:1–3," *Journal for the Study of the Old Testament* 92 (2001): 5–27.

22. See "Circumfession," in *Jacques Derrida*, Geoffrey Bennington and Derrida (Chicago and London: University of Chicago Press, 1993), p. 154. The ambiguation of the "Je suis" seems to draw on Lacan's exegesis of Exodus 3.14, where a Francophone God who says "*Je suis celui qui suis*" leads to an analysis of God's "I" as hidden, and lagging behind his speech (Jacques Lacan, *Le Seminaire, livre XX: Encore*, ed. Jacques Alain-Miller [Paris: Seuil, 1981], p. 324). On the necessary risk and presumptuousness of the "I am/I follow" see Derrida, *Monolingualism of the Other or the Prosthesis of Origin*, trans. Patrick Mensah (Stanford: Stanford University Press, 1998), p. 50.

23. Note how words take on a very physical quality in Amos as they do in Derrida. The book begins with the declaration that Amos has *seen words* (1:1) and goes on to describe the people as "destroyers of compassion and the tearers of anger," as if compassion were a citadel and anger were a fabric (1:11). In a similar vein it warns that "escape" or "flight" may "perish" (2:14), so giving substance to abstract nouns.

24. *Timon of Athens* IV.3 ll.28–30; Shelley, "A Defence of Poetry," cit. Gayatri Chakravorty Spivak, "Speculations on Reading Marx: After Reading Derrida" in *Poststructuralism and the Question of History*, eds. Derek Attridge, Geoffrey Bennington, and Robert Young (Cambridge: Cambridge University Press, 1987), pp. 30–62 (61, n. 29).

25. Catherine Keller, "Revealing Violence: Empire and Atrocity in the Christian Apocalypse," forthcoming in *JAAR* 72:4 (2004).

26. I (YS) share Catherine Keller's reservations about how the phrase "religion without religion" may set off unintentional echoes in Protestant ears. As Keller warns in her essay in this volume (see Keller and Moore "Derridapocalypse"), "religion without religion" resonates all-too-easily with well-known Protestant hymns to pure faith, or faith alone. And it seems to come perilously close to Karl Barth's hugely influential distinction between Christian faith versus the earthbound, manmade idols and structures that constitute what he disparages as "religion." My question—as someone who is most familiar with Christian language in its Protestant idioms and inflections—is how an antidogmatic, nonreified, and in many ways thoroughly Romantic nonconcept of "religion without religion" can escape what Walter Lowe, in this volume (chap. 7), locates as the traditional and essential Christian element of "anti-Judaism" (see Lowe, "Christianity and Anti-Judaism"). More specifically, how can it escape the particularly Protestant language of the dead letter/external ritual that Derrida describes himself as having taken in, into his thoroughly Christian *insides*, in *Monolingualism of the Other*? (Compare Derrida's circumfessional: "I used to think that I was dealing with a Judaism of 'external signs.' But I could not rebel … I could not lose my temper, except from what was already an insidious Christian contamination: the respectful belief in inwardness, the preference for intention, the heart, the mind, mistrust with respect to literalness or to an objective action given to the mechanicity of the body, in short, a denunciation, so coventional, of Pharisaism" (*Monolingualism of the Other*, p. 54).

27. Shalom M. Paul, *Amos* (Hermeneia; Minneapolis: Fortress Press, 1991), p. 177.

28. Wisdom theology is the distinctive form of theology that governs Proverbs, Job, and Qoheleth (or Ecclesiastes) but that also exerts a strong and partial influence on other biblical literature. The governing principle, by no means uncontested within the genre, is that God is revealed not through dramatic intervention, but through a world designed around the principles of justice. The created order naturally rewards those who live in tune with its intrinsic order and also—equally naturally—recoils against the one who acts unjustly or foolishly. The book of Amos pushes this thesis to its most extreme conclusions, postulating a highly sensitive universe in which the slightest injustice threatens to cause the earth to sink back into primal chaos. As Susan Gillingham observes, "There is in the book of Amos a profound link between the natural order and natural justice, and it is this which distinguishes the actions of Amos's God from the actions of other gods; to put things starkly, the preservation of justice and righteousness throughout all humanity is more important than the perpetuity of the natural order for its own sake" (Gillingham, "God and Creation in the Book of Amos," *Scottish Journal of Theology* 45 [1992]: 165–184 [182–183].)

29. In Amos 7:10 the priest Amaziah complains לא־תוכל ארץ להכיל את־כל־דבריו, "The land cannot contain all his words." The verb כול ("to contain") suggests that the words are being compared to a liquid rather than to a lead weight, as suggested, for example, in the NRSV translation, "The land is not able to bear all his words."

30. John D. Caputo, *Against Ethics: A Contribution to a Poetics of Obligation With Constant Reference to Deconstruction* (Bloomington and Indianapolis: Indiana University Press, 1993), pp. 18, 80.

31. On the question of whether the audience hears the "you" of Amos as an "us" or "them," see "Warning: It's As If They're Already Dead. We're the Only Ones in the World," this chap.

32. Jacques Derrida, *Glas*, trans. John P. Leavey Jr. and Richard Rand (Lincoln and London: University of Nebraska Press, 1986, 1st ed. 1974), p. 243.

33. See *The Gift of Death*, pp. 97–115. For a discussion of Derrida's analysis of the relationship between the economies of earth and heaven, see Tyler Roberts' "Sacrifice and Secularization: Derrida, De Vries, and the Future of Mourning" in this volume (chap. 16).

34. The Isaianic paradox, which resonates so provocatively with what we are discussing here, can be made to mean (without too much coercion) "We have made a deal with death; i.e. we have humanised and mollified death," or "We have chosen an alliance with death over and against an alliance with God," or perhaps, "We are as irrevocably joined to death as we are to God—i.e. the two are in a certain sense the same." In order to banish the more unsettling readings, commentators have over-leant on what Derrida calls the "guardrail of context," preferring to read "death" as a mere synonym for "Egypt" or "ancestor worship" or as shorthand for the "cult of the dead." (For discussion, see Francis Landy, "Tracing the Voice of the Other: Isaiah 28 and the Covenant with Death," in *Beauty and the Enigma and Other Essays on the Hebrew Bible*, JSOT Supplement Series 312 [Sheffield: Sheffield Academic Press, 2001], pp. 185–205 [186–187]).

35. In Hebrew, this difference revolves around the unmarked difference between the jussive and imperfect sense.

36. "Johannes Climacus" (Søren Kierkegaard), *Philosophical Fragments*, eds. and trans. Howard V. Hong and Edna H. Hong, Kierkegaard's Writings VII, (Princeton: Princeton University Press, 1985), p. 30. Climacus' prooftext is Exodus 33:20 where Yahweh says to Moses: "You cannot see my face, for man cannot see me and live," but he could equally have appealed to the book of Amos.

37. Lévinas, *Totality and Infinity*, pp. 234–35.

38. Jorg Jeremias, *The Book of Amos: A Commentary*, trans. Douglas Scott (Louisville: Westminster John Knox Press, 1998), pp. 154–58.

39. A revelation should, after all, be revealing, as Martin Luther complained of the Apocalypse of John. For a discussion of literature as a request for forgiveness for not having said, see Jacques Derrida, "La littérature au secret: Une filiation impossible," *Donner La Mort* (Paris: Editions Galilée, 1999), pp. 161–209.

40. For a more detailed analysis of this metalepsis, see Herbert Marks, "On Prophetic Stammering," in *The Book and the Text: The Bible and Literary Theory*, ed. Regina Schwartz (Oxford: Basil Blackwell, 1990), pp. 60–80 (62).

41. Derrida says that death is "the most tempting figure" for the "absolute secret" ("I have a taste for the secret" in *A Taste for the Secret*, Jacques Derrida and Maurizo Ferraris, trans. Giacomo Donis, eds. Giacomo Donis and David Webb [Oxford: Polity, 2001] pp. 1–93 [58]). Cf. Derrida, *The Gift of Death*, p. 10, n. 5: "Literature concerning the secret is almost always organised around scenes and intrigues that deal with death."

42. Sheol in Old Testament/Tanakh is the place of "shades" and nonbeing.

43. This is my own very loose translation of a notoriously difficult Hebrew passage, attempting to convey the element of drama, performance, even improvization [YS].

44. There are three emphatic silences in the book of Amos. Compare the injunction at the end of the fruit-corpse vision ("Women wailing; corpses lying everywhere. Hush!" [8:3]), and the enigmatic "Therefore the wise man will keep silent in such a time; for it is an evil time" (5:13).

45. Lévinas, *Totality and Infinity*, pp. 157, 172; cf. n. 11 and Wyschogrod, "Autochthony and Welcome: Discourses of Exile in Lévinas and Derrida" in this volume (chap. 3).

46. Jeremias, *The Book of Amos*, p. 159.

47. James Luther Mays, *Amos: A Commentary*, Old Testament Library, (Philadelphia: SCM Press and Westminster Press, 1969), pp. 165–166.
48. Compare Derrida's comments on Plato's Timaeus in "Avances" in Serge Margel, *Le tombeau du dieu artisan: sur Platon* (Paris: Editions de Minuit, 1995), pp. 11–43.
49. Derrida, *Le Toucher, Jean-Luc Nancy* (Paris: Galilée, 2000), p. 301; *Donner la Mort*, p. 168. Cf. Derrida's earlier comments on Jabès' "God in perpetual revolt against God" and "God as an interrogation of God," in "Edmund Jabès and the Question of the Book," in *Writing and Difference*, trans. Alan Bass (London: Routledge, 1990, 1st ed. 1978), pp. 64–78 (68). See also *Donner La Mort*, pp. 161–209 (esp. pp. 185–202).
50. Julius Wellhausen famously described Amos' editorial appendix as "Rosen und Lavendel statt Blut und Eisen" (cit. without full reference in Paul, *Amos*, p. 288).
51. Derrida, "Edmund Jabès and the Question of the Book," p. 69; Jacques Derrida, *Cinders*, trans. and ed. Ned Lukacher (Lincoln: University of Nebraska Press, 1991), pp. 39, 59; "Unsealing (the old new language)," in *Points*, pp. 115–131 (118).
52. Derrida, "I have a taste for the secret," p. 23.
53. In J.L. Kugel, "Two Introductions to Midrash," in *Midrash and Literature*, eds. Geoffrey H. Hartman and Sanford Budick (New Haven: Yale University Press, 1986), pp. 77–103 (77–78). Compare Robert Gibbs's analysis of how Jewish interpretation "saves" the biblical text by interrogating it with the concept of resurrection. See also his comments on interpretation as negotiation and disappointment (Gibbs, "Messianic Epistemology").
54. *Mekilta* 4.2.221.
55. See for example *Pesikta de Rav Kahana* 16, 125b; *Pesikta Rabbati* 33, 150b; *Midrash Vayikra Rabbah* 10:2 where Amos as is described as פסילום בלשונו. Another (albeit only partial explanation) is that the verb עמם ("to load" or "to carry a load") is so close to the verb נשא in meaning that the fortuitous coincidence is hard to resist.
56. For the Jewish understanding of the ideal prophet see *Mekilta de Rabbi Ishmael, Pisha* and Sherwood, *A Biblical Text and Its Afterlives*, pp. 120–121. For a discussion of the double identification and the stammering of the prophets see Marks, "On Prophetic Stammering." (Marks alludes to Amos but is unaware of the fact that he too was diagnosed by the Rabbis as a stammerer.)
57. *Genesis Rabbah, Lek Leka* 39:6.
58. Jacques Derrida, "Living On. Border Lines," in *Deconstruction and Criticism*, Harold Bloom, Paul de Man, Jacques Derrida, Geoffrey H. Hartman and J. Hillis Miller (New York: Continuum, 1992), pp. 75–176 (109–110).
59. Nothing would have prevented the southern kingdom from being as effectively destroyed as the northern; nothing would have prevented these texts from being lost forever, which did not happen.
60. See Derrida, "Of an Apocalyptic Tone," p. 24.
61. For the argument of which this statement is a reductive précis, see Immanuel Kant, *Metaphysics of Morals*, trans. Mary Gregor (Cambridge: Cambridge University Press, 1991), pp. 110–111.
62. See Derrida, "Of an Apocalyptic Tone," p. 24.
63. Shalom Paul tells us that "Excavations at Samaria have unearthed the opulence of these buildings with their plethora of ivory inlays" (Paul, *Amos*, p. 126). The statement is remarkable not only for its confidence in the fact that this ivory (such as it is) and Amos's textual "ivory" are equivalent, but also for the assumption that the text can be authenticated and authorized by the testimony of archaeology. For the most part, Biblical Studies continues to work out the relationship between the Bible and modernity on historical/archaeological grounds, still resolutely bracketing out the conflict between the ethical and the religious that Kant, Hegel, and Kierkegaard saw as the main site of conflict.
64. For a denunciation of commentators' sleights of hand in placing themselves outside Amos' ethical and economic critique—delivered in a tone at least as fiery as that of the prophet Amos—see David J.A. Clines, "Metacommentating Amos," in *Interested Parties: The Ideology of Writers and Readers of the Hebrew Bible*, David J.A. Clines, Gender, Culture, Theory 1, JSOT Supplement Series 205 (Sheffield: Sheffield Academic Press, 1995), pp. 76–93. For a discussion of ways in which the "Old Testament" is sometimes used by Christian theology or Biblical Studies as if it were a colonial outpost, in which the inhabitants are conceived of as both the "imitation" and the "antithesis" of the Christian self, see Sherwood, *A Biblical*

Text and Its Afterlives, pp. 77-87 and "'Colonising the Old Testament' or 'Representing Christian Interests Abroad': Jewish-Christian Relations across Old Testament Territory," in *Christian-Jewish Relations Through the Centuries,* eds. Stanley E. Porter and Brook W.R. Pearson, JSNT Supplement series 192, Roehampton Papers 6, (Sheffield: Sheffield Academic Press, 2000), pp. 255–283.

65. Emmanuel Lévinas, "Toward the Other," in *Nine Talmudic Readings,* ed. A. Aronowicz (Bloomington and Indianapolis: Indiana University Press, 1990), pp. 12–29 (16).

66. For a useful survey, see Paul R. Noble, "Amos's Absolute 'No,'" *Vetus Testamentum* 47 (1997): pp. 329–340.

67. Paul Ricoeur, *Figuring the Sacred* (Minneapolis: Augsburg Fortress, 1995), p. 236.

68. Derrida, "The Eyes of Language," p. 196.

69. Derrida, "The Villanova Roundtable," p. 21.

70. Jacques Derrida, *Acts of Literature,* ed. Derek Attridge (London and New York: Routledge, 1992), p. 14.

71. Derrida, "Jacques Derrida: Deconstruction and the Other," in *Dialogues with Contemporary Continental Thinkers: The Phenomenological Heritage,* ed. Richard Kearney (Manchester: Manchester University Press, 1984), p. 123.

72. Certainly the theologies of the Old Testament/Tanakh seem to resonate in provocative ways with Ellen Armour's discussion of how the sovereignty of man is constructed in complex relation to its racial and sexual others, to the animal and to God (see her "Touching Transcendence: Sexual Difference and Sexuality in Derrida's *Le Toucher*" in this volume). If the God of Amos gives an Exodus to other nations and tribes, does that imply that he is, or at least *may be*, a racial stranger? And might the OT/Tanakh figures of God-as-animal or God-as-woman suggest, from the very midst of the biblical, a certain contestation of what are assumed to be solid, "Judeo-Christian," "biblical" constructions of the being of man and the being of God?

73. For a detailed critique of the "biblical theology" movement on these grounds, see James Barr, *The Concept of Biblical Theology: An Old Testament Perspective* (London: SCM Press, 1999).

74. Cf. Heidegger's critique of onto-theology on the grounds that "we can neither pray nor sacrifice to this god [of philosophy]. Before the *causa sui,* man can neither fall to his knees in awe nor can he play music and dance before this god." See Martin Heidegger, *Identity and Difference,* trans. Joan Stambaugh (New York: Harper and Row, 1969), p. 72.

75. Marcel Proust, "The Fugitive," *A la récherche du temps perdu,* trans. C.K.S. Moncrieff (New York: Vintage Books, 1970), p. 54.

76. Derrida, *Monolingualism of the Other,* pp. 21–22.

CHAPTER 15

The Word Becomes Text: A Dialogue between Kevin Hart and George Aichele[1]

KEVIN HART AND GEORGE AICHELE

Kevin Hart: We decided a while back to talk about John 8:1–11, a very familiar story, usually known as the "woman taken in adultery." We see the woman only for a moment or two, and then only in stark relief. Was the discovery of her adultery set up by her husband so he could get a divorce? Or is her husband an injured party? Where is the man with whom she was found? None of these things are mentioned in the story, but they press upon it, and that pressure helps to make it such a powerful narrative. Like so many biblical stories, it leads us to speculate what happens outside the narrative frame. Did the woman become pregnant? If so, what happened to her and her child? Where did the woman live after she was dismissed by Jesus? And what happened to the child when he or she was born?

Doubtless these questions are idle, but one of the questions I have posed intersects the story at one or two precise points, though at the level of reception rather than theme. For it needs to be said, right at the start, that this story is what some biblical scholars call an "orphan text." It has no secure home. If I can trespass a little on your ground, I understand that the story has no early Greek witnesses, that there is no support for its inclusion in John among Old Syriac or Coptic documents. One manuscript has it appearing after John 7:36, another has it at the end of the gospel. Some scholars say it is more in keeping with Lucan than with Johannine narrative, and it is, after all, to be found after Luke 21:38 in one important source. So the story of the woman taken in adultery is itself promiscuous. Yet all orphans have a father, even if they do not have a home. And so I thought we might begin today by asking: Who is the orphan's father?

George Aichele: I find this phrase, "orphan text," awkward and more than a little perplexing—after all, how can any text be an orphan? Or rather, as Socrates suggested, every written text is an orphan, until its "parent" comes to "rescue" it.[2] How else can we talk about the orphan's father? In this light, it is especially interesting that so many commentators on the gospel of John refuse to discuss John 7:53–8:11, or else they relegate this passage to footnotes or appendices. For them it is not so much an orphan text as an illegitimate one. Perhaps these scholars do not want to be named as accomplices in a paternity suit?

But perhaps the "orphan" that you are questioning is the unmentioned child of the adulterous woman. I am intrigued by the connection that you have hinted between the text's orphan status, and the status of the woman in this story. Given the strong interest in the gospel of John in the connection between the Son and the Father, it may be significant that the father does not appear here. Or it may not: there is a widely noted lack of "fit" between this story and the remainder of the gospel—its odd terminology, the wide variations in the placement or even the presence of this passage in ancient manuscripts. This is a text that blurs the edges of the canon of scriptures—and by blurring those edges, it makes the concept of canonical totality problematic. How can any text be both in and not in the canon? This is a profoundly theological issue. And this too may be why some commentators are reluctant to speak about this text in John's gospel. To comment on a text is to "canonize" it. It may be convenient that this troublesome story is of questionable canonical value, for this makes it easier for the commentators to avoid saying anything about it.

In addition, it seems to me that there is another "orphan text," one that is not this passage itself, but rather that only barely appears within the passage. It is the text that none of us can read—the words or doodles that Jesus writes on the ground. Here we have a text that not only doesn't "fit" in the Bible but that is indeed entirely illegible—completely beyond rescue, as Socrates might say. And yet despite its illegibility to us, who are John's readers, we are told that it is a text, a writing (*egraphen*, John 8:8, see also 8:6). Its "parent," Jesus, is even present in John's story, but he does not speak about this text. Or does he? It is as though we see here signifiers without a signified, or rather, we see Jesus' inscrutable signifiers only as a part of the signified that is this story.

Kevin Hart: The expression "orphan text" simply indicates that our story has no fixed home but is found in several early sources. The Eastern Fathers didn't recognize it: Origen, Cyprian, Chrysostom, and Nonnus all pass over it in silence, and for the first millennium there is no Orthodox commentary on it. The orphan fares much better with the Western Fathers: Ambrose and Augustine wanted it to have a home in the Catholic tradition. The adoption is concluded by Jerome who includes it in John, and since the Vulgate determines the canon for Catholics the orphan's past is largely forgotten today except by biblical scholars. Once in the canon, the story becomes a central reference for Christian understanding of forgiveness; and one could even say that the orphan was left out in the cold for so long because it spoke of forgiveness in a way that did not fit the early Church's strict understanding of penance. So we have two big theological issues that have come to light: the authority and the function of the canon and the nature of Christian forgiveness. If we put the two together, we come up with a third issue: the relation between biblical exegesis and theology.

You seize on a fourth issue, Jesus' doodling or writing in the dust. It is an arresting image since we are no more used to seeing Jesus write than Socrates. Those marks on the dust have called forth all manner of interpretations! Oddly enough, the interpretation I find most productive is by an exegete I don't usually like, Adrienne von Speyr. To my mind she runs theology—and if you're not familiar with her, let me say that she urges a very conservative Catholic theology—rather hard over the gospel, showing no interest in textual problems or even in the gospel as a text. What I like about von Speyr's reading, though, is that she stresses that Jesus writes on the ground in order to be incomprehensible. Is Jesus recalling the action of YHWH on Mt. Sinai, writing the decalogue before giving it to Moses? If so, he is asking the crowd to recognize the gravity of Torah: justice does not offer itself quickly. Or is Jesus recalling the act of a Roman magistrate, writing the sentence before pronouncing it? If so, he is appealing to Roman law to indicate that justice must be considered before being enacted. The crowd that wishes to trap him with regard to the conflicting claims of Jewish and Roman law in this difficult situation is being reminded, with regard to both codes, that their action is inappropriate. The trap is sprung merely by tracing a finger in the dust. I'm talking about only the first time that Jesus writes in the dust; there's a good deal more to say about the second time. But perhaps you want to follow one of the other issues we've discovered …

George Aichele: It seems to me that if readers—or at least, scholarly readers!—continue to be troubled by the "orphan" status of this text, and in some cases go so far as to refuse to include it in their commentaries, then its canonical status is still troubled, regardless of its inclusion in editions of the Bible or its approval by official church bodies. The fact that we are conscious that this passage may not properly belong to the gospel of John, and that we need to address this discomfort, says something not only about John 7:53–8:11 but also about the ideological viability of the canon of scriptures for us. A canon requires clarity about what is included and what is excluded. To the extent that this text in John is both included and excluded (or neither included nor excluded), then the canon itself is in trouble.

That Jesus writes inscrutably in the dirt in this passage is not merely coincidental. John's gospel is explicitly, quintessentially logocentric. Yet here we have Jesus, himself the incarnate Logos, writing illegible words on the ground. It is as though the process of the incarnation of the Word has now reached a kind of terminus, a purely physical text from which all trace of meaning (the *logos*) has been removed, in which no meaning could ever appear—an asemic text. In Derrida's terms, it is writing as a wound, as a trace, as the edge of language—only here made explicit, enacted by none other than the Logos of God!

There are two other texts in the gospel of John that also present something like this failure of logocentrism. These are not "orphan" texts, strictly speaking, but they are also points at which John's construction and canonical integrity are problematic. Many scholars have argued that this material was also added, somewhat later, to the text of the gospel, and the coincidence between these two texts and Jesus' two acts of writing (John 8:6, 8) intrigue me: might these two texts somehow be what Jesus wrote? These texts are the two endings of John, 20:30–31 and 21:24–25, which serve as brackets enclosing the alleged epilogue in John 21. Each of these endings announces in its own, self-referential way the incompleteness of writing, but precisely in the form of an assurance to the reader that John's text is authoritative.

Kevin Hart: I don't think that the question of canonicity can be separated from the question of authority. At Trent it was declared that "God is the author" of the forty-five books of the Old Testament and the twenty-seven books of the New Testament. Were we to follow that line, we would have no difficulty determining the paternity of the orphan: it would be the Father! I don't say this to mock the Council, only to make the point that, from the point of view of biblical canonicity, it doesn't make much difference if the story belongs in John or in Luke. One can go further. Divinely inspired or not, the orphan text has always been exposed to the possibility of misunderstanding, including being misunderstood as an authentic part of a sacred corpus. Because the orphan was adopted rather late there are always going to be doubts about whether it is a sacred text or whether it has been sacralized. It would fit into a "canon of preaching" or a "canon of spirituality." It would have to fit somewhere, since it is unimaginable, this late in history, not to have that text informing Christian ideas of forgiveness.

For their part, theologians often work with a "canon within the canon": the synoptics or certain epistles of Paul are taken as regulative, and the rest of the Bible is interpreted from that perspective. Now this leads us to the vexed issue of the relation of exegesis and dogmatics: is this a box we want to open today? Perhaps it is too late and we have already opened it, like Pandora's box. While those spirits flit about the room, let me say that modern biblical scholars will feel very uneasy, and rightly so, with having our story in the canon of the Bible. Some like Raymond Brown will imply that it is deutero-canonical, others like Rudolph Bultmann will excise it altogether. The Fellows of the Jesus Seminar, who are not known for their humor, cut this story from their edition of the fourth gospel but add that they assign it "to a special category of things they wish Jesus had said and done."

The fourth gospel is, as you say, quintessentially logocentric. But when you focus on Jesus writing in the dust, and we both know that the passage in question is more likely to be Lukan than Johannine, it seems to me an odd thing to focus on. Someone determined to defend the logocentrism of the gospel will surely say, "Oh well, that passage, and the other ones you mention, are not really part of John." (Again, you see, the spectre of the canon within the canon floats by.) Were one to attempt a deconstructive reading of John, one would have more than enough writing to deal with, even without the image of Jesus writing. Actually, though, I suspect that we could go further and more quickly in that direction by considering the scene of forgiveness in our story.

George Aichele: Well, then, let's look at the question of forgiveness, but before I do so, one quick comment about exegesis. I've said elsewhere[3] that I regard the concept of exegesis as an ideological or theological illusion, part and parcel of the romantic notion that meaning is somehow hidden in the text, waiting there for some careful reader to draw it out. To claim to exegete is to refuse to confront the subjectivity and partiality of one's own eisegeses, to deny eisegesis by asserting that a neutral or objective careful reading, using a rigorous and justifiable methodology, can access the truth within the text. To admit that there is only eisegesis, never exegesis, is among other things to recognize that biblical study cannot exist apart from the theological or ideological interests of the reader. I read this text, and indeed any text, within the concrete limits of my situation, and so does every reader.

On to forgiveness: is this passage really about forgiveness? I know that's what everyone says, but the more I think about it, the less I believe it. Jesus replies to the Pharisees' question with the maxim, "Let him who is without sin among you be the first to throw a stone at her" (8:7). This is not a request for them to forgive her. Jesus does not advocate mercy as such, but rather that those who punish should themselves be righteous. However, a legal system that requires its judges and executioners to be sinless is quite impractical, for who would be qualified to judge the sinlessness of the judges? This concept of sin-free judgment self-destructs. Still, if there is anyone present in this scene in John 8 who is "without sin," it is the Word of God, the light shining in the darkness, Jesus himself. But Jesus apparently casts no stones. Does this mean that he has forgiven this nameless woman?

The questioners leave while Jesus is writing, and although John doesn't tell us why they left, the commentators love to explain that they must have felt guilty or some such. I don't think anyone has suggested that the people left because *they* forgave the adulterous woman. Jesus then asks the woman whether anyone has condemned her, and she replies—her one little speech—that they have not. To this Jesus responds, "Neither do I condemn you: go, and do not sin again" (8:11, RSV). But is this noncondemnation the same as forgiveness? Not really. If Jesus has not judged her, then how can he tell her not to "sin again?" Although he has not thrown a stone, he still seems to be in a position of judgment—which is a theme that John develops elsewhere.

So does forgiveness simply mean not casting the stone?

Kevin Hart: I can't go along with you when you say that one only reads into texts and not out of them. Of course, there is no natural meaning that abides in the text and is just waiting to be extracted. Meaning comes about by way of an intentional rapport with a text: we are always in contact with the world outside us, and in reading that requires us to acknowledge social codes and literary conventions that are in the text and that can be brought to light. We can see ways in which the codes and conventions are followed, see when they are transgressed, and so on. Needless to say, no text is isolated from its intentional horizons; it is embedded there, and if we reflect on those horizons we can become more finely aware of our concerns in reading the text, even perhaps why we are reading *this* particular text and not another. So consciousness is outwardly directed, yet it can reflect on itself and clarify why the intentional object is meaningful. Even if the social codes and literary conventions in a text are contained in subjectivity, they are not able to be manipulated at whim. The subjectivity at issue is not empirical but transcendental, and is linked to an inter-subjective community.

Turning to forgiveness, I think it is important to take this issue very slowly. I'd like to start by stressing the context in which the story is told. As I suggested earlier, this is one of those gospel stories where the scribes and Pharisees try to trap Jesus. Their trap is elegant: if Jesus judges according to Jewish law—Leviticus 20:10, Deuteronomy 22:22—then he will be in trouble with the Roman authorities; but if he judges according to Roman law, then he cannot be taken seriously as a Jewish teacher. Now Jesus is shown not to be interested merely in getting out of the trap or in exposing that the scribes and Pharisees are more concerned with trapping him than with obtaining justice. His response exceeds that. For the first time in the story, he makes an intelligible response; he speaks, "He that is without sin among you, let him first cast a stone at her." Notice what is said: there need be only *one* of the witnesses who is without sin for the woman to be put to death. Those witnesses who admit to being sinful are at liberty to cast all the other stones, the ones that in all likelihood would kill her. But there is no one who can begin the act. So I don't think that Jesus is being utopian; in fact, he is proposing a low standard for justice. Is there not even *one* person in this crowd—a crowd that partly consists of scribes and Pharisees—who has followed the Law and is free from sin? As you rightly say, the Johannine theology at work in structuring the story invites us to see Jesus, the Logos, as the sole sinless person in the temple. The story is concerned then to reveal Jesus as sinless and to let us see how a sinless man would act on this occasion. One thing he does is suspend the rule of law, or, rather, the rule of laws, both Jewish and Roman.

Has Jesus judged her? Yes: he says, "Go, and sin no more." There is no doubt that he believes adultery to be a sin, and the woman makes no attempt to deny that she has sinned. I do not think the theme of judging something to be a sin conflicts with the theme of forgiveness. Taking this issue slowly, we need to distinguish whether we are viewing a scene of mercy or a scene of forgiveness. One could argue, after all, that Jesus shows mercy but does not offer forgiveness. I would go further and say that forgiveness is implied. Are we not invited to see Jesus forgiving the woman, *and only Jesus*? For von Speyr, the woman is the only person in the crowd who admits to having sinned, and in her view this amounts to the woman making a silent confession. Indeed, von Speyr sees in the latter half of the story a foreshadowing of the sacrament of reconciliation, and so she is hardly reticent when it comes to laying a theological frame over the text. Putting that frame to one side, we might pose some questions. Does the woman need to confess in order to be forgiven? Does there have to be a word spoken—"your sins are forgiven"—for forgiveness to take place? And since Jesus suspends the rule of law, what is the relation between the law and forgiveness?

George Aichele: I'm afraid that our dialogue is in danger of splitting and becoming more than that, since we now have two topics on the table: the question of exegesis and the question of justice and forgiveness. But the more I think about it, the less sure I am that they are really two separate matters.

As I understand you, you argue that in this story, Jesus has suspended both the Roman and the Jewish laws, but that he has judged the woman nonetheless. That's a plausible reading, although I don't see any reference to Roman law and it looks to me like the test here is to see whether Jesus will interpret the Torah or not in a way that would be acceptable to the Pharisees and scribes. Of course, the Romans might have some interest in judgment as well, but Jesus is in the Temple in Jerusalem, and as far as I can tell, no Romans are present. Jesus judges the woman but he does not condemn her. The gospel of John tells us that Jesus' judgment is superior to that of the Pharisees (8:15–16), and that it is just (5:30), but I'm having trouble understanding how any judgment can be just unless it is according to some law. Likewise in the matter of forgiveness: how can there be forgiveness without law? Are you suggesting that Jesus judges in terms of some higher law, not a law of flesh or of appearance, but the truth of "right judgment" (7:24, 8:15–16)? That would be a rather Johannine claim.

Indeed, Jesus himself does give us a law: "Let him who is without sin among you be the first to throw a stone at her." Even though that statement is, as I mentioned earlier, an impractical law, an unworkable one, it is still a law. Jesus is here engaged in a matter of exegesis, or dare I say eisegesis! Whether this law that he announces is an acceptable interpretation of the Torah, I don't know, because even Jesus' opponents have become speechless by this point in the story. The King James translation tells us that they all left because they were "convicted by [their own] conscience(s)" (8:9), picking up on one of those numerous little variations within this orphan text—an orphan within the orphan, as it were. Their dark consciousnesses have been brought to gospel light. The Revised Standard Version and other modern translations omit this phrase, leaving the reason that the opponents left unclear. Has Jesus passed their test? Has their own self-awareness convinced them that he is right? Or to return to your comments about the text and the reader's consciousness, is this a point where locution becomes perlocution and where readers become conscious, along with Jesus' opponents, of our own need for forgiveness?

When you talk about exegesis, you make it sound as though the text is alive: when we read, we seek an "intentional rapport" with the text, respecting the codes and conventions embedded in it. Is this what makes Jesus' judgment "right" or "true," that he is in living harmony with his

Father? Who is better suited to interpret the Torah? After all, he is the living Word, according to John. Surely he understands the intentions of God, the true author of the Torah, better than any other. But on what basis can *we* judge Jesus' judgment about the law? If only the one who is attuned to the will of the Father can judge rightly, how dare we make any judgment? If our consciences convict us, then we cannot judge. And if we don't accept *John's* judgment about these matters, then the problem remains.

Yes, we disagree here. I think that written texts are dead, that they only look alive when we animate them using our own codes and conventions. Socrates says something rather like this. Which is not by any means to say that "anything goes." I can't read John's gospel or any other text in any way that I want. No matter how conscious I am of my codes and conventions—and I agree that consciousness of them is a good thing—I am still bound by them. In the language of this text, I am not "without sin": my intentional rapport is finally only with myself. I am trapped, just as the Pharisees are trapped by Jesus in this story, and I am forced to acknowledge the failure of my rapport with the text. This may be why I have trouble seeing justice or forgiveness in this text. I find myself reading John's gospel, with its grandiose claims about truthful testimony and reliable signs, with a great deal of suspicion. In the midst of all that, I find this little story about Jesus writing in the dirt to be a refreshing interruption, a narrative moment when all of John's grandiosity falls apart and what we are left with is something close to a bare text, simple scratch marks on the ground that refuse all of our interpretations. The living Word produces an inscrutable text!

Kevin Hart: I agree entirely that the question about forgiveness and the question about exegesis are bound together. So let me begin by clearing up a possible misunderstanding to do with exegesis. If consciousness has an intentional structure, as I think it does, then one always and already has a rapport with the things of the world, whether they be inanimate, living, or dead. It's not a matter of *seeking* a rapport: it is our condition as conscious beings. The act of reading turns on both noesis and noema, if I can use the vocabulary of Husserl's *Ideas* I, although in reading I also have an experience of writing, as Derrida would say, one that displaces the concepts of phenomenology. In a general sense, this experience of writing influences our reading of the fourth gospel and brings up some of the problems that we've been talking about.

The Roman law? Again, I entirely agree that it is not explicitly mentioned in the passage. We are dealing, though, with an extremely concise text that was most likely composed when its audience had an all too clear understanding of what "Roman Law" meant and what infringements of it could mean. As a people occupied by a highly efficient and violent military administration, the Jews in the story knew that all too well, surely much better than Roman citizens. I think the pressure of Roman Law is felt in the passage, almost as much as Jewish Law. But I am evoking "fingertips criticism." You know that wonderful passage in Nietzsche where he declares himself to be a slow reader? "Philology," he says, "is that venerable art and connoisseurship of the *word* which has nothing but delicate, cautious work to do and achieves nothing if it does not achieve it *lento*." And he goes on to tell us what it means to read well, "to read slowly, deeply, looking cautiously before and aft, with reservations, with doors left open, with delicate eyes and fingers ..."[4] I cite this partly in honor of your charming thought about the orphan within the orphan and partly because I feel the pressure of Roman Law in my fingertips as I read our story. Maybe, though, you think I am simply making smudges with my fingertips! I'm joking, since I don't doubt that given world enough and time we could work out the balance of truth in my claim, even though we might disagree about the exact proportions.

But here is the point where perhaps we disagree the most sharply. If I understand you correctly, you are saying that forgiveness is a matter of following a rule or a law, that justice also is a matter of rule following. You stand in a tradition in saying that, to be sure, one that minimizes differences between law and justice, though it is not the tradition in which I find myself at home. Justice and forgiveness strike me as *exceeding* rule or law. That view has a long tradition as well—it is certainly bound up with Christianity—though in our time the names that come to mind as representing it are Lévinas and Derrida. Those two philosophers are both thinkers of the gift, a notion sufficiently familiar to theologians, and maybe we need to say something about that. At the very least, though, we need to acknowledge that "forgiveness" contains a reference to giving. I think that Jesus, in our story, tries to suspend the law, both Jewish and Roman, in order to escape from the nasty trap in which he finds himself. He does not abolish the Jewish law: as we agree, he maintains that the woman has sinned. She does not dispute the judgment, and we are not invited to do so either. And yet Jesus in saying, "Neither do I condemn thee" exceeds the law. He could say, "If there is to be justice, then the Law must be followed scrupulously; but since the Law is not being followed with all due respect, the sentence cannot be carried out." But he does not say that; he goes much further than saying "not proven" and instead says "Neither do I condemn thee." It is in that very excess that I find forgiveness, although it is not said in so many words.

George Aichele: I'm a great admirer of Nietzsche, and I do find that as I get older, so I also read slower—but that may not be what Nietzsche had in mind!

I have no problem with the idea of forgiveness as exceeding the law, although I'm not persuaded that that is an entirely adequate definition. After all, there are other ways to exceed the law! But given that definition, I think that there can be no exceeding of the law unless there is a law to exceed. So in that sense, forgiveness requires a law. True, there is no law of forgiveness as such, i.e., "you ought to forgive these people under those conditions," but as excess, forgiveness is not possible without law. Or to put it another way, you cannot forgive unless you have been harmed under the law (although that is one point at which I find this definition troublesome). That itself is a kind of law, I suppose, not a law requiring or specifying forgiveness, but a law limiting the possibility of forgiveness.

On the other hand, I also cannot understand justice apart from the law, except in a purely hypothetical way. This story in the gospel of John is not about an abstract concept of justice, but rather a concrete encounter between a specific man and a specific woman. The law specifies in practical terms what justice is. Without law, justice is pure abstraction, and while we could still argue about the definition of that abstraction, I would not find the argument very interesting unless it had practical implications for how people live.

Thus, justice and forgiveness are both bound to the law, but in different ways. By exceeding the law, forgiveness exceeds justice. It is unjust. It is not always good to forgive. In a sense, it is not ever good to forgive, even though it may sometimes be better to forgive than to demand justice. Here again we may disagree, for I understand you to be saying that Jesus' words to the woman, "neither do I condemn you," represent in this story not only forgiveness but also justice. If "neither do I condemn you" means, "I do have the right to cast the first stone, in fact I alone have that right because I alone am without sin, but I choose not to do so," then yes, Jesus forgives her. In so doing, he acknowledges both the law of Moses that requires stoning (John 8:5) and his own law that requires that only sinless people can cast the first stone (8:7) and he exceeds both of these laws at once. It is not clear how that is just. In contrast, if "neither do I condemn you" means simply "I don't think you did anything wrong," then Jesus both rejects the law of Moses and apparently contradicts what he says next: "do not sin again." Either Jesus exceeds his own law or else he contradicts his own judgment of the woman.

I am willing to grant that even this is forgiveness, and maybe contradiction is at the heart of forgiveness, but it is still a rather puzzling sort of forgiveness. What then is the point of the maxim in John 8:7: "Let him who is without sin among you be the first to throw a stone at her?" Note that this saying is bracketed, as it were, by the two times that Jesus bends down to write upon the ground (8:6, 8). Is this arrangement of John's text a way of highlighting this saying, and if so why is the saying specially deserving of such treatment? Or are these words perhaps the ones that Jesus wrote?

Why does Jesus even bother to utter this rule that apparently applies only to himself, and that he apparently does not intend ever to invoke for himself? Is Jesus here defining an abstract concept of justice that has no practical significance? That's what I argued earlier. An alternative is possible, namely, that this is yet another weirdly ironic Johannine way for Jesus to say something important, in this case, "Don't ever throw stones at people!" or more broadly, "You ought always to forgive sinners?" But if that's the case, then Jesus has indeed made forgiveness into a law! And if that is what Jesus means by these words, or rather what John means by this story, that forgiveness is the law, that the law itself is that you should always exceed the law, then those who are bound by this law can no longer exceed the law. When forgiveness understood as not condemning people becomes the law, then forgiveness understood as exceeding the law becomes impossible.[5] Therefore either justice is impractical, or forgiveness is impossible.

Not all forgiveness exceeds the law. And, I suspect, not all forgiveness is a gift. Returning again to our story, and to your comments, what has Jesus given to this woman? Has he taken away her sin (John 1:29)? Has he somehow healed her, like the sick man whom he also tells to "sin no more" (5:14)? Does she now have faith, the belief in Jesus as the Christ that this gospel is evidently trying so hard to signify (20:31)? Does she have "life in his name?" Jesus has saved her life, to be sure, but that seems almost incidental in this story. Jesus has not condemned her—but is that a gift?

Kevin Hart: I don't think this is a story oriented around the end of the sinner coming to have faith that Jesus is the Christ. To be sure, the Johannine context puts all sorts of pressures on it, including those that you have mentioned, but we have already agreed, I think, that this text participates in the fourth gospel but does not belong to it unless, of course, you take Jerome's signature as the definitive sign of canonicity and authority. When Jesus asks, "Hath no man condemned thee?" the woman replies, "No man, Lord," and one could argue that in calling Jesus "Lord" the woman accepts that Jesus is the Christ. Indeed, if you push hard enough—I can imagine Meister Eckhart doing this—you could take her response to be, "No *man* has condemned me, but I know, as I stand here in your presence, that you, the *Logos*, know that I am sinful and have every right to condemn me." But

I don't want to engage here and now in that sort of reading which, I know, you would say is reading *into* a text not *out* of it; and you would have good reason to say so, even though I'd like to keep open the possibility of that style of reading in different circumstances.

Let me make a general comment, and then I'll say something about justice and forgiveness. One of the things we agreed to do in having this conversation is to keep in the back of our minds how an awareness of Jacques Derrida's writings might help one read the story about the woman caught in the act of adultery. I think we've been doing that, and incidentally it is interesting to see how his ideas can be worked into our different responses to the story. Derrida observed some years ago that deconstruction cannot be "applied" (to biblical criticism, for instance) because it is not a method or a theory in the first place, yet because deconstruction is not a self-contained theory it exists only in its applications, in its life in fresh contexts (like biblical criticism). That's a compelling aporia, and I sometimes think that Jacques must feel very torn when hearing a conversation like ours. On the one hand, it must be intriguing to see deconstruction being resituated and debated in a field that is not his own; while, on the other hand, it must cause some anxiety to see some texts that he has signed passing out of his hands, being put to uses that he might not agree with or might wish to distance himself from. That said, I think that if Jacques were on stage he would want to emphasize that neither forgiveness nor justice should be taken as given. The entire thrust of deconstruction, with regard to these crucial ideas, is that there might not *be* such a thing as forgiveness or justice. They might belong, if they belong anywhere, to an economy foreign to philosophy. At the most, Derrida will say: *if* there is such a thing as forgiveness or justice, then ... So let me say, that if there is such a thing as forgiveness, then it takes the form of a gift; and the gift is not something that can be given in the present. Were that so, it would immediately enter the circuit of exchange. If I say, "I forgive you," I am certainly not giving anything; I am covertly asking for gratitude. Perhaps this opens up whether we can consider our story as a scene of forgiveness, and, if so, what that would mean. As we agree, Jesus does not explicitly say that he forgives the woman, but does that mean that forgiveness has not taken place?

Your comments on Jesus having a law or a rule that applies only to himself are interesting, not least of all because the very idea of a rule that applies only to oneself is a long way from being self-evident. In response, I'd like to evoke Otto Weber's distinction between the exemplary Christ and Christ as exemplar (and I'd like to thank Elisabeth Moltmann-Wendel for pointing it out to me). How do we put the story we're discussing into action? Not, I think, by regarding Jesus as exemplar but by seeing him as exemplary in his response to the crowd's demand for quick justice, for an unthinking application of the Law.

George Aichele: Now perhaps it is my turn to clear up what may be a misunderstanding—although if every understanding is a misunderstanding, then perhaps I shouldn't trouble! I don't object at all to eisegesis, whether on your part or anyone else's. All reading is reading into, eisegesis. In fact I am very interested in creative eisegesis, or "intergesis" as Gary Phillips and I once called it, for I think that the only sort of reading that is worth paying much attention to is a reading that shows us something different and worthy of further consideration about the text, a reading that makes the text new for us. This is why I value deconstruction, which I understand to be a reading that explores the possibility and the limits of the text, the relation between what is said and what is not said, and the limits of reading itself. It is a reading that acknowledges itself as situated—as some actual person reading some specific text using some particular set of codes. Jesus' reading of the law of Moses in this passage is such a reading, and the consequence is not a universal model of forgiveness but an encounter between two individuals.

What I object to is the claim, explicit or more often implicit, that some eisegesis is in fact exegesis—such as the claim that we encounter from those readers who talk as though they have discovered the true meaning of some text. However, as I said before, I don't think that "anything goes," and I do believe that every reading must stay responsive to the actuality of the text, just as every reading is confined to the reader's ideology. It is in this tension between ideology and text that new thoughts and further considerations become possible.

Furthermore, as we have previously noted, the canonical ambiguity of this particular text—this "orphan" text in John—also puts it in tension with larger structures of the gospel of John. What is "the actuality of the text" in this case? Are we obliged to read this story in all of its uncertainty as part of John's larger narrative, or are we free to delete it from John, as some commentators have done, and either disregard it altogether—that would be simplest—or treat it as some third thing, neither canonical nor noncanonical? As I have come increasingly to the belief that the Christian canon is no longer viable today—as an authority, the canon no longer exists for me (or for many others)—I am drawn to read this story as part of John's gospel, not because I have to but because that allows me to upset established, canonical notions, of what the gospel of John is all about. It makes John interesting to me. Here I have an opportunity for creative eisegesis.

No doubt part of my overhasty and inconsiderate response to your previous comments on forgiveness, for which I apologize, derives from my own experience growing up in a Protestant church where this very passage would be invoked to demonstrate Jesus' love and forgiveness for sinners, as opposed to the narrow legalism of those cruel Pharisees. Not that we Methodists were any more charitable or any less narrow-minded than anyone else, of course, but this passage and others like it all joined together for us in the great canonical chorus that proclaimed the truth and the superiority of our sort of Christianity.

I completely agree with you that, whether in this passage from the gospel of John or as general concepts, neither justice not forgiveness can be taken as givens—and there too we have the gift, or rather the nongift, the nongivenness of these concepts. In fact, I am somewhat uncomfortable talking about justice or forgiveness at all, for this is a kind of discourse in which I rarely engage any more. But the nongivenness of this passage—whether as canonical, or as Johannine, or even as meaningful in any way—that is what continues to draw me back to it. And nowhere does that nongivenness appear more clearly, paradoxical as that may be, than in the image of Jesus writing something that we readers cannot read, cannot exegete or eisegete, and therefore cannot deconstruct.

To return to your final question, the distinction that you suggest between exemplar and exemplary is not clear to me. I agree that Jesus is not an exemplar of anything in this story. Is it precisely that which makes him exemplary? Is it because his own creative eisegesis (if I may) of the law of Moses has allowed the crowd, from the eldest to the youngest, to see something in the law that they hadn't seen before?

Kevin Hart: Like you, I value those readings that make a difference to what we are reading, though I think they can be of very different styles, and—I suppose here we differ once again—my initial impulse as a reader is to submit to the law or the laws of the text, to get a feel for its structures and its limits, its tone, and its relations with other texts. It seems to me that reading begins from the side of the text. It is contained in subjectivity but as "nonreal" as Husserl would say.

Can reading be creative? In *Le Livre à venir* Maurice Blanchot tells us that when we read we experience a lightness and an innocence, a "weightless yes"; we experience "the joy of plenitude, the sure evidence of complete success, the revelation of the unique work." So in a very sharp twist of Romantic aesthetics, Blanchot sees reading, rather than writing, as the better evoking "the divine aspect of creation." There is something strange and original in these remarks, I think; but what Blanchot affirms in reading is a certain passivity, as well as an avoidance of the "original experience," a brushing against the threatening realm or nonrealm of the imaginary. That said, I think you are evoking something quite different, something much more active, something more akin to "creative writing" than Blanchot has in mind. You are more of a Romantic than Blanchot in this, even though, I suspect, you would prefer not to be seen as Romantic at all. With that in mind, my main worry about "creative reading" with respect to the Bible or any writing is that you can't seek to do it or commend it as a program: a reading is either creative or it isn't. Usually it isn't, because creativity in any field is very scarce. As intellectual history grows longer and longer, it becomes harder and harder to be original. Derrida has some very interesting things to say about creativity. His early work on Husserl's essay, "The Origin of Geometry," makes some acute remarks about misunderstanding and historical transmission that suggest an intriguing view of originality, not unlike the one that Harold Bloom was to develop on very different ground; and I would cite Derrida's fascinating little book on Condillac, as well as his more recent essays on invention.

I'm intrigued when you say that the canon no longer has authority for you. Deep down, I've never quite understood why Protestants should think the biblical canon is authoritative in the first place. Your doubts about it, I imagine, are scholarly and—I don't use the word lightly—political. Perhaps you want to question the borders between intracanonical and extracanonical texts, perhaps you wish to query or reject the processes of canonization and the Church that authorized them. And so on. I imagine, in other words, that your doubts go a lot further than the canonical or deutercanonical status of the story we are talking about. It might help our discussion of that story if we were clear about our different attitudes to the canon. I'm not talking about our confessional differences, though they certainly inform how we regard it. Rather, I'm wondering about the relation of "canon" and "authority." Are your doubts exclusively to do with the canon of the Bible? Or to canons in general?

A dozen or so years ago there were very lively discussions about the canon of English literature. Who controls the canon? At the time, the consensus answer was this: an unholy mix of the genteel academy and the more powerful publishers. After a while, some big teaching anthologies, which are crucially linked to canon formation, were expanded to include more people of color, more women, more minorities; and I recall there was a big sigh of relief here and there. The canon had been expanded! I might add that the canon had been expanded by American academics and American publishers with a relentless focus on American interests. There was no contestation of the canon, only a contemporary American take over or make over of the canon. So I think that "canon" and "authority" are hard to separate, especially since "power" is hiding behind the milder word "authority." At the same time, in Australia, I remember one department of

English vigorously rejecting a canonical understanding of English litera-ture, and reforming the curriculum so that students could readily avoid having to study a good deal of Chaucer and Langland, Shakespeare and Milton, Pope and Johnson, Austen and George Eliot. Very soon after, the department issued a quite strict series of rules pointing out the students had to know Raymond Williams and Roland Barthes, Stuart Hall and Gayatri Spivak, and so on: a canon of "cultural studies" had in effect replaced the canon of English literature, and it was enforced with rather more zest than the old canon had been.

I tell these stories partly because I enjoy their irony and partly because I want to know how you see the relation of "canon" and "authority" with regard to the Bible. I realize that I haven't said anything directly about for-giveness. Just think of me as a man taken in the act of thinking.

George Aichele: It seems that the further we get into this dialogue, more and more topics open up for us. This could be dangerous! As Richard Rorty suggested many years ago, dialogues are in principle endless.[6]

I very much agree that canons are matters of power. And while I am interested in many canons, my main interest is in what is arguably the old-est canon still around, the canon of the Christian Bible. I also suspect, as your story about the Australian university English department suggests, that canons of one sort or another are inevitable in any culture in which writing and reading play the kind of role that they still do today, although with the emergence of electronic culture, the need for and the nature of our canons may change considerably. Canon concerns the question of identity—not only the identity of the canonical texts themselves, but the identity of the community that holds them to be canonical. So yes, I think that confessional differences will always be involved when it comes to mat-ters of canon, in English departments as well as in churches and syna-gogues. But I also believe that the canonical power of the Bible is rapidly fading away from our world, except in highly homogeneous communities that are in effect Christian reverse ghettoes, holding the world out.

That's why, I suspect, Protestants can't do without the canon, although I would also argue that the modern demise of the Christian canon begins with the birth of print culture, which coincides historically with the Refor-mation. If you really believe in the principle of *sola scriptura*, you need to be very clear about what counts as scripture. Just as in English depart-ments, not every writing is "literature," so in the churches, not every writ-ing is "scripture." My own doubts about the Christian canon are, as you say, both scholarly and political, and they reflect among other things my rejection of Christianity. And this, oddly enough, brings me back to the gospel of John, because one thing that I want to do at this point in my life is to see what biblical texts such as the gospels look like when they are no longer in a canon—when the canon ceases to control their meaning. I think that some biblical texts—including the gospel of John—may still be well worth reading outside of the canon, or in the absence of a canon. A groundbreaking book in this regard was written by the very person who has organized this conference, and who even served as the "matchmaker" for our dialogue, Yvonne Sherwood. That book is titled *A Biblical Text and Its Afterlives: the Survival of Jonah in Western Culture.*[7] It's also my understanding that an issue of the journal *Semeia* on "the recycled Bible" is in the works—I hope it is. I think we need to study further the afterlives of biblical books, how and whether they get recycled in a world where the canon itself is losing its power.

Back to the first point of your last comment, I agree that reading starts from the "side of the text," if by that you mean that we have to acknowledge that the text is in some sense outside of our control. Reading is a constant struggle for control over a text that is always resistant to our desire for meaning. It is eisegesis. That struggle can be innovative and creative, or it can be committed to reinforcing the beliefs and values of some traditional community. I believe that one important function of the Christian canon is to keep the texts in the control of the community that is the church—in other words, to subdue the biblical texts, to make them safe and properly meaningful for their readers. That's why I think this story in John 8 is fascinating, for here the scripture itself tells of a text that can never be subdued or controlled, that resists every attempt to read it. The speculations by commentators as to what Jesus actually wrote on the ground are rather amusing,[8] but they are also telling symptoms of this need for control. The commentators inevitably think that Jesus wrote something thoroughly canonical, perhaps a quote from the Torah or the Prophets—never something noncanonical, much less nonsensical, like "do wah diddy diddy." Go figure ...

Kevin Hart: I agree with J.-B. Metz when he associates Jesus with a "dangerous memory." There is something profoundly irruptive for the Church as well as for everyone else in anything to do with the words and acts of Jesus. Of course, the Church officially tries to keep a tight control on the interpretation of scripture; and a part of that control is a response to the sheer danger that Jesus represents for what is centered on the self, the institution, the nation, and so on. Jesus' preaching of the *basileia* cuts across our desire to form closed totalities; it is dangerous, as can be seen by recalling the history of the reception of the *basileia*, which is largely a history of accommodation, even within the Church, and by simply pointing to the many people who have been tortured and murdered because they have preached it. I think that our story, the "first stone" pericope, squares with the preaching of the *basileia*, even if it is not formally part of that group of parables and sayings. The danger of Jesus is that his preaching of the *basileia* lets us glimpse what God wants in the world, and that is a frightening thing as well as a joyful thing.

So you wouldn't expect me, a Catholic, to agree that the Bible is not or cannot be a site of power in the world today! But let's bracket confessional commitments and much that follows from them. I wonder if it makes good sense to say that the Bible no longer functions as a site of power in the world. My first reaction is that it would be hard to understand our world, in any sense, without the Bible. Of course, many, many people don't know their way around the Bible, don't own a Bible, and have never opened a Bible. Yet could anyone get close to even the vaguest of understandings of the horrors that beset Palestinians and Jews without at least knowing the story of the children of Israel and the Canaanites? Could one even begin to understand American politics without having some awareness of the Bible and its interpretations? One would have to admit some wayward interpretations, it is true, in order to grasp the actions of some recent Presidents. Some of those very interpretations, though, come from not having read the text, from having caught an interpretation much as one catches the flu. I'm inclined to say that since the world, including the conflict in the Middle East, is dominated politically by America it is thereby dominated by an implied understanding of the Bible, doubtless one that no halfway decent reader of scripture could square with the Bible. When it comes to global politics I'm inclined to agree with everything you say about "reading into" the text! Against that ground, a careful and informed reading of a biblical text is political as well as spiritual, if *that* distinction makes sense. Since so much of Jesus' work was concerned with the *basileia*, I find it hard to draw a distinction at a deep level between politics and spirituality. I'm very sympathetic to attempts by biblical scholars to develop fresh readings of biblical texts. For my part, I think there are all sort of things that biblical scholars can learn from literary critics, although I hope I'm not provincial enough to think that we literary critics don't have things to learn from biblical scholars. Having said that, I have a flicker of concern when I hear you talk about some readings being "outside the canon." That's not because I can't imagine adventurous and compelling readings of biblical texts that don't abide by ecclesial authority and that don't follow ecclesial interests. European literature give us many examples of just that, both in the inch and in the mile. I simply doubt that one can draw a clear and firm line that separates the canon from its outsides. A few years ago when one of my favorite Australian writers, Helen Garner, wrote a book about feminism and forgiveness, based on a specific incident in a university college only minutes from where I used to live, she called it *The First Stone*. The book caused quite a furor, and it was willfully misunderstood in all sorts of ways, though I cannot recall anyone not catching the allusion in the title. I have no doubt that one of the vanishing points of that brave book was precisely the story that has intrigued us today, the story we now look for in the fourth gospel.

References

1. This article was prepared from an exchange of e-mail messages over a period of several weeks during the summer of 2002. Since that dialogue, the content has been revised only slightly.
2. Plato, *Phaedrus*, trans. Walter Hamilton (Harmondsworth, Middlesex: Penguin Books, 1973), p. 97.
3. George Aichele, *The Control of Biblical Meaning: Canon as Semiotic Mechanism* (Harrisburg: Trinity Press International, 2001), pp. 61–83; see also George Aichele and Gary A. Phillips, "Exegesis, Eisegesis, Intergesis," *Semeia* 69/70 (1995): 7–18.
4. Friedrich Nietzsche, "Preface," *Daybreak: Thoughts on the Prejudices of Morality*, trans. R.J. Hollingdale, intro. Michael Tanner (Cambridge: Cambridge University Press, 1982), p. 5.
5. On this matter, see also John 20:23.
6. Richard Rorty, *Philosophy and the Mirror of Nature* (Princeton: Princeton University Press, 1979).
7. Yvonne Sherwood, *A Biblical Text and its Afterlives: the Survival of Jonah in Western Culture* (Cambridge: Cambridge University Press, 2000).
8. For a summary of some of these speculations, see Rudolf Schnackenburg, *The Gospel According to St. John*, vol. 2 (New York: The Seabury Press, 1980), pp. 165–166.

CHAPTER 16

Sacrifice and Secularization: Derrida, de Vries, and the Future of Mourning

TYLER ROBERTS

Grieve for me, therefore keep me enough to lose me as you must.

—Derrida, *Given Time*[1]

At a Villanova conference on "Forgiveness," in the roundtable discussion, Derrida spoke of sacrifice: "I am constantly against the logic of sacrifice, especially in the question of forgiveness. I am trying to deconstruct the logic of sacrifice ... So I try not to be *simply sacrificialistic* but at the same time I cannot deny that sacrifice is unavoidable."[2] Derrida was responding to a question from John Milbank, the major figure behind one of the most controversial and intriguing theological movements in recent memory, "Radical Orthodoxy."[3] Milbank had asked Derrida whether his notions of forgiveness and responsibility were not "too moralistic," whether, more generally, his stress on the purity of ethical was an insistence on a "pure absolute self-sacrifice" that obliterates the self and "encourages a kind of masochism."[4] With this question, Milbank picked up on his relentless, critical, and complicated engagement with Derrida and with others he considers to be exemplars of "nihilistic postmodern philosophy." In a recent article, "The Midwinter Sacrifice," Milbank elaborates on the place of sacrifice in Derrida's thought by claiming that Derrida's is an "ethics of

sacrifice" that is "first, immoral, second, impossible, and third, a deformation ... of the Christian gospel."[5]

Is Derrida's an "ethics of sacrifice"? The statement from Villanova
would suggest that this is a complicated question, for here we see Derrida
both "against" the logic of sacrifice and acknowledging that sacrifice is
"unavoidable." This essay will work through these complications in light of
Milbank's criticisms. By tracing the links among a series of themes—sacrifice,
ethics, religion, responsibility, hospitality—I shall argue that Derrida
works "against" the logic of sacrifice not by seeking to escape it in any final
sense, but in a "classic" (if I may use this term) deconstructive gesture, by
twisting away from it in a certain repetition, a sacrifice of sacrifice. With
this, I will also show that by focusing too exclusively on what he views as a
problematic imperative to "purity," Milbank is led to a one-sided reading
of Derrida's ethic. In short, Milbank is wrong to claim that this ethic is
"immoral." Moreover, although Derrida's ethic *is* "impossible" and a
"deformation of the Christian gospel," it is so only in senses very different
from what Milbank argues.[6]

To make these arguments, I will engage in some detail with what is
arguably the most ambitious and philosophically sophisticated reading of
Derrida to date, Hent de Vries's recent two-volume effort to chart the
complex movements of Derrida's recent "turn to religion" and to tie this
turn to pressing questions of ethics and politics.[7] Where Milbank overemphasizes the imperative to purity in Derrida's work on gift and responsibility, de Vries argues the necessity of attending to the aporias of gift and
responsibility to see how the imperative to purity is always and necessarily
countered by an imperative to "betray" that purity. In working through
this idea, with the help of de Vries's treatment of the "sacrifice of sacrifice"
and "reverse implication," I will argue, finally, that the confrontation of
Der-rida and Milbank not only allows us to clarify crucial points of Derrida's ethic, but it also allows us to consider how this confrontation is not,
as Milbank would have it, a confrontation between secularism and religion. Whether that means it is a confrontation between religion and religion is, however, a question that needs to be complicated and displaced,
rather than simply answered.

Milbank's Argument

Although Derrida is the primary target in "The Midwinter Sacrifice," Milbank also is concerned more generally with an ethical tradition stretching
from late antiquity to contemporary post-Kantian ethics of intention and
altruism in Heidegger, Lévinas, and Derrida. He argues that the imperative
to self-sacrifice emerges with the rejection of classical eudaemonism

(e.g., by the Stoics) for its vulnerability to the contingencies of destiny and happiness. This new ethical perspective located ethical identity in the non-alienable capacity to form pure other-directed intentions. Inflected in a Heideggerian direction—with the idea of our death as that of which we absolutely cannot be robbed—and taken to its logical conclusion, this ethical perspective means that "to be ethical is to offer your life as a gift without hope or return in time."[8] One's altruism, that is, is guaranteed in the purifying act of self-sacrifice, of "giving oneself death." Milbank acknowledges the intuitive and logical power of this position, acknowledges, indeed, that it dominates modern ethical thought, but he argues that it can be deconstructed to show that what appears to be absolute altruism is, in fact, in its insistence on the absolute purity of intention, a desperate attempt to possess oneself.

Milbank clarifies his view of the immorality and impossibility of the sacrificial economy by identifying faulty assumptions and unacceptable conclusions. First, he claims that ethics cannot in the end ignore happiness, at least not the happiness of the other, because a moral act "which fails to make the other happy surely ceases to be a moral act."[9] Second, a sacrificial ethic ends in a loss of self because an absolute altruism cannot imagine the consummation of relationship in which the self finds some satisfaction in itself. Third, such an ethic also loses the other since, as Lévinas has argued, the other can only fully appear as other in his or her absence, especially in his or her death, at which point, however, another crucial aspect of his or her otherness—the ability to respond to me—disappears.[10] Milbank concludes that "there is no true respect for the other involved here, since the gesture which allows the other to persist outside of his communication with you is seen as more definitive of the good than the living communication which you enjoy with the other."[11] On this reading, Derrida reduces exchange to contract instead of distinguishing, as Milbank says we must, between different forms of exchange. Such a distinction would allow us to think about gift in terms of its content, where what is crucial is not the purity of the act of giving but the thing given as it expresses caring attention to the particularity and desires of the recipient.[12] To give, in this sense, is a matter of knowing what is an appropriate gift for this particular person—as someone related to me—at this particular time. Derrida, though, according to Milbank, ignores the content of the gift and the concrete reality of the recipient of the gift, and focuses only on pure intention. This is immoral because it is really a self-interested attempt to secure one's virtue and, therefore, oneself. And, if self-sacrifice is the only way to prove the good and possess ourselves, then "we need the misfortunes of others to demonstrate our worth."[13]

Christianity, argues Milbank, avoids the ethics of sacrifice, for, "unlike stoicism, [Christianity] was able to stick with and even augment the goal of happiness or beatitude through a novel abandonment of the goal of self-possession, even in its mode of ethical reduction [i.e., in an ethic of self-sacrifice]."[14] From this Christian perspective, the ethical life is never a life that just gives, but always a life that also receives, for which, in fact, all giving gives out of plenitude, from already having received. One gives oneself up, therefore, only to an ever-circulating divine grace. From one perspective, then, this takes us back to the problem of classical ethics and our vulnerability to fate and chance.[15] For Milbank, though, the Christian difference is faith, which transforms fate into grace. In one sense, then, Milbank does not deny the need for a certain kind of self-sacrifice: "... in a fallen world the only path to the recovery of mutual giving will always pass through an element of apparently 'unredeemed' sacrifice and apparently unilateral gift."[16] But this is not, first of all, self-sacrifice for the sake of the other person, but sacrifice to God that is made out of faith in a return. Milbank goes on: "but the point is that this gesture [of self-sacrifice] is not in itself the good, and indeed, I have argued, is not good at all outside the hope for a redemptive return of the self."[17] For Milbank, one must recognize that on one's own one does not have the capability to give fully and purely to the other. The focus is on God and God's gift to us, not on the possibility or impossibility of my own perfect altruism. Even though Milbank acknowledges that all human lives are marked by tragedy since the Fall, he refuses to ontologize this condition, as he thinks happens in pagan religion and modern and postmodern secularism. And in Derrida, who therefore can articulate only a vague hope for true giving, a hope continually postponed. The Christian, by contrast, believes in God's gift of grace by which "it will ... be given to us to be ethical, given to us again to receive and again to give in such a way that a certain 'asymmetrical reciprocity' or genuine community, will ceaselessly arrive (for now in part and eschatologically without interruption)."[18]

Milbank argues forcefully that an ethics predicated on a self-sacrifice that ends in loss—gift without return, death—needs scarcity and egotism and violence as the condition of being ethical. This is an ethic, in other words, "secretly in love with" humankind's tragic condition. What is required instead, he argues, is the imagination of consummation, an ultimate affirmation of life, such that we give out of plenitude, not lack. For Milbank, it is not that we sacrifice our life and are *therefore* given a reward of a better life in heaven, rather, it is that "a final surrender of an isolated life, a life indifferent to the pain of others *issues of itself* ... in a better more abundant life."[19] From this affirmative standpoint, Milbank imagines gift giving and ethical relationship as reciprocal, and not just one-way.

The Aporia of Responsibility

There is, I think, a powerful ethical and religious vision being articulated here that raises hard questions about reciprocity and plenitude that need to be posed to Derrida. At the same time, however, I do not believe that Derrida's ethic falls prey to Milbank's criticisms. To put it simply, Milbank misreads the significance of two terms crucial to Derrida's work: singularity and responsibility. His reading of *The Gift of Death* misunderstands Derrida's "singularity" because it too quickly conflates Derrida with Heidegger and Patocka on being-toward-death. While it is the case that Derrida follows these thinkers in linking singularity to an "apprehensive approach to death," he also follows Lévinas in questioning whether I apprehend my singularity in a confrontation with *my* death or with the death of the *other*.[20] Indeed, according to de Vries, Derrida even pushes beyond Lévinas with the claim that it is mourning, not death, that is fundamental in the constitution of the self: mourning, says Derrida, is "more originary than my being for death."[21] Thus the question of singularity for Derrida becomes complicated and, decisively, is not a matter of the kind of self-possession asserted by Milbank. Rather, it is a matter of thinking the self only as it is *both* its own and an other. "The singularity of the 'who' is not the individuality of a thing that would be identical to itself, it is not an atom. It is a singularity that dislocates or divides itself in gathering itself to answer to the other, whose call somehow precedes its own identification with itself …"[22] Whether death or mourning, for Derrida the distinction between what is my mine and what is the other's becomes impossible to discern in any final way. As de Vries puts it, "the very difference between *jemeinig* and *jeanders* becomes obsolete."[23] The self always escapes itself and so is always unknown to itself, it is a "secret" to itself.

With singularity, Milbank does not sufficiently distinguish Derrida from his predecessors. With responsibility, Milbank overemphasizes Derrida's purity and so Derrida's views on self-sacrifice. This issue requires detailed consideration. It certainly is the case that responsibility, in Derrida's view, places upon us an infinite demand: to give altruistically to the other, without expectation of return, aneconomically. And this means that there is a sacrificial imperative in Derrida's view of responsibility. Let me turn to this imperative first, but only while keeping in mind that it is not the end of the story.

In *The Gift of Death*, Derrida argues that "the account of Isaac's sacrifice can be read as a narrative development of the paradox constituting the concept of duty and absolute responsibility."[24] This paradox involves a conflict between duty—the ethical imperative to generality and universality—and "absolute responsibility"—the imperative of singularity, that it is *I* who must decide and act, face to face with God, as it were, and so without the support of rules, whether teleological or deontological, that would tell me what to do or allow me to calculate the "proper" response. Faced with absolute responsibility before God, Abraham is willing to sacrifice everything, most importantly his greatest love, Isaac (as well as his relationship with Sarah, to whom he cannot explain his actions). Responsibility, here, is to "give death." At the same time, and crucially, the relationship with God does not erase the ethical demand (to not murder), it only "suspends" it, meaning that it continues to be affirmed, even as it is transgressed. As de Vries puts it, the point is that in "every genuine decision the ethical must be sacrificed" that is, "suspended 'in the name of' an ab-solute duty or obligation that is always 'singular' and for which the name—the proper name—would be 'God.'"[25] Thus, the only thing that allows us to distinguish Abraham's act from the act of a murderer—a distinction we must make with some trepidation, mirroring Abraham's own "fear and trembling"—is that his was an act done in faith.

Now, when we read the aporia of responsibility from this perspective, it seems that Milbank may have a point, for we have here a conception of responsibility that tears us out of our relationships with others as we turn to face God. Yet I want to argue that we cannot leave the aporia of responsibility with this reading, for there are elements of both *The Gift of Death* and Derrida's work on the gift, especially in *Given Time*, that complicated this aporia even further, suggesting that every act must involve not only a "suspension of the ethical" but also a betrayal of God and therefore of purity and sacrifice. Here, I note de Vries's emphasis on the figure of the "*adieu*," with which he, following Lévinas and Derrida, describes a movement that is at once toward God (*à dieu*), away from God (*adieu*) and in the face to face with the other of God (*a-dieu*). Responsibility does involve a kind of infinitization, a suspension of the universal in affirming a relationship with the absolute, a turn toward God, but it also involves a turn back to the finite, a willingness to engage economy and so a "sacrifice of sacrifice."

Sacrificing Sacrifice

Derrida's examination of sacrificial responsibility in *The Gift of Death* leads him, at the end of the book, to Christian altruism and to the question of whether it is possible to give without the promise of reward. Milbank argues that because of his infinitization of responsibility and gift,

Derrida erases the Christian promise of resurrection, thus "secularizing" the Christian message and offering only crucifixion without resurrection, that is, pure sacrifice and purity through sacrifice. On this reading, Derrida can note the complexity of the view of giving articulated in the Gospel of Matthew only to then question whether it goes far enough. Thus, according to Derrida, for Matthew "one must give ... without knowing, or at least by giving with one hand without the other hand knowing, that is, without having it known, without having it known by other men, in secret, without counting on recognition, reward, or remuneration. Without even having it known to oneself."[26] Yet, Derrida then notes that Matthew's God is the witness who sees into our hearts, who not only "seeth in secret" but shall "himself shall reward thee openly."[27] As Milbank reads it, this is Derrida's last word on Christian sacrifice: while it questions the world economy of reward and self-interest, it does so only in the assurance of a different, divine economy of reward in which I will get a return for my sacrificial gift of death. Derrida, though, according to Milbank, wants to push sacrifice even further, in a purifying move of outbidding that secularizes by canceling the God who sees in secret and rewards with resurrection.

But is "reward" Derrida's last word on Christianity? And so does he, in fact, see the only hope for a sacrificial ethic in the secularization of the gospel? I think matters are more complicated. Derrida proceeds from his reading of Matthew to suggest that the juxtaposition of two economies—worldly and divine—is not *simply* to be understood in terms of the exchange of one economy of exchange for another. Instead, the relationship between the two is one of "excess" and "essential instability," one where "the *same economy* seems sometimes faithful to and sometimes accusing or ironic with respect to the role of Christian sacrifice ... [a] hyperbolic form of this *internal critique* of Christianity that is at the same time evangelical and heretical."[28] I suggest that, for Derrida, the Christian gospel stages two incommensurable readings. Contra Milbank, this reading sees Christianity as repeating without resolving the aporia of responsibility, thus subjecting itself to a kind of hyperbolic, never-ending, internal critique.

Yet, when Derrida turns to Baudelaire and Nietzsche in the final pages of the book, one will be tempted to reject this suggestion for the more familiar secularizing move for which Milbank argues, for it appears that with the turn to these figures Derrida is affirming their demystifications.[29] This temptation, however, should be resisted, for even as he makes this move, even in his reading of Nietzsche's *Genealogy*, Derrida continues to hold to the "hyperbolic form" of Christianity's "internal critique," reversing our expectations by recommending it, as it were, to Nietzsche. He reminds us that Nietzsche pursues his demystification of Christianity to the point of God's own sacrifice, where "God personally immolat[es] himself for the debt of man."[30] It is precisely at this point that Derrida seems to think that the instability of the Christian economy both manifests and questions its demystification at the hands of Nietzsche. From a secret calculation that God will reward my responsibility, we find revealed here a turn to God's responsibility, a responsibility for belief, a belief that (at least for the Augustinian, Lutheran, Kierkegaardian tradition upon which Derrida depends) is not so much an act of the individual but a gift of God's grace: God not only sacrifices himself, but God credits us with belief, makes it possible for us to believe in God's sacrifice/gift. This is a point crucial to Milbank's own view of giving: ultimately, God gives through us.[31] Nietzsche, of course, does not believe this, asking what all indications suggest is a rhetorical question: "Can we credit this?" But Derrida is not satisfied with leaving Nietzsche's question to this reading because he thinks the question must already presuppose faith or commitment, what Derrida describes in other contexts as an "originary affirmation." As he puts it in a different context, he understands this affirmation in terms of a "'yes' or of an 'en-gage' … that answers before even being able to formulate a question."[32] When we speak, we are already responding, so for Derrida even Nietzsche's rhetorical question about belief already presupposes belief, for in order for Nietzsche to know what he is saying when he asks the question, he must already know what belief means, must already be engaged with an economy of language and meaning to which he has assented and is always assenting again whenever he speaks, even if it is to question the acts of speaking and assenting. "The question, the request, and the appeal, must indeed have begun, since the eve of their awakening, by receiving accreditation from the other: by being believed."[33]

In short, Derrida's readings of Christianity and Nietzsche bring us to the same place, from different directions. Although one clearly finds the idea of divine reward in Matthew, one also finds a hyperbolic internal critique of the desire or expectation of such reward. Even though Nietzsche pursues a radical demystifying critique, he too, believes. Where does this leave us on the questions of ethics and sacrifice?

In *Given Time*, after explaining why the gift can never be present as such, why the effort to transcend the economy of exchange always fails, Derrida points us toward a "thinking" of the "impossible." The impossible, he ventures, is the "proper element of thinking." His point is that we can, and we must, think the gift even if we cannot know it or ever experience it as such. I would add that this also can be said about responsibility, for both gift and responsibility are what de Vries calls an "index of the aporia" at issue here.[34] About the gift, Derrida writes, "One can desire, name, think in the proper sense of these words, if there is one, only to the immeasuring extent that one desires, names, thinks still or already, that one still lets announce itself what nevertheless cannot present itself as such to experience, to knowing: in short, here a gift that cannot make itself (a) present."[35] Such thinking is for Derrida a kind of faith, not a fideism that would simply assert and cling to that which it cannot know, but rather a commitment to or engagement with the aporia of the gift despite the impossibility of knowing it, and more, of knowing what one *can* of the gift, thus holding to both the demands of thought and the demands of knowledge and resisting temptations to paralysis or mere pragmatism. In other words, it would be:

> [A] matter … of responding faithfully but also as rigorously as possible both to the injunction or the order of the gift ("give") as well as to the injunction or the order of meaning (presence, science, knowledge): Know still what giving wants to say, know how to give, know what you want and want to say when you give, know what you intend to give, know how the gift annuls itself, commit yourself even if the commitment is the destruction of the gift by the gift, give economy its chance.[36]

"Give economy its chance." Even as one lets the gift, sacrifice, responsibility "announce" themselves in all their infinite purity—calling for gift without return and calculation, for the sacrifice of self and economy—the response to this call of responsibility must be an act or decision that sacrifices the sacrifice of economy, that gives economy its chance. Here is the *adieu,* of which de Vries writes, embedded within the decision itself, made only as one both turns toward and away from God. The purity one seeks with sacrifice, the face to face, unmediated relationship with the absolute, must be sacrificed out of … responsibility. Responsibility demands that one (not) sacrifice oneself. As de Vries puts it, "a certain egoism is good for the other, is necessary for being good to the other, indeed for being separate from and other than the other."[37] Responsibility involves the sacrifice of self in exposing oneself to the infinite, singular demand of responsibility that exhausts language, philosophy, and knowledge in a gesture that Derrida and de Vries compare with kenosis and apophatics. But because responsibility also demands the betrayal of this infinite demand, it also requires a sacrifice of this sacrifice in decision and action.

But in this sacrifice of sacrifice, the thought of the pure gift or the pure sacrifice must not be lost, we must hold onto it as we let go of it, in the

modality, Derrida will argue, of a mourning. To seek to be done with sacrificial logic, once and for all, would only fall back into it, for it would
involve one in the endless outbidding of sacrifice. Instead, as we saw at the
start, Derrida acknowledges that "sacrifice is unavoidable" even as he tries
"not to be *simply sacrificialistic*."

Sacrifice and Secularization

Milbank is mistaken in his claim for the "immorality" of Derrida's "sacrificial ethic" because it is not based on the drive for self-possession. And
Milbank's second claim, that such an ethic is "impossible," while not simply wrong, is based on a limited and so misleading view of Derrida's
"impossibility." Milbank reads Derrida's "impossibility" as meaning that
responsibility will never be fully realized, always postponed, always
demanding further sacrifice in a futile quest for purity. But this is to
overemphasize the imperative to purity while trivializing the counter-
imperative to "give economy a chance." Milbank does not ignore the
counter-imperative altogether, noting that for Derrida one must "embrace
the impossibility of the ethical and yet the necessity of temporary ethical
conventions."[38] But he trivializes this point by failing to examine the significance of the way the "impossibility" orients us to these "conventions,"
which, as I show below, become for Derrida and de Vries more than mere
conventions. For now, I will make the basic point that for Derrida the
impossibility of gift or responsibility is, paradoxically, a condition of their
possibility. Impossibility, in other words, is an ordeal through which the
giver must pass, not a barrier to passage. The movement from the demand
for infinite sacrifice (as the condition of pure gift) to the sacrifice of this
sacrifice is the ordeal of the undecidable, a movement made in the faith
that holds to the orders of both thought and knowledge, in which we
decide and act in the modality of what Derrida and de Vries call "testimony": "the act of faith demanded in bearing witness exceeds, through its
structure, all intuition and all proof, all knowledge."[39] Note, however, that
testimony "exceeds," but does not necessarily do without, intuition and
knowledge. Here faith is understood by de Vries to be a mode of "repetition" and "spontaneity after reflection."[40]

If, for the moment at least, we can grant that the Derridean response
traced above gives reasons for suspecting the plausibility of Milbank's
accusations of immorality and impossibility, then we can move to his
third, and perhaps his most interesting claim, namely, that the ethics of
sacrifice is a "deformation of the Christian gospel." By this, Milbank refers
to Derrida's purported secularization of the gospel in his effort to purify it
of reward. As I have indicated already, though, it is not at all clear that

Derrida makes such a secularizing move, at least not in the straightforward sense argued for by Milbank.

As it is invoked in "Midwinter Sacrifice," as well as in his other discussions of Derrida, and "postmodernism" more generally, the "secular" is for Milbank a key concept, one that helps illuminate his ambivalent but ultimately critical view of postmodernism. On the one hand, according to Milbank, postmodernism is an advance over modern secularism because it has dispensed with the illusion of rational or empirical foundationalisms that were promised by modern philosophers and social theorists. Milbank argues that any comprehensive theory of human life, to be fully explanatory, must define the telos of human beings and that visions of the human telos ultimately cannot be grounded in reason alone but must depend on "mythical" narratives and wagers of faith. Thus, both Christianity and secular social theory necessarily rest on narratives of human origins and human possibilities. These narratives, he argues, convince only through rhetoric and persuasion, not through rational proof. "Christianity does not claim that the Good and the True are self-evident to objective reason, or dialectical argument. On the contrary, it from the first took the side of rhetoric against philosophy and contended that the Good and the True are those things of which we 'have a persuasion,' *pistis*, or 'faith.'"[41] But while postmodernism shares this orientation towards rhetoric, Milbank argues that it also shares with modern secular social theory a variant of pagan myths of primordial violence.[42] Christianity, by contrast, rests on a myth of primordial peace, a story of God's loving, peaceful act of creation.

While the appeal to foundational myths means that Milbank essentially rejects the secular/religious distinction (as a distinction between mythical "religious" foundations and rational "secular" foundations), he continues to draw a sharp contrast between Christianity and all other "religious" and "secular" ideologies with the claim that true peace and genuine hope for such peace are only possible for Christians.[43] But in my view, Derrida is not a "secularist" in either of the senses at stake here: he neither seeks to "purify" or "secularize" the Gospel in the sense Milbank claims, nor does he subscribe to a primordial myth of violence. Consequently, I will suggest, his hope is not as vacuous as Milbank believes.

It is here that comparing de Vries's and Milbank's readings of Derrida can be most helpful. Where Milbank relies on sweeping generalizations about Derridean philosophy as the culmination of nihilist secularism and sacrificial ethics, de Vries's painstaking reconstruction of Derrida's engagement with thinkers like Kant, Heidegger, and Lévinas, among others, makes it possible to identify with great precision both the significant connections and the telling distinctions between these thinkers. Especially when viewed through his reconstruction of Derrida's "turn to religion," de Vries makes it clear that any effort to characterize Derrida's ethics in terms of "secularity" and "sacrifice," though useful to a degree, always will demand that we also think in terms of religiosity and the sacrifice of sacrifice. Indeed, for de Vries, Derrida's "turn to religion" involves a complex effort to deconstruct settled oppositions between the religious and the secular, as well as between the theological and philosophical and the ideal and the real. When de Vries talks of the philosophical turn to religion, he is not simply advocating a "return" to (a particular) religion as, perhaps, a grounding for philosophy or an ethico-political authority. For, as he says, somewhat elliptically, "to turn to religion is also to turn religion around." This means, I think, that there is an imperative to exposure here that goes both ways: to turn to religion (or God) is always also to turn away from or against (any particular) religion. In this sense, argues de Vries, "religion" returns even in a secularization that questions all foundational dogmas and narratives, even amidst a reductionist discourse that exposes the all-too-human origins of so much that has claimed to be transcendent and eternal. Religion is, in other words, "the abstracting and formalizing movement that brings this virtual death about ... In religion's perpetual agony lies its philosophical and theoretical relevance."[44]

At the heart of de Vries's engagement with Derrida is the claim that Derrida's most important philosophical contribution—taking shape in his early engagement with Husserl's concept of "transcendental historicity" and developing especially in his more recent work on religion and responsibility—has been to decisively rethink the Kantian transcendentalism that has had such an impact on modern philosophy.[45] For Kant and his followers, transcendental conditions of possibility and subsequent reformulations of this idea (such as Heidegger's existentials) are universal, ahistorical presuppositions of all empirical, historical phenomena. Thus, it was possible for Kant and Heidegger to view themselves as secularizers of theological discourse—uncovering theology's "pre-religious" philosophical conditions of possibility. But de Vries argues that rather than embrace this "logic of presupposition" in its transcendental or ontological form, or in its inverse form, an empiricism or historicism that views all ideal structures as the product historical, empirical phenomena, Derrida claims that the real and the ideal are mutually implicated in one another, that each is the condition of possibility of the other.[46]

De Vries illustrates this well with respect to the idea of responsibility, arguing that any simple genealogy of the term is ultimately inadequate for

> [I]t suggests a linear development of concepts and themes where there is in fact a far more convoluted trajectory, in which what

seems a single leitmotif—unlimited, infinite or absolute responsibility—is unfolded only to be folded in again, in varying ways
depending on the context, the specific occasion of an interrogation,
or the urgency of a certain clarification. Derrida insists, time and
again, that responsibility, although unrestricted and hence categorical or even transcategorical and excessive, relies on a general structure of iterability in which it is singularly traced and retraced and
only thus attains a certain ideality. What might thus be considered
Derrida's single most wide-ranging insight—infinite responsibility,
as Lévinas would have said, and its necessary betrayal in repetition—is presented in an in principle incomplete series of "examples" or, better, instantiations, whose plurality respects the
uniqueness of pragmatically determined situations.[47]

De Vries contrasts the logic of presupposition guided by genealogical,
transcendental, or phenomenological philosophies of history with a
different mode of philosophical accounting that works out of a "logic of
substitution." This logic accounts for the "examples" and "plurality" de
Vries writes about here; it is a notion of history as a series of nonsynonymous substitutions, each of which both points to and necessarily perverts
the universal.[48] The philosophical task, then, would be to trace "a series of
linkages that allows no single concept or figure of speech to be privileged
ontologically, axiologically, aesthetically, theologically, or ethically and
religiously."[49] It also demands a process of what de Vries calls "reverse
implication" by which transcendental and ontological structures are
"folded back into—once again implicated in—the history of the tropes,
topoi, and even commonplaces that [they] had been thought merely to
open up, so as to provide it with a dimension, a horizon, and the condition
of its possibility."[50] The logic of substitution is, for de Vries, a "hospitable"
or "responsible" logic, for it opens a space for the freedom of testimony,
that is, for those acts of responsibility that testify to the infinite precisely in
betraying it, by giving economy its chance, that gesture toward God *(à
dieu)* even as they turn away from God *(adieu)*. In this moment of
decision, one commits oneself to the past, links oneself with a series of
nonsynonomous testimonies only by giving testimony of one's own and
thereby breaking from the past.

This logic of substitution is, if we are careful to keep in mind the deconstruction of the secular/religious binary, "religious," in the sense of
Derrida's "religion without religion." Through the figure of *adieu*, de Vries
shows that "God," like responsibility, is an index for the aporia we already
have explored under the name responsibility and gift.[51] More important,
while there are, on Derrida's account, no grounds for assuming that the

Christian (or the Jewish, or the Islamic) way of naming and relating to this aporia is the "only" or the "best," the "religions of the book" have structured Western thought, including Derrida's own conceptions of the universal, the ontological, the trace, etc. Derrida is part of this tradition, is, in fact committed to it and always responding to it. And it should be evident by now that this "belonging" cannot be seen as a simple secularizing of the tradition since any account of the tradition that would claim a "secular" rather than "religious" grounding, or that would claim to be atheist rather than theist or philosophical rather than theological, would itself be grounded in a testimony, in a leap of faith, in a sense then, would already be religious. This is the key to Derrida's "religion without religion": the engagement of the aporia that goes by the name of "God" or "responsibility" (as well as others). This engagement is "faithful" in its refusal to prioritize the transcendental/ideal or the empirical/real, taking the risk of action without historical or metaphysical guarantees. Even when the turn to action and decision, away from the infinite and toward the worldly, is made in atheistic or secular language, it is a movement that has already moved through the "religious."

We encounter here the limits of the secular-religious distinction precisely at the point where the imperative to purity and thus to sacrifice is always and inevitably betrayed by a counter-imperative to worldliness, negotiation, and action. In the end, this likely is still not enough faith or enough God for Milbank, but it does demand of him a different reading of Derrida.

Mourning and Hope

My argument so far has not fully addressed Milbank's primary concern: the postmodern appropriation of primordial violence. In "Midwinter Sacrifice," Milbank invokes this idea when he emphasizes that genuine ethics is possible only through faith in the resurrection and claims that when "modern secularity gets rid of [all intimations of the after-life it] perfects pagan logic, a logic of sacrificial obliteration of self either for an ideal, or for the city, or for both."[52] This claim clearly is linked to Milbank's earlier claims about primordial violence since it is only a benevolent Creator who can guarantee the peaceful afterlife of Christian resurrection. But, at least in the case of Derrida, we need to question whether Milbank's claim is justified, for, in the final chapter of *Religion and Violence*, discussing his recent engagement with "hospitality," and responsibility as hospitality, de Vries argues that Derrida diverges from the Kantian (and more generally modern) claim that peace must be instituted over and against the "bellicose state of nature."[53] Instead, Derrida follows Lévinas, who de Vries shows, "starts out from a nonnatural yet originary—or, better, preoriginary—peace rather than from a natural state of war."⁵⁴ What does this mean?

To understand this position, and its significance for my argument, we need to stay with the idea of "reverse implication" a bit longer. Again, the basic idea is that the ideal is not simply the condition of possibility for the real (which would leave us with a Milbankian faith in which God serves as transcendental signified guaranteeing and making possible the ultimate peace and order of the cosmos) nor is it only made possible by the real (which would leave us with a simple pragmatism). Instead, as I have indicated, "the quasi-transcendentality" of responsibility (or of God, hospitality, friendship, peace)⁵⁵ "in its perfection or 'to come' … cannot stand on its own but demands its own interruption and, as it were, instantiation."⁵⁶ In other words, these quasi-transcendentals are not "pregiven and stable" structures or ideals that one's acts may succeed (more or less) in approximating.⁵⁷ Rather, to take the example of peace, the "peace to come" only exists in and through our present acts, which always repeat and revise what is past. Guided by traditions and concepts of peace from the past that we continue to affirm even as we tear ourselves away from them (we "forget without forgetting"⁵⁸), that we affirm in tearing ourselves away from them, it is only in the faithful, partial instantiation of peace that the "to come" comes. Thus, says Derrida in *Faith and Knowledge*: "no to-come without heritage and the possibility of repeating … some sort of iterability."⁵⁹

De Vries argues that at this point Derrida comes quite close to Kant. And he also brings me back to my earlier engagement with the Baudelarian and Nietzschean "demystification" at the end of *The Gift of Death* and to *Given Time's* "give economy a chance." Even though all finite expressions of friendship, generosity, hospitality, etc. are in some sense betrayals of the ethical demand and as such are only "tokens" or "counterfeit coins" subject to a demystifying analysis, they are not, for all that, to be dismissed as "merely illusory" or gestures made in bad faith. Instead, according to Derrida, such gestures establish a history that "begins in a non-truth and should end up making non-truth true."⁶⁰ That is, one needs to think and work in a double-register, thinking critically and demystifying, to be sure, but also seeking to turn such counterfeit money into "gold." Thus Derrida, "The crime against humanity would be to disdain currency, however devalued, illusory or false it may be; it would be to take counterfeit money for counterfeit, for what it is, and to let it come into its truth as counterfeit money. The crime would be not to do everything in one's power to change it into gold—that is, into virtue, true friendship."⁶¹

Rather than simply perpetuating the nihilism or the secularism of which Milbank accuses secular social theory and postmodernism, Derrida points us here to a "post-critical" faith, even, as de Vries hints, to a second "naivete."[62] The ascesis of suspicion and demystification is not rejected, but neither is it the last word. Instead, it is a discipline of vigilance by which we keep in mind that in some real sense we "make up" history, that our genuinely ethical acts and decisions are leaps of faith that can never be fully proven or rationally grounded (though this does not preclude them from being thoughtful, critical, and philosophically and ethically informed). Such testimonies create stories and ideals that then have empirical, historical effects, effects that then in their turn call forth, without determining, the revisions and ruptures of new testimonies. Such stories thus become real; de Vries describes them in terms of "renaturalization or defictionalization."[63] This is not, then, to claim an originary, natural, or ontological peace or a natural state of war. Both claims would adhere to a logic of presupposition. Instead, it is to commit to a "preoriginary," "non-natural" peace, a commitment to peace that operates as an "absolute performative, which initiates (and consists in nothing but the creation of) the very conditions of its own (im)possibility."[64] This is a proleptic act that gestures not only to the future, but also to the past, attesting to its link with the past, its faithful repetition of the past, but faithful only in the sense of a mourning that holds onto the past by breaking away from it: "Grieve for me, therefore keep me enough to lose me as you must."

The difference between Milbank and Derrida is *not* that Milbank grounds his hope for a peace to come in belief in an originary peace and that Derrida's hope is rendered ineffective by belief in originary violence or in a tragic view of life; it is, rather, that Derrida's orientation toward a "preoriginary peace" and to a related "peace to come" allows a more radical openness—hospitality—to the future than Milbank's. In one sense, Milbank certainly is right to say that Derrida produces a certain "deformation" of the gospel. And this should not be surprising for a philosopher of Jewish heritage who claims to "rightly pass for an atheist." But the heritage Derrida affirms does extend to and engage with Christianity—even as it does also to Judaism; Platonism; the Enlightenment; and, in recent works, Islam. But for Derrida only a kind of "deformation"—from his perspective a "substitution" or a writing of the tradition "otherwise"—enables one to genuinely affirm the tradition, in the modality of mourning, in a way that opens it to the—new, unexpected, different—the other. This claim, as de Vries points out over and over, disrupts the distinction between orthodoxy and heterodoxy, which makes his reading of Derrida particularly challenging to those, like Milbank, who claim orthodoxy. We might say, then, that for Derrida one meaning of sacrifice is the renunciation of the assurance of tradition without, though, giving up the memory of or commitment to the tradition. This takes place through a "relation without relation" to the tradition, a relation that is at once a "rupture" and a "continuation," that engages both sides of the aporia of responsibility and thus enlivens the tradition. Again, the *adieu* captures this movement simultaneously toward and away.

Clearly, the notions of tradition and heritage are being complicated here. As it is with human selves, traditions are for Derrida never unified or whole, but always multiple and divided against themselves. Here Derrida stands in stark contrast to Milbank, for whom the deformation of the gospel is an unambiguous evil, evacuating all possibility of the good. This, I think, gives us reasons to be suspicious about the perspective from which Milbank determines "the Christian gospel." Despite his critique of self-possession, Milbank's "radical orthodoxy" is premised not only on his ability to identify a truly orthodox Christian tradition, but also on the claim that true ethics and true religiosity must be, can only be "Christian." And he claims to possess this truth with a tenacity that denies a genuine plurality of past and future Christianities or the ethical and religious truth of any other tradition.[65]

Perhaps one must agree with Milbank that the hope he is able to maintain is in some sense "richer" than Derrida's, issuing as it does from a vision of plenitude and resurrection instead of a vision of interminable mourning. But one would have to consider two factors in making this kind of judgment. First, as I have tried to show, it is definitely not the case that Derrida's hope is ineffective, mystical, or simply infinitely postponed, for it is a hope that demands and enables self-critical, engaged action here and now. Second, given Milbank's claims to orthodoxy and his deep Christo-centrism, one has to ask about the cost of his hope. Isn't it the case that when we become sure of the future we seek to create, when God serves as presupposition instead of aporia, we lose our openness to the other? A hospitality grounded in a logic of substitution, however, enables more openness to the shifts and surprises of history that may demand a substitution, a new leap of faith, a new way of imagining and realizing the demand of the infinite, and thus new ways of creating peace. The real comparison between Milbank and Derrida, therefore, begins with the contrast between Milbank's ultimately assured affirmation of a story told once and for all and Derrida's passionate mourning/affirmation of tradition (better, of traditions) that must constantly be repeated anew in reaching forward to the future and outward toward the other.

References

1. Jacques Derrida, *Given Time*, trans. Peggy Kamuf (Chicago: University of Chicago Press, 1991), p. 57.
2. "On Forgiveness: A Roundtable Discussion with Jacques Derrida," in *Questioning God*, eds. John D. Caputo, Mark Dooley, and Michael Scanlon (Bloomington: Indiana University Press, 2001), p. 67.
3. Milbank's major work *Theology and Social Theory* (Oxford: Blackwell, 1990) was described by Richard Roberts as "perhaps the most brilliant, ambitious—and yet questionable—work to have emerged in English theology since the Second World War" (in "Transcendental Sociology?" *Scottish Journal of Theology*, 46[1993]: 527–35).
4. *Questioning God*, pp. 64–65.
5. John Milbank, "The Midwinter Sacrifice," in *The Blackwell Companion to Postmodern Theology*, ed. Graham Ward (Oxford: Blackwell, 2002), p. 108.
6. John D. Caputo and Mark Dooley have responded persuasively to Milbank's criticisms of Derrida on forgiveness. My response here, though taking a different tack, is indebted to their work. See Dooley, "The Catastrophe of Memory" and Caputo, "What Do I Love When I Love My God? Deconstruction and Radical Orthodoxy," in *Questioning God*.
7. Hent de Vries, *Philosophy and the Turn to Religion* (Baltimore: The Johns Hopkins University Press, 1999); and *Religion and Violence* (Baltimore: The Johns Hopkins University Press, 2002).
8. Milbank, "The Midwinter Sacrifice," p. 110. Thus, Milbank distinguishes between two versions of this sacrificial ethic. In stoicism, for example, one sacrifices the lesser for the greater. In the other, of which Derrida is an example, one finds a gesture of "absolute sacrifice" that renounces any return. Milbank suggests that proponents of the latter think that through this radical sacrifice they thereby "escape" the sacrificial economy, p. 108.
9. Milbank, "The Midwinter Sacrifice," p. 112.
10. Milbank, "The Midwinter Sacrifice," p. 113.
11. Milbank, "The Midwinter Sacrifice," p. 122.
12. Milbank, "The Midwinter Sacrifice," p. 123.
13. Milbank, "The Midwinter Sacrifice," p. 113.
14. Milbank, "The Midwinter Sacrifice," p. 111.
15. Milbank thus rejects readings of Christianity that see it as aligned with stoicism in trying to secure an ethical invulnerability. See, for example, Martha Nussbaum's reading of Christianity in *The Fragility of Goodness* (Cambridge: Cambridge University Press, 1986).
16. Milbank, "The Midwinter Sacrifice," p. 123.
17. Milbank, "The Midwinter Sacrifice," p. 123.
18. Milbank, "The Midwinter Sacrifice," p. 116.
19. Milbank, "The Midwinter Sacrifice," p. 123, emphasis mine.
20. Jacques Derrida, *The Gift of Death*, trans. David Wills (Chicago: The University of Chicago Press, 1995), p. 43.
21. De Vries, *Philosophy and the Turn to Religion*, p. 302.
22. Jacques Derrida, "'Eating Well,' or the Calculation of the Subject," in *Who Comes After the Subject?* ed. Eduardo Cadava, Peter Connor, and Jean-Luc Nancy (London: Routledge, 1991), p. 100.
23. De Vries, *Philosophy and the Turn to Religion*, p. 301.
24. Derrida, *The Gift of Death*, p. 66.
25. De Vries, *Religion and Violence*, p. 158.
26. Derrida, *The Gift of Death*, p. 107.
27. Derrida, *The Gift of Death*, p. 108.
28. Derrida, *The Gift of Death*, p. 109, emphases mine.
29. Derrida, *The Gift of Death*, p. 112.
30. Derrida, *The Gift of Death*, p. 114.
31. And so, at this point at least, I think Derrida is much closer to Milbank than Milbank would want to acknowledge.
32. Derrida, *Eating Well*, p. 100.
33. Derrida, *The Gift of Death*, p. 115.

34. Thus Derrida echoes what he says about the gift in the following on responsibility: "The concept of responsibility is one of those strange concepts that give food for thought without giving themselves over to thematization … it gives itself without giving itself to be seen, without presenting itself in some…phenomenological intuition" (de Vries, *Religion and Violence*, p. 189, citing Derrida, *The Gift of Death*, p. 27. De Vries has modified the translation).

35. Derrida, *Given Time*, p. 30.

36. Derrida, *Given Time*, p. 30.

37. De Vries, *Religion and Violence*, p. 316.

38. Milbank, "The Midwinter Sacrifice," p. 116.

39. Jacques Derrida, "Faith and Knowledge," in *Religion*, eds. Jacques Derrida and Gianni Vattimo (Cambridge: Polity Press, 1997), pp. 63, 47.

40. De Vries, *Religion and Violence*, p. 174.

41. Milbank, *Theology and Social Theory*, p. 398.

42. Thus, for example, Milbank's criticism of Derrida on sacrifice in some key respects mirrors his criticism of another significant theory of sacrifice, René Girard's. From the position that human violence is caused by unavoidable mimetic rivalry, Girard has argued that in pre-Christian cultures the only route to the amelioration of this violence was sacrificial catharsis, the sacrificial death of a surrogate victim or scapegoat. This, for Girard is the terrible secret, "hidden since the foundation of the world," and because "religion" supports sacrifice, Girard argues that religion first makes social solidarity possible. Milbank argues that this view of religion relies on the problematic (and quintessentially modern, liberal) assumption that desire is arbitrary, only mimetic and never for the "objectively desirable." If, though, following Milbank, we agree that there is objective desire or "benign eros" religion looks quite different (*Theology and Social Theory*, pp. 394–395).

43. See John Milbank, "The End of Dialogue" in *Christian Uniqueness Reconsidered* (Maryknoll: Orbis Books, 1990).

44. De Vries, *Philosophy and the Turn to Religion*, p. 3.

45. De Vries, *Philosophy and the Turn to Religion*, p. 183.

46. De Vries, *Philosophy and the Turn to Religion*, p. 163. In this respect, though he does use the term "quasi-transcendental" at times, I think de Vries's reading of Derrida's "transcendentality" differs from that of Gasché and Caputo, who both emphasize the fact that Derrida's "quasi-transcendentals" are simultaneously conditions of possibility and impossibility. This is the case for de Vries as well, but what he adds is the idea of mutual implication, that the transcendental and the empirical condition each other.

47. De Vries, *Religion and Violence*, p. 294.

48. De Vries, *Philosophy and the Turn to Religion*, p. 92.

49. De Vries, *Religion and Violence*, p. 303.

50. De Vries, *Philosophy and the Turn to Religion*, p. 147.

51. As de Vries reminds us, for Derrida the terms *trace* and *différance* are not philosophical master-terms but strategic terms aimed at specific contexts. In different contexts, different terms perform the function of *différance*: we have, then, not a master-term but a series of "nonsynonomous substitutions." Derrida's turn to religion, for de Vries, is the latest of such substitutions. Thus, where the deconstruction of the writing/speaking binary in Derrida's early work produced a "generalized writing," the deconstruction of the religious/secular binary produces a "generalized religion" or "religion without religion" (*Philosophy and the Turn to Religion*, p. 434).

52. Milbank, "The Midwinter Sacrifice," pp. 125–126.

53. De Vries, *Religion and Violence*, p. 338.

54. De Vries, *Religion and Violence*, p. 308.

55. It is important here that Milbank's vision of peace in "Midwinter Sacrifice" is related, above all, through the figure of friendship.

56. De Vries, *Religion and Violence*, p. 381.

57. De Vries, *Philosophy and the Turn to Religion*, p. 311.

58. De Vries, *Philosophy and the Turn to Religion*, p. 311.

59. Derrida, "Faith and Knowledge," p. 47.

60. De Vries, *Religion and Violence*, p. 383.

61. De Vries, *Religion and Violence*, p. 384. The difference with Kant, though, would be that Derrida's position does not hold to a gradualism by which finite acts of peace gradually

come closer and closer to a transcendental peace. This is because each instantiation of peace reshapes the ideal of peace. For Derrida, viewing peace as a "regulative ideal" that we gradually approach is not hospitable enough because it "anticipates or predicts what is still to come" (*Philosophy and the Turn to Religion*, p. 328).

62. De Vries, *Religion and Violence*, p. 305.
63. De Vries, *Religion and Violence*, p. 385.
64. De Vries, *Religion and Violence*, p. 385.
65. Given more space I would need to carefully qualify these claims. Indeed, there are resources in Milbank and his radical orthodox colleagues for thinking seriously about issues of identity and difference that might even have certain parallels with what de Vries calls a logic of substitution. But, all in all, the polemic, rhetorical, and conceptual thrust of Milbank's writing works against this possibility. For a treatment of some of these complexities, see my "Secularism Undone: Locating Religion and Politics In the Post-Secular," in Ann Pelligrini and Janet Jacobson (eds.) *World Secularisms at the Millennium* (Minneapolis: University of Minnesota Press, 2005).

CHAPTER 17
Secrets and Sacrifices of Scission

INGE-BIRGITTE SIEGUMFELDT

I have titled this essay "Secrets and Sacrifices of Scission" and am going to offer a perspective on Derridean thought in which these three notions converge on a single figure: the figure of circumcision. This has bearing on the theme of this section of the Society of Biblical Literature and the American Academy of Religion conference, "Other Testaments: Derrida and Religion," but only insofar as we view Derrida's "religion"—marked by quotation marks, of course—as an affiliation with nonaffiliation, some-what along the lines suggested in John D. Caputo's *The Prayers and Tears of Jacques Derrida*: a "religion without religion."[1] Or more specifically, a cutting to which is also a cutting from: a scission that involves secrets and sacrifices.

The primary cue for placing the theme of circumcision centerstage in my work on Derrida derives from a particular statement in "Circumfes-sion."[2] The statement is this: "*Circumcision, that's all I've ever talked about* …" Now, what could this remarkable piece of personal testimony conceivably entail? While the figure of circumcision has clearly become increasingly prominent in Derrida's later work, it can also be traced through the entire body of his writings as a kind of subtext, where it seems to furnish an image for the practice of deconstruction. As an instance of severance it can be related to the problematics of the proper name; for example, to Derrida's preoccupation in *Signeponge* with the "i" as a split sign, marked, like the Jew, by a cut. It also appears to function as a trope for familiar

283

Derridean themes such as openness and indeterminacy, especially if we take a closer look at *Archive Fever*, where the paternal inscription in Freud's family Bible becomes at once an excision and an incision, illustrative of a reconfirmation of the Jewish covenant. Closely connected to these issues, is the notorious question of the cryptogram repeatedly flaunted as an integral part of *The Post Card*. Here I will tentatively offer a "decipherment" of this secret code (insofar as decipherment is possible in this context) in terms that tie Derrida's secrets and scissions into a notion of ritual sacrifice.

The question of the role of circumcision in Derridean thought has been addressed by several commentators from various perspectives, but often only in passing. While "thinking in Jewish," Jonathan Boyarin briefly mentions Derrida's discussions of circumcision in "Circumfession," though he is predominantly concerned with what he describes as the "pretentious way in which Derrida speaks of Jewish themes while wavering, as it may suit him, between identification and non-identification with the Jewish community."[3] More exotically, Reverend Philip Culbertson announces that he has "peeked into Derrida's underpants" in order to discover the truth about "Circumcision, Textual Multiplexity, and the Cannibalistic Mother."[4] James Boon feels that he must mention Derrida in a footnote to his account of "Muslim/Hindu, Judeo-Christian, and surgical/antisurgical positions in discourses of circumcision/uncircumcision."[5] Gideon Ofrat locates lost foreskins in all areas philosophical, theological, and psychoanalytical in his, shall we say, *midrashic* commentary on Derrida's *oeuvre*, but at least we find here a book length study that "circles around" the figure of circumcision.[6] A sound and focused study of this aspect of Derridean thought is John D. Caputo's *The Prayers and Tears of Jacques Derrida*. Caputo's discussion of circumcision as a double or dialectical movement of opening and closure, belonging and nonbelonging, is very interesting indeed, and I have little to add to it, other than the specifically Judaic perspective.[7] This, however, does not mean that I have any stake in placing Derrida among the sages of Judaism. Nor have I any interest (and perhaps this should be emphasized in the context of this particular conference) in claiming Derrida for any "religion" or "religious" framework—far from it. I am simply interested in the interfaces between aspects of Derridean and Jewish thought, and one of these is "circumcision."

Let me begin with selected Rabbinic sources, and with a passage from *Tanhumah*:

> All of Israel who are circumcised enter the Garden of Eden, for the Holy One, blessed be He, has placed His Name in Israel so that they will enter the Garden of Eden. And what is the name and the seal

[*ha-shem v'ha-hotem*] which He placed in them? It is [the name] [*ShaDaY (shin-dalet-yud)*].[8]

There are several explanations as to why this particular set of consonants denotes this particular name of the Divine, but most of them turn on the morphological correspondence between letters and the parts of the body on which they are placed. Thus the form of the letter *shin* (שׁ) is seen to resemble the nostrils, *daleth* (ד) the human hand, and the *yud* (י) is overlaid on the limb that it most resembles—namely the "place of circumcision"—with some versions claiming that the *yud* resembles the ritual cut itself.

What is interesting to us here is that this constellation of three Hebrew letters placed on the human body together form a name, a seal, a signature (*ha-shem v'ha-hotem*): namely the "divine name which is written on each and every one" (*ha-shem katuv al kol ehad v'ehad*) to mark the covenant with God. Circumcision is referred to as *hatimat milah*, that is, the "signature of the word/circumcision," where the roots *mem-lamed(-lamed)* (to circumcise) and *mem-lamed-heh* (word; relate, tell) undecideably oscillate. Moreover, "circumcision is made like a *yud*"[9] and *yud*, in turn, is regarded as the "letter of the holy covenant" (*ot brit kadosh*). It is also the first letter in the Tetragrammaton in which the secret Holy Name is occulted, and so intimates the *sod YHVH*, the "secret of the Lord" that "is made known to those who fear him" according to Psalms 25:14.

So, we have here several terms denoting the Israelites' covenant with God: name and signature, the secret word, the letter *yud*, all marking the alliance. And it is this concealed, protective mark (the word or name of God sealed in the flesh) that grants passage to the Garden of Eden: circumcision is literally a password, a shibboleth. As such it is closely connected with a secret mark of alliance and a sacrificial scission: it both cleaves to and divides. It marks both adherence and division, for the descendants of Abraham are bound through scission, by a wound, and belonging roots itself in that which no longer belongs.

Let us turn to look at the Derridean figure of "circumcision," keeping in mind these notions that cluster around the motif of the covenant: the secret name and the shibboleth carved in the flesh, granting passage to an alliance that offers only exile.

And let us begin with the name. In linguistics and the philosophy of language the proper name has no meaning; only a referent to which it is contingently attached, with the identity of the bearer indicated only by the circumstantial context of its utterance. Derrida goes further in emphasizing that the term "proper" existentially implies a notion of property, that which is uniquely mine, thus exploring the paradox of a semiotically empty signifier experienced—or "felt"—as a fullness of subjectivity. These are familiar issues in Derridean thought: the dissemination of the illusions of property and belonging invested in the proper name, the related erasure of the signature, and the subversion of naming as an act of calling into being. *Glas*, for instance, with its many divisions, is in many ways a rehearsal of the loss involved in the act of naming. The proper name is inherently divided, Derrida says in *Glas*,

> The given proper (sur) name relieves the head that falls (to the tomb) on the scaffold, but simultaneously redoubles, through the decision to nominate, the arbitrariness of the sentence, consecrates and glorifies the fall, cuts one more time, and engraves—on a literary monument.[10]

One of the questions that then arises is whether we can relate this notion of the name to Derrida's own. I am thinking here of his Jewish name, Elie, which, he claims, was kept secret throughout his childhood. "Elie: my name—not inscribed, the only one, very abstract, that ever happened to me, that I learned, from outside, later, and that I have never felt, borne, the name I do not know ..."[11] Here, in his "circumfession," Derrida reveals his name, hidden, "never felt" once discovered: the name of a (non)identity, yet the name—and this is crucial—of his biblical namesake, Elijah. In Jewish tradition, the prophet Elijah is the guardian of circumcision, that which is "all Derrida has ever talked about." This name, its initial concealment and later discovery, is arguably the site where all of Derrida's contradictory feelings about Jewishness converge in terms that consistently stress the sense of nonbelonging:

> I no longer belonged to them from the day of my birth, that linked with this double sentiment that has always preceded me: I was both excluded and infinitely, secretly preferred by my family who had lost me, from the beginning, through love, whence a series of ruptures without rupture with the family, impossibility, insured from the start, of an endogamous marriage and family, after the debate I shall have to recount, the noncircumcision of my sons. The prophet Elijah is nonetheless the guardian of circumcision (12-23-76)?[12]

Derrida's secret name, Elie, would seem to carry a wealth of significant associations and connotations. While referring directly to circumcision, the ritual combining the naming of the male infant with the excision of his foreskin, it also carries the paradox of affiliation as disaffiliation, or belonging as both difference and deferral—that is, the very emblem of *différance*.

If then we turn back to an earlier source, *The Post Card,* we recall that its opening pages draw attention to a secret associated with the proper name. Here it takes the form of fifty-two blank spaces that repeatedly recur throughout "Envois"—a number that makes up what Derrida declares to be a cryptogram whose codes of decipherment he teasingly claims to have forgotten. The cryptogram "buried" in the text is itself a kind of illegible postcard sent to his readers without any accompanying means of interpretation. As Derrida well knew,[13] the meanings that can be ascribed to fifty-two blank spaces are endless, and any attempt to crack the code will inevitably be left stranded in indeterminacy, leaving the cryptogram as a mere instance of impenetrable Derridean idiosyncrasy.

Nevertheless, there may be virtue in persistence here.[14] Given that a familiar image of Derrida's philosophical strategies is the rabbinic model of proliferating interpretations, perhaps[15] the question of his secret Jewish name, itself in part an autobiography or a story of secret Jewishness, is, after all, closely aligned with the signifying games of esoteric Judaism. And the potential arbitrariness of a kabbalistic reading of the cryptogram in *The Post Card* seems far less so when we take into account the information made available ten years later in "Circumfession." The disclosure of the concealed name opens a belated, but still tantalizing, way into the cryptic void of *The Post Card*: Elie is the French version of Hebrew "Eliahu" and if, by following the simplest of strategies in gematria, or Hebrew numerology, we add up the numerical value of the letters in Derrida's biblical namesake, Eliahu, (rather than Frenchified "Elie"), the result is fifty-two.[16]

The fifty-two blank spaces, repeatedly occurring as a void integral to the text, thus exactly match the structure of Derrida's secret name. Moreover, as we already know, this secret name directly evokes the drama of circumcision—not only as the name of the guardian of the covenant, but, in more formal terms, as itself a blank space, hidden in the cryptogram, excised from the official record of that which is uniquely his—Derrida's "identity." The cryptogram thus stages both the concealment and the cut which epitomize Derrida's "Jewishness," through circumcision, through the secret, through deferral and difference. The void of fifty-two blank spaces is, I suggest, the signature of (Jacques) Elie (Derrida) inscribed in *The Post Card,* which, as Derrida points out, "imprints itself on my language circumcised in its turn,"[16] to the point, indeed, of migrating obsessively through the entire body of his work.

Surely all this cannot be put down to mere coincidence. We have here a name initially excised and hidden from its bearer, then subsequently discovered, and in turn concealed by him. It is buried in a cryptogram, the unravelling of which is made possible by an exercise in kabbalistic numerology: the French version of the Hebraic guardian of the covenant, itself marked by the sign of excision that is circumcision. As such it seems to make perfect sense of Derrida's claim that circumcision is "all he has ever talked about." The question then is what bearing this strange constellation might have upon Derridean thought in general?

Circumcision would seem to furnish a symbolic model for the practice of deconstruction. It functions, more specifically, in its association with the "Jewish" motifs of name, prophet, and blank space, as a marker of the constitutive aporias of deconstruction. Jewish in derivation, it is mobilized in the service of all disaffiliation—including dissociation from Judaism in any of its fixed doctrinal forms. It signals the paradox of an origin and an identity that are neither origin nor identity: the notion of the Jew as never "himself" but cut adrift as the "wandering Jew," captured and undone in dispersion, diaspora. The name is therefore not the site of an embodiment, but (like the name of the Jewish God) points to an identity that is always elsewhere, beyond the reach of definition.

The associations at once carried and concealed in the name therefore appear to offer a crucial opening to Derridean thought in general, and if my reading of the cryptogrammic blanks is plausible, it does provide a new perspective on what Derrida calls the "interrupted verticality"[18] of his writing. This is unmistakably an allusion to the wounded penis as the emblem of writing, which is a striking feature in many of his texts. In *Glas*, for instance, writing is seen as citation that displaces "the syntactic arrangement around a real or sham physical wound that draws attention to and makes the other be forgotten." "What bands this text erect," he continues, "seduces and troubles doctoral discourse ..."[19] Citing, as well as dating, signing, and prefacing, is associated with an act of appropriation, a taking or doing away, thus wounding the erected structure. Although opaque, these references turn on the phallic associations of the graphic shape of the letter "i" and the related problematics of the self-representation of the male subject: the lack of correspondence between the signifier and signified in the name, and ultimately the "explosion" of singularity of the "I": "*Je/tombe*, I/fall(s), I/tomb."[20] Elsewhere Derrida picks up from Francis Ponge the play on the "I" as the erect penis and the lower case "i" as its wilted form marked by the dot, the "liquid drop or accent." "This I is my likeness[...]; in lower case, taking it off in order to write, [...]; playing with its frail or fresh erection..."[21]

If then, following the explicit invitation here, we pursue the identification of the shape of the "i" with the penis further and associate the wound of circumcision with the point at which it is severed, the gap can be perceived at once as the cut dividing the dot from the main stem and as a mark of alliance: that which makes the "i" an "i," just as circumcision is that which makes the Jew a Jew. Derrida's concern with this particular letter is no doubt rooted in the fact that graphically it is a "split" sign. Its main part is severed from the crowning dot, thereby embodying a rupture, a deferral, or inherent difference, which relates it preeminently to differance—"*the point detached and retained at the same time*," as he says in "Circumfession," "false, not false but simulated castration which does not lose what it plays to lose and which transforms it into a pronounceable letter, i and not I ..."[22]

In English (with which Derrida himself plays in the original French), the capital "I" of course also refers to the first person pronoun. Accordingly, the difference between the lower case "i" and the capital "I" marks the difference between the split subject and the Subject that, in what Derrida calls the logocentric tradition, has formally, but deceptively, been "raised" from a divided sign to a united one. "[T]he *I* is carried away," he says in *Glas*, "moved aside in(to) the trait that relates it to anything whatsoever. Undecidable it too in its signature."[23]

However, the question of the "i" can also be approached from the perspective of kabbalah. Here, creation began as God printed his name on the primordial void, beginning with the initial letter of the tetragrammaton IHVH, the Hebrew "i," the *yud* which graphically is not a "full"-size sign but resembles rather a comma or an apostrophe, or indeed a rounded scar. According to kabbalistic cosmogony, this minute sign carries within it the entire alphabet, all signs and combinations of signs, and contains within it the entire creative power of God. Creation begins in the *yud*, but also ends there, for the process is ruptured as the emerging vessel inevitably breaks, only to begin again, turning on its inherent fracture. The *yud* thus binds the perpetually self-repeating process of creation to rupture. For the kabbalists this single point contains everything. For Derrida the *yud* closely links the preliminary wound of circumcision with the N/name, since God began creation as an exercise in writing by carving his signature on the primordial ether. Derrida writes:

> In question might be a proper name or a punctuation mark, just the apostrophe that replaces an elided letter, a word, one or several letters, in question might be brief or very long sentences, numerous or scant, that occasionally were themselves originally unterminated.[24]

As the point at which formation and breakage are combined, and where the outcome is always perpetually deferred, the *yud* can be seen as the emblem of Derridean *différance*, the moment that carries within it continuity as discontinuity, beginning and end. It is the sign of the writer inscribing his signature in the text, "displacing the syntactic arrangement around a real or sham physical wound,"[25] just as Derrida is always playing with the incorporation of his name, indeed as (Jacques) Elie (Derrida) occults himself throughout *The Post Card,* a game also played in and between the columns of *Glas* and with increasing intensity in his later writings.

The letter "i" *"detached and retained at the same time,"* the signature "desingularised,"[26] the erection rising from the fall, circumcision marking an alliance only through scission—all these notions converge on a particular form of binding that takes place in the secret "crypts" of Derridean thought: the binding of the name to its own erasure.

If we look specifically at *Glas,* circumcision entails the paradox of severance as a simultaneous adherence, where the cutting off is at once a cutting to, to itself, indeed to scission itself. Derrida describes it as "a determining cut":

> It permits cutting but, at the same time and in the same stroke, remaining attached to the cut. The Jew arranges himself so that the cut part remains attached to the cut. Jewish errance limited by adherence and countercut. The Jew is cutting only in order to treat thus, to contract the cut with itself.[27]

Erasure here involves both disjunction and conjunction, in a sense forming a "contract with itself." From this perspective, the Jewish covenant marks an alliance with God, but with a God who is already removed beyond the reach of those binding themselves to this law by the ritual act of excision. The Jew, as Derrida here suggests, "treats" the wound of absence with another, thus perpetually filling in the vacated space with blanks. As such the crural cut involves not only an excision of the foreskin but a simultaneous incision, the inscription of the "non" onto the void. Naturally, this could be seen as in part explaining Derrida's declarations of nonaffiliation to the Jewish tradition as in fact a form of adherence, or contract, whereby the Jew "arranges" or "treats" himself, so that nonbelonging in effect involves a form of belonging, and exile itself becomes an abode, a kind of "strong"hold for the (Abrahamic) uprooted, for as Derrida continues: "What remains of/from a cut becomes stronger."[28]

But then, we might ask, what is it that "remains of/from a cut?" The memory of what once was, augmented, "strengthened," by loss? Perhaps what remains is a trace, but in the Derridean sense of that which refers only to its own effacement, making or marking itself only by losing itself: "[t]race destines," as Derrida says in *Cinders,* "like everything, to disappear from itself, as much in order to lose the way as to rekindle a memory."[29]

This too is a form of "treating" a severance by another: the trace remaining from what is not, binding itself to its own dissemination.

This notion of binding through scission, cleaving to by cleaving, forging belonging through sacrifice, is brought to bear on a range of figures in Derridean thought. In *Glas*, for instance, it illustrates the two sacrificial rituals that strengthened Abraham's covenant with God—circumcision (the "Abrahamic cut") and the sacrifice of Isaac, the latter notably named the *Akedah*, the "binding"[30]—so combining the loss of the foreskin and the near-loss of the son. "Circumcision and the sacrifice of Isaac," says Derrida, "are analogous gestures."[31] In both cases the patriarch's alliance with God is determined by self-bereavement, and in the latter case the son is tied up (bound) before the strike. So, according to Derrida, severance, sacrificial and otherwise, binds through the substitution of one erasure by another.

If, in conclusion, we turn to *Archive Fever*, the theme of circumcision, deployed in a discussion of the agonistic relationship between father and son as central to both psychoanalysis and Judaism, eminently illustrates this notion of alliance. Focusing on a copy of the Bible handed down through the filial line in Freud's family, inscribed by the father and bound in new skin for each generation, Derrida describes it as a characteristically Jewish gift of paternal love, which reaffirms the covenant by simultaneously restoring the lost skin to the son and contracting him anew to the Law: "Again inscribing inscription, it commemorates in its way, effectively, a circumcision." This "incision *right on* the skin: more than one skin, at more than one age"[32] on the first blank page—that is before the beginning of the book—is a scission, a wound, marked by the paternal signature. Therefore, as an opening before the beginning, an origin before origin, like the trace, or the cut severing the dot from the stem of the "i," every epigraph becomes such an incision, every seam in Derrida's books a rehearsal of the circumcision of the "writing I." And so we must read Derrida's own headings in *Archive Fever* and everywhere else in precisely this manner: "Exergue," "Preamble," "Foreword" as "new skins" inscribed by "Jewish" fathers, or writers, as wounds opening the text, again and again: the incision on which the (B/)book turns and returns.

There are many examples of how the figure of circumcision can be seen to "mark" Derrida's writing. Here I have touched upon only a few: the notional and morphological resemblance of the Hebrew *yud* to the crural cut; the split sign of "i" which marks the name, secret, divided, encrypted; and the notion of binding as both cleaving and cleaving to an alliance. Naturally, these examples are not randomly chosen. They are all reflected in a particular passage in "Circumfession":

"... [*T*]*he circumcised is* the proper" (12-30-76), that's what my readers won't have known about me, the comma of my breathing henceforward, without continuity but without a break, the changed time of my writing, graphic writing, through having lost its interrupted verticality, almost with every letter, to be bound better and better but be read less and less well over almost twenty years, like my religion about which nobody understands anything ...[33]

"[T]*he circumcised is* the proper," Derrida maintains. If we see the "proper" here as referring to the name, indeed the truncated and encrypted name bound to secret, scission, and sacrifice, it is that which his "readers won't have known about [him]." It is "the comma," the small rounded mark that both separates and combines sentences, at once providing "continuity" and "break"; the mark that "binds" in the sense of the *Akedah*: and the act of cleaving and cleaving to, like the *yud* that is signed in the place of circumcision. It marks "the changed time of [his] writing, graphic writing, through having lost its interrupted verticality," that is, informing a kind of writing doubly severed or, by the same token, doubly bound, where the "signature is desingularized"[34] and the letter "i" "*detached and retained at the same time.*" Derrida's writing has thus been "bound better and better" but has been "read less and less well over almost twenty years like [his] religion about which nobody understands anything."

It is not my claim that Derrida here implies that his writing has been increasingly "bound," like Freud's family Bible, to the paternal Jewish tradition, but rather that it has been bound "better and better" to its own "interrupted verticality," to its own scission: the encrypted sacrifices, the cuts that separate and bind. In other words, it has been increasingly "bound" to the loss that inscribes itself in loss—to the figure of "circumcision" and everything it entails.

References

1. Jonathan D. Caputo, *The Prayers and Tears of Jacques Derrida: Religion without Religion* (Bloomington: Indiana University Press, 1997), p. xxi.
2. Geoffrey Bennington and Jacques Derrida, *Jacques Derrida*, trans. Geoffrey Bennington 1993 (Chicago: University of Chicago Press, 1996), p. 70.
3. Jonathan Boyarin, *Thinking in Jewish* (Chicago: University of Chicago Press, 1996), pp. 140–60.
4. Rev. Philip Culbertson, "Pee(k)ing into Derrida's Underpants," *Textual Reasoning* 10 (Spring 2001).
5. James Boon, "Circumscribing Circumcision/Uncircumcision," in *Implicit Understandings*, ed. Stuart Schwartz (Cambridge: Cambridge University Press, 1994), p. 556; see also footnote 18 p. 562.
6. See Gideon Ofrat, *The Jewish Derrida*, trans. Peretz Kidron (Syracuse: Syracuse University Press, 2001).
7. Personally, I prefer the homograph with the open diphthong of "tears" in Caputo's title, so as to refer to the various Jewish rituals of "tearing," but also to the tears and cuts and seams in the Derridean *oeuvre*.

8. *Midrash Tanhumah, Parashat Sav, 14; Parashat Sh'mini, 8.* See also E.R. Wolfson, "Circumcision and the Divine Name: A Study in the Transmission of Esoteric Doctrine," *The Jewish Quarterly Review,* lxxviii, no. 1–2 (July–Oct. 1987): 78. My italics and square brackets.

9. See Rav Avraham ben Natan ha-Yarhi's *Sefer ha-Manhig,* Toledo 1204; ed. Y. Raphael (Jerusalem, 1978): 2, pp. 579–580.

10. Jacques Derrida, *Glas,* trans. John P. Leavey Jr. and Richard Rand (London: University of Nebraska Press, 1986), p. 9b.

11. Bennington and Derrida, *Jacques Derrida,* pp. 90, 83.

12. Bennington and Derrida, *Jacques Derrida,* pp. 94–95.

13. "I know in advance," he says, "all the types of reaction that this will not fail to induce all around" (*The Post Card,* trans. Alan Bass [Chicago: University of Chicago Press, 1987], p. 5).

14. As I have shown in "Re-Circumcising Derrida," *Orbis Litterarum,* vol. 56, no. 1 (2001): 1–16. The following passage is freely adapted from there.

15. After *Politics of Friendship* we can no longer use "perhaps" idly as a mere marker of interpretive modesty; it must be seen here as marking the paradox of affiliation and disaffiliation.

16. Eliahu comprises the five letters *alef-lamed-yud-heh-vav* which correspond to the numbers 1-30-10-5-6.

17. Bennington and Derrida, *Jacques Derrida,* p. 72.

18. Bennington and Derrida, *Jacques Derrida,* p. 154.

19. Derrida, *Glas,* pp. 215b, 216b.

20. "The play of the anth-erection by which I waken to, embark on my name supposes that, in more than one stroke, I crush some flowers and clear the virgin thicket of erianthus toward the primitive scene, that I falsify and reap the genealogy." (Derrida, *Glas,* p. 175b).

21. Jacques Derrida, *Signéponge—Signsponge,* trans. Richard Rand (New York: Columbia University Press, 1984), p. 28. See also the following passage in *Signéponge.*

22. Bennington and Derrida, *Jacques Derrida,* p. 72.

23. Derrida, *Glas,* p. 127b.

24. Derrida, *The Post Card,* p. 4. Also "… but absolutely refusing to *speak* of this by putting the dots on the i's"; "… small dots lost over our immense territory"; "… a single dot on a single I, infinitely small in a book infinitely big" (pp. 45, 26, 22).

25. Derrida, *Glas,* p. 215b.

26. Derrida, *Glas,* p. 171b.

27. Derrida, *Glas,* p. 41a.

28. Derrida, *Glas,* p. 41a.

29. Jacques Derrida, *Cinders,* trans. Ned Lukacher (London: University of Nebraska Press, 1991), p. 57.

30. The traditional Jewish term for what Christian tradition terms the "sacrifice" of Isaac is *Akedat Yitshak,* "the binding of Isaac." Relatedly, perhaps, Latin *religio* means "bond," "obligation."

31. Derrida, *Glas,* pp. 41a, 42a.

32. Jacques Derrida, *Archive Fever: A Freudian Impression,* trans. Eric Prenowitz (Chicago: Chicago University Press, 1996), p. 20.

33. Bennington and Derrida, *Jacques Derrida,* p. 154.

34. See *Glas,* p. 171b.

SECTION VI
Revelation(s)

CHAPTER 18
Deconstruction, God, and the Possible

RICHARD KEARNEY

You, God, cannot help us but we must help you and defend your dwelling place inside us to the last.

—Etty Hillesum[1]

In a conversation held at New York University in 2001, Derrida responded to my question about the relationship between deconstruction and resurrection as follows:

> I am not against resurrection. I would share your hope for resurrection, reconciliation and redemption. But I think I have a responsibility as someone who thinks deconstructively to obey the necessity—the necessity of the possibility—that there is *khôra* rather than a relationship with the anthropo-theological God of Revelation. At some point, you Richard translate your faith into something determinable and then you have to keep the "name" of the resurrection. My own understanding of faith is that there is faith whenever one gives up not only any certainty but also any determined hope. If one says that resurrection is the horizon of one's hope then—since one knows what one names when one says "resurrection"—faith is not pure faith. It is already knowledge … That is why you have to be an atheist of this sort (someone who "rightly passes for an atheist") in order to be true to faith.[2]

297

Later on the exchange, Derrida compares my eschatological notion of the God-who-may-be with his own deconstructive notion of the Perhaps, touching on what I believe to be a common theme in both our thinking:

> The "perhaps" (*peut-etre*) refers to the unconditional beyond sovereignty. It is an unconditional which is the desire of powerlessness rather than power. I think you are absolutely right to attempt to name God not as sovereign, as almighty, but as precisely the most powerless. Justice and love are precisely oriented to this powerlessness. But *khôra* is powerless too. Not powerlessness in the sense of poor or vulnerable. Powerlessness as simply no-power. No power at all.[3]

What particularly interests me here is the difference between God as powerless and *khôra* as powerless, given that for both Derrida and me the highest form of possibility—which stands higher than actuality—is the possible as more-than-impossible and less-than-power. All this requires a thorough rethinking of the traditional categories of possibility as found in modal logic, the ontology of potency/act and the rationalist epistemology of representational *possibilitas* (as in Leibniz's theodicy of possible worlds). It requires a move beyond metaphysical tendencies to consider the possible as a lack striving toward actualization in the real, reconceiving it instead as an alterity beyond being, and by implication beyond the accomplished order of things: an otherness that comes toward us as unpredicable event or surprise. I think that Derrida's recent reflections on this subject are immensely helpful for a new way of thinking the divine in terms of *posse* rather than *esse*. And while Derrida himself does not embrace a religious affirmation of the God of the Possible—preferring the cooler climes of indeterminate *khôra*—he certainly seems open to dialogue with those who do.

In an essay titled "As If It Were Possible, 'Within Such Limits …'" (1998), Derrida reinterprets the notion of possibility in terms of what he calls the "irreducible modality of 'Perhaps' (*peut-être*)."[4] Cautioning against all talk of "last words," in philosophy no less than in history, Derrida declares this "perhaps" to be the necessary condition of possibility of every experience—to the extent that every experience is an event which registers that which comes from the unpredictable otherness of the future. Such an experience of the "perhaps" is at once that of the possible *and* the impossible. Or as Derrida puts it, the possible as impossible. If what happens is only that which is possible in the sense of what is anticipated and expected, then it is not an event in the true sense. For an event is only possible in so far as it comes from the impossible. An event (*événement*) can only happen, in other words, when and where the "perhaps" lifts all presumptions and assurances about what might be and lets the future come as future (*laisse l'avenir à l'avenir*), that is, as the arrival of the impossible. The "perhaps" thus solicits a "yes" to what is still to come, beyond all plans, programs, and predictions. It keeps the ontological question of "to be or not to be" constantly in question, on its toes, deferring any last word on the matter. But if deconstruction suspends the security of ontological answers, it also, Derrida insists, eschews the levity of a purely rhetorical "perhaps" (*peut-être/vielleicht*). The "perhaps" sustains the survival of the question. But what might such a possible-impossible actually mean?

In *The Politics of Friendship* (1994), Derrida had already ventured some kind of response to this question. Picking up on Nietzsche's talk of a "dangerous perhaps" as the thought of the future, Derrida argues that such a thought is indispensable to friendship precisely as a category of futurity. Distinguishing between the bad possible (of predictability) and the good possible (of impossibility), Derrida affirms that it is only the latter that can safeguard true friendship as a commitment to what is to come. It is also only the good possible (that is, the impossible possible) that can respect the dual fidelity of friendship to undecidability and decision.[5] Without the openness of a radically indeterminate "possible"—which like the phenomenological reduction brackets our prejudices about the future—there could be no genuine decision. But, equally, no decision could be made without somehow also lifting the "perhaps," while retaining its "living" possibility in a kind of living memory. Consequently, if no real decision—ethical, political, juridical—is feasible without conjuring the "perhaps" that keeps the present open to the coming event, there could be no decision either—no committing of oneself to one possible rather than others—if there were not some *limiting* of this opening "perhaps," which serves as condition of the possibility of decision![6]

This circle is what Derrida calls the "lucky aporia of the possible impossible."[7] In "As If ...," he expands on this aporia, as first outlined in the *Politics of Friendship*. In the event of decision, he writes here, "only the im-possible takes place; and the unfolding of a potentiality of possibility already there would never constitute an event or invention."[8] Why? Because, explains Derrida, "a decision that I *can* take, the decision *in my power* and which merely manifests the acting out (*passage à l'acte*) or unfolding of what is *already possible* for me, the actualization of my possibility, decision which only derives from me, would it still be a decision?"[9] The answer is no, because genuine decision—like genuine responsibility—is not just about *my* possibles but is also about *others'* possibles intervening, which may well represent the impossibility of my own possible. Whence Derrida's preference for a paradoxically *receptive* decision, recalling Lévinas's notion of a *"difficile liberté"* which allows for the irruption of the other in the self. He notes: "the responsible decision must be this im-possible possibility of a "passive" decision, a decision of the other in me which removes none of my liberty or responsibility."[10] Moreover, Derrida insists that every responsibility must traverse this aporia of the impossible-possible which, far from paralyzing us, mobilizes a "new thinking of the possible."[11]

Later in "As If ..." Derrida gives further examples of this aporetic logic. He cites, for instance, the fact that an *interpretation* is only possible if it remains to some extent inadequate (that is, if an adequate interpretation is impossible). For an interpretation without any default—closed therefore to the possibility of misinterpretation—would represent not only the end of interpretation, as an on-going process of exploring meaning, but also the end of a historical future in any sense whatsoever. Closing off the future, it would make everything impossible.

Derrida notes a similar interplay of possibility and impossibility in the instance of *invention*. Invention is always possible in so far as it is the invention of the possible; but invention is really only possible when it does not invent something new out of itself—in which case it would not be new—but rather allows something *other* to come, occur, happen. Now, given the fact that this otherness that comes to it is not part or parcel of invention's own resources of possibles, it means that the "only possible invention would be the invention of the impossible."[12] Of course, we may object that the invention of the impossible is impossible; but in fact, insists Derrida, it is the only kind possible. "An invention must pronounce itself as invention of what does not appear possible," short of which it would be little more than an explicitation of a "program of possibles in the economy of the same."[13]

A similar logic of impossible-possibility applies to Derrida's analysis of "pardon." Here we cross the threshold from epistemological aporias to ethics. Pardon, Derrida claims, is only possible, as such, when faced with the unpardonable, that is, where *impossible*. For pardon—like hospitality, gift, justice, etc.—is an unconditional that has to deal with conditions as soon as it becomes an act or decision. In such instances, the possible "is" impossible. Or to put it in more formal, quasi-transcendental terms, the condition of possibility of pardon or hospitality is also and at the same time the condition of its impossibility.[14] The possibility of pardon or hospitality, therefore, requires us to *do the impossible*, to make the impossible possible. But this must occur, says Derrida, without resorting to some sort of morality of rules and prescriptions, of oughts or obligations.

Pardon and hospitality must, by their very unconditional nature, remain unpredictable and gratuitous (*gratuit et imprévisible*).

In all of these examples, Derrida argues that im-possibility is not the mere contrary of possibility but rather its mark of renewal and arrival as event. No event worthy of its name is simply an actualization of some precontained potential program. For an event to be possible, it must be both possible (of course) but also impossible (in the sense of an interruption by something singular and exceptional into the regime of preexisting possibles understood as immanent powers and potencies). The event happens not just because it is possible, qua ontological acting-out of some inherent *dunamis* or *potentia*, but also because something impossible—hitherto unanticipated—comes to pass. It is precisely the impossibility of formerly predictable possibilities which makes new ones announce themselves beyond this very impossibility. The impossible reminds us, therefore, that *beyond our powers* the impossible is still possible. There are impossible possibles *beyond* us, never dreamt of in our philosophies. Or as Derrida puts it in *Politics of Friendship*: "Perhaps the impossible is the only possible chance of something new, of some new philosophy of the new. Perhaps; perhaps in truth the *perhaps* still names this chance."[15]

So how might we relate all this to the religious question of God? Derrida does not directly engage, it has to be said, with the eschatological or theological implications of this issue. But he does leave us one or two tantalizing hints. In a note that refers to my own notion of the "may-be" in *Poétique du Possible* (1984), and to our discussion of Heidegger's "loving possible" (*des mögende Vermögens*), Derrida makes mention of the possible as that which is "more than impossible" (*plus qu'impossible* or *plus impossible*). And he refers us here, tellingly if only in passing, to the mystical maxim of Angelus Silesius: "*das uberunmöglichschste ist möglich*" (God as the more than impossible is possible). The deeply theological connotations of this claim are not addressed by Derrida here alas! But he does allude to his discussion of the "name of God" in "Sauf le Nom." And he does add this sentence—recalling the opening claims about the "desire of God" in that essay—"All the aporias of the possible-impossible or of the more-than-impossible would thus be 'lodged' but also dislodging 'within'(*au-dedans*) what one might calmly call the desire, love or movement towards the Good etc."[16]

The "etc." resists any temptation to pronounce a "last word" and leaves open, in our view, the option of adding a "possible God"—a God whom we might now be inclined to refer to, along with Silesius, as a *more than impossible God*. Indeed, it might be noted that Derrida himself does allude here to a certain connection between the possible-impossible aporia and the undecidable aporia of who/what which he relates to the question of *khôra* (which precedes the distinction who/what). This question of *khôra*, as we have had occasion to remark elsewhere, is deeply linked in Derrida's work, as in Caputo's, to the question of God.[17] But such an eschatological possibility is not, it must be said, explored or extrapolated by Derrida himself.

What Derrida is trying to do, it seems to me, is to think a postmetaphysical category of the possible by rethinking the category of the impossible in a way that is not negative or disabling. The impossible needs to be affirmed because, as we have noted above, it is precisely im-possibility which opens up possibility and makes it possible. Strangely, however, this can only occur when my power of possibility undergoes its own death as "my" possibility—acknowledging in mourning, passion, suffering, and anxiety that it is this very impossibility which allows a new possible, another possible, another's possible, an im-possible possible, to come, or to come back. This "other" possible returns, says Derrida, as a specter. It assumes the guise of a *revenant*, rising up from the grave of my own possible in the form of an in-coming other. And we experience this as surprise, gift, openness, hospitality.[18]

In one especially charged passage, Derrida offers a more phenomenological take on this moment. Here he endeavors to describe the more affective dimension of the impossible-possible aporia:

> It names a suffering or passion, an affect at once sad and joyous, the instability of disquietude (*inquiétude*) proper to every possibilisation. This latter would allow itself to be haunted by the specter of its impossibility, by its mourning for itself: the mourning of the self carried in itself, but which also gives it its life or survival, its very possibility. For this *im*-possibility opens its possibility, it leaves a trace, at once an opportunity and a threat, in what it renders possible. The torment would signal this scar, the trace of this trace … All this recurs with respect to Freud's concept of *Bemachtigung*, of the limit or the paradoxes of the possible as power.[19]

Derrida even goes so far as to identify this paradox of the impossible-possible with the experience of *faith* itself. For how is it, he asks, that that which makes possible makes impossible the very thing it makes possible? How is it that promise is so related to ruin, affirmation to death, renewal to deprivation? "The *in* of the im-possible is no doubt radical, implacable, undeniable," he replies. "But it is not simply negative or dialectical; it *introduces* to the possible … it makes it come, it makes it revolve according to an anachronistic temporality or incredible filiality—a filiality which is also, he avows, the *origin of faith*" (my italics).[20]

But why, we may ask, should Derrida introduce the question of faith at this juncture? Because, he explains, such incredible filiality both "exceeds knowledge and conditions the address to the other, inscribing every theorem in the time and space of a testimony ('I talk to you, believe me')."[21] But, we may further ask, why *testimony*? Why *attestation*? Because we can only possess and practice faith in a possibility never adequately or fully *present*, but always already anachronistic (remembered) or still to come (promised). In this sense, Derrida's relating of "virtuality" to "the origin of faith" alludes, one suspects, to a general "spectral" structure of all human experience rather than to any *specially religious* experience of a loving God.[22] As such, it may have as much to teach us about the postmodern phenomenon of virtual reality—simulations, simulacra, and cyborgs etc.—as about the revealed reality of Yahweh or Jesus. In short, deconstruction may have as much to say about phantoms and phantasms as about prophecies and prayers.

I have argued somewhat differently in *Poétique du possible* (1984) and more recently in *The God Who May Be* (2001), that the impossible-made-possible signals the promise of new thinking about the "possible God." Resurrection rather than deconstruction—or at least resurrection in addition to deconstruction, for we would not deny that the former traverses the latter and has constant need of its purging powers. There is not opposition here, in our view, but difference. And the difference is one of emphasis as much as of substance. Derrida sees in the play of impossible-possible a structure of "experience in general." (Indeed at one point Derrida admits that his entire reflection on the impossible-possible may be little more than a gloss on his early exegesis of Husserl's phenomenology of the possible as a never-adequate intuition; see his *Introduction to the Origin of Geometry*).[23] We, by contrast, would want to claim it marks a specifically *religious* experience of God. And we would want to suggest that this is a difference not only of *rhetori* (language games) but also of "reference"—that is a difference not just of names and signs but of certain truth claims (however provisional and tentative). *Différance* and God, as Derrida is the first to remind us, are *not* the same thing.

While Derrida's reflections on this subject do open up new ways of thinking about faith and eschatology, it does not particularly interest Derrida—a self-avowed atheist—to pursue these issues in a specifically theological or theistic manner. It would appear that Derrida admires and applauds thinkers like Caputo, Hart, Olthuis, and others who do this, but it is not *his* thing. Yes, he will go so far as to declare the impossible-possible paradox of pardon/gift/justice/hospitality as a general "messianic" structure of all experience; but he will not see it as his business to pronounce on the authentically theistic or atheistic import of any given *messianism*. The closest Derrida's reflection comes to religion is in the guise of his "messianicity without messianism," a form of vigilant openness to the incoming events of *all our experiences*—sacred or profane; good or evil; loving or violent. Derrida, in short, is more concerned with the everyday (every moment) incoming of events than in the truth or otherwise of some divine advent. The other that leaps towards you from this in-coming moment may be a "monster slouching towards Bethlehem to be born" (Yeats) or a God of peace who lays down his life for love of mankind. There is no real way of judging.

It is for this reason that Derrida refrains from responding one way or another to any particular God-claim. He speaks of the "spectral" rather than specifically "revealed" structure of such incoming. But what his deconstructive reading of the impossible-possible certainly does help us to perform is a thoroughgoing purge of all "purist" or "dogmatic" notions of possibility as an immanently unfolding power blind to the invention of otherness which alone makes events happen. And this deconstructive critique of inherited ontotheological notions of both potentiality and presence marks, we believe, an invaluable opening to a new eschatological understanding of God as *posse*. Derrida points to such possible paths but he does not choose to walk them. In the heel of the hunt, he prefers ghosts to gods. He prefers, as is his wont and right, to leave matters open. He reserves judgment.

This is where we part company. But I would insist that, on this matter, anyone concerned with tolerance—religious or otherwise—would do well to take Derrida very seriously indeed. The indispensable lessons to be learned from deconstruction here are vigilance, patience, and humility.

Conclusion

Derrida's reading of the possible gestures in interesting ways, I believe, toward a new *eschatological* understanding of "the possible God." Derrida exposes the intriguing enigma of the impossible-possible—and even links this to the "origin of faith"; but the faith in question is a deconstructive belief in the undecidable and unpredictable character of incoming everyday events (what he calls "experience in general") rather than in some special advent of the divine as such.

Despite his reservations on the religious front, however, and his preference for *khôra* over God, I believe that Derrida's approach offers crucial signposts for a new eschatology of the divine—what I term "the God who May-Be." For Derrida provides a powerful reminder that the conventional metaphysical concepts of the possible—as *dumanis, potentia,* or *possibilitas*—fail to appreciate its force as something higher rather than lower than the actual. We may read him accordingly as suggesting, even if he does not pursue this suggestion, that since onto-theology defined God as the absolute priority of actuality over possibility, it may now be timely to reverse or deconstruct that priority. The consequences are far-reaching and we have attempted to explore some of them elsewhere in some detail.[24] Suffice it to note here, in summary, the following salient implications of such a "possible God," understood—after deconstruction—as eschatological May-be:

1. The God-Who-May-Be (*posse* or *possest* in Cusanus's famous formulation) is radically transcendent—guaranteed by the mark of its "impossible-possibility."

2. The May-Be remains historically "possible"—in spite of its impossibility—only if we have *faith* in the promise of advent (the scandal of "impossible" incarnations and resurrections!): indeed, the divine May-Be reveals itself as what "possibilizes" such messianic events in the first place; it is the more-than-impossible possible. But God cannot be God if we are not God's witnesses.

3. The divine May-Be calls us—Where are you? Who are you? Who do you say that I am? Why did you not give me to drink or eat?—in the form of an on-going personal vocation; it solicits us to be made flesh, so that its kingdom may come; it summons us to be hospitable to its divine arriving. That is why we should heed Walter Benjamin's counsel to treat each moment as a portal through which the messiah may enter. God (unlike *khôra*) is constantly knocking but cannot cross the threshold into the flesh of action and passion unless we open the door.[25]

4. Finally, the eschatological May-Be unfolds less as a can-be (*Kann-sein*) than as a should-be (*Sollen-sein*)—in short, less as an ontological power of immanent potency laboring toward fulfillment than as an ethical power of the powerless that bids us remain absolutely hospitable, that is, open to the possible Divinity whose gratuitous coming—already, now and not yet—is always a surprise and never without grace.

Our most immediate task then would be to practice and promote an ethic of hospitality—for the least we might do, as Rilke reminds us, is "to make coming into existence no more difficult for God than the earth does for spring when it wants to come."[26]

References

1. Etty Hillesum, *An Interrupted Life* (New York: Owl Books, 1996), p. 176.
2. Jacques Derrida in conversation with Richard Kearney, "Terror, God and the New Politics," in *Traversing the Imaginary: An Encounter with the Thought of Richard Kearney,* eds. John Manoussakis and Peter Gratton (Lanham: Rowman and Littlefield, 2004).
3. Derrida, "Terror, God and the New Politics."
4. Jacques Derrida, "Comme si c'était possible, 'Within Such Limits …'" *Revue Internationale de Philosophie,* vol. 3, 1998, no. 205, pp. 497–529 (henceforth referred to as "Comme si").
5. Ibid. p. 498. See also *Politique de l'amitié* (Paris: Galilée), 1994 (*Politics of Friendship,* [London/New York: Verso, 1997]), p. 46: "Or la pensée du 'peut-être' engage peut-être la seule pensée *possible* de l'événement. De l'amitié à venir et de l'amitié pour l'avenir. Car pour aimer l'amitié, il ne suffit pas de savoir porter l'autre dans le deuil, il faut aimer l'avenir. Et il n'est pas de categorie plus juste pour l'avenir que celle du '*peut-être*'. Telle pensée conjoint l'amitié, l'avenir et le peut-être pour s'ouvrir à la venue de ce qui vient, c'est-à-dire nécessairement sous le régime d'un *possible* dont la *possibilisation* doit gagner sur l'*impossible*. Car un possible qui serait seulement *possible (non impossible),* un *possible* surement et certainement *possible,* d'avance accessible, ce serait un mauvais *possible,* un *possible* sans avenir, un *possible* déjà mis de côté, si on peut dire, assure sur la vie. Ce serait un programme ou une causalité, un développement, un déroulement sans événement. La *possibilisation de ce possible impossible* doit rester à la fois aussi indécidable et donc aussi décisive que l'avenir même."
6. Derrida, *Politique de l'amitié,* p. 86.
7. Derrida, "Comme si," p. 498.
8. Derrida, "Comme si," p. 515.
9. Derrida, "Comme si," p. 498.
10. Derrida, "Comme si," p. 498.
11. Derrida, "Comme si," p. 519.
12. Derrida, "Comme si," p. 516 (citing "Invention de l'autre" in *Psyché, Inventions de l'autre'* [Paris: Galilée 1987], p. 59). It is useful to compare and contrast Derrida's position here with that of Whitehead; see W. Dean, "Deconstruction and Process Theology," in *The Journal of Religion,* vol. 64, 1984, pp. 1–19, and D. Griffin, "Postmodern Theology," in *Varieties of Postmodern Theology,* eds. J. Holland, W. Beardslee, and D. Griffin (Albany: SUNY Press, 1989), pp. 29–61.
13. Derrida, "Comme si," pp. 504–05.
14. Derrida, "Comme si," p. 520.
15. Derrida, *Politics of Friendship,* p. 36.
16. Derrida, "Comme si," p. 505. See also John D. Caputo and Michael J. Scanlon, "Apology for the Impossible: Religion and Postmodernism," and John D. Caputo, "Apostles of the Impossible: On God and the Gift in Marion and Derrida," in *God, The Gift and Postmodernism* (Bloomington: Indiana University Press, 1999), pp. 1–19 and 185–222. "For Derrida, the experience of the impossible represents the least bad definition of deconstruction … everything *interesting* for Derrida is impossible, not simply, logically or absolutely, impossible, but what he calls *the* impossible … That is why Derrida can say he has spent his whole life "inviting calling promising, hoping sighing dreaming. Of the gift, of justice, of hospitality, of the incoming of the wholly other, of *the* impossible" (pp. 3–4). This leads Caputo to contrast "the impossible" with the "possible" in the form of a polar opposition or exclusion, e.g., "experience is really experience when it is an experience of *the* impossible, not when it experiences the possible" (p. 191). But while there are indeed passages in Derrida which can suggest such a move, the more nuanced position outlined in "Comme si" shies away from such a polar alternativism and speaks instead in terms of a chiasm of "impossible possibility." Of course, if one intends the "possible" in the traditional metaphysical and logical senses of *potentia* and *possibilitas,* then Caputo is correct to oppose it to "*the* impossible"; but as will be clear from the above, we are speaking in this essay—as is Derrida when he speaks of the "perhaps" in "Comme si"—of a radically postmetaphysical notion of possibility as *posse*: at once the possibility *and* impossibility of God/alterity/transcendence/infinity/ incoming event. That is why, eschatologically understood, the divine *posse* or "may-be" is

both already here *and* always still to come (again), *both* incarnation *and* in-coming. In short, the God of eschatological possibility is simultaneously given *and* not given, possible *and* impossible—or to put it in denominational terms, Christian *and* Jewish. For Caputo's characteristically feisty, intriguing and challenging discussion of Derrida's notion of the impossible, in comparison with Marion's concept of "saturation," see "Apostles of the Impossible," pp. 199–206.

17. See our essay, "*Khôra* or God?" in *Questioning God*, John D. Caputo, Mark Dooley, and Michael J. Scanlon (eds.) (Bloomington: Indiana University Press), 2001.

18. Derrida, "Comme si," pp. 516–517.

19. Derrida, "Comme si," pp. 516–17. The aporia of the impossible-possible may be said to be another name for deconstruction: "the beating pulse of the possible im-possible, of the impossible as condition of the possible." From within the very heartbeat of the impossible, writes Derrida, "one could thus hear the pulse or pulsion of deconstruction" ("Comme si," p. 519).

20. Derrida, "Comme si," p. 519, my italics.

21. Derrida, "Comme si," p. 519. This crucial passage reads in full as follows: "Mais comment est-il possible, demandera-t-on, que ce qui rend possible rende impossible cela même qu'il rend possible, donc, et introduise, mais comme sa chance, une chance non négative, un principe de ruine dans cela même qu'il promet ou promeut? Le *in-* de l'im-possible est sans doute radical, implacable, indéniable. Mais il n'est pas simplement négatif ou dialectique, il *introduit* au possible, il en est *aujourd'hui l'huissier;* il le fait venir, il le fait tourner selon une temporalité anachronique ou selon une filiation incroyable—qui est d'ailleurs, aussi bien, l'origine de la foi. Car il excède le savoir et conditionne l'adresse à l'autre, incrit tout théorème dans l'espace et le temps d'un témoignage ('je te parle, crois moi'). Autrement dit, et c'est l'introduction à une aporie sans exemple, une aporie de la logique plutôt qu'une aporie sans exemple, une aporie de la logique plutôt qu'une aporie logique, voilà une impasse de l'indécidable par laquelle une décision ne peut pas ne pas passer. Toute responsabilité doit passer par cette aporie qui, loin de la paralyser, met en mouvement une nouvelle pensée du possible" ("Comme si", p. 519). At a practical level we might draw a parallel here with Leonardo da Vinci's "impossible machines"—from flying and diving apparatuses to a system of shafts and cogwheels for generating enormous heat to rival the sun—which were sketched in his unpublished notebooks but whose "possibility" remained a perpetual promise and spur to further creativity and inventiveness (see Owen Gingerich, "Leonardo da Vinci: Codex Leicester," *Museum of Science* magazine [Boston], Winter 1997).

22. Derrida, "Comme si," pp. 518–519.

23. Derrida, "Comme si," p. 517: "possibilité de l'impossible, impossibilité du possible, l'expérience en générale etc." See Derrida's admission of his debt to Husserl's notions of possibility/impossibility on p. 521, note 27: "J'avais d'ailleurs, il y a bien longtemps, dans l'espace de la phénoménologie husserlienne, analysé de façon analogue une possibilité de forme apparemment négative, une im-possibilité, l'impossibilité de l'intuition pleine et immédiate, la 'possibilité essentielle de la non-intuition', la 'possibilité de la crise' comme 'crise du logos'. Or cette possibilté de l'impossibilité, disais-je alors, n'est pas simplement négative: le piège devient aussi une chance: '… cette possibilité (de la crise) reste liée pour Husserl au mouvement même de la vérité et à la production de l'objectivité idéale: celle-ci a en effet un besoin essential de l'écriture'" (*De la grammatologie* [Paris: Minuit, 1967], p. 60; *Introduction à l'Origine de la géométrie de Husserl* [Paris: Presses Universitaires de France, 1962], p. 162 *passim*).

24. See my *Poétique du Possible* (Paris: Beauchesne, 1984) and *The God Who May Be*, (Bloomington: Indiana University Press, 2001).

25. Derrida himself does not entertain or embrace, to my knowledge, such a personalized relationship between the Perhaps and human selves. The deconstructive structure of messianicity remains removed from such messianist commitments, preferring *khôra* to God. And as he puts it, "you cannot address a prayer to *Khôra*, only to someone or something" ("Terror, God and the New Politics").

26. Rainer Maria Rilke, *Letters to a Young Poet*, trans. Stephen Mitchell (New York: Vintage Books, 1986), p. 63.

CHAPTER **19**

The Revelation According to Jacques Derrida

JOHN P. MANOUSSAKIS

> Today once again, today finally, today otherwise, the great question would still be religion and what some hastily call its "return."[1]

Which day is precisely this "today?" Which is the day that religion—in "power and great glory" (Matthew 24:30)—will make its return to our enlightened, secular world? How do we reckon that day that reckons the days—the day of reckoning? Will it be a Day of Judgment of some sort? And although we are told, "The exact day is not yours to know" (Acts 1:7) persistently we ask "for a sign" to be given to us (Luke 11:29). In his "Faith and Knowledge," Derrida offers us no less than twenty-five such signs, or "crypts" as he calls them—conflating, perhaps, the words "cryptic" and "scripts," (a gesture that aptly indicates yet another way among the many that one could read this text, namely, as a cryptic scripture, or as a Revelation which, like all revelations, conceals more than it reveals).

"Faith and Knowledge" was presented as Derrida's contribution to a colloquium that took place at the island of Capri. His remarks, however, on the mechanical operation of religion and on its possibility for evil and terror, made Capri sound more like Patmos. Apocalyptic and, even more, prophetic, if one takes into account that, eight years later, this "today" of the question about religion assumed a dramatic urgency that day which has become known by no other name but that of a day: *September 11.*

309

A month after the events of September 11, Richard Kearney and I met with Jacques Derrida in New York for a prearranged discussion.[2] A double column of smoke rising in the clear October sky and the burnt smell still hovering over the city kept reminding us of what had happened there. The discussion soon turned to the new situation the world had found itself in, to the war against an elusive and yet all-too-well-known enemy: terror. At least in two instances during the course of conversation, Derrida made a reference to his "Faith and Knowledge" (the only references to his work during the discussion), firmly locating the problem of terror within the context of religion and its, in this case, violent return.

On September 11 what we call today "the return of religion" became all the more visible and "emblematized." The event itself assumed religious dimensions in its sublimity as a *mysterium tremendum et fascinans*. It was immediately accounted to two religious registers: Islamic fanaticism, which "provoked" and "justified" it, and Christian fundamentalism, which proclaimed that the West was under attack and vowed to protect it. As the name of "God" was time and again invoked by politicians and common people alike (a "God" notably cleansed from any religious or denominational differences), as "ground zero" became more and more a *hallowed* ground with interfaith services and memorials to attest to its holiness, gradually September 11 became less and less a political case, simply because such an impossible event could not be appropriated by political language[3]—in order to face it, to come in terms with it, one would need to have recourse to a religious discourse.

We feel that we have to ask, then, *what* kind of religion is that which is returning and to *where* does religion return? At the same time, however, a different set of questions arises: how and when, for example, does religion become a question for philosophy and what are the implications of a discourse on religion that claims, nevertheless, *not* to be religious?

* * *

"Faith and Knowledge: the Two Sources of 'Religion' at the Limits of Reason Alone,"[4] as the full title runs, hints already at three major philosophical texts that Derrida engages with: "Faith and Knowledge" alludes of course to Hegel's homonymous *Glauben und Wissen*; the "Two Sources of Religion" is a reference to Henri Bergson's *The Two Sources of Morality and Religion,* and, finally, the third component of the title unmistakably alludes to Kant's *Religion Within the Limits of Reason Alone.* These are the three philosophical inheritances that, among others, form the basic substance of the loom around which the fabric of Derrida's text is meticulously woven.

Derrida built his text as a *machine*, that is, with the impressive symmetry and precise function of a mechanism—but also as a machine that works independently (i.e., automatically). Here is how he describes, in his own words, the genesis of this text:

> Let us choose, then, I told myself, a quasi-aphoristic form as one chooses a machine, the least pernicious machine to treat *religion* in a certain number of pages: 25 or a few more, we were given; and, let us say, arbitrarily, to de-cipher or anagrammatize the 25, 52 very unequal sequences...[5]

His essay consists of fifty-two "joinings" that simulate the links of a chain, as the one refers to the next, according to a certain technique of scriptural hermeneutics known as a *catenae* of scripts. Derrida employs twenty-five *crypts* that follow twenty-seven italicized paragraphs (*Italics*); between these two the document is divided into equal halves. The importance of this text cannot be fully assessed within the restrictions of the present essay. We have to single out, however, one theme that we intend to discuss at some length precisely because it is of such concern to Derrida, and recurs (or returns) throughout his text: "[I]t is this mechanics, this machine-like return of religion, that I would here like to question."[6]

"The return of religion," then, is a phantasm that haunts this text; "the return of religion" as a question, as a problem and as an aporia *returns* more and more violently upon this text—a philosophical text, to be sure, and perhaps more than once (and more than one) since we already counted three different philosophical currents in its substratum. Is the "return-of-religion" the return *of* the Other (a quasi-Second Coming, of sorts, or "the return of the—alienated—Spirit to itself" as Hegel puts it) and therefore, the pronouncement of some kind of messianism? Or is it a return *to* the promised land of the Same, a nostos that reaches its tauto-logical Ithaca, the prodigal son that returns to the paternal home? Both movements amount to the same: a performance of what Derrida calls the *mechanical*. In other words, the exclusion of the other, the expelling of the different, the circular multiplication of the self-same. For the question of the *machine*, the in-genuity of the en-gine is nothing more but this: the generation of genus, re-production, and productivity. At the same time, it is a question of autogamy, autonomy, automatism, and autism. But how are we to understand this return that occurs, according to Derrida's statement cited above, like a *machine*? What can be possibly *mechanical* in religion?

My approach, as I attempt to untangle these questions, is by no means exhaustive; on the contrary, I shall have to limit my discussion to just three motifs that, time and again, recur in the text that I am reading here: (1) the interplay between Faith and Reason (or religion and philosophy), (2) the double operation of the religious, and (3) the possibility of radical evil (as a possibility of or for religion).

Three Readings

It has been said that all problems and questions of religion should be understood as problems and questions intrinsically *philosophical.* The question-of-religion cannot be posed in any satisfactory way but only to the extent that it is posed philosophically: not for any other reason but simply because "the question of religion is first of all the question of the question."[7] Neither faith nor revelation are in a position to raise questions; what they can do at best is to provide answers—but only to such questions that one could have never asked.[8] Even the question-of-God itself and theo-*logy*, to the degree that they do not cease to be formulated as a question and as a *logos,* can attain their proper meaning only within a philosophical grammar, outside of which even the very concept of "God" is rendered nonsensical.

But God is not only that, nor always just that, a "concept." One could rightly contest, then, that the God of the religious experience, that God to whom the whisper of prayer is addressed amidst the darkness, has nothing to do with the "God of the philosophers." Granted. But only for so long as one remains within the limits of the unmediated, ineffable experience. For at the moment that one attempts to express that experience, at this very moment, one is already and unavoidably referring to terms and categories of philosophical thinking, one is already speaking the language (the *logos*) of philosophy. To do otherwise, we are in need of an entirely *other* idiom, of/in which we have not yet learned how to speak.

The turn-of-philosophy-to-religion is not, therefore, a "turning-away" from what constitutes the proper element of philosophical thinking; on the contrary, such a turn signals the "re-turn" of thought to that question that is *the* philosophical question *par excellence*: the question of God.

Within the question of God these two different, but not mutually exclusive, modes should be brought, with respect to their disparity, *together*: the concept of "God" and the "experience" of God. The one is lacking the other and the one is yearning for the other. No language can ever articulate (describe, communicate, or explain) the "experience of God" without turning that very experience into an idea or a concept governed by the logic of language. And what else can language be but that which, before God, is destined to fail? Are we not speaking of this failure every time that we are speaking of God? Is it possible, then, that the (philosophical) *logos* could ever be able to think God outside language? Is it possible, then, that religion could be, in this or that way, *thinkable* at all? The turn-of-philosophy-to-religion does not aspire to re-turn to the discourse and the question of God (which it has never forsaken, anyway) but attempts something far more radical: to say the unsayable, to think the unthinkable, to make possible what remains impossible, for it is this God outside language and signification (a *theo*-logy without its *logos*) that becomes the impossible towards which the possibility of thinking strives. Philosophy's turn to religion indicates, ultimately, a locus or a moment of "turning-back," of retraction (*retractare*) within thinking itself.

Of the Two Sources

This "return," however, on another level, can be discussed not only in terms of the-return-to religion but also as the-return-*of*-religion (or the religious); a multifarious return occasioned by the advent of techno-science and of what Derrida mystically calls *the mechanical*, though he qualifies it thus: "'Mechanical' would have to be understood here in a meaning that is rather 'mystical.'"[9] The return-of-religion is not so much, as one first might think, the return of faith, spirituality or any type of fundamentalism to a society that, since the Enlightenment, has been proclaimed (and ought to be) *secular*, that is, "pure of all religiosity."[10] On the contrary, Derrida seems to argue that not only is there no such purity (of and from the religious) but also that such fundamental structures of the Enlightened, secularized state as the concepts of sovereignty, the citizen-subject and the distinction of public/private space "still entail what is religious, inherited in truth from a determined religious stratum."[11] Let us remind ourselves here of such cursory examples as the "sacredness" of the flag, the "scriptural" authority of the constitution, the "veneration" of the nation's founding fathers, the "hierarchy" of the governmental structure, and the "ritual" in public acts and ceremonies. Furthermore, the very criteria on the basis of which the separation between the Church and the State or the distinction between the sacred and the profane becomes possible "remain religious or in any case theologico-political."[12]

The war that fundamentalism wages against liberal forces, civil rights and so on, religious wars, and even terrorism *but also* globalization, capitalism, and technology are all—and equally—symptomatic of this double mechanization of the religious: protecting itself from anything that might threaten it (immunitary) and protecting itself from what protects it (auto-immunitary). "Religion today," Derrida writes, "allies itself with tele-technoscience, to which it reacts with all its forces."[13] It is a strange logic that "mechanically" duplicates itself and hints at the controversial formula that holds faith *and* knowledge as having the same source[14] and, in a different calculation of the same arithmetic, divides faith and knowledge as constituting the two sources from which religion springs. (Hence the "two sources of religion" as stated in the title of his essay.) Working along the same trajectory of argument, Derrida believes that "one would blind oneself to the phenomenon called 'of religion' or of the 'return of the religious' *today* if one continued to oppose so naively Reason *and* Religion, Critique or Science *and* Religion, technoscientific Modernity *and* Religion."[15] To remain blind to this intercontamination between Religion and Reason would simply amount to an unreflecting embrace of ideology.

Of the One Possibility

The ratio between these two, Religion and Reason (or faith and knowledge), could also be given analogically in the relation between two other phenomena as they are considered in a related idiom: revelation (*Offenbarum*) and revealability (*Offenbarkeit*). The latter offers the possibility to revelation—a possibility that is open (and opens itself) as precisely this place (*lieu, khôra*) that allows revelation to take place. But the possibility of revealability, the possibility of the possibility of revelation, is an unconditional possibility and thus, absolute. Such a possibility is not bound to or limited by anything, (not to/by revelation itself or to/by revelation alone) and it could even negate revelation, becoming, thus, and by the same gesture, the possibility of radical evil.

"The possibility of radical evil," Derrida writes, "both destroys and institutes the religious."[16] The religion that radical evil institutes, and, in turn, is instituted by, is the religion inaugurated by the Kantian categorical imperative (which overthrows and replaces the divine law) and its autonomous subject (who becomes independent from God). It is Kant's natural religion that first proclaims the death of God, even prior to Nietzsche, since the moral subject is supposed to act *as if* God did not exist. God is nothing more than a useless prosthesis to such a religion—reduced as it is to a rational morality—and he can, then, be properly discarded. Here we have neither the time nor the space to discuss how Kant's reaction to Newton's mechanical universe resulted in a system whose mechanics mimicked those of its rival. For the moment, suffice it to say that Derrida characteristically speaks of Kant's *Religion within the Limits of Reason Alone* as "a book on radical evil,"[17] since it is radical evil that such morality presupposes, without which "good would be for nothing" (*sans lequel on ne saurait bien faire*).[18]

Throughout these pages two specters of religion arise—two cruel twins in similarity and in difference—the one is that of religion that runs as a "theological machine, the 'machine for making gods'";[19] the other, its twin (that is to say, the same and yet different) is religion that operates as "a machine of evil, and of radical evil."[20] At first, this duplicity seems to be evocative of a Gnostic dualism between a good God and a divine Evil. In terms of such equivocal language the two opposites could meet, if not coincide, as they both go beyond similarity and beyond difference. Their advent is virtually indistinguishable: "the coming of the other"—one does not know yet *which* other, *what kind* of other—"can only emerge as a singular event when no anticipation *sees it coming*, when the other and death—and radical evil—can come as a surprise at any moment."[21] Therefore, radical otherness and singular eventfulness are those parameters that define "God's" and "Evil's" common structure. Perhaps, if one of the two occurs, when one of the two arrives, we would only know that "it" has finally come—unable always to say *what* that "it" is.

"In this sense, the technical is the possibility of faith, indeed its very chance. A chance that entails the greatest risk, even the menace of radical evil."[22] If there is something that will give us a chance to think of God, to offer us a *place* (*lieu*) from which such thinking may become possible, then this cannot be anything else but precisely that risk that is revealed in the dark light of revealability that lies open in the desolate expanses of *khôra*. That is why, at the end, "instead of opposing them [the religious and the machinal], as is almost always done," Derrida suggests that "they ought to be thought *together*, as *one and the same possibility* ..."[23]

Radical evil, as a possibility for religion, opens up in the positing of precisely such a Kantian God, that is a conceptual God, "universal" and therefore, impersonal. For radical evil and a conceptual God share the very same structure: that of radical otherness. A God who lacks a face (and consists only in the dictation of the moral imperative) is a God who prohibits or demands but cannot promise—it is only in promise, however, that there is memory (as remembrance of the promise given) and hope (as anticipation of the fulfillment of the promise). Without memory and hope, without past and future, this God becomes imprisoned in the stillness of the "now." Without memory and hope, there is also no imagination, for there can be no image of the immemorial or of the unexpected. Hence the iconoclastic prohibition against images—for the image mediates the Absolute, it seeks to befriend what is alien in otherness. It is precisely at this point that the alliance of the three Abrahamic religions breaks up: Judaism and Islam, seeking to safeguard the absolute otherness of the Other, forbid the iconic representations of God.

Christianity's *Shibboleth*: the Death, the Flesh, and the Icon of God

Let this be considered not as a minute matter of difference in artistic taste. There is a difference indeed—and Derrida's acute insight locates it on another plane, namely that of the "death of God." He says:

> In my short essay "Faith and Knowledge" I ask the question of Islam in relation to the other religions. We have the Judeo-Christian couple as opposed to Islam but, on the other hand, we have the Judeo-Islamic couple as opposed to Christianity. The death of God is Christian, neither Jew nor Muslim would ever say that God is dead. There is, then, this confrontation between the three Abrahamic traditions.[24]

The possibility of divine representation and the death of God are not as dissimilar as it first appears, for the latter presupposes the former. To understand how this is so, we need to think of that historic event which, although it took place in two different moments, in two different geographical coordinates, separated by a few centuries, remains, nevertheless, the same event.

The first "moment" is well known: it takes place in first century A.D. Athens. It is the moment when Paul, in Acts 17, stands in front of the wise of Greece announcing what we know today as Christianity. What exactly happened there has been evaluated by history's textbooks; the "heretical" faith of a few Jews meets with that cultural system that would later allow the revealed Truth to speak the language of the Academy.

The second "moment," while it is the other side of the same event, also consists of an announcement but this time not through the voice of the apostle, but through the sermon of the madman, the madman that Nietzsche depicts in his *Gay Science*.

> Have you not heard of that madman who lit a lantern in the bright morning hours, ran to the market place, and cried incessantly: "I seek God! I seek God!"—As many of those who did not believe in God were standing around just then, he provoked much laughter. Has He got lost? asked one. Did He lose His way like a child? asked another. Or is He hiding? Is He afraid of us? Has He gone on a voyage? Emigrated?—Thus they yelled and laughed.
>
> The madman jumped into their midst and pierced them with his eyes. "Where is God?" he cried; "I will tell you. *We have killed Him*—you and I. All of us are His murderers. (…) God is dead."[25]

In both these moments, the apostle as well as the madman received the same reaction from their audience: a scornful laughter. "When they heard about the raising of the dead, some laughed at him" (οἱ μὲν ἐχλεύαζον) writes the author of the Acts (17:32). It seems that the kerygma of the death of God and that of the risen God constitute a common phenomenon, in front of which the Agora, that is the Polis, knows of no other reaction but to laugh. Of course, this is a laughter indicative of a deep anxiety, of the kind that one experiences when one is faced with a radical reversal, or caught by surprise by an unexpected event, after which nothing can ever be the same again.

What is this reversal? In the case of Paul, his message refers to the end of the epoch of idols that were "everywhere in the city" (Acts 17:16). Paul's speech aims at the subversion of the idolization of God, and he attempts it not by overthrowing the physical idols themselves (he doesn't turn against the statues and the sanctuaries of the gods), but by criticizing the reasoning that establishes them: "If we are indeed God's offspring, we ought not to think of divinity as something like a statue of gold, or silver or stone, or a product of man's mind and his art" (Acts 17:29). It is this likeness (ὁμοίωσις) of God with stone, silver or gold that Paul contests here. At the same time, however, another idol comes to light, the one that had always remained imperceptible (and for this reason, the most dangerous of all) because, unlike the rest of the idols, it was *invisible*. The conceptual idol, the idol produced by the human mind (ἐνθυμήσεως ἀνθρώπου), is the cause of a wholly different idolatry: the one that, especially after Kant's enlightenment, propagates the autonomy of the individual's reason, subjugating nature, thinking and God under the categories of its critical omnipotence. In the Athenian aeropagus, Paul is not interested in the πράττειν of the Athenians (that is, their actions) but in the νομίζειν, that is, their *thoughts*. "... We ought not to *think* of divinity as ..." Then, one might ask, *how* ought we to think of God?

But first, how ought we *not* to think of God? The answer is offered by the contemporary evangelist of the death of God. Nietzsche knows very well that the distance from God (*Gott*) to the idol (*Götze*) is a short one. The passage from the one to the other occurs easily as well as often. And the bridge that facilitates the passage is nothing other than the *idea* of God. An "idea" indicates a seeing (from εἰδεῖν, to see)—Nietzsche's genius, however, lies in the fact that he reverses the classical position on seeing the divine. In antiquity, to see a god (as, for example, Actaeus sees Aphrodite) means death, for to see a god is to die. We find the same prohibition already in the Bible. Yahweh warns Moses as he is about to ascend Mt. Sinai, not to look on him for "a man cannot see my face and live" (οὐ γὰρ μὴ ἴδη ἄνθρωπος τό πρόσωπόν μου καὶ ζήσεται) (Exodus 33:20). For Nietzsche, what happens is the exact opposite: when we have an *idea* of God, when with the eyes of our intellect we seek to see God, it is God who dies.[26] This is the death of God that the madman announces, the death of the God-Idea, the death of God by means and because of the Idea. And who is to blame for such a terrible act? Nietzsche is very clear:

> All that philosophers have handled for thousands of years have been concept-mummies; nothing real escaped their grasp alive. When these honorable idolaters of concepts [*diese Herren Begriffs-Götzendiener*] worship something, they kill it and stuff it; they threaten the life of everything they worship.[27]

In the history of philosophy from Plato onwards, God ceased to be a person and was turned into an abstract idea, a "concept-mummy." Although he always occupied the highest place in the conceptual hierarchy, this didn't prevent philosophy from placing him among the rest of its concepts (that are usually attributed to him as predicates) such as the One, the Good, Being—so signing, so to speak, his death certificate and confirming his irrevocable admission to the pantheon of idols.

This rather long detour has shown, I hope, that the death of God is not irrelevant to the question of God's representation (be it iconic or idolatrous). It is not accidental that Judaism and Islam according, at least, to Derrida, part ways with Christianity precisely on the question of the death of God. It is no caprice of history that death befalls the Christian God but not the God of Judaism and Islam. For Islam and Judaism there is no "death of God" because it is prohibited to depict God: radical otherness results in radical iconoclasm, which in turn opens up the possibility of radical evil. To re-state this conclusion, we could say that the absence of relation (with the Other) is the very root of the possibility for radical evil. An encounter with the divine without relation, that is, without some form of iconic representation, would not be different in any way from an encounter with sheer evil, an encounter with utter destruction.

The issue is complex, for the semantic differential between Christianity and the Judeo-Islamic couple—Christianity's *Shibboleth* so to speak—is made up of three interrelated factors. We have already seen the first two—the death of God and the possibility of iconic representation—and the third is that of the Incarnation. It is precisely thanks to the Incarnation that the iconic representation of the divine becomes possible: the Incarnate God, Christ, is "the *icon* of the invisible God" (εἰκὼν τοῦ θεοῦ τοῦ ἀοράτου, Colossians 1:15). It is never the Father or the Holy Spirit that are depicted in icons, for they do not partake in the incarnation. Only Christ can be depicted by merit of his flesh[28]—the same flesh that allows us to "see" God while at the same time, like a screen, protecting us from the lethal rays of the (unmediated) divine.

It is precisely this mediating character of the Incarnation that Derrida picks up in a later essay[29] in order to emphasize Christianity's break with the other two monotheistic religions: "[t]his, I think, stands in a certain structural relation to what probably distinguishes the Jewish or Moslem religion from the Christian religion, which is to say, the incarnation, the mediation, the *hoc est meum corpus*, the Eucharist: God become visible."[30] The mediation of Incarnation and Eucharist is, for Derrida, structurally parallel with, if not responsible for, what he calls "globalized mediatization of religion," which is also "fundamentally Christian and not Jewish, Islamic, Buddhist, etc." Thus, he sees a common structure between the "live" broadcasting of a television program ("the simulation of 'live' transmission which has you believe … that you are before 'the thing itself'; you are there …"[31]) and the "here and now" of the Eucharist; that is, the assumption that we are witness of an event that is always supposed to take place before our eyes, at this very moment:

> During a Christian mass, by contrast, the thing itself, the event takes place in front of the camera: communion, the coming of real presence, the Eucharist…the thing actually takes place "live" *as* a religious event, *as* a sacred event.[32]

> Such "direct," "live" presentation, translated into the Christian code, is the "real presence," the "transubstantiation" or the "Eucharist," and, in a more general way, a phenomenon of incarnation: deictic and sensible *immediacy* of the mediator, here and now, in the *this*, the making present of mediation or of reconciliation.[33]

Such remarks call for some kind of a response. Derrida's unsophisticated understanding of liturgical time fails to distinguish between vulgar, everyday *Chronos* and eschatological *Kairos*. The "here and now" of the Eucharistic event has nothing to do with the order of chronological time (as the "live" televised event), but it essentially belongs to kairological time (together with Plato's *exhaiphnes*, Heidegger's *Augenblick* and Benjamin's *Jetztzeit*). Moreover, the repeated claim that in the Eucharist or in the Incarnation "one is confronted with the thing itself"[34] is rather a hasty observation. Isn't this precisely the "folly" and "paradox" of Incarnation, that when God wished to reveal Himself, He did so by *hiding* Himself behind the human flesh? What we *see* in Christ is *only* a man's face and in the Eucharistic element *only* a piece of bread—it is in the freedom of one's faith that one receives the bread and the wine of the communion *as* the body and the blood of Christ. Far from being "the thing itself," the consecrated bread and the incarnate God are actually the very opposite: screens for protecting against the terrifying reality of the Real.

Derrida, however, has tried to anticipate this argument by assigning both Eucharist and the Incarnation (and also the Resurrection) to the strange logic of what he calls, as we have already seen, *auto-immunization*:

> Whether it is a question of the cenotaph, of the tomb without corpse, or of the void of *kenosis*, that absence or emptiness, the disappearance of the body does not necessarily contradict the appeal to visibility or to the image. In a certain manner television itself would be the figure: the appeal to the media is the disappearance of the body, whether because there is no longer a corpse…or because it has become wine and bread, wafer, spiritualized blood and body, spectralized, virtualized, sanctified, and consumable. Certain Christian theologians can denounce, no doubt, television as a perversion. But that does not necessarily go against this logic. Theology always has more resources than one believes. Television is conjured not as a spiritualizing spectralization but as the temptation of a new idolatry, a pagan cult of the image. Evil, for this theology, is the carnal temptation of the idol, not the spirituality of the icon.[35]

It becomes more and more evident here that Derrida seems to show a preference for the invisible voice that commands "Hear, O Israel …" or proclaims "La ilaha illa 'llah …" Or, to be more precise, a preference for the *transcendence* of the voice over the *immanence* of the image. This kind of preference—evidenced again and again under a variety of rubrics, be it the *infinite* Other, *absolute* justice, *unconditional* hospitality, or *pure* gift—justifies placing Derrida (as recently Giorgio Agamben did)[36] in that tradition of transcendence that goes, via Lévinas and Husserl, back to Kant. But by pursuing such Kantian Ideas as the infinite, the absolute, or the pure, don't we sacrifice at the end what constitutes a concrete human experience? And without the concreteness of human life (which is always to be understood historically and corporeally), aren't we left susceptible to the abstractions of fundamentalism and fetishism (e.g., the Qur'an that is untranslatable or the Torah that is untouchable)? And isn't evil all the more possible once we have traded the person for the Idea (even if that is the "idea of God")?

* * *

In an recent exchange with Yvonne Sherwood, she (rightly, I believe) reminded me that no faith and no tradition is immune to the collapse of fetishism or fundamentalism—the way certain Protestant denominations read the Bible, as a text outside context, is undeniably fetishistic and this proves that fundamentalism is by no means endemic only to Islam or only to Judaism. My argument here is not to identify what I believe is a certain pathology of our theologies with this or that religious community, but rather to show that any imbalance in the chiasmus between transcendence and immanence constitutes the inception of ideology, that the two, flesh and spirit, should be better taken as the christic formula that Chalcedon advises, "without division and without confusion."

And doesn't the flesh sometimes turn into a text? Sherwood contests. And every time we read the Scriptures (be it the Torah, the Gospels or the Qur'an) doesn't a curious intercontamination between the body of the text and the body as flesh take place? After all, both constitute a *corpus*.

> And as they were writing he took papyrus, and blessed, and tore it, and gave it to them, and said "Take, this is my body." And he took ink, and when he had given thanks he gave it to them, and they drank of it. And he said, "This is the blood of the New Testament, which is poured out for many."[37]

I would be delighted, as another John in Patmos, to "take the scroll" of his body "and eat it" (Revelation 10:9). My problem lies precisely with that attitude that *in principio* prohibits even the *possibility* that there ever be such a thing as His body and blood (textual or otherwise). Even if this is taken to be—and here Derrida, I think, would agree with me—a possibility for the impossible.

References

1. Jacques Derrida, "Faith and Knowledge," in *Religion,* eds. Jacques Derrida and Gianni Vattimo (Stanford: Stanford University Press, 1998), p. 39.
2. To appear in *Traversing the Imaginary,* eds. John P. Manoussakis and Peter Gratton (Lanham: Rowman & Littlefield, 2004). See also Richard Kearney's in-depth analysis of terrorism from a philosophical point of view in his "On Terror," *Strangers, Gods and Monsters,* chap. 5 (London: Routledge, 2003).
3. Or any language for that matter. The experience of the event had left people "speechless," simply because the nameless event falls outside language. It will be a task for another day to show how September 11 gave us a glimpse of what Lacan calls the "Real"—one, the most elusive, of his three registers, among the Imaginary and the Symbolic. If so, however, the collapse of the Twin Towers offered to those who experienced it a sense of what the encounter with the divine might be like: for, in Lacan's thought, God cannot be placed but in the Real.
4. "Foi et savoir: Les deux sources de la 'religion' aux limites de la simple raison," in *La Réligion,* eds. Jacques Derrida and Gianni Vattimo (Paris: Éditions du Seuil, 1996), pp. 9–86; trans. *Religion,* pp. 1–78. I follow here the main argument as presented in my review essay of Derrida's text (see "Religion's Machine," *Religion & the Arts* 6:3 [2002]: 375–382).

5. Derrida, "Faith and Knowledge," p. 40.
6. Derrida, "Faith and Knowledge," p. 14.
7. Derrida, "Faith and Knowledge," p. 39.
8. See Heidegger's remark in the *Introduction to Metaphysics*: "Anyone for whom the Bible is divine revelation and truth has the answer to the question 'Why are there essents rather than nothing?' even before it is asked: everything that is, except God himself, has been created by Him. God himself, the uncreated creator, 'is'" (trans. Ralph Manheim [New Haven and London: Yale University Press, 1987], pp. 6–7).
9. Derrida, "Faith and Knowledge," p. 41.
10. Derrida, "Faith and Knowledge," p. 25.
11. Derrida, "Faith and Knowledge," p. 26.
12. Derrida, "Faith and Knowledge," p. 25.
13. Derrida, "Faith and Knowledge," p. 46.
14. Derrida, "Faith and Knowledge," p. 28.
15. Derrida, "Faith and Knowledge," p. 28 (his emphasis).
16. Derrida, "Faith and Knowledge," p. 65.
17. Derrida, "Faith and Knowledge," p. 41.
18. Derrida, "Faith and Knowledge," p. 47.
19. Derrida (reading Bergson), "Faith and Knowledge," pp. 51, 41.
20. Derrida, "Faith and Knowledge," p. 56.
21. Derrida, "Faith and Knowledge," p. 17.
22. Derrida, "Faith and Knowledge," p. 47.
23. Derrida, "Faith and Knowledge," p. 48.
24. In the interview with Richard Kearney, in *Traversing the Imaginary* (see above).
25. Friedrich Nietzsche, *The Gay Science*, p. 125, trans. Walter Kaufmann (New York: Vintage Books, 1974), p. 181.
26. "In Nietzschean terms no one can see God without God dying" (p. 29). See Jean-Luc Marion's excellent analysis of the "death of God," to which I am indebted here, in *The Idol and Distance*, trans. Thomas A. Carlson (New York: Fordham University Press, 2001).
27. Friedrich Nietzsche, *Götzen-Dämmerung oder Wie man mit dem Hammer philosophiert*, "Die Vernuft in der Philosophie"; trans. Walter Kaufmann, *The Twilight of the Idols*, in *The Portable Nietzsche* (New York: Penguin Books, 1982), p. 479.
28. In his *Refutation* against the iconoclasts, the Patriarch of Constantinople Nicephorus makes clear that the iconic *inscription* of Christ is by merit of His incarnational *circumscription*: "it therefore follows that Christ, having truly taken on a body like ours, is circumscribed by His humanity" (see the Appendix in Marie-Jose Baudinet's essay "The Face of Christ, the Form of the Church," in *Fragments for a History of the Human Body*, Part One, eds. M. Feher, R. Naddaff and N. Tazi [New York: Zone Books, 1989], p. 158).
29. "Above All, No Journalists!" in *Religion and Media*, eds. Hent de Vries and Samuel Weber (Stanford: Stanford University Press, 2001).
30. De Vries and Weber, *Religion and Media*, p. 58.
31. De Vries and Weber, *Religion and Media*, p. 63.
32. De Vries and Weber, *Religion and Media*, p. 58. We should accept here, in part at least, Derrida's criticism about the "live" televised Mass. It seems that the Church herself has forgotten that the Eucharist is not an event open for everyone to see. The first Christians worshipped in secret and that secrecy was despised by Roman society, which began to fabricate notorious stories about cannibalism and incest. In both liturgies of the Eastern Rite (i.e., the Liturgy of John Chrysotom and Basil the Great), before the celebrant uncovers the Eucharistic gifts he exclaims τάς Θύρας τάς Θύρας, ἐν σοφίᾳ πρόσχωμεν—an order for the doorkeepers of the church to shut and watch over the doors, because what is about to be revealed is not for anyone to see (not even for the catechumens who are supposed to leave the church at that point). In the Orthodox churches, the icon-screen that separates the altar from the rest of the church, reinforces even further that protective secrecy that keeps what is going on in the altar away from the curious gaze even of the faithful themselves.
33. De Vries and Weber, *Religion and Media*, p. 62.
34. De Vries and Weber, *Religion and Media*, p. 64.
35. De Vries and Weber, *Religion and Media*, p. 93.

36. Giorgio Agamben, *Potentialities: Collected Essays in Philosophy,* trans. Daniel Heller-Roazen (Stanford: Stanford University Press, 1999), pp. 220–239.
37. Stephen Moore, *Mark and Luke in Poststructuralist Perspectives: Jesus Begins to Write* (New Haven: Yale University Press, 1992), p. 84. Quoted by Yvonne Sherwood in our correspondence.

CHAPTER **20**

Aporia or Excess?
Two Strategies for Thinking r/Revelation

ROBYN HORNER

In recent times the problem of the gift has received a great deal of philosophical attention. Its scope is set out powerfully by Jacques Derrida in *Given Time. 1: Counterfeit Money*, where the conditions of possibility of the gift—that it is completely free and that it is present, or identifiable *as such*—are simultaneously its conditions of impossibility—no gift that is ever present is completely free, and if it is not present then we cannot know it as a gift.[1] The gift structurally exemplifies what Derrida calls "the impossible," where conditions of possibility meet with conditions of impossibility in an aporia. This aporetic quality of the gift has been the subject of a debate during the last decade that seems inevitably to spill over from the academic arena into the daily lives of its protagonists, if such a distinction between academia and daily life can in fact be made. I sometimes wonder whether Derrida suffers much for having written about the gift. In my own case, at least, and despite anything I might have said or written, any gift-giving on the part of friends or family is now often humorously but cautiously accompanied by the disclaimer, "but of course, we know that there's no such thing as a gift!" In this spilling over we begin to see, nonetheless, what is at stake in the question. The possibility of the gift seems so incredibly obvious that to problematize it is to make too much of it, to take it too seriously. No one, the anecdotal evidence would suggest, *really* thinks of the gift as something that must never be returned. At the same time, however, in the face of this challenge to the all-too-obvious, there is often expressed a deep sense of being affronted, a sense that betrays nothing other than the deadly seriousness of the desire to "really" give.[2] [*]

The gift polemic, especially insofar as it touches a sensitive nerve running through a commitment to the plain *common sense* of the economy, opens usefully onto other important debates. First, it serves to focus contemporary philosophical discussion about the nature and limits of phenomenology. Is phenomenology inherently metaphysical, as Derrida seems to suggest, because it ultimately seeks to reduce phenomena to presence, a presence that is ultimately reliant on representation by a theoretical consciousness?[3] And must it thereby be doomed to fail, since the phenomenological reduction inevitably promises what it cannot deliver?[4] Or following the position developed by Jean-Luc Marion, does phenomenology offer a way forward for philosophy beyond metaphysics? In brief, the argument from Marion's perspective runs something as follows. A reading of Edmund Husserl's phenomenology through a Heideggerian lens, especially as this reading is informed by Derrida, reveals Husserl's metaphysical focus, where phenomenology is oriented solely towards a reduction of the ontic according to the horizon of its object-ness or presence. Martin Heidegger's subsequent two-phased reduction is an attempt to move beyond the ontic and to manifest what is not present, sheer being, which brings-into-presence but itself withdraws in the same movement. Yet Heidegger, too, remains implicated in the metaphysics he seeks to go beyond, and this for Derrida as much as for Marion, although with slightly different inflections.[5] In part drawing from the work of Emmanuel Lévinas, Marion is critical of the way in which Heidegger absolutises being, blind to the possibilities of what is not given according to the light of being. Rehabilitating Husserl's work, Marion claims to find in it resources for a third reduction. While in *Reduction and Givenness* Marion describes this as the reduction to the call, in the two subsequent volumes of his phenomenological trilogy, *Being Given* and *In Excess*, it has become the reduction to sheer givenness.[6] Phenomenology, he claims, offers a postmetaphysical possibility in its emphasis on the utter self-givenness of phenomena to the reduced consciousness, *l'adonné*, the "gifted," the one given over to the self-giving phenomenon. With this emphasis on the priority of the given in place, and with a consequent de-centering of any constituting subject, Marion maintains that a whole range

---

[*]My thanks to Stephen Curkpatrick, Kevin Hart, and Tony Kelly for their helpful comments on earlier drafts of this chapter

of phenomena can show themselves as given, without making any concession to metaphysics. Such phenomena potentially might include phenomena of revelation. In Marion's analysis, much will rest on his exploitation of Husserl's use of *Gegebenheit*, givenness, and the constellation of terms that might resonate with it, including not only the given, but also the gift.

For Derrida, there cannot be a phenomenology of the gift because for him phenomenology attempts to reduce to presence, and a present gift, losing its essential characteristic of freedom, would no longer be a gift.[7] Nevertheless, he does not give up on the gift.[8] If the gift leads to an aporia, then while it may not be known, it might still be thought as the impossible, and risked according to desire and decision. While I could never know for sure whether or not I had given, or whether or not I had received, and would never be able definitively to identify a gift *as such*, I could risk giving or receiving on the basis of an undecidable trace, and with the same desire that risks the perfection of love, or justice, or forgiveness. For Marion, on the other hand, phenomenology can deliver the gift, since the phenomenological reduction to givenness operates to remove the gift from the schema of causality that implicates it in metaphysics. The problem of the gift as Derrida has articulated it is overcome through the suspension of any one or two of the gift's three constituent elements: the giver, the gift object, or the recipient. It is removed from the cycle of metaphysical causality either because it loses its giver through the reduction of its transcendence, or because it loses its object-ness and is no thing as such, or because it ultimately has no recipient determinable by the giver. While Derrida requires these three conditions to operate simultaneously, Marion demands that only one or two of the three is operative at any given moment.[9] The difficulty with Derrida's position is that the risk of the gift is also the risk of deception: if I do not know for sure but instead only have a kind of faith in the gift, I may be seriously mistaken about it. Yet for the gift to be possible from Marion's perspective, any one or two of the elements of giving, the gift, or receiving, can always be identified, and hence the gift is always and already undone according to Derrida's conditions.

The second debate onto which the gift polemic opens is a theological one, and this in a number of ways. Christian theology makes much of the category of gift when it comes to God; grace is nothing other than God's self-giving, and we could, of course, go on to speak about gift and sacrifice, the gifts of the Spirit, and so on. But if we limit the discussion simply to the idea of grace, we find that the aporia is doubled here. If God is, as theology claims, on the one hand desirous of a loving relationship with human beings, and always and already giving Godself as the offer of that relationship, and on the other hand, beyond all capacity of human understanding, then a particular problem emerges with regard to relationship with God. A loving relationship seems to be characterized by freedom, that is, an absence of coercion, and by presence, where the relationship between parties can be recognized as such. Yet God's presence would destroy the very possibility of the relationship being free, for it would override the limitations of human knowledge and would therefore eliminate the possibility of choice to enter into relationship.[10] The conditions of possibility for relationship with God are also its conditions of impossibility. It is not surprising that "gift" is the word used to characterize this relationship, since God and gift are similarly aporetic. The thought of God is a thought of the gift.

This is apparently confirmed by Marion in his theological works, where he resists a thinking of God according to being and advocates a thinking of God according to love, expressed in terms of gift.[11] For example, in *God Without Being* we read:

> God can give himself to be thought without idolatry only starting from himself alone; to give himself to be thought as love, hence as gift; to give himself to thought as a thought of the gift. Or better, as a gift for thought, as a gift that gives itself to be thought. But a gift, which gives itself forever, can be thought only by a thought that gives itself to the gift to be thought. Only a thought that gives itself can devote itself to a gift for thought. But, for thought, what is it to give itself, if not to love?[12]

This revelatory self-giving of God is a theme that Marion later insists can only be worked out strictly on the basis of Revelation (capital R), and on many occasions, he is at pains to point out both that capital R Revelation cannot be phenomenologically deduced, and that theological questions lie properly beyond the scope of phenomenology.[13] Nevertheless, as I have just indicated, in his phenomenological works Marion is still drawn to consider the possibility of phenomena of revelation (and this is ambiguously written, sometimes with a small and sometimes with a capital R).[14] Evidently the question of the relationship between phenomenology and theology is complex, and the gift polemic serves to highlight ways in which the two debates outlined above can in fact be superimposed.

Marion's strategy for thinking r/Revelation phenomenologically involves the use of what he calls saturated phenomena, phenomena that exceed the capacity of the recipient to constitute them in any ultimately definitive way. *In Excess* deals with each of these phenomena at length: the event, the idol, flesh, and the icon, all of which are contained within a fifth, super-type—Revelation.[15] In the context of a phenomenological approach to mystical theology, Marion observes:

> The intention (the concept or the signification) can never reach adequation with the intuition (fulfillment), not because the latter is lacking but because it exceeds what the concept can receive, expose, and comprehend. ... According to this hypothesis, the impossibility of attaining knowledge of an object, comprehension in the strict sense does not come from a deficiency in the giving intuition, but from its *excess*, which neither concept nor signification nor intention can foresee, organize, or contain.[16]

In other words, phenomenology is capable of sustaining the givenness of phenomena that cannot be contextualized according to the Kantian categories, and which therefore cannot be understood as any-*thing*. Such phenomena appear only as dazzling, overwhelming, or excessive. This coincides with what is given in mystical theology, where "... God remains incomprehensible, not imperceptible—without adequate concept, not without giving intuition. The infinite proliferation of names does indeed suggest that they are still there, but it also flags as insufficient the concepts they put in play and thereby does justice to what constantly subverts them."[17]

While Marion argues that phenomenology can do no more than sketch the conditions for the possibility of revelation with a small r, rather than the actuality of Revelation with a capital R, his work raises a number of questions. I will address only those that concern Marion's commitment to theology in his working out of phenomenology. First, we need to observe Derrida's ongoing reservations about the possibility of that commitment:

> My hypothesis concerns the fact that you use or credit the word *Gegebenheit* with gift, with the meaning of gift, and this has to do with—I will not call this theological or religious—the deepest ambition of your thought. For you, everything that is given in the phenomenological sense, *gegeben, donné, Gegebenheit*, everything that is given to us in perception, in memory, in a phenomenological perception, is finally a gift to a finite creature, and it is finally a gift of God.[18]

Second, we also need to take into account the concerns of Dominique Janicaud, who maintains that Marion's frequent use of a capital letter when he speaks of r/Revelation seems to suggest that he is not interested merely in the possibility of revelatory phenomena, but in their actuality; and further, that to isolate such phenomena as ultimate paradoxes would require that their theological truth claims be given consideration.[19]

Marion's response to the first issue is to reassert that while it may be that "between the givenness, if any, in the phenomenological meaning of the word, and the gift, there is nothing but pure equivocity," his intent is to read the gift from givenness, and not vice versa.[20] In other words, his association of the gift with givenness and the given does not rely on any semantic continuity, but on the structure of thinking according to givenness. With Marion's analysis, then, we observe the gift as an extreme instance of the phenomenal given. The structural features of both given and gift are that they exclude transcendence, lose any object-ness, and are not given to a constituting I but to *l'adonné*, with givenness as a horizon.[21] What complicates matters is that in *Being Given*, the gift is addressed prior to the two sections dedicated to the given, and so it seems that the given might be thought according to the gift. Perhaps this confusion is why, at the beginning of the debate at Villanova in 1997, Marion quickly declares that he is no longer interested in talking about the gift![22] This does not, however, address the other part of Derrida's concern, which is that Marion always has a surreptitious Giver in mind. Now, while it is possible to read Marion's corpus and to become quite convinced of the coherent emergence of what Derrida calls "the deepest ambition of [Marion's] thought," we can only take Marion at his word when he claims that he does not seek a theological end for his phenomenology, particularly as he thinks the gift. Nevertheless, this issue will reemerge in Janicaud's set of questions, for it is the case that small r revelation and capital R Revelation are frequently interwoven in Marion's phenomenological texts, including *In Excess*, and that the possibility of r/Revelation is not so easily separated from its actuality. It would seem that to identify any particular phenomenon of small r revelation as such demands a commitment in advance to its actuality as capital R Revelation. At the same time, it all depends on what is meant by the two inscriptions of r/Revelation.

In the context of his writing on religion, I am struck by Derrida's meditation on the question of whether revealability is "more originary than revelation" (he uses a small r for both), or whether "the event of revelation [would] have consisted in revealing revealability itself, and the origin of light ..."[23] This seems to relate to his oscillation between the priority of the possibility of religion in general, and its expression in a determinate religion, as also to the tension within individual religious traditions between the ideal and the historically conditioned.[24] Does revelation consist only in the concrete, determinate, historical expressions of particular religions—what I have been calling Revelation with a capital R? Or does it consist in the revealing of their condition of possibility, revealability, here read as lower case r revelation? Is *khôra* revealability, or the source of revealability?[25] If so, what could we then make of Derrida's attempt to "... interpret, the anthropo-theological reappropriation of the meaning of the gift as the meaning of the event on the groundless ground of ... *khôra*...?"[26] Ultimately, Derrida refuses to choose between, as he says, "the order of the 'revealed' and the order of the 'revealable.'"[27] Yet his professed "respect for this singular indecision," itself aporetic, might open up for us a way through Janicaud's impasse. If r/Revelation in Marion's texts is similarly characterized by this indecision, then he may escape the accusation of dogmatism.

In *Being Given*, where there is an explicit distinction drawn between lower case and upper case r/Revelation, lower case r revelation seems inevitably to refer to revelatory phenomena from the Christian tradition. There are also, of course, many examples of revelatory phenomena given in Marion's theological works.[28] Nevertheless, they are often tentatively deprived of their authoritatively Revelatory force by a number of mechanisms, for example, within phenomenology by virtue of their strictly provisional status, or better and more widely, by their inherent undecidability, which is ultimately due to their saturation.[29] As Marion himself states in the debate at Villanova, "... pluralism is implied in the very notion of revelation [small r]. If there is a real revelation [strangely here, still a small r], no concept could achieve to say and to make intelligible in its own way the excess of intuition."[30] We find small r revelation more broadly redefined, however, in the final volume of the phenomenological trilogy. Here it is simply what happens in the resistance—and he is using the metaphor of electrical resistance—of the *adonné* to the self-giving phenomenon: "The revealed does not thus define an extreme stratum or a particular region of phenomenality, but rather the universal mode of phenomenalization of what gives *itself* in what shows *itself*."[31] Small r revelation is finally demythologized, as it were, and Marion soon adds: "philosophy has neither the authority nor the competence to say more."[32] In this new context, Marion nonetheless insists that he will consider phenomena of capital R Revelation, although he maintains that this is still to be done from the point of view of saturation. Now, if there are phenomena given utterly in excess of my capacity to frame them, what they reveal must be ultimately ambiguous. This means that phenomena of capital R Revelation will therefore still rightfully enter into phenomenology as strictly undecidable, it being the task of theology to determine their status as definitive capital R Revelation. Yet with this approach Marion effectively undoes again the very distinction between small r and capital R r/Revelation on which he relies. The capital R Revelatory aspect of the phenomenon could still only be one of a range of possibilities of the small r revelatory phenomenon. Significantly,

Marion's approach in *In Excess* finally makes much more explicit the inevitably hermeneutical supplement to phenomenology, but it also serves to emphasize that theology, too, is hermeneutics. Marion recognizes this in the chapter drawn from his Villanova paper, where he discusses the divine names, as noted above: "The infinite proliferation of names does indeed suggest that they are still there, but it also flags as insufficient the concepts they put in play and thereby does justice to what constantly subverts them."[33] Even capital R Revelation is not protected from the play of *différance*, or to express this more positively, the absolute otherness of God is protected from our references to God. We find, in other words, that Marion's excessive thinking of r/Revelation is shot through with something like Derrida's aporetic "respect for this singular indecision."

These insights help us to clarify that the problem of the gift, too, always comes down to a hermeneutics. The aporia is not solved but resolved through a decision to commit oneself to the gift, which means reading it in one way rather than another. While Derrida is not writing theology, or at least, not in the same way that I might do, it is my view that his thinking of the aporia of the gift provides a useful approach to thinking God or revelation, one that leaves room for faith and decision. Marion's thinking of the saturated phenomenon, with its hermeneutical supplement made quite explicit, and whether or not we discern that it remains within phenomenology or goes beyond it, might also open onto the impossible. Excessiveness inevitably prompts no less a risk of faith than aporia, and in spite of the many differences between their positions, this seems to me to be a point at which our two protagonists come very close.[34]

References

1. Jacques Derrida, *Donner le temps. I. La fausse monnaie* (Paris: Galilée, 1991); *Given Time: 1. Counterfeit Money*, trans. Peggy Kamuf (Chicago: University of Chicago Press, 1992). Derrida summarizes his position in "On the Gift: A Discussion Between Jacques Derrida and Jean-Luc Marion," *God, the Gift, and Postmodernism*, Richard Kearney, Jacques Derrida, and Jean-Luc Marion, eds. John D. Caputo and Michael J. Scanlon (Bloomington: Indiana University Press, 1999), pp. 54–78, 59. For an extensive examination of the topic, see my *Rethinking God as Gift: Marion, Derrida, and the Limits of Phenomenology*, Perspectives in Continental Philosophy, ed. John D. Caputo (New York: Fordham University Press, 2001).

2. This dilemma is resolved by John Milbank by maintaining that the gift can be really given even (and, in fact, only) where it occasions a return. John Milbank, "Can a Gift be Given? Prolegomena to a Future Trinitarian Metaphysic," *Rethinking Metaphysics*, eds. L. Gregory Jones and Stephen E. Fowl (Oxford: Blackwell, 1995), pp. 119–161.

3. Derrida's critique of Husserl has two main thrusts, the genealogies of which are carefully described in Leonard Lawlor, *Derrida and Husserl: The Basic Problem of Phenomenology* (Bloomington: Indiana University Press, 2002). The first concerns the problem of genesis, which is explored in the only relatively recently published *Le problème de la genèse dans la philosophie de Husserl* (Paris: Presses Universitaires de France, 1990), and which Lawlor summarizes in the following terms: "The irreducible inclusion of retention implies that the constituting is always preceded by a constituted, even though retention issues from the

constituting of primal impression. Supposedly first, intentionality is already actual; supposedly original, consciousness is already invested with a sense; supposedly second, sense is already there. The reduction, therefore for Derrida, cannot capture, within temporal lived experience, the absolute constituting source: genesis" (p. 81). The second thrust of Derrida's critique is developed in terms of language, which is observed in both Jacques Derrida, *Edmund Husserl's "Origin of Geometry": an Introduction*, trans. John P. Leavey Jr. (Lincoln: University of Nebraska Press, 1989), and *Speech and Phenomena and Other Essays on Husserl's Theory of Signs*, trans. David B. Allison and Newton Garver (Evanston: Northwestern University Press, 1973). We see both ideas together in the following example: "The discursive and dialectical intersubjectivity of Time with itself in the infinite multiplicity and infinite implication of its absolute origins entitles every other intersubjectivity in general to exist and makes the polemical unity of appearing and disappearing irreducible. Here delay is the philosophical absolute, because the beginning of methodic reflection can only consist in the consciousness of the implication of *another* previous, possible, and absolute origin in general. Since this alterity of the absolute origin structurally appears in *my Living Present* and since it can appear and be recognized only in the primordiality of something like *my Living Present*, this very fact signifies the authenticity of phenomenological delay and limitation. In the lackluster guise of a technique, the Reduction is only pure thought as that delay, pure thought investigating the sense of itself as delay within philosophy" (Derrida, *Origin of Geometry*, p. 152.) Derrida comments most powerfully in *Speech and Phenomena*: "Do not phenomenological necessity, the rigor and subtlety of Husserl's analysis, the exigencies to which it responds and which we must first recognize, nonetheless conceal a metaphysical presupposition? Do they not harbor a dogmatic or speculative commitment which, to be sure, would not keep the phenomenological critique from being realized, would not be a residue of unperceived naïveté, but would *constitute* phenomenology from within, in its project of criticism and in the instructive value of its own premises? This would be done precisely in what soon comes to be recognized as the source and guarantee of all value, the 'principle of principles': i.e. the original and self-giving evidence, the *present* or *presence* of sense to a full and primordial intuition" (Derrida, *Speech and Phenomena*, pp. 4–5). On the linguistic critique, see especially *Speech and Phenomena*, chap. 4, and the seminal essay in the same collection, "Différance" (pp. 129–160).

4. In the example given above: "... the Reduction is only pure thought as that delay, pure thought investigating the sense of itself as delay within philosophy" (Derrida, *Origin of Geometry*, p. 152).

5. In Derrida, for example, this has to do with Heidegger's idea of "gathering" and "appropriation." See Jacques Derrida, *Points: Interviews, 1974–1994*, trans. Peggy Kamuf, ed. Elisabeth Weber (Stanford: Stanford University Press, 1995), p. 131; *Positions*, trans. Alan Bass (Chicago: University of Chicago Press, 1981), pp. 9–10, 54; *Spurs: Nietzsche's Styles/Éperons: Les Styles de Nietzsche*, trans. Barbara Harlow (Chicago: University of Chicago Press, 1978), pp. 120–21; "The Villanova Roundtable," *Deconstruction in a Nutshell: A Conversation with Jacques Derrida*, ed. John D. Caputo, Perspectives in Continental Philosophy (New York: Fordham University Press, 1997), pp. 3–48, 15. See also *Given Time. 1: Counterfeit Money*, pp. 18–23.

6. Jean-Luc Marion, *Réduction et donation: recherches sur Husserl, Heidegger et la phénoménologie* (Paris: Presses Universitaires de France, 1989); *Reduction and Givenness: Investigations of Husserl, Heidegger and Phenomenology*, trans. Thomas A. Carlson (Evanston: Northwestern University Press, 1998); *Étant donné. Essai d'une phénoménologie de la donation* (Paris: Presses Universitaires de France, 1997); *Being Given: Toward a Phenomenology of Givenness*, trans. Jeffrey L. Kosky (Stanford: Stanford University Press, 2002); *De surcroît: études sur les phénomènes saturés* (Paris: Presses Universitaires de France, 2001); *In Excess: Studies of Saturated Phenomena*, trans. Robyn Horner and Vincent Berraud (New York: Fordham University Press, 2002).

7. Derrida in Kearney, Derrida and Marion, "On the Gift," p. 59.

8. Derrida in Kearney, Derrida and Marion, "On the Gift," p. 60.

9. See Marion, "Esquisse d'un concept phénoménologique du don," *Archivio di Filosofia* LXII.1-3 (1994): 75–94; "Sketch of a Phenomenological Concept of the Gift," *Postmodern Philosophy and Christian Thought*, eds. John Conley and Danielle Poe (Bloomington: Indiana University Press, 1999), pp. 122–143; *Étant donné; Being Given*.

10. This is also the case—though in a very different way—in human relationships, as they are explored by Lévinas and Maurice Blanchot, for example.

11. See, for example, Jean-Luc Marion, *Dieu sans l'être. Hors-texte*, rev. ed. (Paris: Presses Universitaires de France, 1991), pp. 75, 81ff., 225ff.; *God Without Being*, trans. Thomas A. Carlson (Chicago: University of Chicago Press, 1991), pp. 49, 53ff., 161ff.; "Le don d'une présence," *Prolégomènes à la charité*, 2nd ed. (Paris: Éditions de la Différence, 1991); "The Gift of a Presence," *Prolegomena to Charity*, trans. Stephen Lewis (New York: Fordham University Press, 2002), p. 124ff.

12. Marion, *God Without Being*, p. 49.

13. See, for example, Marion, *Étant donné*, p. 337: "Il ne s'agit ici que d'admettre *la possibilité* du phénomène de revelation (et non pas, encore une fois, du fait d'une Révélation)…" Marion, *Being Given*, p. 242. See also the extensive footnote on p. 329 n. 90, p. 367, where Marion is explicit about his "scrupulousness" in utilizing the upper and upper cases in maintaining this difference, and the comments on p. 410/297.

14. In the trilogy of phenomenological works, there is no mention of revelation or Revelation in *Reduction and Givenness*; in *Being Given* revelation is mentioned at pp. 5, 235, 236, 241, 242, 243, 244, 245, 246, and 367 n. 90, and Revelation at pp. 4, 5, 141, 234, 242, 243, 246, and 367 n. 90; and in *In Excess*, revelation occurs at pp. 28, 29, and 29n, and Revelation at pp. 52, 53, 134, 149, 150, and 158n.

15. In the foreword, Marion is clear that chapter 6 refers to "… the possibility of a saturated phenomenon *par excellence*, that of Revelation …"

16. Marion, *In Excess*, p. 159.

17. Marion, *In Excess*, p. 160.

18. Derrida in "On the Gift," Kearney, Derrida, and Marion, p. 66.

19. Horner, *Rethinking God as Gift*, p. 153; Dominique Janicaud, *La phénoménologie éclatée* (Combas: Éditions de l'éclat, 1998).

20. Marion in "On the Gift," Kearney, Derrida, and Marion, pp. 61, 70: "My project attempts, on the contrary, to reduce the gift to givenness, and to establish the phenomenon as given."

21. Of course, this horizon must be only quasi-transcendental.

22. Marion in "On the Gift," Kearney, Derrida, and Marion, p. 56.

23. Jacques Derrida, "Faith and Knowledge: the Two Sources of 'Religion' at the Limits of Reason Alone," trans. Samuel Weber, *Religion*, eds. Jacques Derrida and Gianni Vattimo (Stanford: Stanford University Press, 1998), pp. 1–78, 16. See also: "Light … wherever this arché commands or begins discourse … as much in the discourse of philosophy as in the discourses of a revelation (*Offenbarung*) or of a revealability (*Offenbarkeit*), of a possibility more originary than manifestation. More originary, which is to say, closer to the source, to the sole and same source" (p. 6); "It would accordingly be necessary that a 'revealability' (*Offenbarkeit*) be allowed to reveal itself, with a light that would manifest (itself) more originarily than all revelation (*Offenbarung*)" (p. 15); "If I am interested in the *khôra*, I am trying to reach a structure which is not the *khôra* as interpreted by Plato, but by myself against Plato. I do not know if this structure [*khôra?*] is really prior to what comes under the name of revealed religion or even of philosophy, or whether it is through philosophy or the revealed religions, the religions of the book, or any other experience of revelation, that retrospectively we think what I try to think. I must confess, I cannot make the choice between these two hypotheses. Translated into Heidegger's discourse, which is addressing the same difficulty, this is the distinction between *Offenbarung* and *Offenbarkeit*, revelation and revealability. Heidegger said, this is his position, that there would be no revelation or *Offenbarung* without the prior structure of *Offenbarkeit*, without the possibility of revelation and the possibility of manifestation. That is Heidegger's position. I am not sure. Perhaps it is through *Offenbarung* that *Offenbarkeit* becomes thinkable, historically. That is why I am constantly really hesitating. That is part of—what can I call this here?—let us say, my cross. Since it is impossible for me to choose between these two hypotheses, my last hypothesis is that the question is not well posed, that we should displace the question, not to have an answer, but to think otherwise the possibility of these two possibilities"; "when I referred a moment ago to *Offenbarkeit* and *Offenbarung*, I was sincere but at the same time I am also perplexed. I am also perperplexed without a guide in this respect. The discourse of *Offenbarung* and *Offenbarkeit*, in Heidegger or anywhere else in this context, implies the historicity of *Dasein*, of man and God, the historicity of revelation, historicity in the Christian or

European sense. My problem is that when I refer to *khôra*, I refer to some event, the possibility of taking place, which is not historical, to something nonhistorical that resists historicity. In other words, there might be something that is excluded by this problematic, however complex it may be, of revelation, of *Offenbarung* and *Offenbarkeit* … That is why I refer to what I call the 'desert in the desert.' … This resists even *Offenbarkeit*, which [the desert in the desert, *khôra*, or *Offenbarkeit*?] is not revealed and cannot be revealed, not because it is obscure, but because it has nothing to do with the gift, with revelation, or with anything we are discussing here … I think that this reference to what I call *khôra*, the absolutely universal place, so to speak, is what is irreducible to what we call revelation, revealability, history, religion, philosophy … and so forth" (Derrida in "On the Gift," Kearney, Derrida, and Marion, pp. 73, 76). These reflections, and this hesitation, are all the more important given his comments at the annual meeting of the American Academy of Religion in November, 2002, in response to a question from Kevin Hart on revelation and revealability.

24. "But the gap between the opening of this *possibility (as a universal structure)* and the *determinate necessity* of this or that religion will always remain irreducible; and sometimes [it operates] within each religion, between on the one hand that which keeps it closest to its 'pure' and proper possibility, and on the other, its own historically determined necessities or authorities" (Derrida, "Faith and Knowledge," p. 58). It might also be related to a distinction Lévinas makes between the holy and the sacred, but that is too large a debate to enter into here. See my "Thinking Under a Double Contradiction," in *Naming the Present: The Pastoral Response*, ed. Dennis Rochford (London: T & T Clark, forthcoming).

25. It seems to me that there is some ambiguity in Derrida's work between thinking *khôra* as the source of both revelation and revealability, and thinking *khôra* as the revealability that allows for a thinking of revelation. See note 22 above, but also note 26 below.

26. Derrida in "On the Gift," Kearney, Derrida, and Marion, p. 67.

27. "*Chora* is nothing … The question remains open, and with it that of knowing whether this desert can be thought and left to announce itself 'before' the desert that we know (that of the revelations and the retreats, of the lives and deaths of God, of all the figures of kenosis or of transcendence, of religio or of historical 'religions'); or whether, 'on the contrary,' it is 'from' this last desert that we can glimpse that which precedes the first … what I call the desert in the desert. The indecisive oscillation, that reticence … already alluded to above (between revelation and revealability, *Offenbarung* and *Offenbarkeit*, between event and possibility or virtuality of the event), must it not be respected for itself? Respect for this singular indecision or for this hyperbolic outbidding between two originarities, the order of the 'revealed' and the order of the 'revealable,' is this not at once the chance of every responsible decision and of another 'reflecting faith,' of a new tolerance?'" (Derrida, "Faith and Knowledge," p. 21).

28. For example, in Jean-Luc Marion, *L'idole et la distance: cinq études* (Paris: B. Grasset, 1977); *The Idol and Distance: Five Studies*, trans. Thomas A. Carlson, Perspectives in Continental Philosophy, ed. John D. Caputo (New York: Fordham University Press, 2001); *Dieu sans l'être. Hors-texte*; *God Without Being*; *Prolégomènes à la charité*; *Prolegomena to Charity*; *La croisée du visible*, rev. ed. (Paris: Éditions de la Différence, 1996).

29. As I argue of the icon in *Rethinking God as Gift*, p. 172.

30. Marion in "On the Name," Kearney, Derrida, and Marion, p. 69.

31. Marion, *In Excess*, p. 52. This redefinition can, in fact, already be seen in an earlier work. See Jean-Luc Marion, "Le phénomène saturé," *Phénoménologie et théologie*, ed. Jean-François Courtine (Paris: Critérion, 1992), pp. 79–128; "The Saturated Phenomenon," trans. Thomas A. Carlson, *Philosophy Today* 40:1–4 (1996): 103–124. Here Marion defines revelation phenomenologically as "… une apparition purement de soi et à partir de soi…" p. 127/121. To my knowledge, however, this locution does not appear in *Being Given*.

32. Marion, *In Excess*, p. 53.

33. Marion, *In Excess*, p. 160. I note here John D. Caputo's reading of the Villanova texts in his "Apostles of the Impossible: On God and the Gift in Derrida and Marion," in *God, the Gift and Postmodernism*, pp. 185–222. Caputo argues that Marion's commitment to the givenness of God also implies a commitment to God's ultimate, if not conceptual, presence. "We have contended that Marion and Derrida are agreed in regarding the 'intention' or the 'concept' as an 'arrow' which is aimed at the heart of God from which God must be 'shielded' … or kept 'safe.' For Marion, … this is because the arrow of intentionality is too

weak and narrow to penetrate or comprehend the infinite givenness of God; it would compromise the infinite incomprehensibility of God who has utterly saturated the intention 'God' in a plenitude of givenness. But for Derrida, ... the arrow takes aim at God and never reaches God precisely because the name of God is the name of what we love and desire ... something *tout autre* which is not 'present,' not only in the narrow conceptual sense of conceptual presentation advanced by Marion, but also not *given*" (p. 199). The point is a valid one. Marion, of course, argues that givenness is not equivalent to presence, but his argument only works if what is given gives itself as something like a trace, which redoubles the saturation and the need for a hermeneutic supplement. In other words, if God gives Godself in such a way that intuition is saturated, then this is not only because the thought of God is excessive but because we cannot know whether or not that excessiveness even refers us to God. It is the possibility—rather than the actuality—that God gives, which provides a "content without object" for givenness. Perhaps I am taking Marion further than he wishes to go.

34. While it is not certain that what Marion describes as a "shortage" of intuition is the same as what Derrida means by aporia, it could be argued that Marion recognizes that aporia and excess work effectively in the same way where he observes: "... the alternative between a shortage and a saturation of intuition becomes undecidable" (Marion, *Being Given*, p. 245; *Étant donné*, p. 340).

CHAPTER 21
The Revelation of Justice

REGINA M. SCHWARTZ

I have already been indebted to Professor Derrida when I talked about biblical scenes of writing in the context of iterability. When Moses is given the tablets of the law, before he has even had a chance to promulgate it, he dashes the tablets to pieces. The Law that the people are constantly urged to remember is lost and given again, the Torah itself must be rewritten; the one we have is a copy and it in turn proliferates further copies: whatever was written was not the last word, for there are numerous codes of law in the Bible, never identical. And when we add the proliferation in the "oral tradition," a tradition that is in fact written in the Talmud, a twice-given law suggests not only that the original is destroyed and all we have is a copy and all we can have are copies, but that the copies will keep coming—as the scroll of the book of Deuteronomy is found, as Jeremiah's scroll is dictated again. These stories suggest the infinite in both their narrative of origin, defying the concept of "the original," and their end, defying a final, definitive version. As such, they point to the infinite proliferation of the law. But this is already the chapter of my last book, *The Curse of Cain*, even if I will doubtless endlessly proliferate it, both as a Jew who must endlessly copy out the Bible and as a postmodern critic.[1]

Here, I want to address another aspect of the law: that the Law comes into being as a rupture, an act of violence. People cannot receive this law, are not qualified to receive it, are not deserving of it. So the law is thrown down and they are punished. Not qualified according to what? Is it according to the principle of justice that precedes the law, an impossible justice that must be prior? According to that reading, the story would recount how, having violated justice, the people cannot have the law.

But this reading quickly collapses before one of the most compelling aspects of this narrative: it is precisely the first command of *the law*—the law, and not a prior justice—that they violate, and thereby disqualify themselves for the law. The first law is "thou shalt not make a graven image": they are worshipping idols, and so are not worthy to receive the law forbidding their worship of idols. How are we to understand this?

Derrida has affirmed Kant's understanding of enforceability:

[T]here is no law that does not imply in itself, *a priori, in the analytic structure of its concept*, the possibility of being "enforced" applied by force.[2] Noting that Kant recalls this as early as the *Introduction to the Theory of Right* (paragraph E, which concerns law "in its strict sense, *das stricte Recht*"). There are, to be sure, laws (*lois*) that are not enforced, but there is no law (*loi*) without enforceability and no applicability or enforceability of the law (*loi*) without force, whether this force be direct or indirect, physical or symbolic, exterior or interior, brutal or subtly discursive—even hermeneutic—coercive or regulative, and so forth.

But in the biblical scene of the giving of the law, the enforcement of the law is not a response that follows upon the heels of law-breaking; rather the enforcement is part of the law-giving. The law is broken *even as* it is given, and enforced even as it is given. If the giving of a law is a rupture of transcendence into immanence, it is also a rupture that quickly issues in violence.

And Moses turned, and went down from the mountain with the two tables of the testimony in his hands, tables that were written on both sides; on the one side and on the other were they written. And the tables were the work of God, and the writing was the writing of God, graven upon the tables … And as soon as he came near the camp and saw the calf and the dancing, Moses' anger burned hot, and he threw the tables out of his hands and broke them at the foot of the mountain. Moses stood in the gate of the camp and said, "Who is on the Lord's side? Come to me." And all the sons of Levi gathered themselves together to him. And he said to them, "Thus says the Lord God of Israel, 'Put every man his sword on his side, and go to and fro from gate to gate throughout the camp and slay every man his brother, and every man his companion, and every man his neighbor.'" And the sons of Levi did according to the word of Moses; and there fell of the people that day about three thousand men. And Moses said, "Today you have ordained yourselves for the service of the Lord, each one at the cost of his son and of his brother, that he may bestow a blessing upon you this day" (Exodus 32:15–29).

The price of the law is violence, and the price of justice is violence. Here, where justice is violated, the law is broken. There is no law without justice.

> In his work on justice, Derrida elaborates an aporia between justice and law, between justice (infinite, incalculable, rebellious to rule and foreign to symmetry, heterogeneous and heterotropic) on the one hand, and, on the other, the exercise of justice as law, legitimacy or legality, a stabilizable, statutory, and calculable apparatus [dispositif], a system of regulated and coded prescriptions.[3]

He adds,

> Everything would be simple if this distinction between justice and law were a true distinction, an opposition the functioning of which was logically regulated and masterable. But it turns out that law claims to exercise itself in the name of justice and that justice demands for itself that it be established in the name of a law that must be put to work (constituted and applied) by force "enforced."[4]

Then, in the midst of Derrida's discussion of the instability of justice and law, he has a very brief discussion, almost an allusion—left as quickly as entered—to Lévinasian justice, to the notion of justice as the relation to the other, to that absolute dissymmetry:

> I would be tempted, up to a certain point, to bring the concept of justice—which I am here trying to distinguish from law—close to Lévinas's. I would do so just because of this infinity and because of the heteronomic relation to the other [autrui], to the face of the other that commands me, whose infinity I cannot thematize and whose hostage I am … The Lévinasian notion of justice would rather come closer to the Hebrew equivalent of what we would perhaps translate as holiness [sainteté]. But since I would have other difficult questions about Lévinas's difficult discourse, I cannot be content to borrow a conceptual trait without risking confusions or analogies. And so I will go no further in this direction.[5]

I would suggest that this allusion is unconsciously or perhaps consciously pointing not only to Lévinas, but beyond, to the Talmud and beyond that—not to the aporia, but to the radical identity of the law and justice that characterizes revelation in the Hebrew Bible, especially in Exodus. Because elsewhere the gap between justice and the law is so wide—in Christian theology, which sees the Pharisaic law as inhibiting the realization of justice; in philosophy where from Plato on, law is formal and justice substantive; in political theory, which includes those who endorse "procedural justice" for they have abandoned substantive justice—this radical biblical vision, when the law IS justice, is unique.

Again, what is radical in the biblical instance described in Exodus is that this justice that shows itself as prior to the law also inheres in the law, constituting the law. Without this condition—obeying only one God—there can be no justice, and no law. And the law is: only one God, only his law, only his law is just. The biblical case defies the usual logic that would separate justice from law, the oft-noted importance of reserving the possibility of a justice that would exceed the law, contradict it, or even be indifferent to it. Here the justice so often believed to be beyond the law is also the justice of the law. When one understands how radical the biblical case described in Exodus is—that *justice is the law*—the antisemitic charges of pharisaic legalism become ludicrous. And the biblical case is radical in another sense: the force of the law is executed, in this narrative, on those who are in the very process of receiving it. They are accountable to the law, must answer to the law, but are not yet under the law. This radical understanding of the institution of law—that authority and justice are both outside and inside the law—makes it utterly impossible to reject. This law can and is broken; but it cannot be refused. The option of living within this law or not is not offered. It comes into being in a condition of complete inevitability. While political theory may call this totalitarianism, Judaism has called it revelation. Once it is given, there is no way to be outside of this (divine) justice. Anything else is false, a fake.

If the biblical name for justice is revelation, then the biblical name for injustice is idolatry. The command that signals this radical entry of the law and of justice is clear: not to make idols. What does this preoccupation with idolatry mean? Idolatry is not only the wrong object of worship, but the wrong manner of worshipping. I have already focused on a very strange way of worshipping—possessing—and noted the violent cost of that idolatry. When we imagine that we possess God, we can use him as a legitimating instrument for our violence. Such a God can authorize the slaughter of our enemies. When we imagine that God possesses us, we can explain the terrors of history as his righteous wrath at our infidelity.

The violence of possession proliferates: as God possesses us, so we possess land and men possess women, and all of this ownership leads to anxiety over the borders of possession and inevitable violence. (By the way, if I have been suspicious about the adequacy of narratives about God, it is not only because such narratives tend to be projections of human life, human desire, human possession, and human violence, but also because of the idolatry of any such description. To speak of representation as idolatry is not new; it is several thousand years old. But to speak of the idol, not as a visual representation—a statue, a painting—but a verbal one—a narrative—seems to be still somewhat controversial. And yet it is our narrative idolatries that hold us in their grip and so demand critique.)

But here, idolatry is meant in another although related sense: not possession, control, or the effort to submit to instrumental use that which is ineffable. The identity of justice and the law, the commandment against idols, signals that only the genuine article will do, the one true god who has the true law and true justice, and all else are not admissible. Justice can brook no compromise. This is not denying other idols in an exclusivism grounded by scarcity. To the contrary, this is a claim for revelation that is generous: the difference between the false universalism that excludes and the one that endlessly proliferates is important. Lévinas has shown how the pact that began as particular to Israel is opened up until it becomes universal.[6] The pact of Exodus is revisited (among other places) in Deuteronmy 27 and Joshua 4. Deuteronomy describes the recommendations for a ceremony that is to take place upon the Israelites' entry into the Promised Land (of course, after Moses' death).

> And on the day you pass over the Jordan ... you shall set up large stones, and plaster them with plaster; and you shall write upon them all the words of this law ... And there you shall build an altar to the Lord your God, an altar of stones; you shall lift up no iron tool upon them ... and you shall write upon the stones all the words of this law "very plainly" (ba'er hetev) (Deuteronomy 27:4–8).

And Joshua describes how

> ... Joshua built an altar to the Lord, the God of Israel, as Moses the servant of the Lord had commanded the people of Israel, as it is written in the book of the law of Moses, an altar of unhewn stones, upon which no man has lifted an iron tool ... and there, in the presence of the people of Israel, he wrote upon the stones a copy of the law of Moses, which he had written.

Who receives this law? all of Israel indeed, but all of *Israel*. "And all Israel, sojourner as well as homeborn, with their elders and officers and their judges, stood on opposite sides of the ark before the Levitical priests who carried the ark—and he read all the words of the law, the blessing and the curse, according to all that is written in the book of the law."

When the Mishnah deals with this story, it specifies the blessings and curses that are read:

> They turned their faces toward Mt. Gerizim and began with the blessing: Blessed be the man that maketh not a graven or molten image. And both these and these answered Amen ... And afterward they brought the stones and built the altar and plastered it with plaster. And they wrote there all the words of the Law in seventy languages, as it is written "very plainly."

As Lévinas notes, what had begun as a particular, concrete community is now universalized: the law is written in seventy languages—the law that was broken by some is now given to all. The justice that marks the Hebraic revelation is, in the tradition, universal.

Ever since Hobbes, contemporary political theory has taken refuge in the notion that it is law—not justice—that offers a true universal. Substantive justice is particular, contingent, culturally specific. And because my notion of justice is so different from that which emerges in another culture, we must adjudicate our differences through law. Thank goodness for law, for procedures, for offering us a formal universal. Stuart Hampshire has offered a clear expression of this:

> ... [F]airness in procedure is an invariable value, a constant in human nature. Justice and fairness in substantial matters, as in the distribution of goods or in the payment of penalties for a crime, will always vary with varying moral outlooks and with varying conceptions of the good. Because there will always be conflicts between conceptions of the good, moral conflicts, both in the soul and in the city, there is everywhere a well-recognized need for procedures of confliction resolution ... This is the place of a common rationality of method.[7]

Hobbes unmasks the way this embrace of the universalism of procedure is grounded, not just in conflicting notions of the good, but more fundamentally, in the state of endless war over scarce goods. The contract is a constraining effort to impose peace on this warring state of nature, but of course Hobbes finally understands that because the contract is artificial and fragile, it will ultimately require totalitarianism:

> It is no wonder if there be somewhat else required (besides cove-
> nant) to make their agreement constant and lasting; which is a
> common power, to keep them in awe, and to direct their actions to
> the common benefit. The only way to erect such a common power
> … is to confer all their power and strength on one man, or upon
> one assembly of men, that may reduce all of their wills, by plurality
> of voices, to one will … And he that carrieth this person, is called
> SOVEREIGN, and is said to have sovereign power, and every one
> besides, his SUBJECT.[8]

Justice is emptied; the reign of law has become a reign of terror. If there is a
difference here, it is the difference between this totalitarianism and the
positive monotheism offered in Exodus, that is, the difference between law
as universal procedure and law as universal justice. Here the Bible distinguishes between a true universal—the reign of justice—and a false one.
The true one is most radically realized in Jeremiah where the covenant is
written on the heart:

> "The time is coming," declares the Lord, "when I will make a new
> covenant with the house of Israel and with the house of Judah. It
> will not be like the covenant I made with their forefathers when I
> took them by the hand to lead them out of Egypt, because they
> broke my covenant … This is the covenant I will make with the
> house of Israel after that time," declares the Lord, "I will put my
> law in their minds and write it on their hearts. I will be their God,
> and they will be my people. No longer will a man teach his
> neighbor or a man his brother, saying, 'Know the Lord,' because
> they will all know me, from the least of them to the greatest"
> (Jeremiah 31:31).

This internalization of justice is not the same as the incarnation, as the
Logos of Christianity. Lévinas distinguishes them: "God is real and concrete not through incarnation but through Law."[9] Indeed, for Judaism,
"it is precisely a word, not incarnate, from God that ensures a living
God among us."[10] Because so much of humankind is unjust, the just
man will suffer. But in the end, the "God Who hides His face and aban-
dons the just man, this distant God, comes from within," from the intimacy of one's conscience and the moral law. "This is the specifically
Jewish sense of suffering that at no stage assumes the value of a mystical
atonement for the sins of the world."[11] In Derrida's own version of this
interiorized justice, this transcendence made immanent, he understands
a paradox:

> The inaccessible transcendence of the law [*loi*], before which and prior to which man stands fast, only appears infinitely transcendent and thus theological to the extent that, nearest to him, it depends only on him, on the performative act by which he institutes it: ... The law is transcendent and theological, and so always to come, always promised, because it is immanent, finite, and thus already past.[12]

Lévinas offers a radical corrective to the procedural justice embraced by so much political theory:

> Justice cannot be reduced to the order it institutes or restores, nor to a system whose rationality commands, without difference, men and gods, revealing itself in human legislation like the structures of space in the theorems of geometricians, a justice that a Montesquieu calls the "logos of Jupiter," recuperating religion within this metaphor, but effacing precisely transcendence. In the justice of the Rabbis, difference [between man and God] retains its meaning. Ethics is not simply the corollary of the religious but is, of itself, the element in which religious transcendence receives its original meaning.[13]

In the book of Amos, we are shown the force of this transcendent justice:

> The Lord roars from Zion,
> and utters his voice from Jerusalem;
> the pastures of the shepherds mourn,
> and the top of Carmel withers.
>
> (Amos 1:2)

And as the word of the Lord makes the mountains wither, so a famine of the word of the Lord—of justice—will bring desperation.

> "Behold, the days are coming," says the Lord God,
> "When I will send a famine on the land;
> not a famine of bread, nor a thirst for water,
> but of hearing the words of the Lord.
> They shall wander from sea to sea,
> And from north to east;
> They shall run to and fro, to seek the word of the Lord,
> But they shall not find it."
>
> (Amos 8:11)

The word of the Lord is life-giving; take it away, and Israel dies, thirsting for the revelation of justice.

The biblical Amos also takes pains to separate—as Lévinas does not —religious ritual from keeping the law of social justice. One does not suffice for the other; in fact the hypocrisy of imagining that it could is offensive to God: "they lay themselves down beside every altar upon garments taken in pledge; and in the house of their God they drink the wine of those who have been fined" (Amos 2:8). If the ritual law is only that, and not also the law of justice, it is despicable:

> I hate, I despise your feasts, and I take no delight in your solemn assemblies. Even though you offer me your burnt offerings and cereal offerings, I will not accept them, and the peace offerings of your fatted beasts I will not look upon. Take away from me the noise of your sons: to the melody of your harps I will not listen. But let justice roll down like waters, and righteousness like an ever-flowing stream (Amos 5:21-24).

Not controlling a primordial war for scarce goods; this justice is ever-flowing abundance.

When "I will be your God if you will be my people" is replaced with "Then I will be their God and they will be my people," the Bible distinguishes between a true universal and a false universal, one that is really the terror of obedience to an empty law or the perversion of exclusivity, of murdering the other in the name of God, and the demand for justice that knows no compromise. Idolatry can be read in both ways: under the reign of terror and exclusivism "other gods" are regarded as threatening because multiple gods are threatening. Under the reign of universal justice, "other gods" signal a threat to substantive justice: if the biblical name for injustice is idolatry, the biblical name for justice is God. That is why the first patriarch referred to God as "the Judge of all the Earth."

But justice is not achieved; we are not there yet. Its violation led to the breaking of the law, a graphic depiction of the impossibility of justice. What Genesis Rabbah says about the justice of God makes this clear: When Abraham addressed his plea to God, "Shall not the Judge of all the earth do justly? The meaning of his words was: If You desire the world to continue there cannot be strict justice; if you insist on strict justice, the world cannot endure" (Genesis Rabbah xxxix 6). The failure of justice, the hidden face of God, is both part of the suffering of Judaism and the threat to the entire creation. As Lévinas writes, in Volozhiner's *Nefesh ha'Hayyim* (*The Soul of Life*), published posthumously in 1824, man has a partnership in the creation. For "through God's will, man's acts, words, and thoughts … condition or disturb or block the association of God with the world." God needed man to give life to the beings of the world, to sustain them, "and thereby bring them into existence."[14] How is this participation in the sustenance of the world achieved? Through each act of justice: this is "participation" in divinity, but not in the Augustinian sense. "Let nobody in Israel—God forbid!" wrote Volozhiner,

> [A]sk himself: what am I, and what can my humble acts achieve in the world? Let him rather understand this, that he may know it and fix it in his thoughts: not one detail of his acts, of his words and of his thoughts is ever lost. Each one leads back to its origin where it takes effect in the height of heights … The man of intelligence who understands this in its truth will be fearful at heart and will tremble as he thinks how far his bad acts reach and what corruption and destruction even a small misdeed can cause.[15]

"In this way," writes Lévinas, "man becomes, in turn, the soul of the world, as if God's creative word had been entrusted to him to dispose of it as he liked, to let it ring out, or to interrupt it." This responsibility, with God, for the beings of the world is for Volozhiner the meaning of Genesis 1:27 which describes man as being made in the image of God. Man is not in the image of God in the sense of possessor of the earth, as sovereign with dominion over it—as in Gregory of Nyssa—but is in that image in the sense of being responsible for keeping the created order, for bearing responsibility for the other, in a word, for justice. As Lévinas remarks with wonder, "the contribution of the readers, listeners and pupils to the open-ended work of the Revelation is so essential to it that I was recently able to read … that the slightest question put to the schoolmaster by a novice constitutes an ineluctable articulation of the Revelation which was heard at Sinai."[16] That is, each act of interpretation is understood to be an essential part of the ongoing revelation of justice—a far cry from the idolatry that would use the Bible as a political weapon.

References

1. "Inscribing Identity: Memory," in *The Curse of Cain: The Violent Legacy of Monotheism*, chap. 5 (Chicago: University of Chicago Press, 1997), pp. 143–176.
2. Jacques Derrida, *Acts of Religion*, ed. and intro. Gil Anidjar (New York: Routledge, 2002), p. 233.
3. Derrida, *Acts of Religion*, p. 250.
4. Derrida, *Acts of Religion*, pp. 250–251.
5. Derrida, *Acts of Religion*, p. 250.
6. Emmanuel Lévinas, "The Pact," in *Beyond the Verse: Talmudic Readings and Lectures*, trans. Gary D. Mole (London: Athlone Press, 1994), pp. 68–85.
7. Stuart Hampshire, *Justice is Conflict* (Princeton: Princeton University Press, 2000), pp. 4–5.

8. Thomas Hobbes, *Leviathan,* ed. and intro. J.C.A. Gaskin (Oxford: Oxford University Press, 1996, first published 1651), pp. 113–115.

9. Emmanuel Lévinas, "Loving the Torah more than God," *Difficult Freedom: Essays on Judaism,* trans. Sean Hand (Baltimore: The Johns Hopkins University Press, 1990), p. 145.

10. Lévinas, *Difficult Freeedom,* p. 144.

11. Lévinas, *Difficult Freeedom,* p. 143.

12. Derrida, *Acts of Religion,* p. 270.

13. Lévinas, *Beyond the Verse,* p. 113.

14. Sean Hand, ed., *The Lévinas Reader* (Oxford: Blackwell, 1989), p. 230.

15. Hand, ed., *Lévinas Reader,* pp. 230-31.

16. Hand, ed., *Lévinas Reader,* p. 195.

SECTION VII
La/Le Toucher (Touching Her/Him)

CHAPTER 22

Touching Transcendence: Sexual Difference and Sacrality in Derrida's *Le Toucher*

ELLEN T. ARMOUR

Le Toucher, Jean-Luc Nancy is Derrida's *homage*, as it were, to his friend and colleague, Jean-Luc Nancy. It reaches out to Nancy via a series of inquiries on touch in the philosophical tradition—a theme on which Nancy himself has written. Indeed, each gesture toward the tradition gestures toward Nancy insofar as Nancy's work on touch becomes a critical lens through which Derrida reads the tradition. I say "reaches out" rather than "touches" for specific reasons. First, the gap between *Le Toucher* and *Jean-Luc Nancy* in the title is, it turns out, indicative of a central insight that emerges from following touch through the philosophical tradition. Touch, that most intimate and arguably essential of senses, beckons toward a contact that is profoundly impossible. Yet, as with other figures of the impossible taken up by Derrida over the years, therein lies its significance. The medium is the message, as is often the case for Derrida. As Michael Naas argues, the physical structure of this book mirrors the shape of the analysis that occurs between its pages.[1] Derrida honors Nancy by placing his work in proximity to thinkers from Aristotle to Lévinas, including figures one would expect to encounter (Merleau-Ponty and Irigaray, for example) and some whose presence surprise. (An example that will be of particular relevance to this paper is the scholar Jean-Louis

351

Chrétien, author of *L'Appel et la Réponse*, an analysis of touch in Christianity.)[2] The pages of *Le Toucher* are organized into three major parts: "This is—of/to the other" (Ceci est—de l'autre), "Exemplary Stories of the 'Flesh'" (Histoires exemplaires de la 'chair'"), and "Punctuations: 'and you'" ("Ponctuations: 'et toi'")—bordered by prefaces and a conclusion and separated by a series of drawings by Simon Hantai ("Salve"). Part I considers Nancy's work in the context of that of other philosophers and thinkers in a series of six fairly lengthy essays. Part III carries further certain themes from earlier analyses in *Le Toucher* in three brief and more schematic essays, the last of which concludes by dispersing rather than tying together. Given the enigmatic and untranslatable title "Salve: postscriptum à contretemps, faute de retouche finale," this essay marks *Le Toucher* as quite literally eccentric: untimely (*contretemps* = outside of time) and unseemly (lacking a final touch-up). These parts are separated by a series of five "tangents" linked together as "Exemplary Stories of the 'Flesh.'" Together with the prefaces and conclusion, the book consists of essays of various lengths and purposes that together create a composite of touch.[3] Derrida's discussion of touch carries its readers to terrain that is simultaneously familiar and unfamiliar: the terrain of subjectivity and its limits (the interplay of immanence and transcendence, body and soul, divinity and humanity, humanity and animality, ethics and *eros*).

Given the aim of this book, it is perhaps particularly appropriate that it was selected as the centerpiece of this series of sessions delivered in proximity to one another—but not quite touching—in honor of Jacques Derrida, who honors us with his presence. In keeping with the structure of the book and with its theme, I have constructed my *homage* as an analysis of selected sections of *Le Toucher* brought together with other texts of Derrida's that they border, it seems to me. In what follows, I continue to pursue what has been for me a most fruitful encounter with Derrida via texts and, from time to time, in person; one that continues to help me to think and rethink connections between sexual and racial (in)difference and religion (past, present, and future).

In *Le Toucher*, Derrida takes up once again the figure of the impossible—in this case, also the impassable—as that which has the potential to open toward radical alterity. Alterity is always an elusive target, but never more so than in this text, in which it literally and metaphorically eludes and exceeds our grasp: here (as in many other sites Derrida investigates in search of alterity), sexual difference, racial difference, and religion converge. Though the sections of *Le Toucher* on which I will focus reach back as far as Aristotle and invoke such decidedly premodern figures as the Virgin Mary, the incarnate Christ, and St. John of the Cross (just to name a few), they appear in a framework constituted by the post-Kantian philosophical tradition, especially phenomenology and what succeeds it (Heidegger, Lévinas, Nancy, and of course, deconstruction). Given that milieu, one should not be surprised to find that Derrida's reflections on questions about the place of the body, religion, and difference invoke particularly modern concepts: the body/soul dualism, the subject/object split, the subject as master of all he surveys, the dominance of the visual. Approaching these themes through touch exposes *aporias* that surround them and brings these concepts into new focus.

Although the themes of sexual difference and religion appear in various places in *Le Toucher*, I will focus my comments on two sustained discussions of these issues: first, Derrida's discussion of the caress in Lévinas (Ch. IV, "The untouchable or the vow of abstinence" ["L'intouchable ou le voeu d'abstinence"], in Part I, pp. 81–108) and second, his discussion of the thinker whom I mentioned earlier, Chrétien, which comprises the fifth tangent ("Tangente V," pp. 273–293). In bringing these two portions of *Le Toucher* into proximity with one another, I trust that I also extend the book's project in another way. *Le Toucher*'s structure, it seems to me, takes the form of a book to its limits and, in doing so, embodies the (im)possible possibility of touch. The materiality of "book" requires that its subject matter be presented in linear form, but these essays (or forays) reach out to one another through and around their immediate neighbors. In this case, Derrida hints at parallels in the two thinkers' treatments of touch. Though the link is explicit, Derrida leaves it to the attentive reader to pick up the trail and to follow it from Chrétien back to Lévinas. Following this trail exposes a common logic of touch in the work of two very disparate thinkers. Structuring this logic is a fourfold (to borrow a Heideggerian notion) that consists of man and his others: his racial and sexual others, his divine other (God), and the animal. This fourfold links *Le Toucher* with other works of Derrida's that, if read with *Le Toucher*, suggest some important sites to be excavated by projects like mine that see a link between exceeding ontotheology and sexual and racial differences.

At first glance, the projects of Lévinas and Chrétien seem to have little in common beyond their approach to the theme of touch, in both cases launched from phenomenology, terrain that both treatments also ultimately exceed. Lévinas approaches touch through what is if not an everyday occurrence at least a common one: the lover's caress of the beloved. Chrétien, on the other hand, approaches touch through what purports to be a unique occurrence: the traditional Christian claim that God became incarnate in Christ. But Lévinas claims that what seems to be the most accessible to us is actually the most elusive. And Chrétien claims that what seems to be the most improbable contact of all is actually the most real. Lévinas and Chrétien, then, start from opposite corners and move (without recognizing it) toward each other: from immanence toward transcendence (in Lévinas's case), from transcendence toward immanence (in Chrétien's case). Finite-to-finite touch ungrounds what seems to be a fully grounded subject (in Lévinas's case). Infinite-to-finite touch grounds the subject by granting it its essential properties (in Chrétien's case). These two thinkers do not exactly meet in the middle. Yet, as we shall see, Derrida's reading (via Nancy) uncovers a common ground (marked by sexual [in]difference and a certain erotic bearing) that ungrounds both of them.[4]

Touching Touch I: The Caress

I begin, then, with Derrida's invocation of Lévinas who, like Nancy, has been an important conversation partner for Derrida over the years (and the subject of his own Derridean *homage* a few years ago). Our common sense associations with "caress" might suggest that it is a type of touch; one that brings pleasure in a distinctive form through contact with another (human) being. Since it involves a reaching-toward the other, its trajectory starts from within the self (immanence) and moves toward what lies outside the self (transcendence). We take for granted its success; that is, the reach-toward makes contact—flesh to flesh, skin to skin—and achieves satisfaction and release. As contact-with-another, the caress would seem to constitute the most intimate form of intersubjectivity; one that promises intimate knowledge of the Other. It promises to unify the orders of sensibility and intelligibility. It seems, on its surface, utterly benign; indeed, utterly good. Perhaps even ethical.

Derrida's reading of Lévinas's analysis of the caress considers two texts: Lévinas's well known "Phenomenology of Eros" in *Totality and Infinity* (*Totalité et Infini*, published in 1961) as well as *Time and the Other* (*Le Temps et l'Autre*, published in 1946–1947), a text that precedes by some 15 years its more famous counterpart.[5] These two texts are linked by a common logic, as well. In both texts, Lévinas reworks and ultimately challenges our common sense assumptions. In seeking the Beloved (always gendered feminine, Derrida points out), the Lover (always gendered masculine, Derrida points out) is indeed drawn out of himself. The pleasure of the caress is distinct from other pleasures (eating or drinking, for example), in that it is not solitary. But it is not yet social, thus not yet intersubjective. It envelopes the Lover in the closed circle of the couple, a site that at least holds out the fantasy of fusion and is thus, according to Lévinas, "the exceptional place of the feminine," a point to which I shall return later.[6] Fusion is only a phantasm, though, as Lévinas describes the caress.

It is the nature of the eternally feminine to remain forever out of reach and thus perpetually virginal. The Lover's quest also fails to achieve satisfaction beyond the level of phantasm. The two—Lover and Beloved, Caresser and Caressed—remain forever locked in a not-yet-embrace. Lévinas describes the caress as constituting a peculiar kind of transcendence; "contact beyond [au-delà] contact"—a contact that exceeds sensation and knowledge, the order of representation, and the order of intentionality. In short, pursuing the object-to-be-caressed carries the caressing subject to its limits. Derrida quotes Lévinas:

> The caress is a mode of being of the subject where the subject in its contact with an other goes beyond contact. The contact, in as much as it is sensation, breaks with the world of light. But that which is caressed is not touched, properly speaking. It is not the smoothness or warmth of this hand given in contact that the caress seeks. The search for the caress is constituted in its essence by the fact that the caress does not know what it seeks. This "not knowing," this fundamental disorder, is essential to it.[7]

The exposure of limits comes across as both promise and threat. Excess promises insofar as willing dispossession indicates a primordial openness-to-the-other, to the gift. It menaces insofar as willed dispossession loses control as the Caresser descends into a literal "no-man's-land" (in English, in Lévinas' original) of a vertiginous fusion-not-to-be. In following after the eternally feminine Beloved, "caress holds neither a person nor a thing. It loses itself in a mode of being which dissipates itself as though in an impersonal dream without will and without resistance, a passivity and anonymity already animal or infantile."[8] Its immersion in the "false security of the elemental" (ibid.) and in nonknowing—particularly not-knowing its mortality—are the markers of its animality or infantilism.

Elements of Lévinas's analysis of the caress call to mind his analysis of the ethical. However, Derrida argues that, rather than a site of the ethical (that is, the face), Lévinas's description of the caress amounts to an inversion (or even perversion) of the ethical. Both exceed the order of knowing and representation. Both carry the subject-as-master toward its limits. The demand of the Face that constitutes the ethical brings the subject up short, while the caress culminates in a blind dissipation of both self and other. Both also involve a relationship to death. Whereas the caress yields a forgetting of mortality, the Face presents itself as the demand "Do not kill me."

The erotic bearing of this scene is no doubt apparent, and Derrida finds it troubling. He is not, of course, the first to criticize it. Indeed, he refers (in a footnote) to Irigaray's critique of the division it introduces between the feminine and the ethical in "The Fecundity of the Caress."[9] Noting that the caress mirrors the face suggests to Derrida a set of questions that need to be answered. What is the line, if any, between the transcendence (as excess that renders impossible) of the caress and the transcendence (as ground that makes possible) the ethical? Insofar as both gesture toward transcendence, don't they both also gesture toward the ethical? Must the erotic be interrupted for the ethical to take place? Does the structural similarity between the erotic and the ethical link them as tangents of the same impossible? The same desire?

Touching Touch II: The Incarnation

As noted above, Chrétien starts from the opposite corner, as it were. Where Lévinas exceeds phenomenology by following a common everyday experience to its limits, Chrétien exceeds phenomenology by outdoing it. What phenomenology dreams of, theology accomplishes. Phenomenology makes a theoretical mistake when it posits touch between finite creatures as unmediated. Touch of finite to finite is afflicted by veils and intervals; it must be preceded by literal and metaphorical disrobing. Access to unmediated touch requires that one carry phenomenology toward its limits via a phenomenology of ecstasy and mystical love.

The touch *par excellence* is not the carnal touch, but the spiritual touch whose paradigm is the incarnation. In the incarnation, the infinite touches the finite; in becoming flesh, it converts the body from mere flesh to enfleshed spirit. Unlike the carnal touch, the touch of the divine is temporally and spatially immediate (that is, eternal and unmediated). Unlike Lévinas's caress, this touch meets its match—at least, on the surface. Chrétien asserts, via Aquinas and John of the Cross, that there is mutual contact (call AND response, to cite the title of his book). Where Lévinas's touch carries the subject to its limits, Chrétien's touch establishes the limits of the subject; that is, it gives to the subject its essential properties. We are used to thinking of the hand of God as the metaphor based on the literal hand of man. The real physical human touch provides the model for the figurative spiritual touch of the divine. But Chrétien's reading of the incarnation inverts the assignation of the literal and the metaphorical. In becoming incarnate in Christ-the-Son, the merciful hand of God-the-Father literally reaches out to touch—and through touch to become—human flesh. It is that touch that gives to man his proper hand; the hand that, it turns out, marks man as man. As we have known at least since Heidegger's famous analysis of *Zuhandenheit* in *Being and Time*, handedness grounds his ability to know, to discriminate, to organize, to see, to hear.[10]

No doubt, as with Lévinas, certain dynamics of this scene are so obvious as perhaps to go without saying. Derrida notes the anthropo-theo-teleological pattern that dominates this scene. Ontotheology (a system centered around a God whose Word grounds being) and metaphysical humanism—two sides of the same coin, as Derrida notes elsewhere—appear in tandem once again. And just as we might expect, Derrida is not going to let their reappearance go unchallenged. As with Lévinas, Derrida poses a set of questions to expose what remains unthought in Chrétien's project. Is the spiritual touch really as unmediated as Chrétien would like to believe? Are there not passages between that transcend (ground and exceed) Chrétien's assertion of the power of the spiritual touch? Chrétien's theological claim passes first through the philosophical (one gets to Aquinas only through Aristotle). But perhaps more significant for my purposes, theologic itself is constituted by a series of passages that Chrétien passes by without comment. Derrida notes that Chrétien ignores an essential passage between the infinite and the finite, namely, death. The infinite God becomes truly finite by dying on the cross. The meaning that Christian theology traditionally gives to this death links God, Christ, and sinful man via a prosthetic logic of multiple substitutions. God's death in Christ constitutes a sacrifice that replaces that owed by man to God, thus transforming sinner into saint. That transforming sacrifice is, in turn, commemorated and reenacted in the Eucharistic feast where bread and wine stand (in) for body and blood. God becomes man, the infinite becomes finite, saint becomes sinner, bread becomes body, wine becomes blood, sinner becomes saint: a chain of passages repeated *ad infinitum.*

Derrida also brings to our attention a figural logic of fiery desire that carries Chrétien's project along. Chrétien figures the touch of the divine as fire: fire that enflames flesh with desire for union with the divine, that provides illumination, but that will not be possessed. The divine fire consumes all attempts to contain it via representation (as icon or idol). In other words, Chrétien is bound to Lévinas by a certain logic of desire that tends toward ecstasy and excess (of representation and possession). The figural logic of Chrétien's text undercuts its surface logic that aims toward securing the subject by grounding its proper(ty) in the eternal. Chrétien's ostensible project is at least potentially undone by its own figures and forgettings; a scene marked once again by sexual (in)difference (veils, *khôra,* and now fire—one of the pre-Socratic elements) and death.

Derrida is not content simply with pointing out the prosthetic logic that runs counter to the surface logic of Chrétien's text. "Tangent V" concludes, as "L'intouchable" does, with questions and allusions that point toward what remains to be thought. What makes possible passages-between?

What gives place so that passages between may take place? Here, Derrida invokes *khôra,* that enigmatic figure from Plato's *Timaeus* that elsewhere in Derrida's corpus names that which exceeds Christian theo-logic. Chrétien's analysis of touch uses *khôra*'s resources (without knowing or at least without acknowledgement) to construct a prosthetic economy built around sacrifice. Is it possible, Derrida asks, to have an economy of substitution without sacrifice?

Tangent VI

It would, I think, violate the spirit and the letter of *Le Toucher* to offer something along the lines of a conclusion. So, let me offer instead my own tangent: a series of gestures toward what it seems to me this text sets forth for a project that aims beyond ontotheology and beyond our current economies of sexual and racial indifference.

Recently, Françoise Meltzer has remarked upon the current fascination among secular postmodernist theorists with mysticism and with saints. Meltzer reads this as a nostalgia for a union of body and soul in a singular commitment to a divine calling, which seems all but impossible in our (post?)modern fragmented world.[11] It seems to me that these sections of *Le Toucher* expose symptoms of a similar nostalgia; a desire for a firm ground upon which the subject can erect itself and project itself as a knower and a doer. But it also seems to me that *Le Toucher* does more than simply expose a nostalgia that us brave folk who know better can do without. It also calls us to think about—to think through—a reconstitution of the fundamental elements of this nostalgia that is perhaps struggling to be born(e) in two senses. Is it possible that we are struggling to shoulder the coming-into-being of a new configuration of transcendence and immanence, of the human being and (what gives it) its place? I referred earlier to a fourfold that I see in *Le Toucher*: man, his raced/sexed others, his animal other, his divine other. Circulating between, around, and through this fourfold are questions of embodiment, death, and desire.

I am going to take a risk here and propose a hypothesis that I am far from ready to defend, much less develop. I will use epochal language that makes me decidedly uncomfortable. But here goes: is it possible (or helpful or useful) to think of modernity as a certain configuration of these four elements? In this configuration, man occupies the center while the animal, God, as well as man's raced and sexed others, constitute a network of mirrors that reflect man back to himself by supposedly securing his boundaries. A distinctive relationship to death and desire and thus embodiment (different in man's relationship to each of the elements of the fourfold) links and separates one from the other. Perhaps the fact that we can now see this configuration as a hall of mirrors signals modernity's passing. But what new configuration is taking its place? Symptoms of this yet-to-come, it seems to me, appear in *Le Toucher*, especially when considered in relationship to other texts of Derrida's (*Sauf le nom*, "Circumfession," the *Geschlecht* essays, "The Ends of Man," *De L'esprit*, and a seminar Derrida gave at New York University in the fall of 1998 on animality all come to mind), but also in relationship to certain cultural dynamics.[12] The boundaries between man and his others are permeable; they leak. Movements in the name of justice in the name of man's others (raced, sexed, but also more recently, animals) are perhaps markers of that permeability. Of course, reassertion of those boundaries is always a possibility—indeed, a reality. I have argued elsewhere that movements for racial and sexual justice in our recent past and present exhibit just such recapitulations at times.[13] A similar argument could probably be made about certain aspects of the animal rights movement (insofar as it exhibits a tendency to anthropomorphize animals, one of the questions Derrida raised in the NYU seminar). But the permeability of those boundaries also, from time to time, goes in the direction of eroding this particular configuration of man and his others in favor of something-yet-to-come. And this, too, Derrida's analyses in *Le Toucher* and elsewhere also evoke. I have already noted that man's others provide a kind of transcendental ground that makes man possible. But that ground is also transcendent in another way: each of man's others transcends man—in the sense of exceeding him and his mastery—and the boundaries of the fourfold. God gives way to *khôra*, animals look back at us (or do they?) from an abyssal place of otherness, man's sexed other dispossesses him, man's raced other calls man to account by "outjusticing" him.[14] Certainly, one response to this situation is a nostalgic one. But another response is also possible: a staying-with these transcendences (and the reconfigured sense of transcendence that they evoke) alert to what is new in our situation.

Let me close with a brief reflection on what seems to me a particularly salient point of difference: the body. Another risky epochal hypothesis: if the desire to escape the limits of the body is one hallmark of modernity, perhaps one sign of a move beyond is an emergence of discourses and practices that reconfigure a bodily sense of transcendence—in which I would include *Le Toucher*. It seems to me that the return to the body (by all kinds of theorists)—is not always or only nostalgic, but is a response to an emerging reality, a material shift in culture marked by notions of and practices of embodiment as plastic (both malleable and synthetic) that evoke and invoke religious responses. One could list many symptoms of this emerging reality: the phenomenon of transsexuality; the disability rights movement; the prosthetic body; the human genome project; the use of animals in medical research, particularly as farms for raising human organs for transplant; and human cloning (which is making headlines even as I write). Let me stress that these are ambivalent and ambiguous phenomena as redolent of the modern ambition to escape the bounds of mortality as of any willingness to confront them. But to recapitulate is not (simply) to repeat. Embedded in these signs and wonders is, I suggest, a reconfiguration of the fourfold of man and his others that calls—in a still, small, voice perhaps?—for our attention.

References

1. Michael Naas, "In and out of touch: Derrida's *Le Toucher,*" *Research in Phenomenology* 31 (2001): 258–265; 258–259.
2. Jean-Luis Chrétien, *L'Appel et la Réponse* (Paris: Minuit, 1992).
3. Naas suggests that the five tangents represent the five fingers of the hand or the five senses. Perhaps the other five essays could be considered the fingers of the other hand as well.
4. I use (in)difference to signal the residue of sexual difference that can often be glimpsed in contexts that explicitly mask or deny it. Most sites (including the one excavated in this essay) figure sexual (in)difference solely within the (heterosexual) masculine/feminine binary. Within that binary, woman is other to man's self, passivity to his activity, object to his subject. I follow Luce Irigaray (and Derrida, among others) in seeing subversive potential in the residue. I go beyond these other thinkers, I believe, in exposing the (in)differences contained within that binary, a move that I will not make in this essay. For more on these issues, see my *Deconstruction, Feminist Theology, and the Problem of Difference: Subverting the Race/Gender Divide* (Chicago: University of Chicago Press, 1999).
5. Emmanuel Lévinas, "Phenomenology of Eros," *Totality and Infinity,* trans. Alphonso Lingis (Duquesne University Press, n.d.), pp. 256–266; *Le Temps et l'Autre* (Paris: Arthaud, 1947; reprinted, Presses Universitaires de France, 1983). Published in English translation as *Time and the Other,* trans. Richard Cohen (Pittsburgh: Duquesne University Press, 1985).
6. Lévinas, *Le Temps et l'Autre,* p. 82; quoted by Derrida, *Le Toucher,* p. 92, my translation.
7. Lévinas, *Le Temps et l'Autre,* p. 82; quoted by Derrida, *Le Toucher,* p. 93, my translation.
8. Lévinas, *Totalité et Infini,* p. 236, my translation; quoted by Derrida, *Le Toucher,* p. 103. See *Totality and Infinity,* p. 259.
9. Luce Irigaray, "Fécondité de la caresse (Lecture de Lévinas. *Totalité et infini,* Section IV, B, «Phénoménologie de l'éros»), *Éthique de la Différence Sexuelle* (Paris: Éditions de Minuit, 1984), pp. 173–199. Published in English as "The Fecundity of the Caress: A Reading of Lévinas, *Totality and Infinity,* "Phenomenology of Eros," *An Ethics of Sexual Difference,* trans. Carolyn Burke and Gillian C. Gill (Ithaca: Cornell University Press, 1994), pp. 185–217.
10. Martin Heidegger, *Being and Time: A Translation of Sein Und Zeit,* trans. Joan Stambaugh (Albany: SUNY Press, 1999), I.iii.A.15–17, pp. 62–76. Earlier, Heidegger establishes touch as a capacity unique to *Dasein.* He notes that, although we routinely ascribe touch to objectively present things (as in "the chair touches the wall"), "two beings which are objectively present within the world and are, moreover, *worldless* in themselves, can never 'touch' each other, neither can 'be together with' the other" (I.II.12, pp. 51–52).
11. Françoise Meltzer, *For Fear of the Fire: Joan of Arc and the Limits of Subjectivity* (Chicago: University of Chicago Press, 2001).
12. Jacques Derrida, *Sauf le nom* (Paris: Galilée, 1993); "Sauf le nom (Post-scriptum)," trans. John P. Leavey Jr., *On the Name,* ed. Thomas Dutoit (Stanford: Stanford University Press, 1995), pp. 34–85. Jacques Derrida, "Circonfession," in *Jacques Derrida,* Geoffrey Bennington and Jacques Derrida (Paris: Seuil, 1991); "Circumfession," in *Jacques Derrida,* Geoffrey Bennington and Jacques Derrida (Chicago: University of Chicago Press, 1993); Jacques

Derrida, "*Geschlecht*: Sexual Difference, Ontological Difference," *Research in Phenomenology* 13 (1983), pp. 65–83; *Geschlecht II:* Heidegger's Hand," *Deconstruction and Philosophy: The Texts of Jacques Derrida*, ed. John Sallis (Chicago: University of Chicago Press, 1987), pp. 161–196; Jacques Derrida, "The Ends of Man," *Margins of Philosophy*, trans. and ed., Alan Bass (Chicago: University of Chicago Press, 1982), pp. 109–136; Jacques Derrida, *De l'esprit: Heidegger et la question* (Paris: Galilée, 1987); *Of Spirit: Heidegger and the Question*, trans. Geoffrey Bennington and Rachel Bowlby (Chicago: University of Chicago Press, 1989).
13. See Armour, *Deconstruction, Feminist Theology, and the Problem of Difference*, esp. chaps. 1, 5.
14. For Derrida on *khôra*, see "*Khôra*," *On the Name*, pp. 89–127. I use "outjusticing" to describe Derrida's analysis of the political effect of Nelson Mandela in "The Laws of Reflection: For Nelson Mandela in Admiration," *For Nelson Mandela*, ed. Jacques Derrida and Mustapha Tlili, trans. Mary Ann Caws and Isabelle Lorenz (New York: Seaver Books, Henry Holt, 1987), pp. 13–42.

CHAPTER 23

Untouchable

GREGG LAMBERT

I want to begin with a brief bit of autobiography. In the early 1980s, I studied at the Graduate Theological Union at the University of California, Berkeley, a period in which I was engaged intensively in the study of the gospel literature, particularly the gospel of Mark, under the guidance of the New Testament scholar, Herman C. Waetjen. During this period "Liberation Theology" was in its full ascendance and Gustavo Guttierez regularly came to the GTU during the summer to teach a seminar on Latin American Theology; it was also a time when "deconstruction" and Derridean approaches to early testament exegesis were first making their mark. It was also in the early 1980s, finally, that Elizabeth Schüssler Fiorenza published her groundbreaking feminist interpretation of the Pauline tradition of Christianity, *In Memory of Her* (1983), and the various questions around "touching" and the "untouchableness" of gender constituted frequent talking points in classes and in lectures. I am giving you this bit of information in order to reassure you that I am not entirely speaking out of school, despite the fact that I now come from what is often referred to colloquially as "another discipline."

After I left the precincts of theology and biblical hermeneutics, I spent a long period (sometimes it seems like 40 years) studying Derrida's work from a more philosophical and literary perspective. Still, I did not completely leave behind the early influences that shaped my hermeneutic sensibility and so, even in my recent writings on the philosopher Gilles

Deleuze, one can easily find a certain theological resonance. Perhaps the most trenchant sign of this early influence derives from a certain passage that appears at the end of the gospel of Mark, the original ending, in which the women who have come to wash Jesus' corpse discover a young man (*neaniskos*) in the tomb who informs them that Jesus had already "gone before them" to Galilee. Of course, what many readers have already noticed is that the presence (*parousia*) of the resurrected Christ is not directly presented in this narrative account, neither is the famous episode where Jesus (the Christ) himself prohibits the women from touching him. Rather, in the original version of Mark, he is merely absent, and it is equally significant to note that his whereabouts are not described in terms of transcendence (that is, hierarchically), but rather in terms that are purely sidereal and terrestrial—the youth says, "He has gone before you to Galilee" (Mark 16:8). This announcement is picked up by the other gospel writers, with the exception of the writer of John, but more in the sense of a narrative anomaly that needs to be interpreted and explained (and I believe that one might locate, around the meaning of this statement, one of the first origins of the theological impulse in the early Christian tradition that follows). Of course, what we find here is an intrigue whose solution is probably purely historical and could be resolved by understanding the original community to which the gospel of Mark was addressed; nevertheless, as has been done so many times before, I cannot resist foregoing this purely scientific and historically plausible explanation for a more allegorical (that is, philosophical) interpretation concerning the meaning of the touch in the gospels.

A central theme of Derrida's recent *Le Toucher: Jean-Luc Nancy*, is the logic of the touch, which Derrida calls "haptology." The term is derived from Husserl's *Ideen II*, concerning the phenomenological sense of the "*haptique*," which can be described as an elision of the usual privilege accorded to the visual, as well as of the transcendence implied by the dominance of the visual organ; even by a politics that ruled by the visible organization of the body (*le corps*) along a vertical axis. On the contrary, the organization of the body around the privilege of "the touch" is purported to be thoroughly Christian, which is at the heart of the doctrine of incarnation. As Jean-Luc Nancy writes in "The Deconstruction of Christianism," "at the heart of Christianity is the doctrine of incarnation, and [...] at the heart of the doctrine of incarnation is the doctrine of *homoousia*, consubstantiality, the identity or community of being and substance between the father and the son."[1] Following this series of prepositional phrases, which go to the heart of the heart of the Christian doctrine, is the doctrine of the consubstantiality of father and son. Here, one can trace the passage of the semen, which bypasses a body that is touched (in the sense of being tainted or contaminated) by sexual difference.

This is an old story, and so I don't have to go into it in much depth. However, one wonders if the body is touched at all, but merely irradiated, to prevent it from being tainted or mixed up with another body. We might imagine here a process, graphically portrayed in the early Christian litera-ture, in which the Father's semen passes through his own body, directly commingling with the body of the son, so that they are of the same substance. In fact, it does not have to pass from his own body at all, which would imply a moment of *expropriation*, so that the Father's substance must then be reappropriated by the son. Of course, this would expose the Father to death. The solution of the early Church Fathers, as we know, was to resolve things so that the being of the Father and the being of the son were identical in substance; hence, there was no need for generation, for the son to be generated by another being. The Father is the son; the son is the Father. Needless to say, there is more than a scent of gnosticism present in this early Christian doctrine of incarnation; at least, there is a fear of the touch passing between the Father and the son, of a kind of con-tact that would cause the community to become mixed up, confused, con-taminated or polluted. Perhaps this underlines a certain contradiction that is present in the early Christian doctrine, which is set up to guarantee the Father's desire, or even the narcissism of the Father's desire for his own substance, but at the same time, installs the position of the woman's body as a possible point of contagion and as a prohibitive limit to this desire. Therefore, it is around this fear of touching and of being touched, as well as this untouchable mark of a prohibition against a certain kind of touch passing between the father and the son, that refers to the location of the body of woman in the early Christian community. She marks, both at once, the site of touching and the fear of being touched, and her body is determined as the site of this extreme contradiction: that is, between a body that is open to the touch and a body that is determined by the prohi-bition against touching.

Historically, this moment of extreme contradiction in the doctrine of incarnation is produced by the social and religious codes of purity and pollution that belonged to the societies of that time. It is reported in Mark 16:1 that Mary Magdalene and Mary the mother of James went to the tomb with spices to anoint the body of Jesus. In other words, they went to touch and handle a corpse, which was first of all an act that pollutes and contaminates—that enfranchises the boundary between living and the dead, between living body and corpse, or dead animal hide—but one that was open to these two women. In Matthew 28:1 it is said to be Mary

Magdalene and simply "the other Mary." In Luke 23:55 through 24:12, it is Mary Magdalene, Joanna, and Mary the mother of James, and "certain other women" (who are not identified in this account) who visit the tomb to prepare the corpse with "prepared spices and fragrant oils." In John, it is just Mary Magdalene, and here is added the statement by Jesus to Mary: "Do not touch me, for I have not yet ascended to the Father." By contrast, In Matthew 28:9, the women hold onto the feet of the resurrected Jesus and worship him, which is why the Greek sometimes is translated as "to cling" rather than to touch.[2]

In his recent work, *Corpus*, Nancy addresses the problem of the body around this tactile image.[3] What Nancy calls the body's "other sense" must be distinguished from the body's superficial sense (*res extensa*), that is, the body wholly determined from "the outside," whose surface can be touched, and whose parts and members can be cut or segmented, scarred or tattooed, colored or translucent, adorned or profaned. It is this sense of the body that we usually refer to when we say "the body," or "my body," since it is first of all open to perception, including the tactile perception of the touch, and consequently to signification as well. It is this sense of the body, as a matter of the *sign*, that is, to the kind of touch that leaves an indelible trace or mark of a sign that is interposed, or that sticks to the body (as in the sign of race or ethnicity, or the sign of voluptuous, or it's the lack thereof in the sense we talk today of "hard bodies"). However, this sense must be radically opposed to another, more absolute, sense of the body that cannot be identified (or rather "recognized") among the various senses by which the body is determined or signified as is the above examples. Nancy names this opposition of two senses the "antinomy of the body," whereby what is found to be proper to the body is always crossed through and divided by this antinomy.[4]

According to this antinomy, the origin of "the spirit" can be understood to derive from this "other body," as a shadow that is cast from the sense of a body that remains *in every sense* a stranger to the body defined by its external senses (sensation, including "touch," perception, image, memory, idea, and consciousness). As Nancy argues, it is precisely on the basis of this living contradiction that the famous dualism of the philosophical tradition unfolds, from Descartes and Hegel all the way through Sartre and Merleau-Ponty, in which the body is expressed in some fashion as the "obstacle to sense," or where the "Sense of sense" is inextricably bound up with the existential experience of our own bodies.[5] The question I will propose, in the context of the gospels, is whether the sense of this other body should immediately be identified with the body of woman, or whether there is yet another body that precedes even this one, that is, the body marked by sexual difference, and of "one sex," in particular, and, finally, whether it is from this other body that *the sense of the body of woman unfolds* as a problem that marks both the origin and the extreme limit of what Nancy refers to as "our tradition" (i.e., Christianity or "*christianisme*")?

For the moment, in order to illustrate further the two opposing senses of the body, we might find this distinction at the origin of the body's concealed surfaces—the privation of the visibility of its sexual parts, for example—as if, in these locations the body's superficial and extended sense turns inward and approaches the sense of the body's inner sense, that is, the privation of this outward and external sense of the body. These zones of privation and concealment (invisibility) are literally created or produced when a portion of the body's surface is folded back, creating an enclave or cryptic enclosure that is con-fused with the body's inner sense. And yet, the interior of these folds remain located on the outside of the body; they literally appear *on* the body, even though they are bound up with a privation of the merely superficial sense of the body's other surfaces (for example, the surface of my forearm, or calf, of the stretch of the body that runs along my back, or my forehead—and it is interesting that the Latin compound words in English that usually refer to these portions of the body are usually indicated as being "foreward," "up front," of being a side that in some way "faces.")[6] The fact that these folded and cryptically interior portions of the body's surface are the effects of this function of privation, that they are confused and mixed up with the body's other sense, can be easily demonstrated by the uncanny quality that surrounds the visibility of the body's orifices, and not only the so-called sexual orifices, but also the cavity of mouth ("that cavernous mouth"), the nostrils, the ears, or even the eyes. This is particularly true when these orifices appear too close to us—for example, while kissing someone I might focus on one eye, which suddenly appears to me as grotesque, as a yawning cavity—and, thus, no longer remain in the background, as parts set peacefully into the exterior composition of a face or a head.

Given these observations, one wonders if the sexually determined orifices are, in fact, *a posteriori* to this other sense of the body, that is, the metonymically organized effects or the expressions of what Nancy calls the absolute "For-Itself" of the body's own "auto-symbolization." As Nancy writes, "*The* body is nothing less than *the auto-symbolization of an absolute organ.*"[7] If we could perform a phenomenological "reduction" (*epoké*) of the positive attributes that define these exterior-interior zones of the body's surface in psychological and moral representations, of course we would quickly discover that they have undergone (and continue to undergo) a seemingly infinite number of variations between cultures, historical periods, and are even exposed to different vicissitudes on an individual level in the psychoanalytic sense of perversion. This is why I referred to them above as metonymically organized, in order to call attention to the fact that we are speaking about the organization of significations here and not about the body in itself. In fact, we might discover them to be the purest expressions of the manner in which the two senses of the body are folded, or in which these senses are con-fused on the body's surface, causing the overall *Gestalt* (or image) of the body to be shaped, contorted, deformed around the absolute tension, perhaps even the violent contraction, between the infinite openness of the body (to perception, representation, or signification, and touch) and a sense that opposes these predicates of the body's openness, expressing instead an aspect of imperceptibility in which the body remains, to all the senses, untouchable.[8]

In *Corpus*, Nancy writes:

> The body is the Living Temple—the life as Temple and the temple as Living, the one touching the other as a sacred mystery—only by achieving absolutely the circularity that founds it. It is necessary that sense be embodied, in itself and eternally, for the body to make sense—and reciprocally. Thus, the sense of "sense" is bodily, and the sense of the "body" is sensed. Within this circular reabsorption of sense, any established signification is immediately wiped away [...]. The body is the organ of sense, that is, the organ (or *organon*), absolutely (one can also say here: the system, the community, the communion, the subjectivity, the finality, etc.). The body is, therefore, nothing less than the auto-symbolization of the absolute organ. Unnameable as God, never exposed to an exterior understanding, ... unnameable in addition to comprising an intimate texture-of-self towards which every philosophy of the "body proper" exhausts itself ("what we call the flesh, this internally worked over matter, nameless in any philosophy"—Merleau-Ponty). God, Death, Flesh: the trinity of every onto-theology. The body is an exhaustive combinatory, the common assumption of these three impossible names, before which all signification trembles.[9]

Because of this absolute sense accorded to the body as a circularity without foundation, this "For-Itself" and "In-Itself" that defines the body—which, most importantly, can be said to be actual moments of sense that belong to our experience of own bodies (as well as the bodies of others)—Nancy provides a philosophical justification for understanding why the body would become an expression of divinity in *"our tradition,"* meaning our

Christian tradition that is founded upon the doctrine of the incarnation of the sacred in the body of the individual.

I would like to underscore the significance of Nancy's statement for interpreting the status of Christian ontotheology, which in some sense also encompasses the ontotheology of the West. What we call the body, for better or worse, is the common locus or source of the three impossible experiences of the "In-Itself" and the "For-Itself," in short, for three experiences of an Absolute Inside. Of course, these are not experiences, properly speaking, since we cannot "traverse" them, go "beyond" or "outside" of them; as Nancy writes, they constitute a sense before which every signification lapses into nothingness. Therefore, it is the historical and ontotheological characteristic of "*our tradition*" to have consecrated this sense with a form of the sacred, and to have filled it with an experience of mystery and terror. From this moment onward, the body will be positioned as the nexus of these three impossible names: God, Death, and the Living Flesh. (For this last impossible name, however, I might simply prefer the name "Life," or "Life-in-itself," which might be a better translation of *Leib* in order to avoid the archaic moral signification that is attached to the word "Flesh.") Thus, it is in this sense of the word that I sense my body as "circularity without ground," as a living absolute whose finality excludes me. If Nancy refers to this circularity as the "auto-symbolization of an absolute organ," this is because Life makes sense in or with my body in a manner that absolutely excludes any relation to my consciousness or my Ego. That is to say, consciousness does not exist as either a moment of this circulation, or as its end—its relation is always outside or exterior to the relation between the body and life. Therefore, from this moment onward, the body will be the common site of these three names, up to and including this current moment in secular culture where the body is located as the privileged locus of identity and freedom of the sexual subject. I pause to ask, can we imagine a moment outside or beyond "our tradition," that is, beyond a Christian ontotheological "humanism" (as Derrida has phrased our epoch)? If so, then perhaps one would have to imagine an organization of life, or the living subject bound up with the particularity of its relation to Life, in which it would be possible to think that *our bodies wouldn't matter*.[10] In the current moment, however, and within the limits of "our tradition," this remains unthinkable, to the degree that it appears impossible to think precisely *that!* Perhaps this is because "the body" is the name of the most powerful trope introduced by Christianity; the body is a "tropological organism," *par excellence,* already installed as the most primitive articulation of flesh and language, from which every performativity of the flesh (from conversion to sexuation) derives its absolute sense.

Nancy's statements concerning the trinity (God, Death, Flesh) can therefore be interpreted to mean that Christianity makes Death a divine name, just as much as it makes Life a form of the divine—but that wouldn't be too different from other religious systems either in the divinity of Life or of Death. What is specific to the Christian transformation of the divine is neither Death nor Life, nor even the figure of a God, but rather the incarnation of all three senses of the divine within the sense of the body. Henceforth, the sense of the body is inextricably bound up with the senses of these divine names. Death is not identical with abstract death, which as Hegel later said, was like the toppling of a pile of sand, but rather the dead body. Life is no longer Life, but the living body, life embodied. Returning to the end of the gospels, it is significant to note that all three names are thoroughly implicated in what could be called the *parousia* of the new divinity announced by the early Christian religion. In the tomb-scene, we have an event that is first of all bodily, present in the flesh; that is, the emphasis is placed on an experience that took on a form of contact with a living body. As I noted above, the form of this contact (between Mary and Jesus) cannot take place outside the social and moral-juridical prohibitions that gave rise to it and made it both normative and exceptional at the same time.

A woman (or "certain women") goes to a tomb, a place of death (*loculus*, a burial chamber in a tomb) and finds a living body. Once again, I stress the importance of the fact that laws governing contact already make it possible for women to enter into this place, to come into contact with death, even if they will only be surprised at what they find. This would imply that this experience, and thus everything that happens to them, was only possible on the basis of the fact that their bodies were already determined to be open to coming into contact with death, to touching the dead. Concerning the revelation of divinity, or *parousia*, the presence of the divine, I would not place as much emphasis on the poetic and allegorical elements of the accounts—the appearance of the "youth" (*neaniskos*) in Mark, or even of the living body of the resurrected Christ in the later Synoptics and John—but rather on the reactions of the women to what they witness. In Mark, it said they are "stunned" (*eklambestha*), which is also translated as "utterly amazed," or "remaining in a stupor," perhaps implying that the sense of what they witnessed at that moment remained with them for some time, like a shadow that caused the sense of what they experienced to remain strange, if not a cause of their estrangement. Of course, the earliest gospel ends by reinforcing this reaction. I will translate it literally: They ran away, possessed by trembling (*tromos*) and confusion (*ekstasis*), saying nothing to nobody (*oudeni ouden*). In Matthew, the women's reaction, at first, is described simply as one of "fear" (*phobos*), and they are even told that "they need not be afraid" (Matthew 28:5). In John, most interestingly, Mary does not even recognize Jesus at first (literally, she does not comprehend what she sees and is present to her in body and flesh), that is, not until Jesus calls her by name and she responds in the Aramaic, "My Master" (*Rabboni*). In all these passages, it is clear that what is revealed is sensed without receiving clear signification; in each case, the signification refers back to the sense of the experience, which is fear, trembling, confusion, amazement, stupor, and miscomprehension (all words that refer their sense primarily to the body, or express the body's relation to an event), which also might imply that the revelation of the divine has a sense that is primarily addressed to the body, which implies an indirect relation to conscious recognition or understanding.

It is clear that what we have here closely corresponds to what Nancy describes as an experience before which all signification trembles. But this trembling does not concern the neutral or neutered body, of male and female, which does not exist; so we must return to ask where does the sexed body figure in Nancy's account of "our tradition?" When we situate the above schema of the two contradictory senses of the body in the context of social and moral representations, we find a more accurate and revealing portrait of how this tension receives signification and content. These significations are not distributed evenly among all bodies, of course; rather, this tension appears to mark some bodies more forcefully than others. This is particularly true in the case of sexual difference, where the body of woman is socially defined by the contrasting tension of openness (voluptuousness) and by moral prohibition, a trait that is especially remarked in the figure of Mary Magdalene.

The body of Mary Magdalene, according to popular Christian legend, was full of semen, awash with the touch of other bodies. For this reason she incarnates the limit of the touchable, which turns around the prohibition that defines her social class and that of "certain other women." We might ask ourselves—and I would certainly not be the first to raise this question—why did the synoptic gospels constantly underscore the encounter between Mary Magdalene and the figure of the resurrected Christ (who is represented by the *neaniskos* in the gospel of Mark) as the meeting of the two extremes of the prohibitions concerning touch: the expression of the two senses of untouchable? I have only counted two, when there are actually three senses of the untouchable in the ending of the gospels: the untouchable that defines Mary, according to popular Christian mythology, to belong to a class of prostitutes; the untouchable that defines the body of Jesus as a dead carcass, a corpse, or cadaver;

and, third, the untouchable that appears in the gospel of John, which concerns the prohibition to touch the resurrected and yet unsanctified body of the Christ. I have not counted the third, but only because it might be considered as an aberration that belongs to the fourth gospel, or at least a didactic and moral moment that the gospel writer is addressing to the Johannian community. (Perhaps it concerns certain fetishistic practices or beliefs that have developed concerning the body of Christ. In this sense, I would read it as similar to the injunction we find in Matthew: "stop clinging to me," that is, to my body.)[11]

Yet, it is the conversion of Mary Magdalene (perhaps a representative of the untouchable classes) into a living member of the early Christian community that receives its allegorical representation in the conversion of a corpse into a living person. According to the scholarship surrounding the social position of women in early Christian communities, she represents the extreme principal of inversion that defined the *ethos* of the early Christian sects: the incarnation of all the untouchable classes in one body (or community), the reversal and abolition of existing purity codes, whereby the bodies of those who were defined outside the limit contact are incorporated into a new community whose inaugurating principal is the transgression of the prohibitions surrounding touching that shaped the former social and moral order. According to Schüssler-Fiorenza, Mary can therefore be identified as the first apostle ("the apostle to the apostles," or the mother to the church fathers, so to speak) the true witness of the resurrection and the life of Jesus, who lived afterwards in fear of Roman persecution and death, a radical Christian, a *mater familias*.[12] But then, this conversion has had profound repercussions; the canceling of the prohibitions surrounding touch, that is, the conversion of the untouchable into a principle of contact and community, has definitely played havoc in early Christian societies, and even today, between the body defined by sexual contact (*porneia*) and the "body proper" defined by Christian morality.

In what historian Wayne Meeks has identified as a fundamental ambiguity in early Christianity (and particularly in the ascendance of Pauline Christianity), this principle of extreme openness that marked many of the early Christian sects is later brought into tension with Greco-Roman social mores and class distinctions, mostly those belonging to the upper classes.[13] It is by no accident, then, that throughout the history of Christian societies this confusion continues to be expressed by the ambivalence and the extreme contradictions that determine (socially, morally, but then even philosophically) the bodies of women. As Paul wrote, "It is a good thing (*kalon estin*) for a man (*anthropon*) not to touch (*aptomai*) a woman" (1 Corinthians 7:1), which could even be rendered more literally as, "It's a good thing for a man to not touch *one.*" I might even go further to say that the body of woman is engendered to incarnate this extreme division that belongs to the body in general, even to the degree that she is made entirely responsible for it, and that it is this spirit of hatred (misogyny) that underscores almost all the early treatments of the division of the sexes in the writings of Paul, Philo, Aquinas, Constantine, and Lucretius. This history can be understood as the expressions of an extreme "ambivalence" (Meeks) that have shaped both the determination of the body's sexuality and the representation of woman in later Christian societies, including our own. Therefore, if feminism has emerged most forcefully in our century, then perhaps it represents a political body (a community) that was already prefigured in the fateful meeting of Mary and Jesus. In this encounter we already bear witness to a volatile principle of community that is founded upon the contradiction between touch and untouchable, in other words, between inclusion and exclusion. In as much as Christianity is to remain "our tradition," it is this same principle of extreme opposition that continues to haunt every representation of the "political body" today.[14]

References

1. Jean-Luc Nancy, "*La deconstruction du christianisme,*" quoted in Derrida, *Le Toucher: Jean-Luc Nancy* (Paris: Galilée, 2000), p. 273.
2. This might also be interpreted as the gospel writer's message to the early Christian community he is addressing: "stop clinging to my body," perhaps even in the sense of preventing the body of the Christ from becoming a mere fetish. "I am not there," we might hear Jesus saying to Mary Magdalene, who could very well represent a certain sect of the early Christian community who might be "clinging" to the idea of the bodily resurrection of Christ.
3. Jean-Luc Nancy, *Corpus* (Paris: Métalié, 2000).
4. Nancy, *Corpus*, p. 71ff.
5. Nancy, *Corpus*, p. 61.
6. Derrida has commented on this Latin root in relation to the psychoanalytic theory of introjection, or cryptonomy, in "*Fors.*" See Derrida's preface to Nicolas Abraham and Maria Torok, *The Wolf-Man's Magic Word: Cryptonomy* (Minneapolis: University of Minnesota Press, 1986).
7. Nancy, *Corpus*, p. 64.
8. We might imagine that these folded points function as vortices *in* the body—Nancy himself refers to them as "black holes"—and the effects of distortion they produce could be similar to the organization of the body in the paintings of Francis Bacon, where the body is visibly pulled and pushed around certain opaque points in the center of the composition (although it is important to note that these points never appear visible, only the distorting effects of their presence). What I have been describing above, of course, has been metaphorically represented in the psychoanalytic theory of the mirror stage as the phallic moment of "mis-recognition" that splits the subject into pure façade and the formless presence of the body's drives that subsequently causes the subject to suffer from "feelings of fragmentation." However, precisely because it is metaphorical representation, this psychoanalytic image of the mirror stage must be bracketed as well since it is already a signification that responds to the hypothesis concerning the origin of a particular formation of the ego's bodily image, what Freud had earlier defined as the *Körper-Ich.*
9. Nancy, *Corpus*, pp. 66–67.

10. The above reference, of course, is to Judith Butler's *Bodies That Matter* (London: Routledge, 1993), which according to the above argument could be said to belong to a Christian onto-theological humanism in that it defines the body as an "in-Itself" that is converted into a "For-Itself," that is, a self-consciousness that transforms the body into a privileged site its own auto-symbolization (i.e., "performativity").

11. In general, I tend to read the significance of the different versions of the tomb narrative very explicitly along the lines of their common theme designed to instruct the intended audiences—who were after all, at least for the most part, fairly simple folk—which is: stop looking for me in the Tomb, since I am not there. Stop looking for my body among the dead, because it is a "living body." The gospel writers, as teachers, wouldn't want to confound their students; this task falls to scholars and academics in the centuries that followed, a group that could be classified as a group of "bad students." According to the Christian testament scholar, Herman Waetjen, this judgment can even be found in the portrait of the original disciples, particularly in the gospel of Mark, who as a group come off looking like a bunch of "blockheads" (Herman Waetjen, *A Reordering of Power: A Socio-Political Reading of Mark's Gospel* [Minneapolis: Fortress, 1989], pp. 149–164).

12. Elizabeth Schussler-Fiorenza, *In Memory of Her: Feminist Theological Reconstructions of Christian Origins* (Minneapolis: Fortress, 1983), p. 333.

13. Wayne Meeks, "Since Then You Would Need to Go Out into the World: Group Boundaries in Early Christianity," in *Critical History and Biblical Faith in New Testament Perspective*, ed. T. J. Ryan (Villanova: College Theology Society, 1979), pp. 4–29.

14. At the same time, the political significance that is recently accorded to the body in "our tradition" is in some ways already redundant. As Nancy reminds us, "'the political body' is a tautology" (Nancy, *Corpus*, p. 64).

CHAPTER **24**

Touching (in) the Desert: Who Goes There?[1]

GRACE M. JANTZEN

In this same light and under this same sky, let us this day name *three* places: the island, the Promised Land, the desert. Three aporetical places: with no way out or any assured path, without itinerary or point of arrival, without an exterior with a predictable map and a *calculable* programme. These three places shape our horizon here and now … Whence the apprehension of an abyss in these places, for example a desert in the desert, there where one neither can nor should see coming what ought or could—perhaps—be yet to come. What is still left to come.

—Jacques Derrida, "Faith and Knowledge: the Two Sources of 'Religion' at the Limits of Reason Alone"[2]

This day, however, I want to name only one of these places, the desert. The desert, in the spiritual traditions of Islam, Judaism, and Christianity, is the place of testing, temptation, and illumination; the place where new perspectives can be gained. John of the Cross writes of the mystical wisdom that arises in the "secret abyss" when one is "led into a remarkably deep and vast wilderness … into an immense, unbounded desert …"[3] The desert has been used as a trope, an "aporetical place" that has "no way out or assured path" by many who have struggled in solitude for wisdom and perspective. But which desert? Whose desert? How can we in this city touch it? How does it touch us? And what is still left to come from it, which we perhaps cannot see? When we name the desert, what places do we name? Who goes there?

The desert I know best is the desert of the southwestern United States. Under its wide skies, missile silos house nuclear warheads. A huge air-force base tests for constant readiness every kind of airborne weaponry. In the middle of this gamble with the future of humanity is Las Vegas, where, as Mark C. Taylor said, "what begins in Puritan New England reaches to a certain closure."[4] Around the periphery of this vast and arid region, and in pockets within it, Native North American peoples—Navajos, Hopi—live on "reservations," struggling against massive odds to retain what they can of dignity and ancient ways. "In this same light and under this same sky, let us this day name" this desert, these deserts within a desert, consider how it touches and may yet touch us, ponder "what is still left to come."

Half a world away, stretch the sands that shook under Desert Storm. Over 60,000 tons of bombs were dropped on Iraq in the first two months of 1991; and in the subsequent hundred-hour ground war up the Wadi-al-Batin and the desert to the west perhaps a hundred thousand Iraqi troops perished.[5] The sandstorms that now blow across the desert to Baghdad and the Euphrates valley, or back across the Saudi desert, carry the fallout of hundreds of tons of depleted uranium.[6] Touched by this wind, hundreds of children with malignancies and tumors are brought into hospitals desperately short of supplies.[7] What wisdom, what new perspectives can be gained from an "apprehension of an abyss in these places?"

In sub-Saharan Africa nearly half the population lacks access to safe water and sanitation. Three million people, many of them children, die each year of waterborne diseases. Water courses and oases that once supplied their needs have been polluted, destroyed by warfare, or diverted to provide irrigation for export crops for western markets, often to pay for military equipment or the interest of international debt.[8] What illumination of mystical theology, what knowledge of divine things could stand in this desert with the mothers touching their dying babies, could face down the greed of the western market for the crops which absorb the water or the products of the industries that pollute it?

In the Palestinian Occupied Territories a desert of a different kind is being created. Palestinians are sentenced to a "parched life," while Israel utilizes most of the water resources of the region. In Hebron, where Jewish settlements are interspersed with Palestinians, 70% of the water goes to about 25% of the population: settlers water their lawns and ornamental trees while the Palestinians have to make do with an ongoing severe short-age.[9] In the frequent "crackdowns on terrorists" by the Israeli Defense Force the strategy includes what international aid workers call "systematic targeting and sabotage" of the water infrastructure, cutting off water sup-plies to homes, refugee camps, and even hospitals, artificially creating the most densely packed "desert" on earth.[10] This "water-conflict" is hardly reported in the west: there is resistance to openness about it. "'Where do we draw a line in the sand between deconstruction as desertification of God and as desertion of God?' There is no line… So you have to resist this resistance to openness to a possible monstrosity and to this evil."[11]

If we—privileged western academics in a large and wealthy city—use the desert as a trope, an "aporetical place" that has "no way out or any assured path," these actual deserts that shape the horizon of the twenty-first century must be our place of accountability, the place where we touch base. It is easy to romanitcize the desert: its wide horizons, vast solitude, and starlit nights; and to suppose that in the immensities of such spaces we might find illumination. But what illumination is available in the missile silo or the refugee camp? What aporia of thirst and disease and abjection must the once proud nomads confront as their sources of water dry up and their dying children must be taken to hospitals riding on camels with lumps deforming their necks? These places, too, we must name. Who goes in the desert? How dare we touch it?

And "one must still respond. And without waiting. Without waiting too long."[12] These deserts are neither found in our "Greek memory" nor are they the deserts of Middle Eastern sources of revelation.[13] They are the deserts of modernity, the outward and visible signs of the inward and spiritual dislocation of the human spirit, a dislocation in which the mono-theistic religions and their secular offshoots are heavily implicated. And so the "troubled question" is "What is going on there? What is happening and so badly? What is happening under this old name? What in the world is suddenly emerging or re-emerging under this appellation?"[14]

As has been pointed out, the Abrahamic has a significant place in con-sideration of the desert, connecting sacrifice and gift with a prophetic and messianic future whose past is in the desert. The Abrahamic connects in other ways too: the Jew, the Muslim, and the Christian all claim Abraham and are gathered by him into a hyphenation, which, however, "does not pacify or appease anything, not a single torment, not a single torture. It will never silence their memory … A hyphen is never enough to conceal protests, cries of anger or suffering, the noise of weapons, airplaces and bombs."[15] Indeed, we must go further. Every one of the abominations of the desert to which I have alluded above have implicated that Abrahamic hyphen. In each case the appropriation of the Abrahamic notions of superiority by divine election have turned the desert into hell.

In the Mediterranean context where Derrida and his friends pondered religion and invoked the desert, there was a consciousness of the exclusive nature of the group. They were reminded of the "pressing obligation: not to forget those [of either gender] whom this … 'being together' is obliged to exclude."[16] Obliged? Why? Who or what placed an *obligation* (a duty, a binding agreement—or an indebtedness?) upon the group to exclude women? And if they were thus obliged, then how could they simultaneously be under obligation not to forget those whom they were obliged to exclude? Women will find only too familiar this impeccable courtesy that nevertheless keeps them out and their voices silent. "We should have, we ought to have, begun by allowing them to speak." So why were they silenced? What might they have had to say about the desert—the desert in the desert? And how might that change our understanding of the city, the settled land?

The Demons of the Desert

"The names of the Abrahamic are numerous."[17] Among them are still other desert dwellers: men and women who, from the third to the fifth century CE, left the cities of the Hellenistic world to live in the deserts of Egypt, Palestine, and Syria. Women were not excluded. They were often silenced later, but they were also held up as models of what could "emerge or re-emerge" in the desert. One such woman was Mary of Egypt, whose story (sometimes conflated with legends of Mary Magdalene) was circulated as a model of conversion, a story of hearts of stone being turned in the desert to hearts of flesh.[18]

The legend as we have it begins with Zossima, a complacent monk who had been in a monastery of Palestine since his infancy and now, as a man of fifty-three, began to think that "it seemed as if he had attained perfection in everything and needed no teaching from anyone."[19] But as he thought thus, "someone stood before him and said":

> A greater ordeal lies ahead of you, although you do not know this. And so that you may know how many and varied are the ways to salvation, leave your native land, go out of your father's house, like Abraham, glorious among the patriarchs, and go to the monastery which lies near the river Jordan.[20]

Off went Zossima and presented himself at a monastery near the Jordan. The brothers, he found, were exemplary in the things that most concerned those who left the cities after Christianity had become the religion of state: food and luxury, sexuality, and anger and violence. (We shall encounter all three of these areas more fully below.) But none of this was unusual for Zossima, model monk that he was. At the beginning of Lent, however, the brothers had the custom of leaving the monastery and each one going alone into the desert for forty days and forty nights to face whatever trial might come to him, as Jesus himself had gone into the wilderness to be tempted of the devil.[21] They then reassembled for the Easter feast. So Zossima also kept the rule, trudging into the wilderness across the Jordan: "something in his soul urged him to go deep into the desert," the desert in the desert, a nomad following the example of his father Abraham. And sure enough, after twenty days, while he stopped for his prayers, "he saw the appearance of a devil and he trembled."[22] Zossima met his demon.

But things were not—or were they?—as they seemed. To Zossima's amazement he saw that what he had taken as a demon "was a woman and she was naked, her body black as if scorched by the fierce heat of the sun, the hair on her head was white as wool and short, coming down only to the neck."[23] Now, for many a monk of the eastern desert the slide between the demonic and the female was quickly made. For Zossima to misidentify the woman as a demon was congruent with the misogyny rife among Christians of late antiquity.

It is his reaction that is astonishing. If it was a demon he was confronting, then he should either flee the temptation or stand his ground and struggle with it. Zossima does neither. Instead, he "began to run swiftly in the direction in which he had seen that it was going, and he rejoiced with unspeakable joy."[24] It ran from him, "quickly, into the depth of the desert," Zossima in hot pursuit. There follows an account of farcical proportions: a naked woman runs ever further into the desert, pursued by an elderly monk puffing and panting and unable to catch up, shouting and begging her in tears to wait for him, "an old man, a sinner." Utterly exhausted, he sinks to his knees and begs of her "a prayer and a blessing for the sake of God who despises no one." But the "fugitive," naked, would not turn around. Instead, calling Zossima by name—which greatly increases his anxiety—she instructs him to throw her his cloak. Having wrapped herself in it, she then turns to him and asks, "Why do you want to see a sinful woman, father? What do you want to learn from me or see, that you were not afraid to undertake such a heavy task?"[25] What indeed? The account as we have it does not seem to notice how odd it is that a monk who is expecting to confront demons in a world where there was an easy slide between the demonic and the female should chase after a naked woman not to fight with her (or even with his own temptation) but to ask her for a *blessing!*

The scene quickly becomes even more ludicrous. "He knelt down and asked her to give him the customary blessing. She also knelt down. So they both remained on the ground asking one another for a blessing." Stalemate. There they both kneel, facing one another, each waiting for the other to make the first move. She recognizes him as a monk and priest; he "breathing with difficulty," addresses her: "O Mother in the spirit, it is plain from this insight that all your life you have dealt with God and have nearly died to the world ... pray for me out of the kindness of your heart."[26] And she, announcing that women must be obedient (!) agrees to do so.

Although the writer of the legend seems piously oblivious to the comical aspects of his presentation, he weaves together the female and the demonic with some (unconscious?) subtlety, making clear one of the central themes of desert spirituality: things are not what they seem. Discernment, the willingness to have one's preconceptions and complacency shattered, is both a prerequisite and a gift of the desert in the desert, which is not a place of starlight and wide skies but a place where demons must be recognized and confronted. These demons are not what they seem; and they are not merely private or personal. They are the personification of the powers configuring society, which awaits its transformation.[27]

Zossima's complacency is severely disrupted. In deference to his request, the woman commences to pray, "turning to the East and raising her eyes to heaven and stretching up her hands."[28] Zossima looks down, trembling; but when he glances at her he "saw that she had risen a cubit from the ground and was standing praying in the air." Now, we might expect that this would reinforce for him the recognition of her holiness. But it has exactly the opposite effect. As inexplicable as his first perception of a naked woman as a "Mother in spirit" is his reaction now: "he fell to the ground, covered with sweat and terrified ... troubled by the thought that this might be an evil spirit and the prayer an illusion."[29] When all the signs were of demonic danger Zossima saw a holy woman; now, when all the signs of holiness are before him he thinks he sees a demon.

The woman turns around, helps him up, makes a sign of the cross, and assures him that she is no demon, "just a woman and a sinner." Zossima executes another pendulum swing: he falls to the ground (again!) embracing her feet and weeping.[30] He begs her to tell him her story, "in the name of ... our Lord, born of a Virgin, for whose sake you clothed yourself in this nakedness ..."[31] This woman, though, is certainly not a virgin, as she quickly makes clear. She replies,

> I am ashamed, my father, to tell you about the infamy of my deeds. But as you have already seen my naked body, I shall also lay bare

before you my deeds ... for what have I got to be vainglorious about, having been chosen as a vessel of the devil?[32]

So here is the devil again, and again attention to the nakedness of the female body. Yet through the reversals that have been coming thick and fast the reader is by now prepared for the lesson that the monk, traumatized out of his complacency, is learning in this desert in the desert. The desert requires new perspectives on the demonic.

Zossima, not for the first time nor the last in the story, weeps "without restraint,"[33] "watering the ground with tears."[34] Now, the gift of tears, in the writings of the desert fathers and others of late antiquity, stood in direct contrast to sexual incontinence. According to the medical tradition of the time, the damp humors of the (male) body could become sexual drives, a process that was particularly heightened by food and wine. Contrariwise, by much fasting and discipline and the grace of God they could become tears of contrition and compassion in which "the rigid heart melted."[35] Just as the woman, usually linked with the demonic, has become a channel of the divine, so the sexual arousal a naked body might elicit becomes in Zossima the means of conversion of his complacent heart. In the desert of the desert, semen is changed into tears by the prayers of a woman. When once the woman is allowed to speak, her voice is redemptive. The demons in the desert do not originate with her, but with the lust and violence projected upon her.

Touching Paradise

Mary now tells her story. She had been born in Egypt.[36] In adolescent rebellion she lost her virginity and from then on "I was on fire with untiring and clamorous desire for lust"[37] becoming a prostitute not so much for money as "out of insatiable desire."[38] In exchange for her—eagerly granted—sexual services Mary was given passage on a ship taking pilgrims to Jerusalem for the feast of the Exaltation of the Holy Cross: her account of her sexual activities to Zossima (who is all the while weeping) is graphic and detailed. She went along to the festival, and wanted to enter the cathedral from the forecourt with the rest of the crowd.

> But as soon as I reached the threshold where others were going in without difficulty, I was prevented from entering by a kind of force. I was pushed back and found myself standing alone in the courtyard.[39]

Three times she tried, at first attributing the failure to "my weakness as a woman," but each time the church itself "refused to admit me."[40] Only then did she begin to understand that it was her "sinfulness"; and the gift of tears came to her. "So I began to weep and grieve and beat my breast; I drew sighs and tears from my heart." She prayed to the Virgin, her namesake, contrasting Mary's purity with her own impurity; and she promised that if the Virgin would let her enter the church and "adore the cross" she would thereafter be forever chaste and moreover would go wherever the Virgin would order and lead her, "for I am alone and without any other help."[41]

Her prayer was granted. Mary entered the church, venerated the cross, and then ran back to the courtyard where she had prayed to the Virgin, willing to keep her promise. "'Now therefore, lead me wherever you please; lead me to salvation, teach me what is true, and go before me in the way of repentance.' When I had said this, I heard a voice far off which said, 'If you cross over the Jordan, you will find rest.'"[42] She set off at once, buying three loaves of bread with three pennies someone gave her. She asked directions: "'Where is the road to Jordan and what is it like?' When I was shown the city gates which lead in that direction, I ran out of them, weeping, and set out on my journey." She reached the Jordan and crossed it, praying to the Virgin her Guide. "So I came into this desert and from that time until this day I go further and run on, waiting for my God …"[43]

So here they both are in the desert, the monk turned nomad and the prostitute turned fugitive. Both of them have left a situation in which their hearts were hard, the monk's with pride in his piety, the prostitute's with pursuit of pleasure. Both of them are sent by divine command into the desert of the desert, their sexual energies released in transforming tears, and each recognizing the other as bringing the voice of God to them. The neat literary parallels serve to heighten the shock of the values turned upside down: good and bad are not what they seem; male and female can reach a mutuality of respect and recognition; the piety of religious observance can dull the heart to sensitivity to the divine which obedience restores. There is a reflexivity of perception intended: the monks for whom the account is written are drawn out of their own context to identification with the pair in the desert. Although they are not physically in the desert themselves, their perspective is shaped and their certainties destabilized by those who are; but that depends on listening to the voices of those who are actually in the desert and taking them seriously enough to shatter their complacency. Only thus can God raise from those stones children unto Abraham.

From this point on in her story, Zossima begins to question Mary. How long has she been in the desert? Forty-seven years since she came from Jerusalem, she says—another parallel to the career of the fifty-year-old monk who had been in the monastery from a very early age. And what had she eaten? "The woman replied, 'I was carrying two and a half loaves when I crossed the Jordan, and after awhile they became hard as stones and I have gone on eating a little of them at a time for all these years.'"[44] And did she ever suffer, or find life in the desert difficult? (!) At Zossima's insistence, this questioning brings out further confession. Mary acknowledges her craving for food and wine, and her intense struggle over many years "with the wild beasts of huge and irrational desires."[45] The passions which had made her a prostitute did not disappear just because she went into the desert. Moreover, she says,

> The clothing that I had when I crossed over Jordan tore and fell to pieces with age. I endured much from the freezing of cold and the burning of heat: I was burned by the heat of summer and frozen stiff and shivering in the winter by so much cold; often I fell to the ground and lay there unmoving, without breath, struggling with many and diverse needs and huger temptations but through it all even until this day the power of God has guarded my unhappy soul and body.[46]

Zossima himself had practiced an ascetical regime all his life. Yet even he is astonished at what Mary has achieved.

Now, in relation to the literature about the desert dwellers, this catechizing of Mary by Zossima mirrors the three primary signs of transformation sought as a contrast to the distorted values of the settled land—signs that can be indicated by the terms food and fasting, sexual pleasure and renunciation, and the overcoming of irrational passions, particularly anger and judgmentalism.[47] The sayings of the desert dwellers are full of heroic accounts of fasting:[48] monks attempted to subdue their natural desire for food to the point where they sometimes needed admonition from their elders to be less harsh with themselves. There were several overlapping reasons why fasting was seen as essential to the spiritual life. First, it was a protest against the economic structure of the cities, where affluent Christians could live in comparative luxury while the general populace lived in hunger and constant fear of starvation. The life of the desert showed that it was possible by living very simply and restraining ones appetites to be removed from the "bitter dependence on the marketplace,"[49] recognizing the demonic in the economic structures of society.

Second, the social protest that found its form in fasting was coupled, in late antiquity, with a theology in which greed expressed as gluttony (not sexual indulgence) was taken to be the first sin. Adam, and Eve before him, had forfeited paradise by eating.[50] Repentance, therefore, necessarily must involve fasting. As Abba Moses, one of the famous desert dwellers of Egypt had said, fasts "make the soul humble" so that God can have mercy upon it.[51] By fasting, the penitent turns from sin to the state of humanity before the fall: in the words of Basil of Caesarea, fasting is "the image of the way of life in paradise,"[52] no longer obsessed with food or with the fear of death because food might be unavailable. Such a return to paradise was graphically illustrated in the legend of Mary and Zossima, for whom the desert had become a new Eden, in which, like Eve before the fall, Mary wandered naked. In one of the many alternative versions, Mary invites Zossima to eat from the loaves in her basket, which miraculously do not diminish as they eat and drink together, a new Adam and Eve partaking of heavenly food.[53] As the first Eve gave Adam the food of sin, Mary gives Zossima the food of repentance.

Third, fasting was closely related to sexual renunciation: it was widely held that plentiful food, especially meat, increased sexual desire while strict fasting diminished it.[54] Again as in the case of fasting, celibacy removed men and women from the preoccupations and social expectations of the cities. Particularly in the case of women it could mean an unusual degree of freedom in a world where a woman's duty was to bear as many children as possible.[55] Theologically, procreation was seen as a preoccupation with death: having children was a "great consolation in the face of mortality."[56] Thus, like fasting, celibacy was seen as a return to paradise where procreation was unnecessary because death was not a threat. Although "ordinary" Christians continued to marry and have children with the blessing of the church, those who chose virginity or celibacy like the desert dwellers were thought to have become "like the angels of God, neither marrying nor giving in marriage" (Matthew 22:30). They reverse the effects of the fall. By their refusal to procreate, "virginity halts the power of death,"[57] bringing no more mortals into the world.

In Mary's account to Zossima of her years in the desert her struggle with sexual desire is presented as interconnected with her struggle with the desire for food.[58] Nevertheless, it is a struggle in which she has been victorious. Paradise is regained. Zossima and Mary, like a new Adam and Eve, come together in the desert that has become for them a garden: later in the legend even a lion is tame.[59] The atmosphere has a heavy erotic charge; and their clothing is at best scanty. But they have become "angels in the flesh," as Zossima later says of Mary.[60] Death has no terror; procreation is unnecessary; sexual desire is transfigured into spiritual communion. The world's social order, its expectation of conventional households for the continuation of society, is broken. The intense investment in sexual pleasure written on the body, promiscuity masquerading as freedom, has been shown to be bondage, and that bondage overcome in a new liberty in this hardwon foretaste of paradise.

Violent Passions

When Mary has told Zossima about her life of penitence and answered his questions she says abruptly, "That is enough about me."[61] They weep and pray together, each seeking the blessing of the other; and then Mary dismisses Zossima, sending him back to his monastery. She asks him to return next year at Maundy Thursday, bringing with him "a portion of the life-giving Body and Blood" of communion: she will meet him "on the inhabited side" of the Jordan.[62] "With these words, she asked him to pray for her, and disappeared very swiftly into the depths of the desert."[63]

Zossima does as she asks, remaining in the monastery during the intervening year, and on the appointed day returning to the Jordan with the elements of communion in a chalice and some choice food in a basket. But Mary does not come. Zossima sits down and weeps (again!). He then falls into anxiety and despair worthy of a teenage lover: maybe she will not come; maybe she has already come and gone; maybe she has decided he is unworthy … And if she does come, how will she get across the river? "Alas, I am wretched; who is keeping such beauty from me?" he groans. Again he is in the grip of an unquiet mind, thoughts and anxieties over which he has no control.

> The old man was turning these things over in his mind, when lo, the Holy One came, and stood on the other bank from whence she had come … And again the thought seized him that she could not cross the Jordan, but when he looked he saw her signing the waters of the Jordan with the sign of the Cross. For the darkness was lit by the full splendour of the moon, since it was that time in the month.[64] As soon as she had made the sign of the Cross, she stepped on to the water and walking over the flowing waves she came as if walking on solid land.[65]

The contrast between Zossima's roller-coaster emotions and her Christ-like command not only over herself but even over the water is not lost on Zossima. He is the bearer of the sacrament; but she has herself *become* sacramental. He falls to his knees; and there follows another farcical scene in which they vie with one another as to who shall bless and venerate whom. The situation is resolved by Zossima offering prayers and giving her the sacrament—at Mary's command: the writer of the legend deftly reinforces the priestly role even while introducing every sort of ambiguity of authority.

Having received the sacrament, Mary asked Zossima to come again the following year to the place in the deep desert where he had seen her the first time, in the meantime imploring his prayers and that he "remember me always as a sinner": Zossima, in turn, "begged her to pray for the Church, for the Kingdom and for himself, and so, weeping, he let her go," watching her walk over the waters of the Jordan as she had come.[66] When the year had passed, Zossima "went again into the huge solitude of the desert," praying that God would show him again "that angel in the flesh of whom the world was not worthy."

And then he came upon her, "lying dead, her hands folded and her face turned to the East." In the sand she had left a note to him: "Father Zossima, bury in this place Mary the sinner, return me to the earth of which I am made, dust to dust, having prayed to the Lord for me, who died … on the selfsame night as the Passion of the Lord after making her communion of the Divine and Mysterious Supper."[67] So Zossima realized that Mary had been miraculously transported into the desert of the desert within an hour of having crossed the Jordan, a journey that had taken him twenty weary days.

The miracles were not yet over. Zossima had no tools to dig the grave, and though he did his best with a stick he found, he grew tired and saw that he would not succeed. Zossima despaired. "He sighed from the depths of his soul and raising his eyes he saw a great lion standing by the body of the Holy One … When he saw the lion he trembled with fear …"[68] yet again his thoughts and emotions are out of control. But Zossima has learned a lesson or two. He made the sign of the cross as Mary had done at the River Jordan, and asked the lion to help him. "While he was still speaking the lion had already dug out with his front paws a hole big enough to bury the body in."[69] So Zossima and the lion together conduct Mary's funeral: the legend is at pains to point out that Mary is as naked as when Zossima had first seen her, barring the old torn cloak he had given her with which she had partially covered herself. Having completed the burial, "the lion went off into the depths of the desert as meekly as if it were a lamb, and Zossima went home, blessing and praising God and singing hymns of praise to our Lord Christ," living in the monastery until he was a hundred.

Important as fasting and chastity are in the accounts of the desert dwellers, they are no more than the outward forms of inner transformation. It is the inner control of thoughts, especially anger and judgmentalism, pride and complacency, that lead to violence that are to be replaced with compassion, contrition, and discernment: that is the real aim of the desert dwellers.[70] It is at this level, more than at the level of physical auster-ity, that Zossima finds his complacency shattered by his encounter with Mary and experiences true conversion.[71] The desert in the desert is unsen-timental: it is a place where demons are confronted and hearts are touched so that the world can be changed.

There is among the sayings of the desert fathers an account of a meeting between a monk and some philosophers:

> They sat him down in their midst and questioned him, "What do you, in the desert, do more than we? You fast, and we also fast; you watch, and we also watch; and all you do, we do also. What more do you who live in the desert do?" The old man said to them, "We hope in the grace of God and we guard our thoughts." They said to him, "We are not able to do that." Edified, they took their leave.[72]

Philosophers are able to simulate the desert; but their thoughts—and their world—remain unchanged. Only those practiced in the discipline of iden-tifying and confronting the demons as they wait upon the divine in the deep desert learned to guard their thoughts with discernment. It was this that Zossima found in his encounter with Mary. Though he was a priest and she had been a harlot, the legend shows that this is the point of his true conversion. Like the philosophers, he is edified, touched in the desert by her humility. He returns to effect a change in the settled land.

Not everyone was edified in their encounter with the desert dwellers. Some thought that what the desert dwellers did was marvellous, but did nothing about it themselves. There is a saying by one of the "old men" that "The prophets wrote books, then came our Fathers who put them into practice. Those who came after them learnt them by heart. Then came the present generation, who have written them out and put them into their window seats without using them."[73] There were those who were even more contemptuous: they simply thought that these men and women who lived much in solitude at an angle to the presuppositions of society had taken leave of their sanity. And so, in a sense, they had. If sanity is defined by the conventions and expectations of a society preoccupied with defeat-ing mortality first by securing their own welfare in food and material pos-sessions and then by procreation and establishing households and families that would continue after they were gone, then those who defied these conventions—despised greed, renounced violence, defied death—were mad. Abba Anthony, one of the earliest and most famous of the desert dwellers, predicted: "A time is coming when men will go mad, and when they see someone who is not mad, they will attack him, saying, 'You are mad, you are not like us.'"[74]

But of course that evaluation can be turned around. Who is mad and who is sane when religion is used to justify society established upon greed and an economy of violence? Men and women went to the desert for a wide range of reasons; prominent among them was the desire to gain freedom from and perspective on a society in which "religion circulated in the world" after the conversion of Constantine had ensured the end of martyrdom and christendom had became the religion of state.[75] The desert dwellers tried to find in their own lives and their own bodies an alternative to the "irresistible and imperial" advance of religion that would become "globalatinization." They looked instead for a restoration of Paradise, where they would be like the angels of God and the desert would become a model for a new Eden.

In historical terms, they failed. The future belonged to the christendom of the west and its secular offspring. It saw those who challenge its economy of luxury, greed, and violence as mad. And it is of course this economy which, with the complicity of the religions of Abraham, has generated the deserts of modernity: the deserts of the missile silos and the refugee camps and the radioactive windstorms. Yet even in such a world, the alterity of the desert dwellers can be touched. If contemporary philosophers take their books from the window seats and are open again to a touch of the desert and those who dwell in it, what sort of response, what swearing of the faith do they prompt? Can we, too, learn to name our demons, overcome the violence of our passions, practice hospitality? Are we edified, or do we say to those who could be our mentors: "You are mad, you are not like us?"

References

1. I am grateful to Grayham Cheyney, of the Religious Society of Friends (Quakers) in Bournemouth, for help with the empirical data in this paper.
2. Jacques Derrida, "Faith and Knowledge: The Two Sources of 'Religion' at the Limits of Reason Alone," in *Religion*, eds. Jacques Derrida and Gianni Vattimo (Cambridge: Polity Press, 1998), p. 7; *Acts of Religion*; ed. Gil Anidjar (New York and London: Routledge, 2002), p. 47.
3. John of the Cross, *Dark Night of the Soul* II.17, in *The Collected Works of St. John of the Cross*, trans. Kieran Kavanaugh and Otilio Rodriguez (Washington D.C.: Institute of Carmelite Studies, 1973), p. 370.
4. Mark C. Taylor, "Betting on Vegas," in John D. Caputo and Michael J. Scanlon, (eds.), *God, the Gift and Postmodernism* (Bloomington: Indiana University Press, 1999), pp. 229–243 (230).
5. *Gulf War Facts*, available online at http://www.cnn.com/SPECIALS/2001/gulf.war/facts.
6. The USA-led allies used between three hundred and eight hundred tons of depleted uranium in more than a million rounds of firing. Microparticles attach to the sand, and are carried in windstorms for hundreds of miles. The halflife of depleted uranium is as long as the life of the solar system (Daniel Robicheau "Desert Concerns," Laka Foundation, May 1999.) pp. 229–243 (230).
7. Since the Gulf War there has been a sixfold rise in cancers in the region, especially leukemias and lymphomas. Birth defects have become common, as have plant and animal mutations.
8. See the Rehydration Project, available online at http://www.rehydrate.org.water/2025.htm.

9. http://www/miftah.org/FactSheets/sheets/water2.htm; see also http://www.golan.org.il/water.html.

10. OXFAM and Christian Aid Reports, 17 April 2002, Institute for Public Accuracy, http://www.accuracy.org/press_releases/PRO41702.htm.

11. Taylor, "Betting on Vegas," p. 133.

12. Derrida, *Acts of Religion*, p. 75.

13. Derrida, *Acts of Religion*, pp. 59, 58.

14. Derrida, *Acts of Religion*, p. 75.

15. Jacques Derrida, *Monolingualism of the Other, or the Prosthesis of Origin*, trans. Patrick Mensah (Stanford: Stanford University Press, 1998), p. 11.

16. Derrida, *Acts of Religion*, p. 47.

17. Gil Anidjar, "'Once More, Once More': Derrida, the Arab, the Jew," Introduction to Derrida, *Acts of Religion*, p. 9.

18. But is it really she who speaks? Or do we have men putting their words into her mouth? The Greek text of the *Life of St. Mary of Egypt* was written by Sophronius, bishop of Jerusalem from 634 CE, who had previously been a monk in the desert; it was translated into Latin by Paul, a deacon of Naples in the eighth century. The English translation together with a short introduction is in Benedicta Ward SLG, *Harlots of the Desert: A Study of Repentance in Early Monastic Sources* (Oxford and London: Mowbray, 1987), chap. 3. The Greek text is printed in *Patrologiae cursus completus: series graeca*, ed J. P. Migne (161 volumes; Paris, 1857–66), vol. 87 (3), cols. 3693–3726; the Latin text is in Migne (ed.), *Patrologiae cursus completus: series latina*, ed. J.P. Migne (221 volumes; Paris, 1844–66), vol. 73, cols. 671–90. Sophronius says that the events he recounts were "revealed to me by good men experienced from childhood in godly words and deeds" (Ward, *Harlots of the Desert*, p. 36), monks of the desert of Palestine. Among them had been "preserved this story without writing it down, … offered to anyone who wanted to hear it as a pattern for edification" (Ward, *Harlots of the Desert*, p. 56) as it had been told to them in turn by Zossima, a central character of the legend. So although we are presented with what purport to be the actual words of Mary, what we in fact have is a legend that shows a good deal about male assumptions and preoccupations regarding female holiness, leaving open the question of how accurately these assumptions map on to women themselves. Already in the seventh century there was the exquisite courtesy of recognizing the significance of women's voices that served precisely to silence them.

19. Ward, *Harlots of the Desert*, p. 37.

20. Ward, *Harlots of the Desert*, p. 38.

21. In the time of the martyrs men and women of the cities had been thrown singing to the lions; but now that the cities had become safe it was in the vast expanse of the desert that evil could be identified (John Binns, *Ascetics and Ambassadors of Christ: The Monasteries of Palestine 314–631* [Oxford: Clarendon, 1994], p. 230). As one of the venerated desert fathers, Abba Poemen, said to a young monk troubled by demons: "The demons fight against you? They do not fight against us at all as long as we are doing our own will …" (Benedicta Ward SLG, *The Sayings of the Desert Fathers: The Alphabetical Collection* [revised edition; Oxford and London: Mowbray, 1981], p. 176). According to Bernard McGinn in *The Foundations of Mysticism* (London: SCM, 1991), p. 136, "The desert, traditionally the home for demons and not for humans, was the place where encounter with the spirits of evil—demons of lust, of gluttony, of anger, of desire for possessions and the like—could be more readily encountered and mastered … These demonic powers, always present within the soul, became luminously real in the intense heat and introspective atmosphere of the desert."

22. Ward, *Harlots of the Desert*, p. 41.

23. Ward, *Harlots of the Desert*, p. 41.

24. Ward, *Harlots of the Desert*, p. 41.

25. Ward, *Harlots of the Desert*, p. 42.

26. Ward, *Harlots of the Desert*, p. 42.

27. Contrast John Tavener's opera *Mary of Egypt*, based on the legend of Mary and Zossima, in which the conversion of each is a purely spiritual, private subjective state, with no obvious social or political implications.

28. Ward, *Harlots of the Desert*, p. 43.

29. Ward, *Harlots of the Desert*, p. 43.

30. It is another reversal: Mary Magdalene embraced the feet of Jesus.
31. Ward, *Harlots of the Desert*, p. 44.
32. Ward, *Harlots of the Desert*, p. 44.
33. Ward, *Harlots of the Desert*, p. 46.
34. Ward, *Harlots of the Desert*, p. 45.
35. Peter Brown, *The Body and Society: Men, Women and Sexual Renunciation in Early Christianity* (New York: Columbia University Press; and London: Faber and Faber, 1988), p. 238. As John Climacus had said, tears given by God "purify us, lead us on in the love of God, wash away our sins and drain away our passions" (John Climacus, *The Ladder of Divine Ascent*, trans. Colm Luibheid and Norman Russell [Classics of Western Spirituality; London: SPCK, and New York: Paulist Press, 1987/1982], p. 140). Note also the linkage of tears, conversion, and continence in Augustine's *Confessions*: Augustine's friends weep when they read the account of St. Anthony; Augustine himself weeps; Monica weeps when he tells her about it (Ward, *Harlots of the Desert*, p. 2).
36. Actually, it is Paul the Deacon, Sophronius, the unnamed monks, and Zossima who now tell Mary's story, attributing the words, however, directly to herself. The situation is parallel to that in Plato's *Symposium*, in which Diotima's words are presented as direct quotation, when in fact within the dialogue itself it is clear that they are at best mediated through a long sequence of men and over considerable time.
37. Ward, *Harlots of the Desert*, p. 44.
38. Ward, *Harlots of the Desert*, p. 45.
39. Ward, *Harlots of the Desert*, p. 46.
40. Ward, *Harlots of the Desert*, p. 47.
41. Ward, *Harlots of the Desert*, p. 47.
42. Ward, *Harlots of the Desert*, p. 48.
43. Ward, *Harlots of the Desert*, p. 49.
44. Ward, *Harlots of the Desert*, p. 49.
45. Ward, *Harlots of the Desert*, p. 49.
46. Ward, *Harlots of the Desert*, p. 50.
47. Graham Gould, *The Desert Fathers on Monastic Community* (Oxford: Clarendon, 1993).
48. Ward, *The Sayings of the Desert Fathers*, pp. 33, 66, 226, etc.
49. Brown, *The Body and Society*, p. 221.
50. Teresa M. Shaw, *The Burden of the Flesh: Fasting and Sexuality in Early Christianity* (Minneapolis: Fortress Press, 1998), p. 176.
51. Ward, *The Sayings of the Desert Fathers*, p. 142.
52. Migne, *Patrologiae graeca* 31.168A, in Shaw, *The Burden of the Flesh*, p. 177.
53. Shaw, *The Burden of the Flesh*, p. 31.
54. The sayings of the desert fathers are full of their efforts toward chastity, some of them carrying strong political comment, but others gruesomely misogynistic. One monk, for example, longed for a particular woman until one day he heard that she had died. "When he heard this, he took his cloak and went to open her tomb by night; he soaked the cloak in the decomposing body. Then he returned to his cell bringing this bad smell with him, and he strove against his thoughts, saying 'Here is the desire you are seeking—you have it—be satisfied'" (Benedicta Ward SLG, *The Wisdom of the Desert Fathers* [Oxford: SLG Press, 1975], p. 10).
55. Brown, *The Body and Society*, p. 6.
56. Shaw, *The Burden of the Flesh*, p. 207.
57. Shaw, *The Burden of the Flesh*, p. 193.
58. But we must not forget the series of male voices representing the story, and the rhetoric of virginity that preoccupied the (male) leaders of christendom in late antiquity.
59. Ward, *Harlots of the Desert*, pp. 55–65.
60. Ward, *Harlots of the Desert*, p. 54.
61. Ward, *Harlots of the Desert*, p. 51.
62. Ward, *Harlots of the Desert*, p. 51.
63. Ward, *Harlots of the Desert*, p. 52.
64. Whatever the intentions, conscious or otherwise, of the author, a contemporary reader can hardly miss another allusion to Mary's femininity in this attention to the "time of the month." Whatever did the pious monastic readers make of it?

65. Ward, *Harlots of the Desert*, p. 53.
66. Ward, *Harlots of the Desert*, p. 54.
67. Ward, *Harlots of the Desert*, pp. 54–55.
68. Ward, *Harlots of the Desert*, p. 55.
69. Ward, *Harlots of the Desert*, p. 55.
70. There is among the sayings of the desert fathers an account of an old man, who was asked, "'How can I find God?' He said, 'In fasting, in watching, in labours, in devotion, and, above all, in discernment. I tell you, many have injured their bodies without discernment and have gone away from us having achieved nothing. Our mouths smell bad through fasting, we know the Scriptures by heart, we recite all the Psalms of David, but we have not that which God asks: charity and humility'" (Ward, *The Wisdom of the Desert Fathers*, p. 29).
71. The emphasis on humility, best understood not as self-abasement but as inner clarity that leaves no room for judgmentalism, was central to desert teaching (Gould, *The Desert Fathers on Monastic Community*, pp. 107-38). Amma Theodora, one of the great women ascetics, told of "an anchorite who was able to banish demons; and he asked them 'What makes you go away? Is it fasting?' They replied, 'We do not eat or drink.' 'Is it vigils?' They replied, 'We do not sleep.' 'Is it separation from the world?' 'We live in the deserts.' 'What power sends you away then?' They said, 'Nothing can overcome us, but humility.'" (Ward, *The Sayings of the Desert Fathers*, p. 84).
72. Ward, *The Wisdom of the Desert Fathers*, p. 57.
73. Ward, *The Wisdom of the Desert Fathers*, p. 31.
74. Ward, *The Sayings of the Desert Fathers*, p. 6.
75. James E. Goehring, *Ascetics, Society, and the Desert: Studies in Early Egyptian Monasticism* (Harrisburg: Trinity Press International, 1999); Rowan Williams, *The Wound of Knowledge: Christian Spirituality from the New Testament to St. John of the Cross* (London: Darton, Longman and Todd, 1979), pp. 93–96.

CHAPTER 25

El Tocado (Le Toucher): Sexual Irregularities in the Translation of God (The Word) in Jesus

MARCELLA MARIA ALTHAUS-REID

> Ah … my face felt ashamed …
>
> (Héctor, a *cartonero* from Buenos Aires)[1]
>
> And Moses hid his face, for he was afraid to look at God.
>
> Exodus 3:5

Dark Transcendence: The God of the Rubbish Bins

Every evening, as the day ends and darkness falls upon Argentina there is a transcendental crossing of the borders of the capital city of Buenos Aires. Your heart must fill up if, from your window you observe mysterious shadows starting to move in silence, ghostly silhouettes crossing the street to stoop at your door. Within minutes there are thousands of shadows trespassing, transcending one by one every border of the complex geographies of class, race, private property, and gender of Buenos Aires. The trespassers are the excluded, the people whom global Capitalism intends to make invisible, as they earn their meagre living by looking into the rubbish bins for something to sell, to exchange or to eat. The *cartoneros*[2] (scavengers) are the untouchables of the expansion of Capitalist society, living and dying by touching the untouchable rubbish of the city, as marginalization reduces them to death by hunger or tetanus. Some, like Héctor, may cover their faces while working because of the shame of the miserable living into which they have been forced.[3] Like Moses covering his face in the presence of God, the excluded cover their faces in the presence of economic horror that brings another dimension (or the dimension of the Other) to the Sinai theophany. The untouchables, as did Moses, have seen the god of horror and survived. They have seen what Nancy calls the transcendental in touch, that is "the obscure, impure, untouchable touch."[4] The garbage sites outside the city are their sacred mountain—and their Golgotha.

People who observe their presence in the city may also cover their faces with sadness for the actual conditions of life in Argentina, but also with a feeling of compassion and solidarity. And a sacred, intimate feeling of the presence of God accompanying the destitute masses may then grow within ourselves. God, the ultimate Other and Untouchable, is the God of the rubbish bins.

Latin American liberation theology, which is based on the search for the materiality of transcendence, knows how God is to be found in the presence of the untouchables. Transcendence is an issue from the margins and not from the centers of theological ideology and it is at the margins that God is found as the material excess of innocent suffering. Lévinas could not have stated it better in his "Alterity and Transcendence,"[5] "transcendence" is a movement of crossing over and of ascent. A way for the distant to give itself, to move beyond the border. Here we see the transcendental Other of Lévinas dressed in rags, opening the rubbish bins, feeding their children while collecting refuse in a cart. There are thousands of them, invading the night, transcending the space of life fixed by world economic powers. Transcendence comes from history: it is a category crisis. This explains its subversiveness in deregulating orders and also the horror it evokes, for it is God touching God's own limits in the untouchables from Buenos Aires.

On the Law of Untouchability

Just as Derrida began his reflections on *Le Toucher* with reference to graffiti painted on a wall in Paris ("When our eyes touch, is it day or night?")[6], so I begin my reflection from graffiti found in a newspaper photograph that shows a *cartonero* walking past a Cathedral carrying a big bag of refuse on his head (Figure 25.1).[7] The slim, fragile figure is silhouetted against the white walls of the cathedral on which someone has written: "*Nace Jesus. Renace*" ("Jesus is Born. Reborn.") It is that graffiti that becomes a text for us (the *cartonero's* body obscures whatever else was written) in

Fig. 25.1 After "Cartoneros: Espejo de la Crisis," p. 1, rendering by Gilad Foss.

which economic untouchability and sexual untouchability become related to the disruption of theological ideology. And as such it is related to a law of tact.[8] The law, according to Derrida, is primarily a law of tact carrying in itself the impossibility of the act of touching for it relates the touchable, the untouchable, and a disruption. Or it is a conjunction and a disjunction, expressed in the law to touch without touching which is the way of the law as ideology. This is expressed in the graffiti from Buenos Aires in the words: "Jesus is born. Reborn." God has become in Jesus part of the order of sensuality by tact, by birth. Born of a *virgo intacta* Jesus' birth has its origin in an untouchable woman. Mary is the woman who could neither be touched by men nor by God. It is that condition of untouchability with humanity and with the sacred that makes God in Jesus touchable and untouchable. Jesus' birth is the condition of touching, of tenderness and sexuality not ordered as yet by law or custom because it displaces the idea of sexuality associated with productivity or at least it complicates the idea of productivity. Jesus' birth belongs to a different category because his birth is the result of another kind of sexual act and also because it requires a different (anOther) type of act in sacred literature. The narrative of Jesus' birth in the Gospels disrupts the literary acts of the Hebrew Scriptures that relate to reproductive sexuality. In the New Testament reproduction is dissociated from sexuality.

Curiously, it has been the tradition of the church to condemn nonreproductive sexual acts (such as masturbation and homosexual relations) as alienation from God. For the church nonreproductive sexual acts belong to the category of waste and are therefore associated with pollution or contamination. But in the New Testament narrative, by dissociating sexual acts from birth narratives Jesus becomes a waste-God or a contaminated Messiah. The lineage of Jesus is grace and not reproductive sexuality. The law of productive sexuality (which is enforced through the Hebrew Scriptures) is therefore discontinued in Jesus. Divine productivity belongs to a different order (the order of grace) and therefore Jesus becomes God manifesting Godself through a path not of industry but of waste or gratuitous, free expenditure. The divine economy is an alternative one because the impossibility of touch is present in the untouched mother and in the fact that Jesus is a wasted and outlawed Messiah. The law of tact seems to carry in itself a disruptive divine logic, and Jesus becomes an outlawed, untouchable God of the poor, oppressed by the law that does not accept the deconstruction of justice.

For Jesus to be reborn (resurrected, present in the Holy Spirit or revealed in history) implies precisely the anomaly of the law. Divine birth is faulty in the sense of incomplete because what has been touched has not been enough: there remains a trace of the intact, the not touched, within it. Liturgically it requires a baptism (a new birth) and even a divine resurrection. The anomaly of the law is its disembodied, unchangeable pretence. However, there is a further contradiction or disjunction of the theological law of tact, announced by the fact that Jesus brings together extreme touchability ("The Word becomes a human being") and extreme untouchability by bringing contamination and contagion into Divine revelation. Jesus does this by bringing together not only a disruption of purity laws and the corruption of the law (and of death as the law of life) into the sacred, but also the contamination of the poor as subjects of divine history. This is the contamination of the outsiders. And if we say with Lévinas that for God, "the way of the Other, is his [sic] way of signifying,"[9] could we say other than that Jesus is another Scripture, that is, the contaminated Scripture of the outcast who writes on the walls of an impoverished city? Is Jesus a graffiti of God that needs to be reread in the rush and fear of the authority of the law it disrupts and contaminates? If Jesus (the logos) belongs to a different kind of scripture, then the messiah should be thought of as a category crisis of an extreme order, the transgressor of all law, including affective orderings. Jesus becomes a deep disruption of the invisible law of heterosexual orders in which economics (as an exchange based on relationships) is based. Could Jesus then, as another scripture, be not just graffiti but the origin of all deviant scriptures outside hegemonic orders? Could not Jesus be a sexual graffiti on the walls of Buenos Aires?

Graffiti Jesus

Paraphrasing Derrida, who has said that the principle of philosophy is not philosophy,[10] we could say that the principle of theology is not theology. Derrida says that a kiss should always come first (that is, before philosophy) and we can agree with this. Theology should start with a kiss and a denunciation. The beginning of any theological praxis should be the kiss of sensuality and the act of denouncing the disruption of love and transcendence by the imposition of sexual ideologies and international monetary agreements on reflection concerning the sacred.

In the photograph we are reflecting on the need to consider the ambiguity of graffiti, or the presence of two representations of Jesus. One is the picture of a Jesus who can be seen as the *cartonero* in Buenos Aires (the bag of refuse on his back resembles a cross); the other is the text "Jesus is born. Reborn" on the wall of the cathedral. That double image powerfully disrupts the law of tact because graffiti are tactless, in more than one sense. They are tactless because they challenge elite conceptions where "tact" (as in tact and diplomacy) is a category for silencing the oppressed under aesthetic rules *de buén gusto* (of "good taste") or decency. But they are also tactless because graffiti are scriptures that continuously change. Like the ever changing texts on the walls of public toilets they fiercely resist fixed or permanent meanings. Moreover, graffiti do not have an original form since words, grammar, and punctuation change according to the dynamics of intertextuality: the presence of other graffiti written beside them or crossing over with them and the impact of erasures. They are highly mobile, dependent and also disruptive and subversive texts. You can never touch graffiti twice; it will be an *Other* graffiti. Graffiti are touched/ untouchable living scriptures. A graffiti Jesus may show us the presence of a moving Scripture. As the excluded are crossing the borders of Buenos Aires by transgressing the spatial limits of class and racial configuration in the big cities, there is another Scripture, more fluid, written on walls and sung in public protests, which contrasts with the Scriptures resting at the altar inside a Cathedral. Inside the Cathedral, the Scriptures may be read from the perspective of an "out of touch" Jesus, a Jesus who has been made to reject his outlawness and subversiveness. Yet, the Other Jesus is the actuality of a transcendence as a text, the texture of which is of a crossbordering quality. The way we read a text on a wall depends on how light and color are absorbed and it is among these chromatic parameters that the meaning of textures on the wall of cathedrals and religious texts are manifested. As the black and white of priestly robes are theologically meaningful and contribute ideologically toward the sacralization of a social and political order, the knowledge of the Jesus of the untouchables may also depend on chromatic perceptions. Things such as tactile feelings and how much light the text of the Messiah may or may not reflect may influence our Christologies. Moreover, if sexuality is the first of the social constructions, then the sexual text/texture of the Messiah may require the same darkness as the *cartoneros* doing their job in the darkness of a society that renders them invisible. That sexual texture of Jesus would then make a different contribution to the political and social construction of meaning in the current era of Globalization.

We are referring here to the presence of what heterosexual ideologies would like to make invisible. That is, the incarnation of God in a more fluid sexual epistemology, such as a bisexual Christ coming with a touch of queer dissent. That queer dissent could make of Jesus a "zone of possibilities" in which "a sense of potentiality" is present,[11] thus pervading Christianity with a different opening toward the Sacred, beyond dualism.

This could be the discovery of a more fluid Christology that I have outlined in previous reflections on the presence of a Bi/Christ,[12] or a Christology from a bisexual epistemology that challenges the heterosexual assumptions pervading theology. Bisexual thinking in theology could provide us with the starting point of a different social imaginary in which God might become an alternative instead of a centrality.

Jesus as a graffiti gives us a texture of sexual dissent because it works as the memory of an invisible God canceling God's own sexual representation. Jesus is a shadow of God but a changing shadow, an impermanent supplement in the struggle not to become an original Father, which is also a filiative struggle (or a struggle for disafiliation). Jesus seems to be in a struggle with an original God, otherwise incarnation would be a repetition. Even so a repetition would only prove that there is a sense of incompleteness in God. *Re-peter* is always a second demand. Does the Trinitarian formula, made of repetition and complementarities, somehow express a second desire in the sense that God cannot be contained in Godself anymore? In that case the second demand of God implies a sacred desire not to be unique but disseminated—not in harmony but in struggle.

The fact that Jesus becomes simultaneously revealed (seen) and also concealed (invisible) when moving in the shadows of the excluded reminds us that Jesus' divine alterity is manifested in history.[13] However, one may ask what kind of originality we find in sacred repetitions. For instance, where does the originality of the secondary in God in Jesus begin? It starts not in a point of social justice, already present in the Hebrew Scriptures, but in God's own suicidal departure from Godself. Incarnation (the elective birth of God) actually starts with the voluntary death of God or the end of God's monotonous divine political and sexual identity. That is part of the pedagogical suicide of the God of Novalis[14] and the principle of praxis in theology. There is a birth that makes God depart from Godself in Jesus, thus signaling also a moment in the self-legitimization crisis of God. That legitimization crisis is a questioning of divine ideology on two levels. One level is the crisis in the category of God itself. The other is a pedagogical level, for it shows the process of God's own dismantling of the institutionalized apparatus that relates to the translation of the God-word, especially the sexual translation of God.

To claim that there are sexual irregularities in that translation of God in Jesus implies then that sexuality forces us to rethink not only the biological underpinnings of current theology, but also that sexuality makes us reflect on the sacred and the sexual gestures of legitimization behind the gendered and sexual dressings of God, as well as the economic ones. For an economy is a reflection of human exchanges and affections[15] and the law or discipline of these exchanges. In the situation of poverty and dehumanization that current economic and affective exchange systems have brought to my country, Argentina, there is an alliance for justice coming from people for whom justice is an integral concept. For instance, never has my country seen so many people involved in actions of solidarity, from unemployed workers forming cooperatives and taking over abandoned factories, to people organizing whole bartering markets in which goods are exchanged for other goods and services without the need for money. In the same way, sexual rights activists stand against sexual and economic injustice in a country where only twenty-five years ago even the length of men's hair or the use of trousers by women were regulated by the state through strict gender laws. The point is that *cartoneros* and the sexual rights activists of the Hotel Gondolin[16] in Buenos Aires have a common order under which to suffer and a common disorder for which to struggle. That disorder on which we will reflect belongs to a drag epistemology and as such is part of the theatrical apparatus of the sacred manifested in the contravention of a policed (hetero-) social and religious order.

El Tocado

In the airport in Torino the authorities questioned the entry in my passport. Why did it say "doctor?" It should say *signora* or *signor.* I argued that I preferred to use my title, but I was rebuked. "It is the gender that we need to know. Is it male or female?" I thought of replying that I was a theologian and if Divine Transcendence crosses the borders of sexuality, who am I then to fix my own sexuality? However, I simply replied "I'm complicated."

To think Jesus as *el Tocado* is to think God from sensuality, but also from sensuality at the margins. In Spanish as in English, *el tocado* (the touched one) conveys the meaning of several epistemological irregularities: *tocado* refers to someone outside the logic of a system; a slightly mad person. In Buenos Aires, a gesture of touching your head with one finger conveys the concept without speaking. As the middle ages, made people and fools of God, the ones that God has touched in the head, are associated categories of the marginals. For instance, the term *estar tocado* also refers to someone who has received a bribe and as such it is used for corrupt politicians. It applies to a spoilt (polluted) thing or to the one who has received a supernatural gift, a talent. However, *tocado* also relates to dressing (in Spanish *tocador* means dressing table, dressing room or boudoir) and it refers to the manner of dressing and to the styling of clothes or hair. Somehow Jesus is as material as his clothes, but the clothes of Jesus are also the clothes of his messiahship, his investiture, or conferral of divinity. Or, to put it in a another way, Jesus himself functions in the divine narrative of incarnation as God's investment, as *el tocado.* As such, Jesus represents God as the clothes of crisis and the toilette of disruption in divinity and the text/texture of marginalization. What we have here is a different sexual epistemology, perhaps a cross-dresser way of knowing which is disclosed to us in the kenosis of God and in incarnation. It is as if in *el tocado* we are told of a God who disrupts the orders of representing or greeting (touching) the divine and who needs to be explained not by the heterosexual parameters of *tocadores* but by an epistemology of drag.

Interestingly, in her book *Vested Interests* Marjorie Garber claims that "Transvestism is the crisis of category itself,"[17] that is, not a process or part of a process but the breaking down of categories—appropriate here as we see a God in need of overcoming its own borders, that is a God in crisis. The borders, such as those of Deuteronomy 22:5 (the dressing code) are sexual and political hegemonic borders. The borders of compulsory heterosexuality are made by the duality of the "us here" and "God there" by accentuating the Lévinasian ascendant movement of transcendence, instead of the crossing of borders and the God among us. In Jesus, God's own borders as defined by metanarratives of law are questioned. Let us consider further the drag hermeneutical circle that dresses and undresses God in Jesus and the new touchability that God's crisis of identity acquires. Contrary to what Derrida calls Marion's concern for exactitude,[18] here we are in the presence of the inexact God announcing the unpunctual and disorderly revelation of the sacred in our lives.

Drag Lessons: Theory of Translation

The drag lessons taken from God's incarnation in Jesus relate to the unveiling of a nonessential God. This is no natural God but a God who precisely has movement in identity, which is in itself a category crisis brought upon Godself by a desire of repetition, that is, to have a second demand of trespassing sacrality. Jesus' incarnation is transcendental as part of a divine exercise of cross-dressing, a symbol of liminality and trespassing of the sacred as false consciousness. The graffiti scriptures of Jesus work by exposing and displaying diverse meanings not just in the text, as we previously considered, but also in the act of producing Jesus as God's effect. Reading the ambiguous text of Jesus, we read the text of a God who does not fit Godself anymore and needs to come out of some divine closet, as an immigrant God or a drag God trespassing the law in its sexual and political coding. As we witness the tension of the act of God's divine cross-dressing and the relativization of God's essential being, we are also aware that Jesus disestablishes the false sense of transcendence prevalent in much North Atlantic theology. *El Tocado* represents a disestablished God, a God whose knowledge invites us also to undress the discipline and pedagogy of sexual, gender, and political assumptions about God and about ourselves. The social construction of divinity, sexuality, and politics become unveiled.

El Tocado requires us to read the Other scriptures, the ones in which God is a graffiti on the wall of a poor city, or the picture that shows Jesus dressed as a *cartonero* and not as a white king—a dirty God satiated with horror and misery or the cross-dresser whose way of knowing may have the corporeality that heterosexual ideologies have lost.

A drag epistemology queries somehow the inequality of the translation God-Jesus. That means that in reading God in Jesus rather than in communicating we are constructing a representation. Does Jesus produce an effect of God beyond the text? Is Jesus the God who makes sense only between the parameters of hegemonic practices of approved heterosexual translation? We need to consider how to deviate from a cultural standard translation of Jesus that coincides with a strong heterosexual given culture and how to rescue that element of the nonessentiality of God. Jesus himself seems to get confused in the translation of his own identity, a confusion reminding us of a diglossia, when translation is not possible because reality is constructed differently. The translation of God (the Word) in Jesus requires the same irregularity that is shown in God's own cross-dressing movement: the drag performance of God is manifested in the investment of God in Jesus.

We learn by the gestures of the body of *El Tocado* that "That of God" in Jesus is a touching paradox. As with the poor cross-dresser living in a community and organizing human rights workshops in a run down hotel in Buenos Aires, God in Jesus became a touching place for the marginalized. A place where injustice is challenged by an alternative way of thinking affection, outside the imperialism of heterosexual ideologies. For the *cartoneros* and the poor transvestites, for the ones at the margin of economic and sexual orders, God's transcendence merges with the untouchability of Jesus, which brings the contamination of justice into religious law. That is the promise of an*other* law. This *other* law subverts the cash-payment mentality on which Christian theology based its own logic of production where only dogmas were (selectively) redistributed among people, but not ecclesiastical properties. But *el Tocado* is another way of production and one in which God does not have priority over Godself in its own translation in Jesus. That translation is sexually irregular because it brings corporeality to the Word of God, and a different production of corporeality—a drag production.

Between the *cartoneros*, the "card-collectors" who collect cardboard and paper, which they do not read and on which they do not write, and Jesus as *el Tocado*, we are in the presence of two mutual exclusions of the law of tact: the untouchable people of the global expansion of Capitalism and *el Tocado* as a different, marginal way of a divine economic and affective production based on a nonheterosexual epistemology. The translation of God happens at Golgotha and not at Sinai, that is, outside heterosexual and economic normativity. The *cartoneros* contaminate with their corporeality theology in Buenos Aires. Their scriptures may be made of graffiti on the walls asking for the return of their bank accounts and the cancellation of the external debt. Or for "Jesus born and reborn": an incomplete God denouncing the changeable reality of bodies and societies that theological ideologies like to deny.

In Jesus as *el Tocado*, what is touchable is his untouchability. God can only be touched in the revelation of the untouchables, the ones whose lives are prophetic because they denounce with their presence in the cities the injustice of the present economic and sexual systems. God (the Word) becomes exemplarily irregular in God's own translation in Jesus, a touching God outside the hegemonic affective and economic structures of production. To be able to touch the untouchable means "to ground God in the language that God speaks to us,"[19] which I have tried to do by reading a story of a graffiti in times of social exclusion. The God of the rubbish bins is a cross-dresser Jesus in more than one way. It is a God searching for transcendence while dressed in rags and prophesying in the presence of the marginalized the exclusion of the blessed by society's unjust orders. The "blessed are the excluded" of the New Testament announces not only a different knowledge of the sacred (a different enlightenment), but also the irruption of another Scripture. The bodies of those who starve, who are abused and tortured, speak from their own suffering denouncing a disorder while sometimes (as in the resurrection of Jesus) they also become the witness of a different project of life. The body of the oppressed is a prophetic body. There is something interestingly radical in the fact that Moses and his people left a country that oppressed them but did not engage themselves in changing a political situation. They just left. No desire was shown in them to become active in order to modify political and religious oppressive circumstances. Was the departure of God from Godself in the incarnation of Jesus somehow a similar act? Or at least can we say that it was the deep dissatisfaction with Godself which made of God *El Tocado*, that is, an untouchable, contaminated and transgressive God? *El Tocado* as a living Scripture of a dissatisfied God, is a text about the need of a fundamental economic disorder and a narrative of an affectionate knowledge or "amatory know how" crossing the borders of tact. Here we are confronted by a tactless theology challenging theology as ideological conformity fundamentally an imperial sexual ideology that is deeply related to ways of thinking exchange systems in society. The way we exchange kisses may be related to the way the economy is currently organized.

And at that point a loving theology becomes an economic theology and vice versa. Searching God in Jesus through the untranslatable of *El Tocado* means to understand that the Messiah means a disruption and betrayal of the law, waste, and contamination and that this is where the power of the powerless of liberation theologies may lie. For the prophetic suffering of the excluded (the disposable of society) and their searching for the bread of life in rubbish bins tells us that this is a time of great departures toward different ways of loving and knowing the transcendental presence of God the untouchable in our lives and in the lives of those condemned by Global Capitalism to all kinds of deaths without resurrections. We have said with Derrida that the principle of theology is not theology. Reflecting on Novalis's idea that "the authentic philosophical act is suicide," Derrida adds that we still need to think about a first kiss and suicide, or "the act and the action."[20] The principle of theology is praxis and specifically a praxis of sensuality (materialist interpretation) and also a suicide pact (or a true kenosis). In Jesus as *El Tocado* there is the beginning of a reflection on how in the sacred narratives God appears to have attempted to undo the references of the divine discourse. The transgression of the metanarratives of divine power is inherent in their own construction. Questioning, queering theology functions then as acts of theology, that is, acts concerned with the performance of alterity, subversion, and compassion in relation to all the hunger (desires) of the world and in struggle with the credit system (*credos*) that orders the praxis of love and economic exchange of our societies. The presence of sexual irregularities in the translation of God (The Word) in Jesus speaks of the tension between epistemological and sexual assumptions and its consequences in the economic law without justice of our present world.

References

1. "Cartoneros: Espejo de la Crisis," *Claramente*, (August 5, 2002): 4.
2. These are men, women, and children known as *cartoneros* (lit. "cardboard collectors") who make a living by opening rubbish bags and picking from them what can be sold or reused, from bits and pieces of reusable objects to food still edible. It is estimated that 100,000 people arrive every day in Buenos Aires from the suburban areas to collect usable leftovers from the rubbish bins.
3. When asked if he remembered the first day he went out to look in rubbish bins, Héctor replied: "Uy ... se me caía la cara de verguenza, nunca había hecho algo así" (lit. "Ah ... my face felt full of shame; I have never done anything like this"); cf. "Cartoneros: Espejo de la Crisis," p. 4.
4. Jacques Derrida, "*Le Toucher*: Touch / to Touch Him," *Paragraph* 16.2 (1993): 122–157 (135).
5. Emmanuel Lévinas, *Alterity and Transcendence* (London: The Athlone Press, 1999).
6. Derrida, "*Le Toucher*," p. 123
7. "Cartoneros: Espejo de la Crisis," p. 1.
8. Derrida, "*Le Toucher*," p. 124.
9. Lévinas, *Alterity and Transcendence*, p. 169.
10. Derrida, "*Le Toucher*," p. 140.
11. Annamarie Jagose, *Queer Theory: An Introduction* (New York University Press, 1997), p. 2.
12. For further reflection on a Bi/Christ, that is, a Christ constructed from a bisexual epistemology and its implication for theology and economics, see Marcella Althaus-Reid, *Indecent*

Theology: Theological Perversions in Sex, Gender and Politics (London: Routledge, 2000), pp 112–120.

13. I'm thinking here of Derrida's reflections in *Memoirs of the Blind: The Self-Portrait and Other Ruins* (Chicago: University of Chicago Press, 1990), p. 3, on speaking from blindness. Derrida asks, "What happens when one writes without seeing?" And we may ask ourselves whether Jesus represents a blind writing of God, a trace supplementing an original.

14. Derrida, "*Le Toucher*," p. 141.

15. One needs to remember here, for instance, the economic institution of *El Cariño* (lit. "Tenderness"), which is pivotal for the Ayllus in Perú.

16. The Hotel Gondolin in Buenos Aires is a Transvestite Collective, from where human rights activities are coordinated for the defence of the life of transvestites suffering police harassment in the city. Originally a favorite place for poor transvestites to rent rooms to live, it has now become a site where transvestites live in community and also organize talks, workshops, and human rights political activities.

17. Marjorie Garber, *Vested Interests: Cross Dressing and Cultural Anxiety* (London: Routledge, 1992), p. 17.

18. Derrida, "*Le Toucher*," p. 155.

19. Derrida, "*Le Toucher*," p. 129.

20. Derrida, "*Le Toucher*," p. 141.

INDEX

hearing, 219
Hegel, 55, 67, 117, 310, 311; Hegelian
    modernism, 102
Heidegger, Martin, 43, 113, 267,
    274, 326, 334n23; and *Augenblick*,
    319; and *Destruktion*, 32; and
    dwelling, 56; and naming, 38; and
    Nazism, 117; and ontotheology,
    37; and *Zuhandenheit*, 356
hermeneutics, 332
Heron, Alasdair, 145
Hinduism, 15
History, 275
Hoffman, Lawrence, 22n59
Holland, Nancy, 25n62
Holy War, and Genesis, 66
Hobbes, Thomas, 342
home, 54–56, 221
hope, 31
hospitality, 53–61 *passim*, 73–94
    passim, 276, 278, 300; as act of
    donation, 59; and distance, 53; as
    hosting, 65; impossibility of to
    other faiths, 74; as link to
    justice, 58; and maternity,
    76; and pregnancy, 77; and
    substitution, 76
host, 76–77, 87
human: part in creation, 346; relation
    with animals, 46; as soul of the
    world, 346; telos of, 273
humility, 391n71
hush, 220; God as, 221
Husserl, Edmund, 249, 255, 320, 326;
    Ideen II, 346
hyphen, 16, 17, 18, 377

I

I, 102; as event, 204; and the eye, 160;
    as "i," 283, 289, 290; as negation,
    102; and Other, 203; and penis,
    288; as radical, 102; and subject,
    289; and tetragrammaton, 289
icon, 131, iconic, 315; and evil, 320

idol: as conceptual, 317; and evil, 320;
    idolatry, 340; idolatry and injustice,
    345; idolatry and instrumental use
    of ineffable, 341
identity, 9, 105
Iliad, 66
il y a, 233
impossible, 297–307 *passim*, 325;
    impossibility, as ordeal, 272;
    beyond our powers, 301;
    possible as impossible, 297–306,
    passim; and thinking, 270
Incarnation, 319, 356, 399; and body,
    369 and internalization of
    justice, 343; Incarnate God as
    screen protecting against the
    Real, 320
inclusion, 74
indeterminacy, as infinite, 202
inheritance, 3
interiorization, 101
interpretation, 131, 300
invention, 300
Irenaeus, Saint, 192
Irigaray, Luce, 356
Isaac, 34
Isaiah, 32
Islamic fundamentalism, 310
Israel, 196; as virgin, 214
Israeli Defense Force, 377
Iterability, 137; and biblical scenes
    of writing, 337; law of, 63
Iteration, 160

J

Jabès, Edmund, 143, 178
James, brother of Jesus, 45
Jameson, Frederic, 5
Janicaud, Dominique, 329–330
Jeremiah, Book of, 224
Jerome, Saint, 173n6
Jesus, 47; as another scripture, 297;
    and Christological claim, 47; as
    dangerous memory, 258; as

INDEX OF REFERENCES